The
Olde Daunce

SUNY Series in Medieval Studies
Paul E. Szarmach, Editor

The
Olde Daunce

Love, Friendship, Sex, and Marriage
in the Medieval World

Robert R. Edwards and Stephen Spector
Editors

STATE ❖ UNIVERSITY ❖ OF ❖ NEW ❖ YORK ❖ PRESS

Published by
State University of New York Press, Albany

© 1991 State University of New York

For information, address State University of New York
Press, State University Plaza, Albany, N.Y., 12246

Library of Congress Cataloging-in-Publication Data

The Olde daunce : love, friendship, sex, and marriage in the medieval
    world / Robert R. Edwards and Stephen Spector, editors.
        p.   cm. — (SUNY series in medieval studies)
    ISBN 0–7914–0439–0 (alk. paper). — ISBN 0-7914-0440-4 (pbk. :
alk. paper)
    1. Marriage—History. 2. Marriage in literature. 3. Love-
-History. 4. Love in literature. 5. Friendship—History.
6. Friendship in literature. 7. Sex—History. 8. Sex in
literature. 9. Literature, Medieval. I. Edwards, Robert, 1947–
. II. Spector, Stephen, 1946–   . III. Series.
HQ513.043   1990
306.7—dc20   89–26349
                                                         CIP

10 9 8 7 6 5 4 3 2 1

For Jean Hagstrum

Contents

ROBERT R. EDWARDS
STEPHEN SPECTOR

Introduction

This collection of essays grew out of a conference on "Love, Marriage, Friendship and Sexuality in the Middle Ages," held at the National Humanities Center in April 1986. The impetus for the conference came from Jean Hagstrum, Professor Emeritus at Northwestern University and Senior Fellow at the Center. Professor Hagstrum proposed a series of conferences on the theme of love, beginning with love in the ancient world and moving forward toward the modern period. These conferences would test in the domains of history and literature whether companionate and reciprocal love, love as requisite to marriage, emerged in any significant way before the later seventeenth century. Hagstrum proposed that sanctioned erotic attachments not only preceded any modern ideal of marriage but also made it historically intelligible.[1] The motto he invoked to describe the nature of these attachments was borrowed from the eighteenth-century English poet James Thomson—"esteem enlivened by desire."[2]

The essays in this volume present revised versions of the papers given at the conference on the Middle Ages and essays added subsequently to explore further the contexts of medieval love.[3] The focus of the book, like the initial theme of the conference, has developed through conversation and reflection. Our subject remains desire, friendship, sexuality, and especially the *olde daunce* of love. What we have found, however, is not a petrified ideal of love but an essentially contested term. Love as a social value in domestic and moral life does not remain invariate; it is not an abstract notion simply enacted in history and unambiguously represented in literature. Rather, it functions as part of a diversified cultural discourse. The essays collected here therefore explore medieval love and desire as they relate to diverse issues, including companionship, equality, power, creativity, voyeurism, faith, violence, and even hate.

It makes sense, then, to speak of love as much more than a theory to be examined for its internal consistency and historical application. The fact that medieval culture could imagine legitimized forms of love and erotic reciprocity is clear enough from the historical and literary records. The interpretive question is, what function did they serve? The answer, as our essays indicate, varies with the specific contexts. Accordingly, we have organized the essays into three groups that deal respectively with the historical context of marriage, representations of love and marriage in continental vernacular literature, and Chaucer's treatment of love.

The first group of essays concentrates chiefly on the formulation of marriage given within Church doctrine. They study Augustine's notions of marriage; the concept of *maritalis affectio* in doctrine, canon law, and popular preaching; and the theological debate on marriage in the learned and vernacular traditions. Our concentration complements the work of historians who have documented the experience of medieval marriage and social relations as they were lived in ordinary life. Georges Duby and David Herlihy, for example, have substantially added to our detailed understanding of medieval social reality, especially the reality of everyday practice.[4] At the same time, their work has challenged many of the suppositions governing a historical understanding of marriage. Jean-Louis Flandrin and Philippe Ariès have contested the assumption that Church doctrine offers an adequate picture of medieval practice.[5] Flandrin questions whether doctrine truly reflected medieval practice. One way of reading the vast literature of marriage precepts, he suggests, is to see doctrine as a repeated attempt to enforce and consolidate standards that often differed from behavior. On this view, the exhortations of moralists and theologians witness the conjugal eroticism that the Church wished to discourage.

Ariès sees both continuity and distinction within marriage. He says, "Fecundity, the modesty of the wife and mother, the dignity of the mistress of a household, such are the enduring qualities which, right up to the eighteenth century, have marked the contrast between married love and love outside marriage" (p. 133). Within this continuity, however, he finds profound distinctions between medieval and modern conceptions of married love. It was only after the eighteenth century, says Ariès, that marital eroticism found general approval. Still, he concedes that it is hard for the historian to penetrate the silence concerning love and sexuality in medieval married life:

... marriage existed where a vast area of public life touched on a tiny secret place, secret rather than private. Privacy implies an enclosed space, withdrawn from the external world but known and sought out, accessible in certain conditions. But that which is secret is hidden away, except from a few initiates, as if it did not exist, protected by its cloak of religious silence, which binds the initiates also to silence. Revelation would destroy it: more than unspoken, it is the unutterable. So conjugal love could be one of the secret places of the old society. [p.136-37]

A second distinction can be made, he argues, between custom and doctrine. In the earlier Middle Ages, marriage took two forms. Among the aristocracy, it was a private, familial function centered on a promise and contract that joined not only the principals but also the two families. Its ceremonies, including the bedding of the couple, were conducted within the sphere of feudal, secular authority. Alongside this domestic contract, the Church introduced a second form of marriage, which had sacramental status. Ariès contends that it is not until the twelfth century that the Church fully appropriated the familial form of marriage.

The essays in the first section of this volume in some ways parallel the revisionist history of Flandrin and Ariès. These essays suggest, among other things, that doctrine, like social practice, has its own history and development; hence that it is not a static structure to be contrasted to the changing norms of human behavior. Elizabeth A. Clark's opening essay examines the development of Augustine's ideas about the essential constituents of marriage. Clark points out that Augustine presents rather contradictory views on marriage. His positions were chiefly determined, she argues, by polemics against extreme ascetics, Manicheans, and Pelagians; they reflect as well the age's view of women and confusion in Roman law about the consensual and physical factors in marriage. Clark contends that Augustine possessed a socially-oriented ideal of marriage emphasizing consensual and affective elements, but that theological controversies forced an emphasis on the goodness of the sexual and reproductive domains. Nevertheless, Augustine was the first major Western theologian to assert that the marriage of Mary and Joseph, though celibate, was complete. A marriage is made by "the pledge of affection of the soul," not by the "voluptuous connection of the body," he argued, and mutual consent is in itself sufficient to make a marriage. Had his view not been mediated by controversy and polemic, Clark concludes, Augustine would have developed a theory of marital friendship unique for its time and place.

Michael Sheehan's essay further examines the ideology of marriage by discussing its sources in Scripture and Roman law. Father Sheehan observes that, although the Middle Ages emphasized the importance of consent in marriage, we have scant information about the actual substance of consent. Citing the scholarship of John T. Noonan, Jr., and others, he argues that by the time of Justinian "marital affection" referred to both legal consent and the emotional texture of a relationship. Affection remains, however, an undefined quality within the legal definitions of marriage. Like Clark, Sheehan traces a central idea within a shifting field. Gratian, for example, went beyond Roman law to assert that wherever there was marital affection, a marriage could come into being and nothing short of death could end it. He also developed the crucial distinction that consent involves accepting another person as a spouse while marital affection is the resultant relation of spouses. Pope Alexander III (1159–81) stressed that marital affection ought to thrive within marriage. Sheehan remarks, "a static notion was replaced by one implying the desirability of growth." Turning to confessors' handbooks, liturgical books, and sermons, he finds sources that address the practical moral lives of men and women. Sheehan's guide through this literature, much of which still awaits proper editorial attention, suggests the local circumstances in which ideas like partnership and mutuality took on specific meaning in the Middle Ages.

Erik Kooper's essay addresses the theological and philosophical views that evolved in Church doctrine over the problematic notion of equality in marriage. Kooper distinguishes a monastic-Augustinian view of marital equality from the philosophical-Aristotelian perspective. Hugh of St. Victor, Kooper notes, developed Augustine's and Bernard of Clairvaux's ideas about marriage to assert the near-equality of man and woman. Hugh declared that woman was created as a *socia* rather than a servant or a mistress. The fact that Eve was taken from the middle of Adam's body, not from the highest or lowest regions, indicates her equality of association, said Hugh—though he added that her being made from man's body shows a kind of inferiority. Later interpretation of the "rib-topos," Kooper shows, extended the claim of equality to all human beings. He observes that other commentators, including Thomas Aquinas, connected equality to Aristotelian notions of friendship. Like Sheehan, Kooper finds the abstract concerns of the theologians translated to popular audiences through the homily, and he turns to *ad status* sermons, addresses to people in specific states of life, as a source for ideas about love, equality, and happiness in marriage.

The historical grounding given in the first part of this collection emphasizes the decisive, if complex, role of Augustine, and the elaboration of doctrine in the ecclesiastical culture of the High Middle Ages. The second part turns to the literary representation of love in the vernacular and examines how desire and companionate partnership—what Guibert de Tournai called *dilectio carnalis* and *dilectio socialis* respectively—found imaginative expression in the literature of Europe. Our sense of the expectations of that literature and its audience has been shaped in large measure by the way the literary history of the Middle Ages has been written for much of the last century. Over fifty years ago C. S. Lewis presented in *The Allegory of Love* a highly influential view of the nature of love in the Middle Ages. Lewis stressed that one of the main qualities of such love was that it existed outside of marriage; it was "always what the nineteenth century called 'dishonourable' love."[6] Although he was principally concerned with love as a poetic convention, Lewis suggested that it reflected and derived from actual belief and practice. In medieval life, Lewis argued, passion was often denounced as wicked, and in feudal society marriage had nothing to do with love. From this cleavage between the Church and the court, and between love and marriage, he concluded, emerged the tradition of courtly love, characterized by humility, courtesy, the religion of love, and adultery. Courtly love seemed to exist with equal force as a social practice and as a literary motif. Subsequent studies like Denis de Rougemont's *Love in the Western World* developed and refined the view that a secret and illicit form of love represented an ideal within medieval culture.[7] In many respects, these scholars established the commonplaces by which subsequent writers describe a general notion of love in the Middle Ages.

Later scholarship has challenged such formulations, both in general and in the particulars. Critics have noted that many texts do not conform to Lewis's definition of courtly love.[8] The love courts where this ideal of love supposedly took shape are also very poorly documented. John F. Benton, for example, has cast serious doubt on the notion that Marie de Champagne presided over such a court, or would even have been interested in immoral love.[9] One of the most notable of the courts for which there is some evidence of courtly love conventions in the later Middle Ages, the *cour amoureuse* of Charles VI, seems to have been based on a charter that represents fictional elaborations of a modest original.[10]

If the historical background of the courtly love tradition has proved uncertain, its literary and social dimensions are no less debated. Several scholars have contested the view that courtly love was an ideal within medieval culture. D. W. Robertson, Jr., and other Patristic critics, for example, maintain that the dominant value in literature of the period was necessarily *caritas:* the love of God and of one's neighbor for the sake of God. Secret, adulterous love exemplifies the much inferior *cupiditas,* the love of oneself, one's neighbor, or something for its own sake. From this perspective, an idealized view of adultery can only be an ironic demonstration of its own inadequacy as passionate and unreasoning cupidity. Robertson contends, in fact, that Andreas Capellanus's famous treatise on love, the *De amore,* did not seriously promote sexual sin, but rather was often satiric in setting forth the rules of love. The warnings in the third book of the *De amore,* that concupiscence offends God, injures one's neighbor, and is inimical to charity, make explicit the implications of the preceding books.[11]

E. Talbot Donaldson, who in other contexts offers spirited arguments against the Patristic approach, agrees with Robertson about Andreas's intentions. Donaldson doubts that the proposition that love can exist only extra-maritally ever had much counterpart in reality: Andreas's treatise, he suggests, "has about as much to do with erotic practices in Champagne at the end of the twelfth century as the debate of the *Owl and the Nightingale* has to do with ornithology."[12] Donaldson notes the observation, made by Gervase Mathew and others, that Middle English portrayals of love rarely involve adultery. The notion that love must be illicit, he concludes, is more relevant for Chaucer's fabliau characters than for his serious lovers.

Henry Ansgar Kelly observes that courtly love was a "widespread delusion" even before Lewis wrote, having begun as a "small tumor" in an essay by Gaston Paris in 1883.[13] Paris had asserted that the first characteristic of courtly love is that it is illicit and furtive, and therefore incompatible with the calm and public possession of a lady in marriage. But Kelly argues that it was quite common for medieval marriages themselves to be both illicit and furtive rather than calm and public. He adds that the idea that love required adultery is patently unhistorical, and he notes that there was never a seriously or generally held opinion that love was impossible within marriage.[14] On the contrary, the idea that true love should lead to mutuality in marriage, says

Kelly, was well known by Chaucer's time: it is inherent in Jean de Meun's portion of the *Roman de la Rose*, and Thomas Usk espoused it vigorously in the *Testament of Love*, written a year or so after the *Troilus* (p.67). Chaucer himself was especially careful in matters of sexual morality, he notes, citing D. S. Brewer: "Chaucer nowhere celebrates illicit love"; his serious love stories always contain "an explicit connection between love and marriage."[15]

George Kane demonstrates that there never was a single medieval code of love. Indeed, he argues, the lack of definition in Chaucer's understanding of *fin amour* (which Chaucer calls "fyn lovynge") resulted from initial ambiguity and subsequent modifications of the convention.[16] Kane shows that perceptions of *fin amour* developed in various phases. The Northern French romances, for example, radically transformed the tradition, linking the ennobling force of love to military prowess and taking for granted, in romances after Chrétien, that romantic, exalted love could exist within marriage. Kane also notes that the thirteenth-century French romances displayed a marked interest in the mentality of the lovers and that this analytical tendency is continued in the *Roman de la Rose*. Italian poets had their own distinct conceptions of love, Kane argues. And he adds that fourteenth-century French verse, notably Machaut's, manifests a further adaptation of *fin amour.* The thematic multiplicity in these diverse depictions of love was compounded, Kane observes, by the long-standing awareness that *fin amour* is essentially self-contradictory and preposterous. He concludes that the differences in the representations of *fin amour* would have promoted eclecticism in Chaucer's work, and he adds that nowhere does Chaucer appear to be committed to the cult.

Lewis's claim that courtly love was a distinctly medieval convention, marking one of the three or four real changes in sentiment in Western history, has also been challenged. Peter Dronke maintains that one of the chief characteristics of this love—that it elevates and ennobles the lover—has in fact been present throughout the Western tradition. The notion owes as much to neo-Platonism as to orthodox Christianity, and analogues reach far back into early classical civilization.[17] A more radical critique of the early contentions about courtly love has emerged from structuralist and poststructuralist criticism. These approaches call into question not only the historical foundations of literary representations but the possibility of representation itself.

Paul Zumthor's theory of the "circularity of the song" in the High Middle Ages proposes that the lyric poetry of the troubadours and trouvères is self-enclosed and self-referential. There is no representation of historical reality in poems; biography and fiction alike are discarded, for the "great courtly song" is concerned with neither actual nor imaginary events. The poems present instead, Zumthor suggests, a series of gestures made toward and about a social circle that is identical with the poet himself.[18] The sources for this theory lie in Robert Guiette's essays on the highly formal quality of the Old French lyrics. But the fullest articulation comes in critics like Pierre Guiraud, who finds an equivalence, if not an identity, in the key terms *amar, trobar,* and *chantar.* Love, song, and poetic making thus designate the same act. But on this view it is an act that has no contact with the world outside the text.[19]

Against such views, however, stands Larry D. Benson's argument that by the fourteenth century the conventions and especially the language of courtly love were accepted and practiced in aristocratic circles.[20] Benson confirms that adultery was not essential to this form of love. But the other qualities that C. S. Lewis cited—humility, courtesy, and the religion of love—were fundamental to love as it was by then understood. The reading of romances, Benson observes, became part of the ordinary education of many aristocratic children, and the new courtly culture sought to emulate the speech of love poetry: for the gentlemen of the time, courtly love offered the only words with which to express desire. (This, he adds, led to the first class dialect in English of which we have any clear indication.) Aristocrats fell in love in ways prescribed by courtly literature, and they often sought to earn their ladies' love in the manner of the old romances. As late as the sixteenth century, Benson observes, courtiers were living the lives of courtly lovers. Henry VIII himself tries, without quite succeeding, to use the style of courtly love in a letter to Anne Boleyn: he begins with traditional declarations of love and service, but in the last line Henry declares that he wants to "kiss her duckies"! Here and in the earlier instances, the conception of love and the way it was expressed were often diverse. The affinity, doubtless unwitting, is more to Chaucer's balade "To Rosemounde" than to the *Troilus,* but as Chaucer says in the *Troilus,* "Scarsly ben ther in this place thre / That have in love said lik, or don, all."

The essays in the second and third parts of this collection explore the diverse and sometimes surprising ways in which love, friendship, and sexuality were portrayed in medieval literature. A. C. Spearing examines the moral compromise inherent in writing and enjoying love poetry, specifically the imaginative voyeurism into which the poet and his audience are necessarily drawn. Beginning with Andreas Capellanus's emphasis on sight as the origin of desire (which was later confirmed by Freud), Spearing explores the essential paradox that the stories expose the private, often most secret actions that the characters urgently try to protect. The poet both describes a private life and finds pleasure in observing its secrets. The public nature of literary presentation makes narrative part of erotic discourse, in this case the near equivalent of rumor and scandal spread by the *lauzengeors* who threaten betrayal. Sometimes, as in Beroul's *Tristan* or Chaucer's *Troilus*, the poet writes his act of surveillance into the text in the form of characters who wish to observe the lovers. In the first part of the *Roman de la Rose*, Spearing finds the poet's metaphorical and thematized voyeurism made literal, in the actions of the dreamer: "in order to describe, he has to watch carefully, obsessively even, and the act of watching an erotic performance with such enthrallment obviously has sexual implications." The radical extension of this poetic surveillance lies for Spearing in a work like William Dunbar's *The Golden Targe*, which explicitly shows voyeurism as the only role for a male poet in a courtly dream-world pervaded by his fantasies of female aggression. Yet the fantasy is dangerous, for the women being observed seek to destroy the observer.

Spearing's essay traces a dimension of medieval writing about love that extends from the High to the Late Middle Ages. In his study of Chrétien de Troyes's *Yvain* and the *Lais* of Marie de France, by contrast, R. W. Hanning focuses on a moment of dramatic social change. Hanning contends that the twelfth century saw a profound social transition from aggression and martial prowess to the rediscovered power of love and creativity. Chrétien and Marie offer, he claims, fictional representations of this rejection of culturally-sanctioned violence. *Yvain* tells the story of a knight whose adventures test the limits of ritualized justice achieved through force. In the tale, says Hanning, trial by combat is transformed into an iconography of love and self-sacrifice. And the qualities that effect the reconciliation of the hero and his wife at the end of the tale are love and artfulness. In Marie's *Lais*, Hanning suggests, love and art are also closely aligned. The young knight Guigemar's success in winning his lady in the lai of *Guigemar* depends on his ability to speak eloquently of love. In another of Marie's tales, *Yonec*, a woman finds fulfilling love and escape from a tyrannical marriage in the embodiment of a lover she has wished into existence through the power of her imagination. This creative act, Hanning points out, can be described in the same terms that Marie uses to describe her own art. The tale is thus "an allegory of the artist's travails and ultimate triumphs."

Giovanni Sinicropi's analysis of the story of Nastagio degli Onesti in Boccaccio's *Decameron* traces a medieval story of love and eventual marriage back to its origins in pagan ritual and confirms Hanning's conclusion about the power of love. Boccaccio's tale is the culmination, as Sinicropi demonstrates, of the widespread motif of testing a woman's chastity by a parable of eschatological punishment. Examining the background of the story in Eastern, Western and classical stories deriving from early ritual or myth, Sinicropi shows that Boccaccio regenerates the tradition he received by transforming its ritualistic elements and their repetitious violence in favor of social stability. As they witness the reenactment of an earlier story of thwarted love that ends in suicide and vengeance, his characters choose a different outcome: marriage. This choice represents the point of arrival for the long literary history of this motif. For Boccaccio does not depict the rejection of chastity as submission to the will of a god or acquiescence in sensuality, as in his sources. Rather, he harmonizes the rejection of chastity in the early sources with its idealization in Christian theology. The result is an affirmation of human love and of the power of life over death.

Jerome Mazzaro's study of Dante's transformation of *fin amour* to friendship traces the evolution of literary convention into a view of spiritual love that draws on much of the philosophical tradition used to define the terms of companionate marriage. Mazzaro sees in Dante's early work "the belief in the ennobling force of human love, the beloved's superiority to the lover, and love's emergence as an unsatiated, ever increasing desire." But, following Étienne Gilson, he finds that the discussion of friendship in the *Convivio* allows a reconception of the bonds that connect creatures to each other and to God.[21] Aristotle's *Ethics*, Cicero's *De amicitia*, and Augustine's *Confessions* provide a context for analyzing the multiform relations of love in the *Comedy*, from the reprise of *fin amour* in the Paolo and Francesca episode to Beatrice's "friendship" with the poet to the soul's relation to God. The tradition of friendship, Mazzaro contends, is what permits Dante to go beyond courtly love and the problem of disparate states to imagine a spiritual community infused with both virtue and affect.

The final group of essays deals with the treatment of love in Chaucer, whose work stands as a sustained exploration of the artistic and moral complexities that love presented to medieval poets. The first two essays explore Chaucer's treatment of love, friendship, marriage, and sexual relations with respect to the reading and writing of poetry. Robert R. Edwards begins by examining the retrospective view Chaucer takes of his early poetry in the Prologue to the *Legend of Good Women*. He argues that the Prologue juxtaposes the social and poetic texts of love. The former represents Cupid's attempt to impose a determinate, socially regulated meaning on the materials of literary tradition; the latter insists on the capacity of the stories to overturn narrow definitions and reflect moral and artistic complexity. Edwards's reading of the *Book of the Duchess* emphasizes the self-conscious fabrication of the Man in Black's erotic history, which qualifies the idealized portrait of Blanche. Similarly, the *Knight's Tale* incorporates a complex meditation on desire and social order in its portrayal of a courtly life that reconciles tragedy through a royal marriage. Returning to the *Legend*, Edwards reviews the ways in which Chaucer's retelling of the tales stresses the paradoxes of courtly values while carrying out Cupid's charge to tell stories that reflect the virtues of faithful women.

Chaucer's use of language as a form of sexual politics is the subject of John M. Fyler's essay. Tracing the use of names for man and woman in the Creation stories in Genesis and reviewing commentary on these passages in Hebrew and Latin, Fyler contends that Chaucer played on the ambiguity of *man* as "male" and "human being" and on the traditional relationship between naming and gender differentiation. Chaucer's word choice associates "woman" to a variety of terms and treats women as the victims as well as the causes of woe. The adjectives "manly" and "womanly" define not absolute values but relative qualities, while "man" and "men" often blur the indefinite and the particular. Fyler finds in the *Squire's Tale* Chaucer's most sophisticated treatment of the ambiguity of "man" as a term that hovers uncertainly between genders and species. He concludes that Chaucer is aware of both the confining nature of gender and the ways in which his own voice speaks from motives that cannot be abstracted from gender.

The next two essays offer readings of the *Franklin's Tale*, a pivotal text for an understanding of the role of married love in Chaucer's writings. George Lyman Kittredge regarded the tale as the culmination of one act in the human comedy that he took to be Chaucer's design for the *Canterbury Tales*. He asserted that the Franklin disputes the theory that love was incompatible with marriage because marriage implies mastery: "Love *can* be consistent with marriage, he declares. Indeed, without love (and perfect *gentle* love) marriage is sure to be a failure. The difficulty about mastery vanishes when mutual love and forbearance are made the guiding principles of the relation between husband and wife."[22] Despite scholarly debate over the Marriage Group and Kittredge's assumptions that the tale's announced values are universal ("A better has never been devised or imagined"), the tale remains a touchstone for critical analysis. That our two essays should come to the philosophical substratum of the *Franklin's Tale* from radically different ways is a measure of the poem's evocative power.

Alan T. Gaylord believes that "the story most richly apprehended invites several kinds of reading at once, in a contradictory yet complementary manner," and he demonstrates a method of reading texts "forwards" and "backwards," applying this approach to the issues of love and marriage that inform the tale. Reading forwards, he says, is a compliant and uncritical response to a text that follows its linear succession, as in listening to an oral performance. Reading backwards involves a resistance born of intense awareness: "reading with a certain kind of memory, employing a sifting that requires comparisons and contrasts, re-reading and reflection." It is a backwards reading of this sort that leads Gaylord to probe the "vavasorial temper" of the Franklin's tale, which "gesture[s] towards philosophy on the way to comforts untested by any fire or true pain." Juxtaposing the *Franklin's Tale* and the *Knight's Tale*, he shows how the former's appropriation of the latter blends all principles together as part of a strategy of control that disguises itself as affability.

James I. Wimsatt takes a different view of the philosophical sources behind the *Franklin's Tale*. Establishing a "family history" for Boethius's *Consolation of Philosophy*, the *Roman de la Rose*, Machaut's *Remede de Fortune*, and texts by Chaucer, he traces a "chain of borrowing, the passing on of literary as well as philosophical features" from one text to another. In this context, the Franklin's assertions in the prologue to his tale that marriage partners should be friends and that neither should attempt to assert mastery over the other acquire an authority that scholars must take into account. Wimsatt gives particular attention to the weight of friendship in the philosophical tradition in the tale, and he sees Machaut's *Remede* as a crucial intermediary between the *Roman* and Chaucer. While he stops short of describing the Franklin's account of marriage early in the tale as an ideal answer, Wimsatt concludes that it agrees with medieval authorities on friendship and marriage, appeals to common sense, and provides "a benign and optimistic dénouement for Chaucer's marital discussion."

In the final essays, Stephen Spector and Marie Borroff consider the quality of the love in the *Prioress's Tale*. Noting the contradictions and mislocations that characterize the Prioress's love, Spector examines the intersection of love and hate in her tale. He argues that the profound conflicts in critical responses to the Prioress reflect the contraries in her makeup as well as the influence of modern experience and ideology. Spector briefly reviews the social position and historical experience of Jews in the late Middle Ages in order to challenge the claim that Chaucer necessarily shared in an inescapable intolerance toward Jews. Instead, he presents evidence of a crosscurrent of respect, friendship, and even intimacy between Christians and Jews. But he concludes that Chaucer's own attitude toward Jews is probably irretrievable. The immediate question, therefore, is how Madame Eglentyne's anti-Jewishness functions within her tale. Spector demonstrates a detailed self-referentiality between teller and tale and concludes that this accounts for the nun's empathy as well as her enmity. Borroff's essay, like Spector's, investigates aspects of the Prioress's prayer and tale that disclose the nature of Eglentyne's love. Inquiring whether the Prioress was inclined to or capable of "love celestial," Borroff discusses the simple and reductive polarities that inform the Prioress's vision. The world of the tale is fashioned from binary oppositions between good and evil, infant and adult, affective piety and reason, love and hate, innocence and experience. These contrasts are enhanced, Borroff adds, by complementary imagistic oppositions and by the distinction between song and speech. In this realm, the Christian relates to divine goodness with the thoughtful and instinctual bliss of the child surrounded by the loving care of its parents. This, she concludes, is celestial love as the Prioress knows it.

1

"Adam's Only Companion": Augustine and the Early Christian Debate on Marriage

I

In the heat of the Pelagian controversy,[1] Augustine composed Book XIV of the *City of God*, the book that details the sin of the first couple in Eden and the idyllic life Adam and Eve would have enjoyed had the Fall not intervened. How, Augustine asks, could a male endowed with rationality and free will have been led astray by the "sly seductions" of Lucifer? With help from I Timothy 2:14,[2] he argues that not Adam, but only Eve, the weaker element of that first "human society," was deceived. Then why did Adam fall, if he was not deceived? Because, Augustine asserts, he was faithful to a "social instinct": he refused to be separated from his "only companion."[3]

Embedded in Augustine's exegesis is a social view of marriage that he had evolved over twenty years or more. Had he developed its implications unswervingly, he would have arrived at a notion of marital friendship unique for his time and place. Yet Augustine's vision of companionate marriage was not just balanced, but often overshadowed, by his emphasis upon the sexual and reproductive functions of marriage. His ambivalent conception of the "essence" of marriage, I shall argue, can be traced primarily to the necessities of theological controversy, for it was in the midst of controversies that he formulated his marital ethic. His attempt to mediate between both orthodox and heretical asceticism, on the one hand, and the Pelagians' praise of lusty sexuality, on the other, contributed to his ambivalent assessment. Only in a later era could his vision of companionate marriage be enlisted in campaigns for actual social change.[4]

To arrive at the sentiments expressed in Book XIV of the *City of God*, Augustine had travelled a long road. In his personal life, he had journeyed from years with his unnamed mistress and the joys of male friendship to the lonelier, more demanding ones as bishop of Hippo Regius. There had been a long road of religious controversy as well: before he arrived at his view of marriage expressed in Book XIV, he had mediated the acrid debates on asceticism and had battled Manicheanism. In response to the excesses of the former and the errors of the latter, he had forged a new vision of marriage that would guide the Catholic Church until the mid-twentieth century.[5] With this revised understanding, he had equipped himself to face the Pelagian accusation that his theory of original sin rendered marriage and procreation damnable. Yet under the Pelagian onslaught, especially that levelled by his brilliant opponent Julian of Eclanum, Augustine failed to develop more fully the new "social" understanding of marriage as fully as he otherwise might. Although he did not abandon his view that the essence of marriage lay in something non-physical, it was more urgent for him to defend himself against Julian's charge that his theory of original sin undermined the goodness of reproduction.

In addition to the role played by theological controversy, Augustine's failure to express unambiguously the non-physical essence of marriage rested on two other factors. For one, Augustine's view of women-in-general, typical for his age, did little to advance his nascent argument about the possibility of friendship in marriage. Second, the confusion of Roman marriage law about the relative importance of consensual and physical factors in marriage may also have contributed to Augustine's dilemma. He probably contributed far more to *later* theories of "consent" as the essence of marriage than he was influenced by formulations of "consent" in legal pronouncements up to his own day. Thus this essay explores the circumstances that prompted his theory of companionate marriage and those that inhibited its realization.

II

The *Confessions* makes clear that in his youth, Augustine could not reconcile the claims of friendship with sexual desire. He agreed with classical authors that friendship was a union of souls, that a friend was a "second self,"[6] but in his own life, "the hell of lust" blackened that lofty ideal all too soon.[7] In his adolescent estimation, a woman's love could not make up for the death of his dearest male companion,[8] yet he was nonetheless unable to live without it. Of his mistress, he writes that he had chosen her for no particular reason but that his "passions had settled on her," that their relationship was "a bargain struck for lust."[9] His words sound callous, but less callous than his reported reason for abandoning this faithful partner of perhaps fifteen years in order to become engaged to a ten-year-old girl:[10] the desire for a wife of high social and financial status who could help advance his career.[11] Augustine and his male friends had hoped to establish a commune in which a life of cultured *otium* could prevail, but their utopian dreams foundered on the problem of what to do with their women.[12] Only after his conversion to ascetic Christianity did he find a brief substitute for his failed dream in his retreat to Cassiciacum with male friends,[13] where he whiled away hours discussing the nature of God[14] and the soul.[15] The only feminine presence in this paradise of male intellectuals was Augustine's widowed mother, Monica.[16]

Since the young Augustine tended to link women with the physical realm, it is not surprising that his dramatic conversion in 386 A.D. was a conversion *away* from women's sexuality, away from the ghosts of his old mistresses, his *nugae nugarum* (aptly translated by Kenneth Burke as "toys of toys"),[17] who whispered in his ear, "Will we never be able to do this-and-that again?"[18] Augustine's youthful prayer—"Grant me chastity, but not yet"[19]— was conveniently answered only many years later, when Lady Continence gave him her decisive summons to the ascetic life.[20] In the years before (and some may wonder about those after), he denied that the blaze of friendship that "melts our hearts and welds them into one"[21] was possible with a woman, least of all with a woman with whom one slept.

Augustine's retreat from physical sexuality is also evident in the exegetical writing of his post-conversion years. In his first extant interpretation of the creation story composed in 388–389 A.D.,[22] *On Genesis Against the Manichees*, Augustine so spiritualizes the tale that he nearly loses a flesh-and-blood couple. The reason for his spiritualizing exegesis is known: he wrote the treatise to answer Manichean accusations that the Old Testament contained gross anthropomorphisms.[23] Against this charge, Augustine employed the allegorical exegesis he had learned from Ambrose[24] to "rescue" the text. Thus he asserts that no physical creation took place in Genesis 1; the creation described therein consisted only of the "causal reasons." Bodily creation represented a second stage, arrived at only in Genesis 2.[25] If this was the case,

how were we to explain the fact that God's command to "reproduce and multiply" stood in Genesis 1? According to Augustine,
that command was for spiritual, not for physical, union. Fleshly
union came about only after the Fall.[26] Thus the Old Latin text of
Luke 20:34 was correct in holding that only the children of *this*
(i.e., the fallen) world beget and are begotten.[27] This asexual interpretation of Genesis is still in evidence in 398, when he wrote
Book XIII of the *Confessions*: there the words in Genesis 1:28
about reproduction are taken to mean the diverse thoughts and expressions produced by the fertile human mind.[28] This spiritualized, asexual reading of Genesis caused Augustine discomfort in
his later years, after he had adopted an earthier interpretation of
Edenic relations.[29]

In sum, Augustine's hard-won conversion and early writings
portended a decidedly non-sexual interpretation of God's plan for
the world. Events of the next decade, however, prompted him to
moderate his teaching.

III

Two controversies of the late fourth century led Augustine to
temper his early ascetic leanings. The first was the debate in the
390s between Jerome and Jovinian: surveying it in retrospect, Augustine concluded that Jerome had gone too far in his enthusiasm
for ascetic renunciation. Although Augustine's mentor, Ambrose,
had celebrated Christian virginity in general and that of Mary in
particular,[30] his praise of virginity was not coupled with a relentless attack upon marriage, as was Jerome's. For Jerome, the only
good of marriage was to produce virgins for the Church.[31] He summons up the woes of marriage—screaming children, adulterous
spouses, disobedient slaves, and the like—to deter young people
from it.[32] He styles marriage the "vomit" to which no widow
would wish to return. In tones of high satire, he mocks a young
widow's desire for children: "Do you fear the extinction of the Fu-
rian line if you do not present your father with some little fellow
to crawl upon his chest and drool down his neck?"[33]

Such vituperative lines prompted a rejoinder from a fellow ascetic, Jovinian.[34] According to Jovinian, Christian baptism rendered all persons equal, whether they were married, widowed, or
virginal; no tiers of merit existed to differentiate Christians on the
basis of their ascetic practice.[35] Jerome's slander of marriage
verged on a "Manichean" denial of the goodness of God's creation,
in Jovinian's view.[36]

Against Jovinian's praise of marriage as a divine gift and his citation of Biblical passages proving that our holy forefathers had married,[37] Jerome argued that marriage occurred only after the Fall. God had created Adam and Eve as virgins,[38] and virgins they were presumably intended to stay. The command to "reproduce and multiply" had in any event been replaced in the New Testament by the admonition, "Let those who have wives live as though they have none."[39] Jerome's argument was buttressed with some fanciful exegesis. In challenging Jovinian's use of I Timothy 2:15 (that women will be saved through childbearing if they raise their children in *sōphrosynē*), Jerome argues that the Greek word should be translated as *castitas,* and interprets it to mean that women who raise children for *virginity* can make up for their own lack of excellence through the virginal commitment of their children.[40] Turning to the animal kingdom for illustrations with which to devalue marriage, Jerome notes that it was only the *unclean* beasts who entered Noah's ark two by two.[41] Although Jerome protests that he is no "Manichean,"[42] Christians in Rome were shocked by his violent language. His Roman friend Pammachius scooped copies of the *Adversus Jovinianum* off the market before more eyes fell upon them. For Pammachius' effort, Jerome expressed little gratitude.[43]

Eight years after Jerome's famous response to Jovinian, i.e., in 401, Augustine wrote *On the Good of Marriage* and *On Holy Virginity,*[44] in which (he later claimed) he tried to prove that Christian virginity could be praised without denigrating marriage.[45] He hints that "some" champions of Christian virginity (clearly Jerome) had so implicated marriage that they had lent plausibility to Jovinian's charge of "Manicheanism."[46] Unlike Jerome, Augustine praises marriage and reproduction as "goods."[47] He posits, quite tentatively, that Adam and Eve *could* have had sexual intercourse in Eden even if they had not sinned. Reproduction could be viewed as part of God's plan for the first couple even though they would not have aged or died[48] (thus Augustine precludes the explanation that the purpose of children is to fill up the ranks left empty by the deaths of the old). This new interpretation of Eden is not further developed in *On the Good of Marriage,*[49] but it was to re-emerge soon.

A few years later, Augustine advances the same view, now more definitively, in *On Genesis According to the Letter.*[50] By Book IX, he has moved far beyond his early spiritualized exegesis of Eden to postulate that the first couple would have had sexual relations leading to reproduction even if they had not sinned, although they would not have known the disrupting lust that sexual functioning today entails.[51] In Book IX, he speaks of procreation as woman's "purpose," necessary for the multiplication of the human race even at the world's beginnings.[52] These views he will explicate more fully about a decade later in the *City of God*. Thus Augustine, in tempering the extreme claims of the ascetic movement, champions the goodness of our sexual functions in their essential created state and the reproduction of the species that derives therefrom.

A second reason for Augustine's move away from his earlier sexual views lies in his battles against Manicheanism in the late 380s and 390s. That Augustine himself had been a Manichean for at least nine years[53] and that Christian ascetics were being slandered as "Manicheans"[54] rendered Augustine anxious to differentiate sharply his own views from those of the Manicheans. The Manichean deprecation of reproduction stemmed from their foundation myth: at the world's origin, the power of Light had been defeated by Darkness and entrapped in matter. Reproduction served only to dissipate particles of light further among matter and thus impede its collection and restoration to its heavenly home.[55] The lower ranks of Manicheans, the Auditors, to whom Augustine had belonged, were permitted to engage in sexual relations *if* contraceptive measures were taken to prevent the further entrapment of light in new bodies. That Augustine learned these techniques (a primitive form of the "rhythm" method[56] and perhaps *coitus interruptus*[57]) is suggested not just by his own testimony,[58] but also by the fact that he produced no other children during his long period as a Manichean, despite living with his mistress throughout the duration of his Manichean attachment.[59] The Manichean ethic was thus pro-contraceptive and anti-reproductive.

Augustine as a newly-baptized Christian inverted the Manichean evaluation to champion a pro-reproductive and anti-contraceptive ethic. From his earliest anti-Manichean works, offspring stand as the central good of marriage.[60] Thus Augustine defends the polygamy of the patriarchs against Manichean attack, since (he claims) they were motivated solely by God's command to reproduce at the world's beginning, not by lust.[61] Since offspring are the central purpose of marriage, the use of contraceptive measures is now deemed tantamount to "adultery."[62] In this anti-Manichean context, Augustine develops his now-infamous interpretation of Genesis 38: Augustine levels the story of Onan (who spilled his seed on the ground rather than impregnate his brother's wife, as levirate marriage demanded, and was slain by God for his sinful act) as a warning to Christian couples who practice contraception.[63] In his anti-Manichean writings, Augustine cleverly links the etymology of the word *matrimonium* with *mater.*[64] He also notes that the Roman marriage contract stipulates that children are the first "end" of marriage.[65] Thus it seems no accident that in the *Confessions*, written toward the end of Augustine's anti-Manichean literary activity, he champions the view that marriage is "for" children, and rues the fact that in his own youth he did not live in an honorable marriage that had children as its goal.[66]

In the second decade of the fifth century, Augustine's pro-reproductive schema was played out in yet a different way. In his anti-Pelagian writings from 412 A.D. on, Augustine argued that original sin led to the corruption of the sex act, although its result, offspring, was still blessed by God. The excitation of our sexual members is the constant reminder of that "injury" which entered the world with the Fall and was transmitted to all the descendants of Adam and Eve except Jesus.[67]

This view Augustine develops in Book XIV of the *City of God*. There he writes that if sin had not intervened, the sexual organs would have moved at the command of the will; no tussle between the will and lust would have occurred; tranquility would have prevailed in mind and body during the sexual act.[68] Moreover, no destruction of "virginal integrity" would have occurred and no labor pains would have accompanied childbirth.[69] Although Augustine admits that we cannot now experience the sexual act in this way,[70] his emphasis lies not on imaginary speculation but on the physicality of the intercourse that would have occurred. In Genesis 1:28, God commanded the first human into a genuinely physical relationship, not simply to "spiritual development,"[71] as he earlier had posited.

In the treatises after the *City of God*, the goodness of conception and birth continues to be praised,[72] and marriage is extolled as God's institution.[73] But now Augustine must be on guard against Pelagian claims that his theory of original sin slandered God's created universe. Especially did he need to emphasize the goodness of reproduction in his last works against Julian of Eclanum, for Julian did not hesitate to call Augustine's theory a throwback to the "Manichean" deprecation of the material world and childbearing.[74] Against this charge, Augustine incessantly repeats that reproduction is God's good gift; that even children of adulterers are a good work; that there would have been sexual union for reproduction even if no sin had occurred, albeit without pain or loss of "virginal integrity."[75] He concedes one further point to the Pelagians: possibly—but only possibly—*libido* could have been exercised in a sinless Eden, although there it would have acted in cooperation with the will, not against it.[76]

Thus from his early writings to his last treatise, Augustine was pushed by the demands of theological controversy to affirm the goodness of sexual reproduction. Yet this emphasis, so necessary for him to affirm against Jerome, the Manicheans, and the Pelagian attacks, was somewhat at variance with his more socially-oriented ideal of marriage that he had also developed throughout the years. It, too, is present in his early works and in his later anti-Pelagian writings. It was this second, more social, view of male-female bonding that would later give impetus to theories of companionate marriage.

IV

Paradoxically, it was in Augustine's attempt to refute the Manichean anti-reproductive program that he found the key to his alternative vision of marriage: the marriage of Mary and Joseph. Manicheans who recoiled from envisioning the divine confined to the "filthy womb" of a woman[77] or inhabiting a material body[78] struck hard at the Catholic theory of God's Incarnation in a flesh-and-blood human, Jesus. The Manicheans buttressed their arguments by noting the discrepancies in the genealogies of Jesus listed in Matthew and Luke. Augustine saw their ploy clearly: they appealed to the discrepancies in the genealogies to discount Jesus's birth.[79] Since Augustine as a Catholic staunchly supported the physical Incarnation of the Second Person of the Trinity,[80] he was impelled by the Manichean argument to examine the genealogies more closely. The results of his investigations are found not just in his explicitly anti-Manichean writings, but also in his sermons and in this treatise *On the Harmony of the Evangelists*. His conclusion—that Mary and Joseph had a genuine marriage despite their lifelong lack of sexual contact—prompted a new assessment of the essence of marriage.

The status of Mary and Joseph's relationship had been raised earlier, in 383, by Jerome in his debate with Helvidius. Jerome argued that Mary and Joseph never had experienced sexual relations after the birth of Jesus.[81] In Jerome's hands, the brothers and sisters of Jesus mentioned in the New Testament become cousins,[82] while Joseph himself (in correction of earlier traditions)[83] is transformed into a lifelong virgin to serve as a model for male celibates.[84] Thus Jerome asserts that Joseph acted as Mary's guardian, not as her husband.[85] Although Joseph has almost the *licentia* of a husband, Jerome does not call the relation a *nuptia*.[86] Embedded in Jerome's view is the belief that if there are no sexual relations, there is no marriage.[87] Ambrose's testimony is more ambivalent. Although he avers that it is not *defloratio* but the *pactio conjugalis* that makes a marriage, he does not develop the view that Joseph and Mary were actually married.[88] Augustine thus remains the first major Western theologian to argue that although Joseph and Mary remained celibate, they had a true marriage.

Augustine's treatise *Against Faustus the Manichean*, composed in 397-398 A.D.,[89] is our first detailed evidence for this view. From Augustine's response, we infer that Faustus broached the Gospel genealogies as his first line of attack upon the corporeality of Jesus. In addition to citing the discrepancies contained therein, Faustus points to such Biblical statements of Jesus as "I am not of this world" and "Who is my mother? Who are my brothers?" to establish that Jesus did not have physical kin.[90] Augustine admits that the genealogies contain discrepancies and attempts to resolve them.[91] In doing so, he tries to answer the question why Joseph is called the *father* of Jesus and why the genealogies come down to him when he was not responsible for the physical conception of Jesus. Augustine argues thus: because Joseph acted in the role of Jesus's father, he can be named Mary's *husband*, and this despite their failure ever to have intercourse. They can be called *husband and wife* because "intercourse of the mind is more intimate than that of the body." Fleshly intercourse is *not* the chief element in marriage, he asserts; a couple can be husband and wife without it.[92]

In the *De consensu Evangelistarum*, written two or three years later, Augustine amplifies the point that Joseph and Mary should be considered married. Indeed, they stand as examples to married couples of the present day who by common consent live in continence. They are rightly called married because they have "affection of mind."[93] When Gospel writers call Joseph and Mary "parents" and Joseph a "father"[94] (despite his lack of participation in Mary's impregnation), they confess that he was truly Mary's husband, "without the intercourse of the flesh, to be sure, but in virtue of the real union of marriage."[95] A later sermon makes the same point: since it is conjugal love, not lust, that binds a husband

and wife, there can be true marriage without the sexual act.[96] Augustine will repeat these sentiments in his later writings against the Pelagians, as we shall see below.

Meanwhile, after his battles with the Manicheans, Augustine had turned in 401 to write *On the Good of Marriage* and *On Holy Virginity* in response to the ascetic debate. Here he finds another forum in which to define marriage from a non-reproductive viewpoint. In fact, Augustine even *begins* his treatise *De bono conjugali* by emphasizing the social nature of humanity, in which the capacity for friendship is planted as a "natural good." Adam and Eve are the first tie in this social chain, and although children are the consequence of the union, Augustine states in the first paragraph that there would have been a "friendly union" of male and female even *without* sexual intercourse.[97] Marriage is a "good" not just because of the children that come in its train, but also because of the "natural companionship" of the sexes. If children were essential to the definition of marriage, what could we say about couples who never had any children, or whose children died young? Or about couples whose ardor had cooled but who still enjoyed what Augustine designates as a mutual "order of charity"?[98] The bond between husband and wife, he thus asserts, goes beyond procreation: not even a separation of the pair can rupture it.[99] Here he pits a Christian understanding of the indissolubility of marriage against both Roman and Mosaic divorce law.[100] Augustine goes so far as to state that the "goods" of marriage and sexual intercourse are necessary "for the sake of friendship," but a close reading of the passage shows he means that a large population gained through reproduction will give more opportunity for friendship, rather than that sexual intercourse builds "marital friendship," as modern readers might conclude. For Christians of his own day, Augustine advises that spiritual relationships are preferable to marriage and reproduction.[101] Even though he here continues to defend the procreativity of the patriarchs against Manichean slanders,[102] Augustine balances his defense with the assertion that the sanctity of marriage is more important than fecundity to Christians.[103] Another distinguishing factor of Christian marriage for Augustine is that while *all* humans now use marriage to restrain lust, only Christians have the "sacramental bond."[104] Augustine does not here precisely designate the nature of that bond, but it is the "cement" that makes the marriage unbreakable.[105]

Augustine returns to the discussion of the essence of marriage and to Joseph and Mary's exemplary marriage in his anti-Pelagian writings. In *On Marriage and Concupiscence*, Book I (written before he knew the content of Julian of Eclanum's attacks upon his theory of original sin),[106] Augustine again asserts that Joseph and Mary had a true marriage. The Gospel writers were correct in calling them "parents," and insofar as Joseph is Mary's true husband, there is no problem occasioned by the Gospel genealogies coming down to him rather than to her.[107] Joseph and Mary can rightfully be said to have all three "goods" of marriage: offspring, mutual fidelity, and the sacramental bond, even though they had a sexless marriage.[108] Thus "fidelity" does not necessarily mean that a couple engages in sexual relations with each other. The marriage of Mary and Joseph stands as an example to couples who wish to live in perpetual abstinence. The "voluptuous connection of the body" does not make a marriage, in any event, but the "pledge of affection of the soul."[109] In describing the "sacramental bond," Augustine here compares the "two becoming one flesh" with the union of Christ and the Church.[110] So strong is the bond that neither a separation nor a partner's union with another can cancel it.[111]

Moreover, in Book I of the De nuptiis, Augustine emphasizes the spiritual dimensions of even the first two marital "goods," offspring and sexual fidelity. Thus he writes that it is not just the bearing of offspring that is a "good," but the bearing of them so that they may be "reborn" for God's kingdom. Likewise, "fidelity" does not connote the "ardent pagan love of the flesh," but reminds Christians of the heavenly reward that awaits them for their marital chastity.[112]

Even in a sinless Paradise there would have been reproduction; fidelity would have brought a security to the couple's relationship; the bond likewise would have existed without sin, since even before the story of the Fall is narrated in Genesis, we are told that "A man shall leave his father and mother and cleave to his wife, and they shall become one flesh." In addition, the bond between the partners is that to which Paul refers when he writes of Christ's union with the Church as a "great sacrament" (Ephesians 5:32).[113] In Book I of De nuptiis, Augustine emphasizes the spiritual dimension so fully that he even asserts that lust has its empire in the heart, not in the body; the sexual members are but the "weapons" lust employs.[114] Thus even lust is not in essence a bodily phenomenon.

From De nuptiis Book II onward through the Contra Julianum and the Opus imperfectum, Augustine's discussion of marriage is formulated in response to the attacks of the Pelagian, Julian of Eclanum. Now Augustine is under pressure to defend the goodness of reproduction against Julian's charge that the theory of original sin condemns sexual intercourse and conception, through which the original sin passes to the next generation. Although Augustine is centrally concerned to praise the physical relation of marriage and reproduction, he *also* engages Julian in a debate on the essence of marriage.

According to Julian, the sexual relation, including its lustful expression, constitutes the essence of marriage: "marriage is nothing else but the union of bodies," he wrote.[115] His assertion gives Augustine easy opportunity for rebuttal: if Julian were correct, nothing would separate marriage from adultery,[116] a point scored centuries earlier by Tertullian.[117] Given Julian's understanding of marriage, his attack on Augustine's theory of Mary and Joseph's marriage is logical: for Julian, if there was no intercourse, there was no marriage.[118] (Julian upheld the virginity of Mary and thus concluded there was no marriage.)[119] In response, Augustine repeats his earlier explanation of how Joseph can rightfully be called a "spouse."[120] He adds that in Julian's view, aged couples would have to stir themselves to intercourse in their declining years or they would forfeit their claim to be married![121] (In fact, Augustine prefers that older people abandon sexual relations completely, just as younger ones should temporarily during the wife's menstruation and pregnancy.)[122] According to Julian, the only point in God's creation of the human race in two sexes was so that reproduction could take place.[123] The views of Julian that Augustine reports leave no room for a theory of marital friendship apart from sexual functioning.

The debate on the essence of marriage continues in the *Opus imperfectum*, although here it is buried amidst Augustine's extended argument that his theory of original sin does *not* denigrate marital intercourse and childbearing. Far more of the discussion in the *Opus imperfectum* centers on the physical than on spiritual dimensions of marriage. From this disorganized and highly repetitious treatise, I have gleaned only three passages in which the essence of marriage is directly discussed.

In the first, Augustine repeats his claim that if marriage consisted *only* in the union of sexes, as Julian "raves," then nothing would separate marriage from adultery. In rejoinder, Augustine claims that other things separate adultery from marriage: the fidelity of the marriage bed, and "most important, the good use of an evil thing, that is, the legitimate use of concupiscence of the flesh, which adulterers use illegitimately."[124] Surprisingly, Augustine says nothing here about the *sacramental* bond. Quite the contrary:

he locates the "most important" difference between marriage and adultery in whether sexual lust is used rightly or wrongly. He thus dwells entirely in the realm of the physical.

In the second passage, Julian states that marriage has no *substantia* of its own and is located in the act of the persons. He goes on to assess the begetting of children by parents, which implies that the "act" of which he speaks is the sexual one. Augustine does not here respond, but refers Julian back to an earlier discussion.[125]

In the third passage, Julian addresses the story in Matthew 22 of the woman successively married to seven brothers and her status in the resurrection. Julian claims that Jesus' response ("In the resurrection, they neither marry nor are given in marriage, but are like the angels in heaven")[126] stems from his knowledge that the purpose of marriage is to produce children who replenish the generation that dies; thus Jesus means that when death loses its power over us, there will be no more need for fecundity. Although Augustine criticizes Julian's view of the purpose of marriage (if *all* that was wanted was children, they could be gotten through promiscuity just as easily as through marriage), his answer again falls short of his earlier discussions on the essence of marriage. Here he merely states that not just reproduction, but "family interests" are important in marriage—but by this phrase he means that only in marriage, where the wife's *pudicitia* is protected, can fathers and children be sure of their relationship. According to Augustine, Matthew 22 teaches that when the number of saints is complete, there will be no further need for birth.[127] Jesus did not here intend to explicate the purpose of marriage.

Julian carried his attack a step further. He recognized that Augustine's position on the marriage of Joseph and Mary might imply that Adam and Eve could *also* have been true spouses without sexual relation.[128] Does Augustine imagine that their relation in Eden was ethereal, he inquires?[129] Augustine responds hotly: "I didn't say that!"[130]—and indeed he had not. Quite the contrary: only after long wrestling had he arrived at the conclusion that Adam and Eve could have had sexual relations in a sinless Eden. He had championed the marriage of Adam and Eve against earlier opponents, yet now the logic of his argument on Joseph and Mary called into question his hard-won conclusion on Adam and Eve.

Julian was relentless in his jibes at the elderly Augustine. He renders Augustine's position ridiculous by inventing a tale of sexless reproduction in Eden that he thinks Augustine might prefer. Mercilessly, he mocks Augustine's likening of Edenic reproduction to that of a tranquil farmer (the husband) sowing his seeds upon the readied field (the wife).[131] Why not have Eve fecund all over, like the earth, and let the children sweat forth from her pores and joints (like lice)? No sexual members would be necessary at all: the man could rake her over, harvesting her "forest," not with his genitals but with iron ploughs and hoes! Poor woman! Such teachings, Julian chides, are worthy of Manicheans who despise the bodily organs God gave us.[132]

Poor Augustine! we might add. Either he had lost his grip on the argument or was so afraid of Julian's charges of "Manicheanism" that he failed in his last, extensive treatise to develop the theme of companionate marriage he had pursued earlier. Yet it was this theme, not the insistence upon the sexual and reproductive dimensions of marriage, that would have allowed for a fuller explanation of marital friendship.

From this discussion of the controversies in which Augustine developed his marital teaching, I turn now briefly to note two other factors that probably contributed to Augustine's failure to develop fully the social and companionate theory of marriage he had set forth in several of his works.

V

A second factor that probably contributed to Augustine's failure to develop a full-fledged theory of companionate marriage lies in his estimate of woman's secondary status. Some of his expressions on the subject of womankind have become *topoi* for feminist textbooks, for example, that woman taken by herself, without the male, is not created in the image of God,[133] and that a Christian man should "hate" in his partner all that pertains to her as a wife.[134] Even in discussing the relation of Mary and Joseph, Augustine argues the fittingness of the genealogies coming down to Joseph rather than to Mary in that he was a member of the stronger sex, so that "no harm might be done to the male sex."[135]

Moreover, if we judge correctly, Augustine's view of real-life marriages was highly traditional. His mother was for him the exemplary wife: she meekly submitted to his father's ill-temper and adulteries with nary a whisper of protest, and counseled her female friends to accept the shabby treatment their husbands accorded them, since the marriage contract had put them in a state of submission.[136] From his other writings, we gather that Augustine believed that a married woman was morally as well as legally bound to heed her husband's will. Although he was a champion of ascetic living, the woman who attempted ascetic renunciation without her husband's consent would receive a severe chastisement from him.[137]

Most telling, Augustine never developed a circle of female friends with whom he shared scholarly and emotional concerns, as did Jerome and John Chrysostom. As I have argued elsewhere, the friendly relations that Jerome and Chrysostom enjoyed with their female friends was directly related to the ascetic commitments of all concerned; such relationships would otherwise have been deemed inappropriate in late Christian antiquity.[138] As for Augustine's own sister, we hear not one word about her in the *Confessions*. Elsewhere we learn that she had been head of a group of ascetic women at Hippo Regius.[139] After her death, Augustine wrote two letters to the nuns in her monastery, one of which is usually called his "Rule for Nuns." Far from providing a glimpse of warm and close relations he enjoyed with the women, the letters contain harsh words of chastisement for their misbehavior and lack of Christian cooperation.[140] Last, the probability that Augustine's mistress was from the lower classes and hence uneducated lessens the likelihood that the one woman he knew intimately could have been a partner in his intellectual endeavors.[141] Thus there is little in Augustine's own life that would have provided an experiential basis for a theory of companionate relations between the sexes—and much else, we have seen, that led him instead to stress the sexual and reproductive dimensions of male-female relationships.

A third factor to consider in relation to Augustine's assessment of the essence of marriage is contemporary legal theory. Twentieth-century scholars have debated the ingredients of marriage implied (but not clearly spelled out) by Roman jurists.[142] Whatever the understanding of "consent" may have been in Republican times (about this point the debate has been intense),[143] by the classical era of Roman law (roughly, the imperial period up to Constantine), consent was a necessary condition for marriage.[144] Probably the importance of consent as a factor grew with the gradual abandonment of *manus* marriage and the acceptance of "free marriage," *sine manu*, in this era.[145] Of course, we must question how a girl's "consent" would be construed in that patriarchal period that saw very young marriages;[146] one interpretation from the *Digest* (that the girl is thought to have consented if she did not overtly protest, and that the only grounds on which she *could* protest were if her father chose for her a man of "unworthy and shameful modes of behavior")[147]does not inspire confidence that "consent" meant to Roman jurists what we now take it to mean.

Even if consent were a necessary condition of marriage by late antiquity, was it a sufficient condition, i.e., did consent *alone*, apart from factors such as cohabitation, define a marriage? Considerable debate has surrounded this issue. Older scholars relied heavily on Ulpian's famous phrase, *"Nuptias non concubitus, sed consensus facit,"*[148] to argue that consent was the one essential (i.e., sufficient) condition of marriage and that this notion of marriage dominated even pre-Christian legal theory.[149] Yet many scholars now judge this phrase (and others like it) to be a later interpolation inspired by Christian sentiments and grafted onto pre-Christian law.[150] If contemporary scholars are correct about this point, then the Church Fathers' teaching on consent as the essence of marriage shaped later legal theory,[151] rather than itself having been much influenced by notions of consensuality in Roman law.

Moreover, the contexts in which *consensus* is discussed in ancient Roman law suggest that the jurists are not attempting to define an "essence" of marriage but wish rather to explain the *ease* with which "free marriage" can be concluded: even without the ceremonies and documents necessary for the conclusion of old-style *manus* marriage, they imply, a couple can in their day enter upon marriage.[152] In addition, some scholars now argue that the emphasis on consent, in any event, was an attempt to distinguish marriage from concubinage. The reasoning is this: since it is not sexual relations, cohabitation, that distinguishes concubinage from marriage, something else must, and this "something else" is the *intention* of the parties.[153] Yet there is no evidence in the jurists to suggest that they intended to champion consent *without* sexual consummation (as in Augustine's view of Mary and Joseph's relation) as the essence of marriage.[154] Even texts such as *Codex Theodosianus* 3, 7, 3 that speak of "the consent of the parties" also mention *consortium*.[155] On this line of argument, we can see why Jerome held that Joseph and Mary did *not* have a marriage: they did not have sexual relations.[156]

Thus although scholars agree that considering consent the essential element of marriage was a "trend" by the late classical period, there was probably not a decisive shift from an earlier interest in the objective (i.e., physical) criteria of marriage to a later concentration solely on *affectio* and *consensus*.[157] At least two factors stood against the theory of consent as the *only* grounds for marriage: popular opinion, which always imagined sexual relations to be part of marriage, and Scriptural texts that referred to the becoming of "one flesh" in the sex act, and this on the analogy of Christ's union with the Church.[158]

Thus Augustine's belief that consent alone can make a marriage, as he argued at least in the case of the marriage of Joseph and Mary, if not in all cases, exerted an original influence on later legal theory. Yet his views did little to influence legislation in the century or so after his death: up through the Justinianic era, although penalties for divorce increased, divorce itself remained legally valid, in sharp contrast to Augustine's marital theory.[159] Thus the seeming ambivalence—or perhaps indifference—of Roman law to the question of the "essence" of marriage is also reflected in Augustine's formulation.

In sum: while Augustine's insistence that Joseph and Mary enjoyed a genuine marriage led him to posit volitional factors as prime in the definition of marriage, the demands of controversy with extreme ascetics, Manicheans, and Pelagians pulled him in a different direction to stress the physical aspects. Who knows whether the volitional factors would not have emerged as central if Augustine had not formulated his theories in the midst of controversy? In his description of Edenic marriage—"a faithful partnership based on love and mutual respect"[160]—he nonetheless pointed the way to future considerations of marital friendship.

2

Maritalis Affectio *Revisited*

One of the principal interests in the contemporary study of society is the analysis of relationships within the family. "Family" in this context can be understood both in its nuclear or more extended form, though the emphasis in the discussion within the Western world is primarily on the nuclear group. This analysis includes the various sets of relationships between the sexes within its purview. It understands that, with the passage of time, the quality of these relations varies and that, within the lifespan of a given group, they have their microhistory. Furthermore, it has become abundantly clear that much is to be gained by studying the evolution of the quality of these relationships through the generations: they have a macrohistory that may well be important for our self-understanding.[1]

Within the broad field of social history, one of the areas in which there has been important progress during the last twenty years has been the study of marriage in Western Europe during the Middle Ages. It is interesting not only in itself, but also because it enables us to observe how a developing Christian ideology was joined to powerful means of diffusion so that it came in time to exercise very serious pressures on marriage and, through it, on the family. (Implied in this statement is the notion that ideas run before social change, a position that social historians often tend to avoid or, at least, ignore.)[2] The family was forced to adjust to a much more individualistic attitude to marriage. It is scarcely an exaggeration to say that the consequences of this change still unfold before us in the West.[3] In the large body of recent scholarly literature devoted to the analysis of this development within the history of marriage, there has been comparatively little study of the relationship between the spouses. Since so much of this research has involved the analysis of the role of consent in creating the marriage bond both in theory and in practice, it is something of a surprise to realize how little attention has been paid to the substance of that consent. On the other hand, this omission might well have been expected for the answer, when it is finally available, will likely prove to be a very complex one. In a society such as that of medieval Europe to which so many traditions and so many cultures had contributed and in which there had been no attempt, by and large, to produce a homogeneous society, differences of expectation based on the nation, class, and age of family members were preserved. They have proved to be very tenacious as is perfectly obvious even in America where, in a transplanted European culture, that richness of background is still evident.

The sources available for the investigation of the quality of the relationship that existed between spouses are daunting in their multiplicity and in their volume. The varied sets of documents associated with marriage agreements are obviously of prime importance, and more general information of a similar sort provided by collections of laws and legal treatises is contributory as well. Then there is the whole area of imaginative literature on which so much scholarship has been lavished for more than a century. The list could be extended, but this is sufficient. Let it be said, however, that study of this material has tended to create an understanding of the spousal relationship that makes it secondary to those expected within the blood-line,[4] or to those enjoyed, at least in imagination, by unmarried lovers. The spousal relationship thus understood can, not unfairly, be summed up in the words of Kenelm Foster as "a purely institutional and judicial state which only engages the personality in a relatively superficial way".[5] It is very likely that such a description of marriage often obtained, but it must not be forgotten that the evidence is provided by a rather specialized set of documents and that they relate to a small part of medieval society.

The point was made earlier that the Church developed an ideology on these matters and was in a position to present it to, even impose it on, society. This ideology, as has been demonstrated in the discussion of the role of consent in establishing the marital bond,[6] was capable of application across a varied spectrum of cultural forms and, although it would not oppose, much less eliminate, all local customary expectations on these matters, it could be expected to have a considerable influence. Thus there is much to be said for looking at Christian teaching on the relationship that should obtain between spouses. Beyond, is the more difficult question, that of the degree to which this ideology was accepted by medieval society; but, first, an attempt must be made to describe that ideology.

It is proposed to study this question in the context of the large-scale discussion of questions touching sexuality, celibacy, religious life, and marriage that occurred during the two centuries that followed the Gregorian reform. Often my purpose will be to suggest lines of approach, indicate serious or at least tentative progress that has been made recently and, in a few cases, illustrate some of the conclusions that it is not unreasonable to expect to result from the enterprises that are currently under way.

The medieval discussion of relations between husband and wife was rooted in the Judaeo-Christian Scriptures. Those Scriptures provide a remarkably developed reflection on the matter at issue. There is a description of the creation of mankind and an explanation of the difference of genders in terms of the purpose of their relationship. Furthermore, that relationship had a history, a history in which there were two principal moments, namely the fall of Adam and Eve and the coming of Christ, after each of which sexuality and marriage and the relationship of spouses within marriage took on new meanings and new possibilities. Throughout the Scriptures there is much advice on the substance and quality of the relationship between the spouses, a quality of which the remark of Professor Foster, mentioned above, would not provide an adequate description. Those Scriptures were taken by the Fathers and interpreted in terms of the culture in which they lived and, as well, in terms of their own experience. When, in the period following the Gregorian Reform, the great intellectual enterprise that characterized the era was launched, it included the examination of this tradition, an ordering and interpreting of it and, occasionally, the rejection of parts that were not capable of being fitted into the syntheses created at the time. This enterprise was not based only on the Christian tradition: it involved a huge intake of ancient ideas, some filtered through Arab scholars, some—and this element increased as the thirteenth century progressed—drawn directly from Greek authors.[7] These latter sources not only introduced ancient understandings of social organization as well as of human biology, but more especially an examination of the meaning of friendship that was to prove of considerable importance.[8] It was in this context that there occurred that large-scale reflection on marriage by Scripture scholar, theologian, philosopher, lawyer, artist, and poet, the importance of which has already been mentioned. By and large, research in recent years, much as it has focused on this development, has paid little attention directly to the question that has been posed, that is, to the quality of the relationship between the spouses. The history of exegesis is only in its infancy: not surprisingly, there is as yet little to say of the texts that might be expected to help in this discussion. Similarly, while historians of theology have examined the role of the consent of the principals to the marriage in the creation of the bond and the sacramentality of matrimony, and there has been an important discussion of abusive aspects of the marriage relationship, little is yet available about positive teaching on the life that spouses were expected to live. The recent work of Dom Jean Leclercq is an important exception to this statement and there are several other enterprises under way that can be expected to be helpful.[9]

Thus, while studies of theological speculation on the relationship between spouses are much to be desired, they have only begun. Significant progress has been made of late in areas more directly related to instruction and enforcement of the Christian life at both the level of moral guidance and that of practice. Among the instruments of instruction were confessors' handbooks, sermons, hymns, liturgical books, and suites of illustration and sculpture that commented on marriage in a variety of ways and had a certain amount to say of the relationship that was expected between the spouses. Other literature, notably the canons, was concerned with expressing the rules that the society could be expected to enforce but, especially in its earlier stage, it often took on the mantle of moral guidance as well. Naturally enough, canon law, its jurisprudence and the detailed information on decisions that the records of the ecclesiastical courts supply, often tend to reveal marriage and human sexuality at the point where they pass beyond the acceptable. Thus canonical literature sometimes creates a foreshortening of vision that limits our understanding of what was expected in a positive way and, even more, of what was actually done in the society of the time.[10]

In their examination and enriching of the classical Roman concept of *maritalis affectio*, however, the canonists provided a much more positive approach to questions touching marriage. The fundamental examination of this concept appeared almost twenty years ago in an important article by Professor John T. Noonan, Jr.[11] It will be used to provide the base for the present discussion. Noonan showed how the notion was developed in Roman law as a means of defining a relationship distinguished from concubinage, a union, the children of which were fit to inherit.[12] At first, it probably connoted nothing more than a legal intent, a willing. Implicit in the discussion was the notion that where marital affection had ceased, the marriage ended, but by the time of Justinian that possibility no longer applied. More important for the present discussion was the question of the relationship between marital affection and consent. Were the expressions synonymous? It is clear that both were required. "Marital affection" defined the content of the consent, namely to have the other as spouse. Having discussed the meaning of the word *affectio* in this context, Noonan concluded that, by the time of Justinian, the term implied "not simply a legal will but an emotion-colored intent not far from love," an implication that is important for this analysis.[13] The notion usually implied the intention to procreate, and that the relationship was to be monogamous, exclude promiscuity, and enjoy a degree of permanence; but no intrinsic criteria for judging whether that attitude existed were developed. Roman law was content to fall back on an external expression of marital affection by proper registration, at least in the case of the well-to-do.

This notion was adopted by Gratian, the great canonist of the second quarter of the twelfth century. Collections like his *Decretum* were made up, for the most part, of canons taken from a wide variety of older sources. Gratian's volume had many of the qualities of a treatise, however, for it included an important discussion of the canons as his text progressed. It is in this discussion, the part most directly indicative of his thought, that the use of the term *maritalis affectio* is most common.[14] Like Justinian he used the term to identify a married union, but went beyond Roman law, concluding that where a relationship began with marital affection, the marriage persisted even though a spouse had become a prisoner or a slave. Furthermore, under the same conditions, a marriage bond could be created between slaves. It was in this context that Gratian cited a text of Pope Leo to the effect that such a union was begun in God.[15] Thus he concluded that wherever there was marital affection, the bond could come into being and, once established, nothing short of the death of a spouse caused it to fail.[16] He held that the concept need not include the intent to procreate. Thus in the case of the marriage of Mary and Joseph, the relation was established by affection, an affection that was not procreative, but completely faithful. On the other hand, marital affection could exist where the purpose was simply to satisfy sexual desire.[17] Furthermore, in his discussion of the first, and very confused, stage of the union of Jacob and Leah, Gratian introduced a distinction between consent and marital affection that was to prove of importance: to consent was to accept a given person as spouse, while marital affection referred to the quality of the relationship that, as a result, came into being between the spouses.[18] When it came to the criteria necessary for the law to recognize the existence of that bond and thus, where necessary, enforce it, Gratian fell back, as Roman law had done, on external evidence: the agreed statement of the principals or the observance of visible formalities.[19]

With Alexander III (1159–1181), the notion of marital affection entered papal decretals. It was used as in the *Decretum*, but a further development is quickly discernible. The term was distinguished from consent, the act that created the marriage bond (the wedding). Marital or conjugal affection was expected to endure during the marriage. It was seen, in Noonan's words, "as an active disposition which the spouses had a duty to cultivate".[20] Thus a static notion was replaced by one implying the desirability of growth. With this in mind, and in accord with the Pauline exhortation that husbands love their wives, the Pope was willing to command a certain behavior during marriage. Thus a husband or wife might be ordered to take back a repudiated spouse and treat him or her with marital affection. The modern reader, at least one accustomed to the expectations of Western society, is tempted to judge that such action would hardly resolve the problem revealed. Yet it is clear that this solution was considered desirable, for there is abundant evidence in papal decretals and the records of local ecclesiastical courts that both men and women often demanded the enforced society of their spouse.[21] This fact needs to be underlined for it is an important indication of what some spouses expected of marriage, of what made it desirable and worth defending in court: a sexual partner even though another was preferred, a place in society, shelter and sustinence, etc. A somewhat different point of view is expressed in another of Pope Alexander's decretals exhorting the spouses of lepers (both husbands and wives) to accompany their sick partners and minister to them with conjugal affection. This was not likely intended to be a sexual service, but the kind of mutual care that, the decretal implied, could be expected of those who were married.[22]

A similar understanding of marital affection as the quality that should characterize the relations between spouses during their life together was adopted by Pope Innocent III (1199–1216). He carried the notion considerably further, both in the sense of the substance of consent at the beginning of marriage and of the quality of the relationship that was expected to endure, in his discussion of the marriage and polygamy of pagan peoples. But with him, as with his predecessors, no attempt was made to define its essential qualities or to establish criteria that would make it possible for a court to decide whether marital affection existed or not.[23] The concept would continue to be used, especially as a means to describe external aspects of an ideal. Thus it was often employed against a certain type of behavior (excessive correction of a spouse, mistreatment of a spouse, etc.) as opposed to marital affection. More positively, husbands were ordered to provide suitable dress for their wives, to see to their proper nourishment, etc., as required by marital affection. Thus the concept can be seen to provide a set of rules expressing what was expected and what was not allowed, but the canonical system, especially in its more mature stage, when its role was to express rules that could be enforced, did not seek to become involved with the more intimate positive aspects of the affection that was called marital. No doubt, further research along the lines suggested will refine our understanding of this matter, but it will likely remain a description that rarely moves beyond the external aspects of *maritalis affectio*. The exhortation of Alexander III to the spouse of a leper, mentioned above, did indicate a more internal vision of its meaning; for further evidence of this sort it is necessary to examine other types of literature.

The confessor's handbook, a manual intended to instruct the priest who sought to form the consciences of his flock, correct their faults, and lead them to a life of virtue, seems a likely source where positive teaching on the meaning of marital affection might be expected.[24] This type of literature was derived in part from the ancient Penitentials, texts that had much to say of the abuses of sexuality and marriage, but shed little light on the matter under present discussion.[25] These new manuals began to appear late in the twelfth century and rapidly increased in number and in the quality of their contents, especially after the Fourth Lateran Council (1215). At first, they were mostly given to instruction on the regulations of the Church, sins, and their penances, but as the years passed, they tended to provide instruction of a much more positive sort on the sacraments and on many of the practical problems of the Christian life. Though it remained very important, the legal element was reduced with the passage of the years; many of the notions developed by theologians received statement in a form that would be useful at the level of parish instruction.[26] Much use has already been made of this literature in the study of medieval marriage, especially with regard to the instruction on the requirements for the validity of the union.[27]

A preliminary examination of several of these *Summae confessorum* gives valuable insight into their authors' understanding of the spousal relationship. For example, in one of the earliest, the *Liber penitentialis* of Alan of Lille, completed 1198x1203, several indirect references to the causes of sexual excitement and its moral consequences are mentioned. Thus in a consideration of illicit unions, the confessor is instructed to learn whether the penitent was moved by lust or whether he purposefully set out to excite himself sexually.[28] Sin with a beautiful woman is less serious than with a homely one because her attraction diminishes the sinner's self-control.[29] To yield to passion after a single glance is a more serious offense than to fall as a result of prolonged social intercourse.[30] There is nothing of great moment in these little insights, but they do suggest the reflection on the mechanisms of sexual attraction and the broad understanding of it that lay behind the moral guidance that this type of treatise sought to provide.

A similar awareness of the relations between spouses is suggested in an engaging passage from the *Summa confessorum* of Thomas of Chobham, Sub-dean and *Officialis* of the Diocese of Salisbury, England. The work, completed about 1216, marks a considerable progress on that of Alan of Lille, and its treatment of marriage is a major treatise on the subject. The section ends with a statement on the role of wives as preachers to their husbands: "Quod mulieres debent esse predicatrices virorum suorum," and leaves no doubt as to the author's judgment of when a husband is most likely to be moved by his wife's request. The confessor is instructed to urge women to take up this role, for no priest can be expected to soften a man's heart as a wife can. The text continues:

> Hence the sin of a man can often be imputed to his wife if, through her neglect, the husband does not mend his ways. When they are alone and she is in her husband's arms, she ought to speak to him soothingly, and if he is hard and merciless and an oppressor of the poor she ought to invite him to mercy; if he is a plunderer to detest his plundering. . . .[31]

A considerably more developed reflection on these aspects of marriage is to be found in the *Tractatus de Matrimonio* of John of

Friburg. The treatise is the fourth book of his *Summa confesso-rum*, a highly sophisticated compendium for the confessor published at the end of the thirteenth century.[32] In his definition he adopts the usual text from the *Decretum Gratiani:* "matrimonium est viri et mulieris coniunctio individuam vite consuetudinem retinens" (C.2 q.2 c.1), then goes on to state that the "undivided companionship of life" implies mutual faith, mutual rendering of the marital debt, and "mutuam exhibitionem," which he defines as the obligation of both to provide the necessities of this life inasmuch as they can.[33] Furthermore, in the discussion of the consent that is necessary to create the marriage bond, he explicitly asked in what that consent consisted.[34] He replied that it could not be identified with cohabitation nor with carnal union. The latter need not be explicit in consent, though it should be implicit, since the communion necessary for conjugal society is not only of goods but also of bodies. The marriage of Mary and Joseph is seen as a touchstone for the understanding of matrimonial consent or conjugal society. This he says—and here John falls back on a traditional theme—is evident from the account of the "formation" of Eve in Genesis 2.18–25: she is not taken from the head of man, lest she seem his superior; nor is she taken from his foot, lest she seem his servant. She is taken from his side that he might have both a helper and an associate.[35] Furthermore, John followed the usual teaching that marriage was instituted by God for two reasons: before the Fall for the generation and education of children and, after the Fall, with an additional purpose: the channeling of sexual desire. He added that there could be other, secondary reasons for seeking marriage, such as wealth or a woman's beauty.[36] With regard to the rendering of the marital debt, the Pauline point of view was presented as might be expected. Sexual powers are to be exercised with restraint and with purpose. A practical reflection on the unselfishness and—if one may use an overworked word of the moment—the sensitivity, that was recommended by this approach, is evident in his adopting the observation made by theologians fifty years before: since women tend to be more modest than men in expressing their longing for sexual union, a husband should provide for his wife's wish not only when she asks but also when, though in her modesty she does not express it, there is some indication of her desire.[37]

It is hoped that, from peripheral remarks in the *Summae confessorum* such as these, further clues as to the meaning of that marital affection to which spouses consented will be gained in research projects that are currently under way. But there is a serious limitation to this literature: it was intended for those who were to instruct the laity at the local level, rather than for the laity themselves. Much that was personal, be it exhortation, warning, or command, was presumed and, since there was no need to present it in these treatises, it appeared, if it appeared at all, on the fringe of major discussions.

Other modes of instruction were more directly intended for those to whom this discussion relates, namely the laity. One of the principal modes over the centuries has been the liturgy. Within it, the matrimonial rite, involving instruction of the principals as well as those present at the ceremony, had much to say of the Christian ideal of marriage.[38] Thus far liturgical texts have been analyzed to establish the rate at which the necessity that spouses freely consent to their union became generally expressed. This has been done by exploring the questions put to them, a questioning that, in one case at least, included the enquiry whether there were love between the pair.[39] Similarly, the examination of a variety of graphic treatments of courtship, the wedding, and family life, especially in manuscript decoration, has begun to yield valued indications of the understanding of certain aspects of marriage.[40] But, even here, there does not seem to have been a study of this evidence from the point of view of the present essay.

Perhaps the last major area of medieval literature that has yet to be explored in a thorough way is the sermon. The first steps towards the easy accessibility of this literature have been taken during the last decade and some important studies of the sermon and marriage have recently appeared.[41] It is proposed to devote a few paragraphs to suggest ways in which this literature may be expected to shed light on the question of the relationship between husband and wife that was seen as the norm among the men and women of the time. An article by David d'Avray of Cambridge University, written in cooperation with W. Tausche can be used for this purpose.[42]

Two principal types of marriage sermon have been identified. The first, much the more common, was related to the account of the marriage feast at Cana (John 2:1), read at the Mass of the second Sunday after Pentecost. The second type was the *ad status* sermon, one of a series preached to different classes and groups—the married were included—within medieval society. It is to the latter type that d'Avray and Tausche turn in the article just mentioned. The authors see the sermon as a useful index, not of the highest flights of theology but as a means "to discover what sort of ideas about marriage ordinary men and women were regularly exposed to."[43] Many of these ideas touched the relations between the spouses. Thus, in a sermon of the early twelfth century, Honorius of Autun emphasizes the mutual love of the couple:

> Let husbands love their wives with tender affection; let them keep faith with them in all things; let them abstain from them on holy nights and on the nights of fasts, and at the time when women suffer their natural infirmity. . . . In the same way, women should love their husbands deeply ("Mulieres viros suos similiter intime diligant"), fear them, and keep faith with a pure heart. Let them agree in everything good, like a pair of eyes.[44]

A more developed reflection on married love is found in an *ad status* sermon of Guibert de Tournai, a Franciscan who seems to have been active from c.1235 to his death in 1284.[45] He writes: "There is also a kind of love founded on partnership, and this is the love which husband and wife owe to each other, because they are equals and partners."[46] Where so many other authors pointed out that this equality referred only to the equal sexual rights the spouses possessed, Guibert makes no such restriction, a fact that is in accord with the "optimistic attitude to marriage" that was typical of him. Later he says that husband and wife should, in the words of Proverbs 17, be inseparable; as friends, they love each other at all times.[47] They ought to have a feeling of love that makes separation impossible; love is a guarantee of fidelity; spouses should be able to accept criticism from each other.[48] The citation of this excellent article could be carried much farther, but this should be sufficient to suggest the potential of sermon literature as an indication of the relation of husband and wife that was presented as an ideal.

These reflections are merely a series of probes into various kinds of literature that until recently have not yet been used at all for the study of medieval marriage or, if they have been analyzed, it has been with the purpose of gleaning their information on the marriage bond. Of the quality of that bond, they seem to have had little to say. Yet, from the brief presentation that has been made, it seems reasonable to hope that there is much to be derived from these sources and that a serious attempt should be made to master them. It has been suggested that the investigation of the conception of *maritalis affectio* (and probably of *coniugalis affectio* as well) in canon law and in the records of ecclesiastical courts will indicate the outer shell of accepted relationships; that the *Summae confessorum* will look more to the interior of the marriage but, because of an understanding that is presumed, will not turn to the problem directly, revealing the substance of that presumption only by the occasional remark in passing; that in the sermon, an instrument for the direct instruction of the married, a more fruitful source for the understanding of the ideals presented to the married couple will be found. Enough has been said already to suggest that the various types of literature that have been examined, when taken together and with due attention to their complementarity, present an understanding of the spousal relationship that cannot be described as one that "only engages the personality in a relatively superficial way."

3

Loving the Unequal Equal: Medieval Theologians and Marital Affection

Conpainz, cist fos vilains jalous,
. . .
[qui] se fet seigneur de sa fame,
qui ne redoit pas estre dame,
mes sa pareille et sa compaigne,
si con la loi les acompaigne
et il redoit ses compainz estre
sanz soi fere seigneur ne mestre.
   Roman de la Rose, 9391–9400[1]

"My friend, consider this mad jealous boor. . . .
He makes himself lord over his wife, who, in
turn, should not be his lady but his equal and
his companion, as the law joins them together;
and, for his part, he should be her companion
without making himself her lord or master."[2]

    In a note to this well-known passage from Jean de Meun's part of the *Roman de la Rose*, Charles Dahlberg suggests a parallel with the marriage sermon *De matrimonio* (*post* 1247) by Robert de Sorbon.[3] It is difficult to prove that Dahlberg is right, but a connection between the two is not implausible: during the time in which Robert was a university professor of theology in Paris (1250–1274), Jean was probably connected with the arts faculty for at least part of that period.

The key words in the lines quoted from the *Roman* are *pareille* and *compaigne:* these also occur together in the paragraph of Robert's sermon preceding the one adduced by Dahlberg in support of his suggestion. Because of their interest for the purpose of this paper I give the relevant passages from the two paragraphs below. They are part of Robert's exegesis of Genesis 2:18:

> *Non est bonum hominem esse solum; faciamus ei adjutorium simile.* . . . Dicit etiam *simile sibi;* quod est relativum æquiparantiæ. In quo notatur quod mulier debet esse æqualis viro suo, sive socia, non sub viro, non supra virum.
>
> Item, mulier facta fuit de costa viri, non de inferiori parte vel de superiori, sed de media, ut per hoc significaretur quod mulier debet esse æqualis viro suo.[4]

> "It is not good for man to be alone; let us make him a help like unto himself." . . . Indeed he said "like unto himself"; this corresponds to equivalence. By this is indicated that the woman must be the equal of the man, or his companion, not under him and not above him.
>
> Also, woman was made from man's rib, not from the upper part or from the lower, but from the middle, that by it might be designated that woman must be man's equal. (my translation)

The remarkably positive impression of woman, or, more correctly, of woman as wife, that is created by these lines has its origin in the word *æqualis,* used here not just in association with, but as a synonym of, *socia.* The occurrence of these two words gives rise to a number of questions, e.g. in what sense were husband and wife considered equals, and by whom; are they mere juridical terms, stemming from the marriage contract, or do they also refer to the emotional relation between husband and wife? Naturally it will not be possible to answer all these questions satisfactorily within the scope of this article. I have limited its purpose to a sketch of the development of the idea of equality in the love relationship of the marital partners from the time it was first formulated till the end of the thirteenth century. In addition to that I will address a few related problems of the kind formulated above.

Historically two streams can be distinguished in the development of the equality concept: a "monastic" Augustinian and a philosophical Aristotelian one. Of these, the Augustinian is the older and it is there that we must look for the origin of what D. L.

d'Avray and M. L. Tausche have termed the "rib-topos," the gloss on the creation of Eve from Adam's rib.[5]

One of the less fortunate results of the enormously energetic and creative activities of the canonists and theologians in the twelfth and thirteenth centuries was an ever widening gap between their rather abstract pursuits and the concrete religious life of the individual Christian. A significant example is the Church's attitude toward marriage. The (in itself uncomplicated) copulation of male and female had in the course of time been surrounded by an extensive structure of doctrinal and exegetical material, while the equally important concept of marital affection had received only scarce attention. Edward Schillebeeckx traces this apparent lack of interest to the predominantly canonical orientation of the theological reflections on marriage of the time: by focusing so exclusively on this aspect of marriage, aimed at safeguarding the life after death of the spouses, theologians had lost sight of the needs of the partners in the present world.[6]

Fortunately there are exceptions and one of them is Hugh of St. Victor, the great contemplative religious and scholar. The major influence in Hugh's thinking was Augustine.[7] Hugh agrees with the Augustinian idea that the essence of marriage lies in the personal relationship of the spouses.[8] This view is a natural consequence of Augustine's highly negative appraisal of sexuality, which led him to conclude that the purer a marriage, the better it is.[9] Hugh, who refers to Augustine and to the *De bono conjugali* repeatedly in the chapter on the sacrament of marriage in his *De sacramentis Christianae fidei* (c. 1134), is not as strict as Augustine in his views on the marital relationship. He agrees that husband and wife are not complete equals, for woman was made from man (for which see below), but on the other hand he puts full emphasis on the union of hearts of the spouses, bound by a bond of love: "Conjugium est in foedere dilectionis." He even goes so far as to say that without the bond of love a marriage would be void, whether it has been consummated or not.[10]

From his comments on verses of the Song of Songs it is clear that Hugh was also influenced by Bernard of Clairvaux's *Sermones super Canticum Canticorum*. In these sermons Bernard had expounded that the love between the mystical Bride and Groom leads to a harmony of will in which the inequality of the partners was no longer felt (Sermon 83.3; vol. 4, 182).[11] The phrasing recalls *the* classical definition of friendship, that of Cicero, given in his *De amicitia* (vi.20): "omnium divinarum humanarumque rerum cum benevolentia et caritate concensio" ("an accord in all things, human and divine, conjoined with mutual goodwill and affection"),[12] but even if the notion of a harmony of wills in Bernard's sermons is not a direct echo of Cicero's definition we may probably see it as a form of friendship. In that case it is friendship and (near) equality which constitute the essence of the love of the Bride and the Groom and enable them to be joined not only in the flesh, but, in the spiritual marriage, also in one spirit, as Bernard says in another sermon, basing himself on 1 Corinthians 6:17:

> Love neither looks up to nor looks down on anybody. It regards as equal all who love each other truly, bringing together in itself the lofty and the lowly. It makes them not only equal but one. Perhaps up till now you have thought God should be an exception to this law of love; but anyone who is united to the Lord becomes one in spirit with him. [Sermon 59.2: vol. 3, 121]

In a famous passage in the *De sacramentis*, Hugh elaborates on this idea of the (near) equality in a way that was to become a commonplace in medieval religious and misogynistic literature:

> For since [woman] was given as a companion [*socia*], not a servant or a mistress, she was to be produced not from the highest or from the lowest part but from the middle. . . . She was made from the middle, that she might be proved to have been made for equality of association. *Yet in a certain way she was inferior to him,* in that she was made from him, so that she might always look to him as to her beginning and cleaving to him indivisibly might not separate herself from that association which ought to have been established reciprocally. (italics mine)[13]

In this passage Hugh places the equality of man and woman as human beings created in the image of God before their inequality, which belongs to the order of creation. The italicized clause seems to indicate that Hugh has struggled with this principle of inequality, and we must conclude that he who so highly valued the mutual love between the spouses has not been able to find a solution to this apparently insurmountable difficulty. On the other hand, he could hardly have been expected to do so; after all, there was a sound Biblical basis for the conviction that woman was man's subsidiary, as in Genesis 3: 16, where God says to Eve: " . . . and he [your husband] shall be your master," and also in the repeated admonitions found in the letters of Paul as well as Peter. Seen in this light, Hugh's view, and the way in which it was worded, can be called an important contribution to a higher appreciation of woman as wife.

The influence of both Bernard and Hugh is visible in the first book on friendship since Cicero's *De amicitia*, Aelred of Rievaulx's *De spirituali amicitia* (c. 1160).[14] In this Christian philosophical treatise Aelred shows his great affection for and affinity with Cicero's work by adopting the same form and structure, and a similar ending. His second important source of inspiration was Augustine's *Confessions*, to which he pays an elegant tribute by drawing the opening lines of his Prologue from it. Many of the ideas found in the *De spirituali amicitia* Aelred had first advanced in his earlier *Speculum caritatis*, a written-out version of the lecture notes which he had used as a master of novices at Rievaulx and which he had collected at the urgent request of his own master, Bernard of Clairvaux.[15] In a number of essential points the influence of Bernard is obvious, as in Aelred's assertion that true friendship achieves equality of the friends and unites them so that they become one instead of two.[16]

Aelred distinguishes three kinds of friendship: carnal (or puerile), worldly, and spiritual.[17] The development of carnal friendship is depicted, as one might expect, as a love affair springing from an attraction through the senses (I.39; Laker: 59).[18] The second type, that of worldly friendship, "is born of a desire for temporal advantage or possessions" (I.42; Laker: 60), and as a result it disappears when the hope of profit is taken away. Spiritual friendship, finally, is what all should strive after,

> not for consideration of any worldly advantage or for any intrinsic cause, but from the dignity of its own nature and the feelings of the human heart, so that its fruition and reward is nothing other than itself. (I.45; Laker: 60)[19]

This ideal kind of love proceeds from reason and affection simultaneously and is characterized by mutuality, equality, complete trust and confidence, and perfect harmony in matters human and divine (III.2–8; Laker: 91–93).

Besides the correct form of loving, Aelred mentions another prerequisite for true friendship. The Biblical source and the argumentation built on it sound familiar:

> [And] when God created man, in order to commend more highly the good of society, he said: "It is not good for man to be alone: let us make him a helper like unto himself." It was

from no similar, nor even from the same, material that divine Might formed this help mate, but as a clearer inspiration to charity and friendship he produced the woman from the very substance of the man. How beautiful it is that the second human being was taken from the side of the first, so that nature might teach that human beings are equal and, as it were, collateral, and that there is in human affairs neither a superior nor an inferior, a characteristic of true friendship. (I.57; Laker: 63)

Aelred has used Hugh's gloss on the creation of Adam and Eve and pushed it to its logical extreme to produce an argument supporting the equality of all human beings and man's natural need for a companion.[20] We must not forget of course that Aelred was writing for an all-male audience, his fellow-monks. Nevertheless his interpretation remains highly unorthodox, and unless we assume that Aelred did not fathom the purport of his own words, we must accept that he was aware that this passage might be taken as referring to the hierarchy of man and woman (and was perhaps so taken by Jean de Meun, who after all translated Aelred's treatise and drew on it for the *Roman de la Rose*).[21] Some support for this assumption is found a little later in Book III, where Aelred says that it is "a law of friendship that a superior must be on a plane of equality with an inferior" (III.90; Laker: 115).[22] We shall see that Aristotle and Thomas Aquinas consider friendship possible in such cases, quoting the relation between husband and wife as a typical example.

If we now turn to Robert de Sorbon we make a stride of a hundred years of virtually unresearched territory with respect to the rib-topos, and I do not know how widely disseminated it was before it attracted the attention of Robert.[23] However, even if Robert de Sorbon may not have had a copy of Hugh's *De sacramentis* in front of him when writing his sermon *De matrimonio*, ultimately that work is his source. Although not a monk himself, Robert fits in the "monastic" mould[24] because in his sermon he explicitly addresses himself to the members of the monastic orders, which, as shown by his *exempla*, he puts on a level with the order of marriage [*ordo conjugii*]: if the orders of the black monks and of the Cistercians are to be called noble because of the saintliness of their founders, so much more noble ought to be the order of marriage which was established by God.[25]

A new impulse to the discussion on the quality of the relationship between husband and wife was given by Thomas Aquinas, who throughout his career writes about marriage in terms of friendship. Thus in his early *Summa contra gentiles* (1258-1260) he asserts that the greatest friendship is obviously that between marital partners because "they [also] unite themselves in the flesh by the copula [and not just spiritually]" (III.cxxiii.5; my translation).[26] In marriage Thomas recognizes the *officium naturae*, the natural urge to procreate (*Summa Theologiae* 3a.29,2), and the *officium civilitatis*, which derives its name from the necessity to preserve the state through the generative activity (*STh* 2a2ae.154,2 resp).[27] These concepts also, according to E. Schillebeeckx, comprise the love relationship of the spouses, which combines friendship and mutual assistance, as well as everything touching on the domestic community and subservience to the civic community.[28] Further considerations are to be found in his Commentary on Aristotle's *Ethics*. In the eighth book, on friendship, Aristotle argues that friendship is the most valuable kind of interhuman relationship because "friendship is especially necessary for living, to the extent that no one, even though he had all other goods, would choose to live without friends" (VIII.i.1538; Litzinger: 701).[29] In Lecture vii he discusses the friendship of a superior with a subordinate, under which he classifies the friendship of a father with a son or of an older with a younger person, or of a husband with a wife. With such unequal friendships Aristotle has to face the problem that to him equality is a *conditio sine qua non* for friendship. He answers to this that in such friendships "love must be given proportionately" (VIII.vii.1630).[30] He returns to this point in the next lecture:

> Since friendship consists rather in loving and friends are praised for it, the excellence of a friend seems to be found in loving. For this reason persons who love their friends in proportion to their worth remain friends and their friendship is lasting. In this way, more than any other, those who are unequal will become friends because they will thus be made equal. But then friendship is a kind of equality and likeness. [VIII.viii.1648-9; Litzinger: 740]

On this Thomas gives the following comment:

> He says first that, since friendship consists rather in loving than in being loved, friends are praised because they love and not because they are loved; in fact this is the compliment we pay lovers. [1649] Because everyone is praised for his own virtue, the virtue of a lover should be judged according to his

love. For this reason persons who love their friends in proportion to their worth remain friends and their friendship is lasting. Thus, when people love one another according to their worth, even those who are of unequal condition can be friends because they are made equal in this way—provided that the one who is more lacking in goodness or some other excellence loves that much more. In this way the abundance of love makes up for the inadequacy of condition. [Litzinger: 743]

In the next section Aristotle shows that friendship between virtuous people is the most enduring because, Thomas says, such friends have no need to serve the other in any evil, and he goes on:

But if any evil may possibly occur among the virtuous, one rather prevents the other from doing wrong; for it is characteristic of virtuous men that they neither sin themselves nor allow their friends to commit sin. [VIII.viii.1650; Litzinger: 743]

All the considerations given here are applied together in the chapters on the friendship between husband and wife in Lecture xii. After his approval of Aristotle's statement that friendship seems natural between them because they are "more inclined by nature to conjugal than political society" (VIII.xii.1719), Thomas continues:

[Aristotle] shows how this friendship shares the common reasons for friendship. He observes that . . . conjugal friendship obviously has utility inasmuch as it furnishes a sufficiency for family life. Likewise it provides pleasure in the generative act, as is the case with other animals. But when the husband and wife are virtuous, their friendship can be based on virtue. In fact there is a virtue proper to both husband and wife that renders their friendship delightful to each other. Clearly then friendship of this kind can be based on virtue, utility, and pleasure. [VIII.xii. 1723; Litzinger: 768]

When reading what Thomas has to say about *amicitia* in relation to husband and wife, one gets the impression that he considers marital friendship as an ideal which serves a rather practical purpose.[31]

Summarizing our findings we can say that the characteristic features of the "monastic," Augustinian tradition of Bernard, Hugh, and Aelred are attention for the love relationship between the spouses (or friends, with Aelred), a recognition of their (near) equality, and the rib-topos. The philosophical, Aristotelian tradition lacks the rib-topos, but on the other hand it elaborates on the first two, combining them by means of the ideal of friendship. The obvious question to be asked next is of course whether these two traditions ever came together. It seems they did, and for this we must turn to the popular sermon, the sermon as it was preached to the laity (unlike that of Robert de Sorbon, which was probably intended for his students).

Undoubtedly the most important source of information on all matters pertaining to theological doctrine, both for the nobility and for the common people, was the sermon. In a recent article D. L. d'Avray and M. L. Tausche have reported on their research in the field of medieval marriage preaching.[32] In view of the enormous corpus they decided to start their investigations with what appeared to be a manageable subgenre, the *ad status* collections, that is, the collections of sermons addressed to people of a particular state of life, which usually include sermons for the married. Of the five collections from the central medieval period presently known two are fairly small; one is by Honorius of Autun (early twelfth century), the other by Alan of Lille (late twelfth century). The other three, all more extensive ones, belong to the thirteenth century; of these two will be discussed, one by Jacques de Vitry (or Jacobus de Vitriaco, d. 1240), the other by Guibert de Tournai (Guibertus de Tornaco, d. 1284).[33] The sermons in these collections make a rather uniform impression: each author tends to write down the commonplaces, with a delicate admixture of his own ideas. The result is "that one can only discover the originality of a given writer by labeling the commonplaces he has taken over from the tradition to which he belongs."[34] We shall briefly consider the more important of these sermons.

An original point with Honorius, to start with the earliest, is his emphasis on the love the spouses should have for each other, an idea he may have taken from his contemporary, Hugh of St. Victor, or possibly from Bernard of Clairvaux. We know that in this respect the official view of the Church moved in a different direction, away from this emphasis on love, and it is significant that in the sermon of Alan, some fifty years later, references to love have disappeared altogether.[35]

Jacques de Vitry and Guibert de Tournai are naturally paired, for the latter depends heavily, both for substance and for phrasing, on the *Sermones vulgares* of Jacques.[36] In their sermons "both provide a fairly comprehensive popularization of marriage doctrine to meet the needs of the laity."[37] Both Jacques and Guibert believe that the husband should prove that the male is the more reasonable being and that the wife must obey her husband. On the other hand, they apply the rib-topos in slightly different ways. Jacques follows Hugh of St. Victor in concluding that the woman is to be the husband's partner (*socia*); he goes on to prove with Scriptural texts that wives should be loved and honored, and he concludes that husbands "ought not to despise or illtreat their wives, but should have them as partners (*tanquam socias*), in bed, at the table, and with respect to money, food, and clothing."[38] Guibert distinguishes two kinds of love; the first is *dilectio carnalis*, which he deals with in the first half of his sermon and which covers such questions as when sexual intercourse is permitted. The other type is *dilectio socialis*, and part two of the sermon opens with the following statement: "There is also a kind of love founded on partnership (*dilectio socialis*), and this is the love which husband and wife owe to each other, because they are equal [*pares*] and partners [*socii*]."[39] Guibert's two kinds of *dilectio* call to mind Thomas's two offices of marriage, the *officium naturae* and the *officium civilitatis*. Immediately after this Guibert gives the rib-topos, on which he comments, not that the spouses are partners or equals, for he has already said that, but that woman was not created from the head lest she would become presumptuous, nor from the feet, lest the husband would treat her with contempt. This passage is followed by admonitions to the husbands to love their wives, by means of the familiar quotations from Ephesians 5. We see that Guibert has rearranged the argument of Jacques: it now has the same order as that in Robert de Sorbon's sermon, which could also have provided the idea of the equality of the partners. On the other hand, since the wording of the rib-topos is closer to Jacques than to Robert, Guibert may not have seen Robert's sermon and taken this particular idea, like his two types of love, from Thomas. In the passage mentioned Guibert does not comment on the words *pares* and *socii*, but as the sermon progresses some interesting clarifications are provided. With respect to the motives for marriage, Guibert here produces an argumentation that contains some familiar elements:

> Moreover this love ought to be formed in such a way that the motives for it are pure, so that the husband and wife should not love each other or be joined in marriage for the sake of some temporal gain, or a beautiful figure (*forma*), or to gratify their lust, but so that they may live together (*vivant simul* (!))

happily and decently, so that God may receive honour, and the marriage yield fruit for the service of God. . . . For when they are equal (*pares*), then they live in peace; but when they have got married for the sake of a dowry or for something temporal they always quarrel. So if you want to get married, marry an equal.[40]

The first thing we notice is that Guibert makes quite a point of the right motive for marriage, love between the future spouses, in which he reminds us of Honorius of Autun and of Thomas. In the two motives he rejects we recognize the two false friendships repudiated by Aelred, worldly and carnal friendship, while the description of the happy life that awaits the man and woman who have based their choice on the right motives, love and equality, bears a resemblance to that of Aelred's true friendship, though with a Thomistic, pragmatic touch: the equality of Guibert seems one of rank, of social status, whereas that of Aelred is a truly spiritual one, through which "the rich [can] be in want, the poor become rich."[41]

So far we can only speak about parallels between love and friendship in these lines of Guibert. The final step to an equation of the two he takes when he supports his exhortation that "husband and wife should be inseparable in their affection" by quoting Proverbs 17:17, "a friend loves at all times." To this he adds a few lines later that "those who live an indivisible life ought to have a feeling of love which makes separation impossible"[42]—which is not too different from what Aelred (e.g. in *De spir.am.* I.21) and Thomas say. What follows is again reminiscent of Aelred and of Thomas: "There should be absolute freedom to correct each other, so that a husband may be free to criticize his wife, and she accept it for the love she bears him, and vice versa."[43]

Is it mere coincidence that there are so many echoes of Aelred and Thomas in the sermons of Guibert? In spite of our faulty knowledge of the transmission and dissemination of the relevant texts, it is possible to reach a few tentative conclusions because the historical context has some suggestive facts in store.

The most recent editor of Aelred's *De spirituali amicitia* lists a total of thirteen manuscripts, practically all of them stemming from Cistercian or Benedictine abbeys.[44] Yet at least one manuscript must have been available in Paris, if that is where Jean de Meun translated it.

It is much easier to find evidence for a link between Thomas Aquinas and Guibert. After the first outburst of the conflict between the seculars and the mendicants at the University of Paris had been temporarily suppressed by Pope Innocent IV in 1254, two young professors in theology, the Dominican Thomas Aquinas and the Franciscan Bonaventura, formed a united front in the "vigorous pamphlet warfare" against the seculars, led by William of St. Amour.[45] In 1257 Bonaventura was elected minister general of the Franciscans and his successor to the (one) Franciscan chair of theology was Guibert. Though Guibert's professorship, from 1257 to 1261, may have been less turbulent than that of Bonaventura, it was by no means a dull period, and during the two years in which he was Thomas's closest colleague (Thomas left Paris in 1259) they must have met frequently. If there is any resemblance between academic meetings in the days of Thomas and those of our own age the subject will not have been restricted to faculty issues. When Guibert resigned from his duties in 1261 to devote himself entirely to preaching he must have taken with him many ideas originally developed by Thomas, who after all was the more scholarly of the two.

Robert de Sorbon was a professor of theology in that same period (1250–1274),[46] but as a canon he occupied a "secular" chair. Nevertheless we must assume, for a number of reasons, that he and Guibert knew each other. In the first place neither was, as it seems, personally involved in the conflict. Secondly, both enjoyed royal favor: Robert was "clerc du roi" and possibly even confessor to Louis the Pious[47] and received rich gifts for his colleges from the king,[48] and Guibert wrote his *Eruditio regum et principium* (1259) at Louis's special request.[49] Thirdly, both of them were gifted preachers. Add to this that there were only a dozen professors of theology at the time, and it is evident that Guibert and Robert could hardly have avoided one another.

At the end of their article d'Avray and Tausche come to the conclusion that the additions of Guibert to the sermons of Jacques produce a "picture of marriage [that] is lighter and more optimistic."[50] This coloring he may well have derived from Aelred or from one of his colleagues, Robert or Thomas, whose ideas on friendship so often seem to underlie Guibert's words. Exactly when Guibert wrote his *ad status* collection is impossible to ascertain (although it is unlikely that he wrote them before he left Paris), but in itself it is significant that he, a Franciscan and one-time professor of theology at the University of Paris, should write a model sermon on marital love in this vein at approximately the same time that another professor of theology in Paris, Thomas Aquinas, was working on a commentary of Aristotle's *Ethics*.

A final word about Jean de Meun, with whom this article opened. In 1269 Thomas returned to Paris where he took up residence in the Dominican house of St. Jacques. During the three years he spent at the university he taught from and continued to work on his Commentary on the *Ethics*.[51] In that same period Jean de Meun was probably connected with the Faculty of Arts, working on his continuation of the *Roman de la Rose* and living in all likelihood in a house at a stone's throw from Thomas's domicile.[52] This is not the place to analyze the role of the friars in the *Roman* or Jean's attitude to them,[53] but an intimate relation between Jean and Thomas, in spite of their geographical and intellectual proximity, is not very plausible. Still, even if Jean developed his considerable interest in friendship as an ideal for the love relationship between a man and a woman independently,[54] he certainly found in Paris both the sources and the spiritual climate in which a latent interest in *amicitia* could germinate.[55]

4

The Medieval Poet as Voyeur

... that thow canst not do, yit mayst thow se.
For many a man that may nat stonde a pul
Yet liketh hym at wrastlyng for to be ...
(Chaucer, *The Parliament of Fowls*)[1]

The special part played by the sense of sight in medieval accounts of love is well known. Whether for good or ill, Love's arrow
enters the heart through the eye: Andreas Capellanus, defining
love as "passio quaedam innata *procedens ex visione* et immoder-
ata cogitatione formae alterius sexus,"[2] is so convinced of the importance of sight that he denies that a blind man can fall in love,
while Chaucer, following orthodox penitential doctrine in *The Parson's Tale*, states that lechery begins with "the fool lookynge of
the fool womman and of the fool man" (*Canterbury Tales* X. 852).
There has been less discussion of looking and watching as means
by which, once Love's arrow has become firmly lodged, the private
activities of lovers can be brought to public knowledge, and as actions which may themselves become sexually charged. I think I
can best indicate the potential of this subject not discursively but
by asking you to reflect on two brief examples. The first is a lyric
by Walther von der Vogelweide, a short poem about love, of a kind
that can be found in many languages in the Middle Ages but perhaps rarely expressed with such charm and felicity:

> Under der linden
> an der heide,
> dâ unser zweier bette was,

dâ mugt ir vinden
schône beide
gebrochen bluomen unde gras.
vor dem walde in einem tal,
tandaradei,
     schône sanc diu nahtegal.

Ich kam gegangen
zue der ouwe:
dô was min friedel comen ê.
dâ wart ich enpfangen,
here frouwe,
daz ich bin saelic iemer mê.
kuster mich? wol tûsentstunt:
tandaradei,
     seht wie rôt mir ist der munt.

Dô het er gemachet
alsô rîche
von bluomen eine bettestat.
des wirt noh gelachet
innedîche,
kumt ieman an daz selbe pfat.
bi den rôsen er wol mac,
tandaradei,
     merken wâ mirz houbet lac.

Daz er bî mir laege,
wessez iemen
(nu enwelle got!) sô schamt ich mich.
wes er mit mir pflaege,
niemer nieman
bevinde daz, wan er unt ich,
und ein kleinez vogellîn:
tandaradei,
     daz mac wol getriuwe sin.[3]

Under the lindentree
on the heather
there our bed for two was
and there too
you may find blossoms grasses
picked together.

In a clearing of a wood
tandaradei!
>the nightingale sang sweetly.

I came walking
over the field:
my love was already there.
Then I was received
with the words "Noble lady!"
It will always make me happy.
Did he kiss me? He gave me thousands!
tandaradei!
>O look at my red mouth.

He had made
very beautifully
a soft bed out of the flowers.
Anybody who comes by there
knowingly
may smile to himself.
For by the upset roses he may see
tandaradei!
>where my head lay.

If any one were to know
how he lay with me
(may God forbid it!), I'd feel such shame.
What we did together
may no one ever know
except us two
one small bird excepted
tandaradei!
>and it can keep a secret.[4]

In this brief narrative, the speaker is a peasant girl who tells of an encounter she had with a knight. The encounter has manifestly involved lovemaking, described in a way that mixes allusion with direct statement—on the one hand broken flowers and grass and the impression of her body among the roses, on the other lips red with kisses. The encounter has been secret, and the only witness has been "ein kleinez vogellîn," the nightingale, whose refrain of *tandaradei* reminds us of its presence throughout, and who, the girl says, will not betray her. And yet, of course, she has betrayed herself by speaking the words of the poem; the lyric is a verbal act that makes public precisely what it claims to keep private. No one will ever find out what her lover did with her, she says, and she would be ashamed if anyone knew that he had slept with her. Notice that she says ashamed ("sô schamt ich mich"), not guilty: it is a delightfully cheerful poem, and she is speaking not of any actual remorse at illicit love, but of how her feelings would be affected if what happened were known to others. Yet the poem has to have only one listener or reader for everything to be disclosed and for her to bring on herself the very shame that she says she wants to avoid. And when we become its hearers or readers, we are put imaginatively in the position of the nightingale, the poet's surrogate within the poem: we become onlookers at a sexual encounter in which we have no part.

That is what is commonly known as voyeurism, a term which I do not pretend to use with an accuracy that would satisfy any school of psychology. Freud and others have explained that the wish to look in sexual matters is both a normal stage in the development of the child and a normal element in adult sexuality. As Freud puts it in his formidably scientific way in one of his most important earlier works, the *Three Essays on the Theory of Sexuality* (1905), "Visual impressions remain the most frequent pathway along which libidinal excitation is aroused," and to linger over seeing, like lingering over touching, "can scarcely be counted a perversion, provided that in the long run the sexual act is carried further." Voyeurism (also known as scopophilia, though this term is sometimes distinguished from it in ways I shall not pursue) emerges as a perversion, "if, instead of being *preparatory* to the normal sexual aim, it supplants it"—if, that is, in terms of the quotation from Chaucer that stands at the head of this paper, sex becomes what wrestling is for most people: a spectator-sport.[5] Or, as a popular exposition of Freud's thought puts it,

> Perversions are forms of incomplete maturity of sexual object and aim, which prevent full union of any kind with another individual. Among them may be included voyeurism, where looking at other people of the same or opposite sex naked, watching others having sexual intercourse, seeking to see the genitalia of others, or watching them in the act of urination or defecation, takes the place of a more complete sexual aim.[6]

Obviously, from one point of view, writing about human sexual behavior may itself be regarded as a perversion, a substitute for the "more complete sexual aim"; we have all become familiar with the phallic implications of the pen. But my concern will be with some writings in which looking, for the narrator or some of his characters, seems within the fiction to have supplanted the "normal" sexuality that has physical union as its goal. Now let me turn to my second introductory example.

This is a passage from the novel *Rates of Exchange*, written by the British novelist Malcolm Bradbury and published in 1983. The novel's central character, a British academic named Dr. Petworth, is sent to give some lectures for the British Council in an imaginary Eastern European country. He has assigned to him as his official guide an attractive young woman, Mari Lubijova; in the scene from which I quote, to his surprise, delight, and embarrassment, she joins him in his hotel room, and the following conversation takes place (Mari speaks first):

> "And you know those who watch us and listen to us, they would like us to make some love."
>
> "Who do you mean?" asks Petworth.
>
> "Oh, please, you know them, they are always there," says Mari, "But I do not think it is their business. I think we disappoint them, yes?"
>
> "Yes," says Petworth.
>
> "But I cannot go now," says Mari. "I think we turn out the light and be together very quiet for a bit. And if we say nothing, no one can tell anything of us."
>
> "Who would tell?" asks Petworth.
>
> "Of course," says Mari, "Someone is always telling of you and me. So we are quiet together, and we make no words."
>
> Outside the window there is the noise of the rushing river, and there is a scent of trees in the air. But it is totally quiet and entirely dark in the little bedroom, and there is absolutely nothing to hear or see. A clock ticks, but one cannot tell how much time is passing; certainly it is some time later when Mari, in the dark, says:
>
> "Comrade Petwurt, now I go. You must sleep very nicely, don't forget you must make an early wake, to go on that train to Nogod. Thank you for the drink, thank you to be with me, thank you to be quiet. And perhaps even we did make some love, if not in the usual way."
>
> "Yes," says Petworth.
>
> "But there is nothing to know, nothing to tell," says Mari.[7]

"Someone is always telling of you and me." In one sense, that refers to the spies, the informers, who we may imagine are always present, reporting to the state authorities on the behavior of the visiting lecturer and his guide. But in another sense that someone is the novelist; and "those who watch us and listen to us" are also in one sense spies and in another sense ourselves, the readers of the novel. What follows is a kind of joke by the characters at the expense of the novelist and his readers; Petworth and Mari remain completely quiet, the room is in total darkness, and thus "there is nothing to know, nothing to tell." The novelist and his readers may be eager for there to be a love scene at this point, but the characters cheat them—we don't know whether they make love or not.

In some ways this is a more sophisticated piece of narrative than Walther's lyric. It does not simply present the paradox of concealment and disclosure; it makes the characters themselves—or at least one of them—seem to be conscious of the paradox, and it incorporates the morally ambiguous roles of author and reader into the fiction. It is as though the world of every novel were a kind of police state in which the most private activities are conducted under the eyes of hidden watchers. Late-twentieth-century novelists are notoriously self-conscious about themselves as narrators and about their audience as readers; but many medieval poets, who still had oral delivery in mind as the normal situation, were perhaps even more so. And that self-consciousness or reflexivity is especially likely to emerge when, as in the scene from *Rates of Exchange*, their subject is love, as it so often is. Love is essentially a private experience, if only in the empirical sense that human beings in most cultures choose to conduct their love-relations in private whenever possible; but to "tell" about love is to break its privacy, and to identify oneself with those malicious gossips and slanderers by whom medieval lovers tend to be surrounded. It implies that the narrator (or perhaps the narrator of his source) has somehow been present as a secret onlooker and/or overhearer[8] of the lovers' behavior, and that the readers or listeners somehow share his concealed presence. This is the fundamental paradox of the medieval love-poet; it takes a somewhat different form if his subject is his own love affair, because then the secret observation that constitutes voyeurism is not involved, but the paradox of a public report of private behavior remains in that case, too. I want to discuss a number of different instances where the element of voyeurism in a narrative about love is brought to our attention, so that it functions not as a silent necessity for that favorite kind of medieval narrative, but as something in which we as readers are knowingly implicated, so that the excitement and the shame of voyeurism become parts of the narrative effect. I shall begin with two poets who do not claim literally to have witnessed what they describe, then go on to two whose fictional role is that of literal voyeurs.

My first example is an early medieval French narrative, the *Tristan* attributed to Beroul. Dating from the twelfth century, this is one of the earliest surviving versions of the famous love story of Tristan and Iseult. Not all of it survives, and what does survive in the single manuscript has many peculiarities of narrative technique. In the past these have troubled scholars for whom the classic novel seemed the natural form of fiction, but they are probably more acceptable to those brought up on modernist and post-modernist narratives. Fragmentation of narrative sequence and of causal structure, inconsistency of characterization, abrupt shifts of tone and of narratorial position: all these offenses against classical conceptions of the well-formed narrative are found in Beroul's *Tristan*, but (supposing that "Beroul" is a single author) his narrative syntax is no more peculiar than that of Joyce or Lawrence, not to mention William Burroughs or Kurt Vonnegut, Thomas Pynchon or Alasdair Gray. However one interprets it, voyeurism plays a major part in the story told; it must do so, because it concerns a prolonged illicit love affair, secret not just because lovers prefer privacy but for reasons having to do with feudal law.[9] It is vitally important first that the affair should not become known to Iseult's husband King Mark (who is Tristan's uncle); and then too it is important that, whatever Mark's private suspicions might be, the affair should not become public knowledge and thus force him into public action against Iseult and her lover.

Many of the incidents concern attempts by Mark and his informants literally to *see* whether Tristan and Iseult are committing adultery, to catch them in the act; merely circumstantial evidence of adultery would not be legally sufficient. This is true, for example, of the first surviving scene. Mark's suspicions have been aroused by a group of his barons, who have their own reasons for wanting Tristan to be disgraced; and Tristan has been banished from the court but has continued to have secret meetings with Iseult, arranged by throwing twigs into a stream as messages. A dwarf has told Mark about this, and has advised the king to conceal himself in a tree near the stream, so that he can overhear the lovers' conversation. The image of the king hiding in the tree, secretly spying on the lovers, is a memorable one, sometimes represented in medieval art as capturing the essence of this story—one in which shameful suspense is the constant accompaniment of romantic love.[10] But the scene as recounted by Beroul is more complicated than that. Mark is not really an unseen spy, because, although it is nighttime, Tristan sees by moonlight the reflection of Mark's shadow in the stream; then Iseult sees it too; and the two lovers play out for Mark's benefit a scene intended to deceive him as to their relationship. Iseult rebukes Tristan for summoning her there, saying that it will only encourage Mark to believe those villains who allege that they love each other wickedly, when really she is well disposed towards Tristan only because he is her husband's nephew. What she says conveys to Tristan that she too realizes that Mark is spying on them, and he answers in the same way:

> Qar j'ai tel duel c'onques le roi
> Out mal pensé de vos vers moi
> Qu'il n'i a el fors que je muere. . . .
> Ne deüst pas mis oncles chiers
> De moi croire ses losengiers;
> Sovent en ai mon cuer irié.
>   [109–11, 143–5][11]

❖❖❖

That the king should ever think ill of me on your account grieves me so much that I think I shall die. . . . My dear uncle ought not to believe the slanders that are told about me; it makes me deeply angry to think of it.[12]

He asks Iseult to speak well of him to Mark. That would be a great mistake, she answers, given Mark's existing suspicions, and she makes to leave, saying,

> Grant poor ai que aucun home
> Ne vos ait ci veü venir.
> S'un mot en puet li rois oïr
> Que nos fuson ça asenblé,
> Il me feroit ardoir en ré.
>   [188–92]

❖❖❖

I am very much afraid that someone may have seen us coming here. If the king heard a word of our being together, I should not be surprised if he decided to have me burnt.

Tristan calls her back, begging her to advise him: should he ask the king to release him from his service, so that he could go elsewhere and put an end to the unpleasant situation? Good heavens, no, exclaims Iseult; that would just make Mark certain that Tristan was disloyal to him! She leaves, and Tristan ostentatiously soliloquizes about the unhappiness of his state, unjustly suspected of a liaison he would never dream of entering into. Then he too leaves; and Mark is left to climb down from his tree, totally convinced that the dwarf has misled him with his "fort outrage" (306), and determined to make peace with Tristan and invite him once more to sleep in his private apartment.

In this scene Mark is a concealed voyeur, but so are we, spying on him spying on the lovers; and the fact that the story is *about* an act of voyeurism encourages us to become aware that we too are voyeurs, only more sharp-eyed ones than the king. We share the indignity of his position, knowing what the lovers are saying only because we are also spies; but at the same time we are admitted by Beroul into the lovers' knowledge of Mark's presence and into their motives for saying what they do. This means that we are morally implicated too. The deception the lovers practice on the king is acceptable only if we wish it to be so. And I think we do: we wish Mark to be deceived, we delight in the ingenuity with which he is manipulated, and we are thus manipulated ourselves into sharing the extraordinary view expressed by Brangain, Iseult's maid, in the scene that follows, that the success of the deceit is a miracle wrought by God for the benefit of lovers who are "buen et loial" (380)! Who is watching whom? Who is manipulated by whom? The apparent naïveté and inconsistency of Beroul's storytelling may well have the effect of supreme sophistication for listeners conscious of their own morally questionable role in the fiction. At every point a supposedly impregnable secrecy is penetrated and exposed: Mark is watching the lovers; the lovers watch him watching them; we watch them watching him watching them; and Beroul, whose motives are truly secret (at least to us, eight centuries later—but perhaps they always have been), watches us, exposing in us the disreputable motives of voyeurs who interpret what we see in accordance with our own preconceptions (this is a miracle!), while unaware until too late that our own interpretation is shaped by the cunning of the poet.

The following scene reveals yet another level of voyeurism. Iseult goes to her room (that is, to the *chanbre* she shares with her husband) and confides to Brangain what has just happened. But Mark now joins them, and Iseult tells him what she and Tristan said to each other by the stream, and then pretends surprise when Mark confesses that he overheard the conversation. Mark sends Brangain to find Tristan; she pretends reluctance, because she says that Tristan hates her, and Beroul comments,

> Oiez que dit la tricherresse!
> Molt fist que bone lecherresse:
> Lores gaboit a esscïent
> Et se plaignoit de maltalent.
> [519–22]

❖❖❖

Just listen to the deceitful woman! She spoke like a real swindler. She lied deliberately when she complained about Tristan's ill will.

But as soon as Brangain leaves the room, Beroul reveals that Tristan has been hidden just outside, secretly listening to the conversation with the king. "He caught Brangain in his arms and embraced her, thanking God [that the king was going to allow him] to be with Yseut as he wished." After a suitable delay, filled with more embraces and kisses, Tristan and Brangain return, and Mark forgives Tristan and gives him permission once more to visit his private apartment, thus making it easier for him and Iseult to continue their adulterous relationship. Once again, we have become implicated as watchers and listeners to what is supposedly secret. The concealment on which the story depends is possible, it is worth bearing in mind, because of the existence of (supposedly) private *places:* the pine tree overlooking the stream, and especially the king's private apartment, the *chanbre,* containing the bed where he sleeps with Iseult. Private bedrooms were possessed in the early Middle Ages only by those of the very highest rank, and the room and the bed have a powerful emotional and symbolic charge, embodying simultaneously King Mark's public status and his most intimate being. It is from this *chanbre painte* (549) (literally a room hung with painted curtains, but perhaps with a hint of painting in the sense of deception and concealment) that Tristan is temporarily banished, in this room that he sleeps in a bed at the foot of the king's, and here too that he abuses his loyalty to his uncle and feudal lord by sleeping with Iseult in Mark's bed whenever he gets the chance.

The remainder of the story is full of acts of voyeurism. Three of the king's barons—"Ainz ne veïstes plus felons" (582) [you

never saw more wicked men], says Beroul—often see the lovers lying together naked in King Mark's bed: "El lit roi Marc gesir toz
nus" (594). The dwarf peers through the window at night when
Mark is absent; it is completely dark, "Cirge ne lanpë alumez"
(726) [no lamp or candle was lit] (just as in Bradbury's novel); but
by moonlight he watches Tristan and Iseult making love, and he
quivers with joy at what he sees: "de joie en trenble" (738). Beroul,
with his usual partisanship, encourages us to hate and despise
the dwarf; but in this scene it is inevitable that we should share
this contemptible figure's point of view and participate in his
voyeuristic pleasure. There is another scene later, again a very famous one, in which the lovers are living in exile in the forest (a
symbolic setting the very opposite of the bedroom), and, after
Tristan returns from hunting for their food, they lie down together
in a leafy bower, and Tristan places his sword between them. They
are half-clothed, and Beroul explicitly invites us to become imaginative voyeurs: "Oez com il se sont couchiez" (1816) [Hear how
they were lying], he says, and he gives a detailed description of
their postures:

> Desoz le col Tristran a mis
> Son braz, et l'autre, ce m'est vis,
> Li out par dedesus geté;
> Estroitement l'ot acolé,
> Et il la rot des ses braz çainte;
> Lor amistié ne fu pas fainte.
> Les bouches furent pres asises,
> Et ne porquant si ot devises
> Que n'asenbloient pas ensenble.
> Vent ne cort ne fuelle ne trenble;
> Uns rais decent desor la face
> Yseut, que plus reluist que glace.
>   [1817–28]

❖❖❖

She had put one arm under Tristan's neck and the other, I
think, over him; her arms were clasped tightly around him.
Tristan in his turn had his arms around her, for their affection was not feigned. Their mouths and bodies were close
together, yet there was a space between them and their
bodies were not touching. There was no wind and the leaves
were still. A ray of sunlight fell on Iseut's face where it shone
like glass.[13]

In this moment of enchantment, it is as though we as onlookers are incorporated into the scene: the absence of wind is because we are holding our breaths, the stillness of the leaves reflects our stillness, the ray of sunlight is our glance cast on the sleeping Iseult. Then a forester comes up and glimpses them, and he fetches Mark, who becomes a voyeur in his turn. Once more Mark misinterprets what he sees; from the fact that they are not naked and that the sword lies between them, he deduces that they are not lovers, attributing a symbolism to the sword that was quite unintended by Tristan.

In the final surviving episode of Beroul's version, Tristan emerges from hiding to visit Iseult yet again in Mark's *chanbre*, while the king is off on a hunting expedition. But the three malicious barons are warned by a spy what Tristan is doing. One of them, Godoïne, gets there before him, and once more we are in the position of peering with a concealed watcher through the window.

> La cortine ot dedenz percie;
> Vit la chanbre, qui fu jonchie,
> Tot vit quant que dedenz avoit . . .
>   [4413–5]

He had pushed aside the curtain and could see the bedroom carpeted with rushes and everything inside . . .

When Tristan arrives, with Godoïne still watching,

> Sa chape osta, pert ses genz cors.
> Iseut, la bele o les crins sors,
> Contre lui lieve, sil salue.
>   [4425–7]

He took off his cloak, revealing his well-made body, and the lovely fair-haired Yseut rose to greet him.

But yet again the watcher is watched; Iseult catches a glimpse of Godoïne's shadow, she conveys to Tristan by subtle hints that she has seen a spy, he too sees Godoïne's head "Contre le jor, par la cortine" (4461) [against the light by the curtain], and he draws his bow and shoots him dead. He shoots him, significantly, through the eye; thus voyeurism receives its appropriate punishment, and perhaps at this moment, by vicariously suffering the punishment, we may feel temporarily absolved from our share in its shame.

A privacy which is difficult to achieve; a furtiveness which adds to the relish of a love-affair; the presence within the story of secret onlookers whose existence makes us aware that we too are secret onlookers—these are the ingredients of many medieval narratives of love in a courtly setting. One of the most famous is Chaucer's *Troilus and Criseyde,* where the voyeur within the story is not an enemy but a friend of the lovers, Pandarus, the go-between who brings them together for the first time. Chaucer emphasizes strongly the historical distance of the events he is recounting, and the fact that he knows about them not from any personal experience of love, still less from having been there, but only from the writings of "olde clerkis" (V.1854). This enables him to leave conspicuous gaps in the story—how old was Criseyde? did she have any children by her late husband? did she eventually, having betrayed Troilus, give her heart or only her body to Diomede?—gaps which invite our imaginative participation to fill them. He emphasizes too that his essential subject matter is not public events such as *armes* and *batailles* (V.1766–7) but private behavior and feelings which the participants do their utmost to conceal from public knowledge. The problem of how a storyteller can get reliable information about secret behavior (one that had interested Chaucer at least since he wrote *The House of Fame*) is constantly being brought to our attention, and the lovers are much influenced by the need to avoid storytellers in the other sense—gossips and scandalmongers—in order to preserve Criseyde's honor, her *name.* Indeed, when Criseyde is inwardly debating whether to allow herself to fall in love with Troilus, an important argument against doing so is that "thise wikked tonges ben so prest / To speke us harm" (II.785–6). The two kinds of storyteller eventually merge into one, as the lovers foresee and the poet condemns those malicious repeaters of their story, the *olde clerkis* themselves, who will present it as one of shame and betrayal, not of love and fidelity. At the very moment when she finally commits herself to Diomede, Criseyde soliloquizes,

> Allas, of me, unto the worldes ende,
> Shal neyther ben ywriten nor ysonge
> No good word, for thise bokes wol me shende.

> O, rolled shal I ben on many a tonge!
> Thorughout the world my belle shal be ronge!
> [V 1058–62]

Unlike Beroul, Chaucer makes these paradoxes perfectly explicit.

The gaps he leaves do not, as one might expect, include the lovers' intimate relations. Their first night together is recounted in exquisite detail, in some of the most beautiful erotic poetry in the English language. Metaphor plays its appropriate part: after the bashful Troilus, having swooned and been brought round, finally plucks up courage to embrace Criseyde fully, Chaucer asks what could the hapless lark say when seized by the sparrowhawk? and he goes on,

> Criseyde, which that felte hire thus itake,
> As writen clerkes in hire bokes olde,
> Right as an aspes leef she gan to quake,
> Whan she hym felte hire in his armes folde. . . .
> [III 1198–1201]

Somehow, then, the *clerkes* who wrote the *bokes olde* were in a position to know exactly how Criseyde trembled when Troilus clasped her to him. Pandarus, having at his disposal the dwelling arrangements of a fourteenth-century nobleman, far more lavish than those of a twelfth-century king, has made elaborate preparations for secrecy. Criseyde is to go to bed, separated from her waiting women, in a *litel closet* (III.663) provided with a *secre trappe-dore* (759) through which first he and then Troilus can come to her when everyone else is asleep. But these precautions must have been unavailing, if the *clerkes* got to be so well informed about what went on. And of course the lovers' privacy has literally been broken, indeed has never existed, because Pandarus is not merely in the know all along, he is in the room all along, throughout this climactic love scene.

Pandarus's role in the poem corresponds in many ways to that which Chaucer attributes to himself, as unsuccessful lover, a mere servant of the servants of Cupid (I.15). And Pandarus takes over inside the poem the complicated planning and manipulation necessary to bring two by no means forward young people together in the same bed without anyone else knowing about it. Just as Chaucer or his clerkly authorities are in some imaginative sense actually present throughout all the lovers' dealings—or how else would he be able to tell us about them?—so Pandarus is literally present

as an interested observer. First, he persuades Criseyde to allow
Troilus into the *litel closet* so that she can assure him that he has
no cause for his alleged jealousy of her alleged love for his alleged
rival Horaste; but then, having got Troilus sitting on her bedside,
he does not leave the room himself, but, Chaucer says, commends
this good beginning,

> And with that word he drow hym to the feere,
> And took a light, and fond his contenaunce,
> As for to looke upon an old romaunce
> [III 978–80]

—presumably something about love written by one of the surprisingly knowledgeable *olde clerkis* of Trojan times. It is fortunate
that Pandarus does not leave, because the outcome of Criseyde's
long and moving speech against jealousy is that she covers her
head with the sheet and falls silent, and it is now that Troilus
faints. Pandarus immediately leaps up, pushes him into Criseyde's
bed, pulls off all Troilus's clothes except his shirt (just what one
would do if someone fainted, of course), helps Criseyde to chafe his
hands and moisten his temples, does not discourage her from giving him mouth-to mouth resuscitation; and finally, saying that too
much light is bad for sick people's eyes, he goes back to the fire-
place, taking his candle with him.

There Pandarus apparently stays all night; at any rate, Chaucer does not mention that he leaves, indeed he does not mention
him again at all until the next morning. There is none of the business of peering through bedroom windows favored by Beroul; the
love scene itself is described with the greatest beauty and delicacy.
But when morning arrives, there is an extraordinary scene in
which Pandarus comes back to Criseyde's bedside before she rises,
makes jokes about rain keeping people awake in the night, pries
under the sheet, thrusts his arm beneath her neck, and kisses her.
There are scholars who manage to persuade themselves, though
not me, that at this point Pandarus actually has sexual intercourse
with his own niece. It is perfectly clear at least that Pandarus,
whose personal lack of success in love has become a standing joke
among his friends, has gained and is still gaining a vicarious sexual pleasure from the encounter between his niece and her lover.
He is sexually aroused by being there as a witness to their love-
making. And we are there, too; even when no one else but Pandarus knows that the lovers are together, we are there; and even

when Troilus, earlier, is assuring Pandarus that he will never mention their love to anyone else, asking

> How dorst I mo tellen of this matere,
> That quake now, and no wight may us here?
>
> [III 370–1]

—even then, we are there, hearing him as he says no one can hear
him and watching him tremble as he says it.

We are not only present, we are also given a far larger share of
responsibility for what happens in *Troilus and Criseyde* than we
are as readers of Beroul's *Tristan*. Beroul never explicitly raises the
question how he or we can know what happened in private and in
the dark; but Chaucer constantly raises such questions, precisely
because there is so much that he admits to not knowing. And he
keeps on telling us, as he does in the very middle of the love scene
in Book III, that we know or can guess what is unknown to him:

> Of hire delit or joies oon the leeste
> Were impossible to my wit to seye;
> But juggeth ye that han ben at the feste
> Of swich gladnesse, if that hem liste pleye!
>
> [III 1310–13]

Thus the responsibility for imagining further details of the lovers'
play becomes ours; and in that strange scene towards the end of
Book III, when Pandarus comes to his niece's bedside after Troilus
has left her, if we imagine that Pandarus has intercourse with her,
then that too is our responsibility. Chaucer has said no more than
that he passes over everything that is not worth mentioning—"I
passe al that which chargeth nought to seye" (III.1576)—and if we
choose to construct a scene which would be truly vicious and
shocking, it is our voyeurism, not his, that is to blame.[14]

Troilus and Criseyde is an extraordinary achievement in
many ways, but perhaps especially in the way that it acknowledges
and even foregrounds the element of voyeurism in medieval love-
narrative, while sustaining a treatment of love itself that is beautiful and reverent without being solemn. In a later work Chaucer
returns to the theme of the poet as voyeur, but now in a spirit of
sour disillusion. This is *The Manciple's Tale*, the last but one of
the *Canterbury Tales*, in a sense the last of all, because *The Parson's Tale* is no tale but a treatise whose teller austerely rejects

both fiction and verse. In the course of his prologue the Manciple shows his contempt for the Cook, whom the Host has called on to tell the next tale, but who is so drunk that he can scarcely keep awake. The Host warns the Manciple not to reprove the Cook too openly for his vice, in case the Cook should take vengeance another day by revealing some of the unpleasant truths he knows about the Manciple's creative accounting procedures; and the Manciple beats a hasty retreat, and gives the Cook yet another drink. The outward jollity of *The Manciple's Prologue* is strikingly unfunny, and it is hard to know whom to regard with the greater contempt, the Cook for his swinish drunkenness or the Manciple for his jeering mockery when he thinks it is safe, combined with cowardice when he thinks it is not. These are human beings degraded below the level of animals, and *The Canterbury Tales* as a whole seems to be entering a phase of terminal degeneration. In its sarcastic way, the prologue concerns the danger of speaking freely of what one knows and the greater wisdom of expedient flattery or silence; and this theme, of the subordination of truthful speech to expediency and self-interest, is at the centre of the tale that follows and is put forward with wearying repetitiveness in the moral the Manciple draws from it.

The tale is about Apollo: the god of poetic eloquence, but now almost completely demythologized and deglamorized, dwelling "in this erthe adoun" as a "lusty bachiler" (IX.105, 107) famed for his skill in archery. He possesses a pet crow, which is as white as a swan, and which he has taught to speak, so that it could imitate every man's speech when he was telling a tale:

> . . . countrefete the speche of every man
> He koude, when he sholde telle a tale:
> [134–5]

It is as though Chaucer, in the crow, is describing himself as poet of *The Canterbury Tales*, taught by Apollo (for whose inspiration he had prayed in *The House of Fame*) to imitate the voices of all the pilgrims. But Apollo has another possession that he cherishes even more, a wife whom he loves dearly and does his utmost to please; in vain, however, because she secretly takes a lover,

> A man of litel reputacioun,
> Nat worth to Phebus in comparisoun.
> [199–200]

In Apollo's absence, the wife sends for her lover, and "Anon they wroghten al hire lust volage" (239). They are not alone, however, because

> The white crowe, that heeng ay in the cage,
> Biheeld hire werk, and seyde never a word.
> [240–1]

They think they are in privacy and safety, but the crow (whose cage is presumably in the bedroom, and who must therefore have had plenty of opportunity to witness the primal scene legitimately enacted) is present as an impotent voyeur, precisely the role in which Chaucer so often places himself in his courtly poems about love.[15] The crow might be thought of as a degraded version of Walther von der Vogelweide's nightingale, or of the Pandarus of *Troilus and Criseyde*; but unlike these he does not keep secret the secret things he sees.

When Apollo returns, the crow hints at what has happened, in a line which, in its tactless and cynical way, is surely one of Chaucer's funniest: "This crowe sang 'Cokkow! Cokkow! Cokkow!'" (243). Cuckoo means cuckold, of course—even the crow seems to have been infected by the malice of the prologue—but at first Apollo does not understand what he is being told:

> "What, bryd?" quod Phebus, "What song syngestow?
> Ne were thow wont so myrily to synge
> That to myn herte it was a rejoysynge
> To heere thy voys? Allas! what song is this?"
> [244–7]

And the crow tells him, in words of one syllable, including one word that Chaucer never employs in any of his courtly poems, that his wife has taken a worthless lover, "For on thy bed thy wyf I saugh hym swyve" (256). And he adds that it has been going on for a long time, and that "ofte he saugh it with his yen" (261). One might well ask why in that case the crow did not tell Apollo about it before, but perhaps the pleasure of watching outweighed the pleasure of telling. In any event, Apollo's immediate response is to set an arrow to his bow and slay his wife on the spot. Next he demythologizes himself even further, breaking his bow and arrows and his various musical instruments, and then he turns on the crow.

"Traitour," quod he, "with tonge of scorpioun,
Thou hast me broght to my confusioun."

[271–2]

Now he turns aside, to speak with operatic and self-deceiving sentimentality about his wife; she lies dead, he exclaims, "with face pale of hewe, / Ful giltelees, that dorste I swere, ywys!" (276–7). Like the crow, we know perfectly well that she is not guiltless; Apollo prefers to think otherwise, and he therefore turns on the crow with renewed anger, calling him false thief and traitor. He pulls out all the crow's white feathers, turns him black, deprives him of his powers of song and speech, "and out at dore hym slong / Unto the devel" (306–7). "And for this caas," adds the Manciple, turning it into a Just-So story, "been alle crowes blake" (308). The tale ends with a lengthy moral, in which the Manciple explains that it is an exemplum teaching his listeners, as he says his mother taught him, the wisdom of holding one's tongue. As the moral continues, for line after line, until it is eventually fifty-four lines long (by far the longest of any in *The Canterbury Tales*), it inevitably contradicts itself. It recommends silence in an intolerably verbose way, and it mentions the tongue that is to be restrained so often that one is left with a mental image of a gigantic tongue incessantly babbling. The tongue, frequently mentioned in *Troilus and Criseyde* as the danger the lovers had to fear—'O, rolled shal I ben on many a tonge!'—has now swollen up till it seems to fill the whole space of the poem.

I find it irresistible to speculate about Chaucerian self-reference in *The Manciple's Tale*. The voyeur-poet is rebuked and shamed for telling what he sees, even though it is the truth; and as an upstart crow he is eventually stripped of his feathers and deprived of his poetic power by an angry and foolish god. There is of course no possibility of knowing what real experience, if any, underlies the self-punishing comedy of this fiction. Had Chaucer really reached a state of self-disgust with his role as poet? At any rate, within *The Canterbury Tales*, the end of *The Manciple's Tale* leads in all manuscripts of any significance into *The Parson's Prologue*, and there the whole box of tricks is hastily shut up as the evening shadows lengthen, and the Parson hurries to deliver the last words of the poem in the short time left. He firmly rejects the Host's proposal that he should tell a *fable* (X. 29, 31), and offers instead "Moralitee and vertuous mateere" (38) in plain prose. His tale, as I remarked, is no tale at all, but a penitential treatise; and when that is over we do not return to the fiction of the pilgrimage and the tale-telling competition, but are left instead with the voice of Geoffrey Chaucer, "the makere of this book," speaking from outside the book he has made, and regretting that he has composed nearly all of his most famous works, including "the tales of Canterbury, thilke that sownen into synne." The other works he lists by name as being revoked in these retractions are precisely those courtly poems in which his role has been that of Apollo's crow, spying and reporting on a sexual love from which he is excluded.

In Beroul's *Tristan* and Chaucer's *Troilus* the role of the poet within the fiction is only metaphorically that of a voyeur, and, as I have been suggesting, that metaphor is then literalized in *The Manciple's Tale*, but in relation to a character (the crow) who is only metaphorically representative of the poet. I now want to turn to two cases where the "I" of the poem is literally a watcher of the sexual behavior of others and a listener to their talk in sexual matters. The first example is again French; it is the first part of the *Roman de la Rose*, one of the most influential of all medieval poems, written by Guillaume de Lorris in the second quarter of the thirteenth century. I shall be concerned only with the first section of this part, and since this section was translated by an English poet rather more than a century later, and the poet may well have been Chaucer himself, I shall quote from the Middle English *Romaunt of the Rose*; it is a close and skilful translation, and nothing I have to say about it is affected by the changes the English poet made.[16] Guillaume's part of the *Roman de la Rose*, unlike the continuation written some forty years later by Jean de Meun, has been widely regarded as sweetly and idealistically courtly, with something of the springtime quality of the season in which it is set. There have been some dissenting voices, but mainly from scholars who have regarded it as implying an orthodox ecclesiastical viewpoint which it does not explicitly state, and which has to be regarded as systematically veiled in irony. The choice is between those who see the world of Guillaume's Amant as "a self-sufficient paradise of wit and love and revelry . . . an enchanted garden" allegorizing either "the life of the court" or "the poet's state of mind when, as a young man ready for love, he sees that joy, which is now for him the quest and inspiration of life, is attainable through courtly virtues;"[17] and, on the other hand, those who see the poem as "a warning to heed the voice of reason, and to avoid desire that may lead to hypocritical behavior and adultery in the heart."[18] It is unfortunate, I think, that most of the *Roman's* readers have encountered some more or less scholarly account of it before reading any of the poem itself. That was certainly my own case; and I must say that I do not think it would have occurred to me to see it in either of the ways indicated if I had not been influenced by previous secondary reading. What I want to do now is not to strike a balance between the prevailing views, but to pretend that I am reading the *Roman* for the first time and to give, as best I can, an account simply of what happens in an early section of Guillaume's poem.

It is, of course, a dream-poem, and it is the dream of a young man, not yet twenty. He dreams that it is a May morning, when he wakes up and walks out alongside a river through a meadow. There he finds a garden enclosed with high stone walls. The walls have sculpted images on their outer side, and he gives detailed descriptions and identifications of these images. They are personified figures of vices such as Hatred, Covetousness, Avarice, and Envy, and also of misfortunes such as Sorrow, Old Age, and Poverty. The poet has told us at the beginning that his poem is one in which "al the art of love I close" (40); that idea of enclosure is made manifest in the walled garden, and the images, we may guess, are personifications of the characteristics that exclude one from the practice and enjoyment of the "art of love." Looked at from our point of view, the garden represents both a particular kind of experience (the arousal and prospective fulfillment of male desire—the nearest one can come to paradise on earth, as the young dreamer soon judges) and the socio-economic and cultural conditions that permit a privileged cultivation of experience (entry to an exclusive circle of youthful, fashionable, and wealthy courtiers). There is something inside the garden, which for the dreamer is love and for us is the meaning of the poem, concealed within the walls of allegory; but inside also implies outside, the other realm of all those who cannot get in, and whose exclusion makes what is inside all the more desirable.

The dreamer is naturally eager to enter the garden, all the more so because he can hear such "blisful" (496, 500) birdsong coming from inside. He searches round the wall, until he comes to a little gate, "So shett that I ne myght in gon" (529). His analyst would probably have had no difficulty in telling him what that element in his dream symbolized, even if he did not know that it was going to be about love and that, in Jean de Meun's continuation, it was going to end with a hilariously obscene symbolic account of the sexual act itself. Anyway, he knocks at the gate, and it is opened (of course) by a beautiful girl. The dreamer's adventure has begun, and it opens with a strong emphasis on watching. He observes the girl in great detail, giving what is basically one of those formal, part-by-part descriptions of a beautiful lady recommended by the medieval *artes poeticae:* but, attributed as it is to the poem's first-person narrator, it conveys an especially strong impression of eroticism, with the sense of sight evoking fantasies of the other senses. Her flesh, he says, is as tender as chicken (541), and, as for her neck,

> Ther nys a fairer nekke, iwys,
> To fele how smothe and softe it is.
> [555–6]

In his imagination he is already caressing her, and even sinking his teeth into that tender flesh. Perfectly natural, of course: there is a touch of Dracula about all young men—hence the popularity of the Dracula story.

The girl says that her name is Ydelnesse; and what this means, fairly obviously, is that, in order to enter the garden of love, leisure is a prerequisite. One of the great attractions, and also sources of confusion, in the *Roman de la Rose* is that its characters have meanings of an allegorical or mythological kind, but that they also have bodies, which in many cases are suffused with a literal eroticism. This is clearly true of the portress: whatever moral coloring you attribute to her name, she is also a delectable creature in her person. She remarks that, like many of the beautiful young ladies who haunt the night spots, she cares for nothing

> But to my joye and my pleying,
> And for to kembe and tresse me.
> [598–9]

She explains that the lord of the garden is Myrthe, and that he amuses himself in it with a company of the most beautiful people in the world. The dreamer says that he badly wants to *see* what goes on inside; and she lets him in. There, the first thing that catches his attention is the birds; then, walking down a little path, he finds Myrthe and his company, being sung to by a lady called Gladnesse. Next his eye is caught by people dancing everywhere, and by musicians playing to them. I mentioned night spots just now; and it is true that in the dream all this is happening early in the morning and in the open air. But what is described to us in the form of a dream is of course the dreamer's own night-life; and in any case, we could suppose if we wished that, since the beautiful people in the dream are at it so early, they must have been dancing

all night. I should like you to imagine, in order to clear your mind
of scholarly prejudice, that the young man in his dream has entered a fashionable discotheque called, let us say, The Garden of
the Rose or The Enchanted Garden. The exclusiveness that is so
strongly emphasized by the images on the outside of the walls fits
in well here, because the really fashionable club has to have
crowds of people outside trying to get in, and being excluded because they look too old, too poor, too ugly, and so on.

The next thing the dreamer sees is a remarkable performance,
arranged, we are told, by Myrthe himself: two lithe girls, very
young, dressed only in their kirtles, are dancing together, and

> That oon wolde come all pryvyly
> Agayn that other, and whan they were
> Togidre almost, they threwe yfere
> Her mouthis so that thorough her play
> It semed as they kiste alwey.
>
> [784–8]

One way to interpret this dance is no doubt to see it as in keeping
with what one scholar has called "a sense of virtue immune to the
vice and tribulations of the world."[19] I must say, however, that that
is not what immediately occurs to me. It strikes me that what
Myrthe has arranged is a suggestive, quasi-lesbian performance,
involving the corruption of under-age girls. Needless to say, the
dreamer is there, watching the show with great enthusiasm and
extremely reluctant to depart:

> Ne bede I never thennes go,
> Whiles that I saw hem daunce so.
>
> [791–2]

At this point, one of the company, a lady called Curtesie,
courteously invites him to do more than watch. He does so, joining in the dance; yet at this very moment he inserts an even stronger emphasis on watching rather than doing:

> Thanne gan I loken ofte sithe
> The shap, the bodies, and the cheres,
> The countenaunce and the maneres
> Of all the folk that daunced there,
> And I shal telle what they were.
>
> [812–16]

He watches, and then he tells. Once more, what underlies this is a perfectly normal convention of medieval poetry: the *effictio,* the detailed, point-by-point, largely pictorial description. Yet, once attributed to this young man, it inevitably has voyeuristic associations: in order to describe, he has to watch carefully, obsessively even, and the act of watching an erotic performance with such enthralment obviously has sexual implications. I cannot discuss in detail everything the dreamer sees in Myrthe's night club, but I will mention a few of the more telling features. We learn a little more about Myrthe himself and his girlfriend. Myrthe is a handsome, beardless young man, dressed in the height of thirteenth-century fashion; and his girlfriend is Gladnesse, the young woman described as singing earlier. She has granted him her love, we are told, since she was twelve; and then there is a passage about her flesh similar to that about Ydelnesse's flesh, only going a little further:

> She semed lyk a rose newe
> Of colour, and hir flesh so tendre
> That with a brere smale and slendre
> Men myght it cleve, I dar wel seyn.
> [856-9]

This is plainly a sadistic fantasy on the dreamer's part: he drools over the tenderness of the girl's flesh, and as he does so momentarily fantasizes about what it would be like to whip her.

Myrthe and his chief guest, the God of Love himself, are men, but most of the other dancers mentioned—it is hard to tell whether to think of them as guests or performers—are women. The dreamer is of course also male, and what he dreams (the night-life he devises for himself in his dream) is naturally a male erotic fantasy. His entrance into the garden of love is an encounter with female sexuality, defined as perceived by the young male. Thus the God of Love is accompanied by a "bacheler" called "Swete-lokyng" (918, 920), who carries two bows and ten arrows. The looks this "bacheler" personifies are the messages conveyed by female eyes; he himself needs to be not female but male in order that he can appropriately be armed; but the choice of this way of allegorizing female looks, as weapons, used aggressively against the male, is of course a male choice. And in general (to move for a moment outside the section of the *Roman* I am concerned with), what Guillaume's allegory does is to fragment the girl who arouses the dreamer's sexual interest and to masculinize her, by projecting on to her his perception of sex as aggression. She is represented in the allegorical fiction not as a person, like Amant, but in two other ways: as an object, the rose, and as a collection of male personifications. This mode of representation is far from neutral: it implies certain attitudes which are built into the poem's total system of signification and which therefore tend to escape notice. (They may well have been occluded for Guillaume himself.) To symbolize a girl as a rose is to evoke her beauty and its transience; it is also to see her as the passive object of male desire, something to be plucked, possessed. And to divide her up into male personifications is in a sense to violate her still further: she exists *only* as perceived by the insecure young male who desires her. In the *Roman* there is none of the empathy with the inner life of a woman that can be found, for example, in Book II of *Troilus and Criseyde*. In the long run one consequence of this is that the poem does not distinguish between the girl's wishes and the wishes of her male proprietors; its whole imagining of sexuality and relations between the sexes is permeated by the assumptions of a society in which males are dominant.

To return to the night club section. There not all the females are performing for the benefit of the male clients. The God of Love's partner in the dance is, it is true, a slender-waisted girl called Beauty, whose body, as we might expect, once more makes the dreamer's mouth water: "Hir flesh was tendre as dew of flour" (1013). His mental undressing of her affects his memory in terms not just of sight but of "savour" (taste, or possibly smell):

> A ful gret savour and a swote
> Me toucheth in myn herte rote,
> As helpe me God, whan I remembre
> Of the fasoun of every membre.
> [1025–8]

However, "Biside Beaute yede Richesse" (1033); and Richesse is not a man but a noble and much-esteemed lady, who has power over the whole world; she is expensively dressed, and her belt has a buckle made of a precious stone with the marvellous power of protecting the wearer against poison and is trimmed with another that cures palsy, toothache, and blindness. Such magic jewels are common enough in medieval romances, but when they are worn by a lady called Wealth the meaning is obvious: only the wealthy can afford the best medical treatment, and the jewels must be the medieval equivalent to her private health insurance policy. But

Richesse has another, even more precious possession; she leads about by the hand

> A yong man ful of semelyhede,
> That she best loved of ony thing.
> [1130–1]

Guillaume explains that this young man was much given to extravagant purchases of clothes and horses, and that his aim in life was to spend freely without working; that was why he desired the acquaintance of Richesse. What he did for her in return is not mentioned, but is not difficult to guess. It may perhaps be a comfort for the feminist reader to know that in the Garden of the Rose a woman does not necessarily have to provide sexual services for men; provided she is rich enough, she can buy a young man to serve her. That at least is the literal meaning of this section; on the allegorical level it personifies as a woman the seductive and unscrupulous power of wealth in the world, and that is no more complimentary to women than anything else in the poem.

Finally, let me say a word about the last item in the description of the garden's clientele, before the dreamer comes to the fountain of Narcissus and becomes something more than a voyeur. It concerns a girl called Youthe,

> That nas not yit twelve yeer of age,
> With herte wylde and thought volage.[20]
> [1283–4]

Youthe is dancing with her sweetheart, who is no older than she, and of similar disposition. We are told that he kisses her whenever he pleases:

> That all the daunce myght it see.
> They make no force of pryvete,
> For who spake of hem yvel or well,
> They were ashamed never a dell,
> But men myght seen hem kisse there
> As it two yonge dowves were.
> [1293–8]

We must take account of historical differences in assumptions about the age at which sexual activity becomes proper and legal; we must also bear in mind that what is being described here is manifestly not something furtive but something Guillaume presumably intends to be the innocence of the Golden Age. But innocence is a quality very difficult to represent in art, because it implies the absence of artifice, and this innocence is on display. This pair of eleven-year-olds are performing their erotic dance innocently but exhibitionistically, and much to the dreamer's pleasure. Once innocence is consciously displayed, it ceases to be truly innocent; and in the lines quoted the mention of "pryvete" and shame, in order to deny their relevance, unavoidably encourages us to use them as criteria of judgment. Paedophilia evidently has its place along with voyeurism in Amant's fantasy-world.

Guillaume de Lorris may well not have recognized the voyeuristic implications of his treatment of the courtly world of love, but by the later Middle Ages the role of the poet as a spy upon and overhearer of intimate relations from which he is himself included becomes far more explicit. This is especially the case with poets who, like Chaucer, present themselves as socially inferior to the courtiers who form their implied audiences. One especially clear example of this in pictorial form occurs in the illuminated frontispiece of a fifteenth-century manuscript of Laurent de Premierfait's French translation of Boccaccio's *Decameron*.[21] Here the company of ten courtly young people who are the storytellers of Boccaccio's collection are shown taking their ease in a garden enclosed by a stone wall, with one of their number telling a story to the rest. But Boccaccio himself, unlike Guillaume's dreamer, has not been admitted to the courtly garden (and indeed Boccaccio in the *Decameron*, unlike Chaucer among the Canterbury pilgrims, is not a character in the framing narrative of his own collection of tales). More soberly clad, in clerkly fashion, he sits outside the wall, unknown to the people inside, carefully listening to what they are saying and copying it down on a scroll. His role is inferior and undignified, that of a concealed "auditeur"; and my final example is of a still later medieval poem in which this undignified role is fully realized and is made more undignified still by being combined with sexual voyeurism. The poem is *The Goldyn Targe* by William Dunbar, a Scottish poet who wrote at the highly sophisticated court of King James IV in the early sixteenth century. The tradition of the *Roman de la Rose* was still alive, nearly three centuries after Guillaume de Lorris began it, and some of Dunbar's poetry is written as a further development of that tradition; but Dunbar had a more compelling reason than either Chaucer or Boccaccio to represent himself as an outsider to the celebration of secular love, because he was a priest.

The Goldyn Targe is a dream allegory consciously related to the tradition that Guillaume began. It is much influenced by Chaucer and Lydgate, who were themselves writing in that tradition and to whom Dunbar pays explicit tribute in his poem, but it also goes back behind its English sources to the *Roman* itself. Like much of the best post-Chaucerian poetry, *The Goldyn Targe* is richly allusive, a kind of palimpsest of traditions, in which we are expected to be able to read several layers of allusion, one inscribed upon and within another. What happens in it, briefly, is that the poet one May morning wanders through a beautiful meadow full of young roses. He stops to rest beside a rose bush near a river among singing birds, falls asleep, and dreams. In his dream he is in the same landscape. Guillaume would have felt entirely at home in it, except that his later Scottish namesake emphasizes much more strongly than he does that the landscape is one of literary artifice. Dunbar sees a ship come sailing along the river, and from it disembarks a company of a hundred ladies, enticing creatures "With pappis quhite and mydlis small as wandis" (64).[22] They include all the female deities imaginable—classical goddesses, muses, spring months—ruled over by two goddesses who play crucial parts in the *Roman de la Rose,* Nature and Venus. The birds sing to Venus, "lufis mychti quene," "ballettis in lufe, . . . With amourouse notis lusty to devise" (102–04), while Dunbar remains a silent onlooker. But now another company appears, consisting entirely of male deities, led by another central figure from the *Roman*, "Cupide the king wyth bow in hand ybent" (110). They too play and sing, and the male and female companies join in a dance; it is like a pagan fertility ceremony, and Dunbar, excited by it, creeps through the leaves to have a closer look; but his voyeurism proves to be his downfall:

> Thair observance rycht hevynly was to here:
> Than crap I throu the levis and drew nere,
> Quhare that I was rycht sudaynly affrayit,
> All throu a luke quhilk I have boucht full dere.
>
> [132–5]

Venus catches a glimpse of him as he crouches in the bushes, and has him arrested by her archers, who let fall their mantles to reveal their terrifying bows. Like Guillaume's dreamer, the poet perceives female sexuality as a form of aggression, but unlike him, though the bows are doubtless phallic, he personifies the aggression itself as female. There follows a listing of the Amazonian archers who represent female attractions; two of them have the same names as the arrows with which Guillaume's "bacheler" Swete-lokyng is armed. Against them Dunbar's only ally is Reason (again a key figure in the *Roman*, as opponent of Cupid and Venus), who defends him with the golden shield from which the poem takes its name. Venus makes a series of attacks on the helpless Dunbar with her artillery, in an allegorical action which represents the increasing threat posed by the female to the male as she grows from a girl to a woman to a lady of high rank capable of exerting all her wiles. First comes tender Youth with her virgin followers Innocence, Bashfulness, Dread, and Obedience, but they pose little real threat: this dreamer seems not to share the paedophiliac tendencies of Guillaume's Amant. Then Womanhood attacks with her more mature supporters, such as Nurture, Discretion, "Benigne Luke"(167), and so on; their arrows damage Dunbar a little, but still Reason's shield protects him. Next "Hie Degree" (172) enters the battle, assisted by the concomitants of the aristocratic lady, such as Estate, Will, Wantonness, and Wealth; but they too are repulsed. Finally, Venus decides that the only way to pierce the golden shield is by appointing Dissymilance (dissimulation) as leader of the next attack. Dissymilance chooses as her archers Presence (meaning, presumably, the irresistible attraction of the female's physical proximity), Fair Greeting, Cherishing, and Hamelynes (intimacy), and she brings Beautee once more into the field. These apparently charming female qualities are the most dangerous of all, but still Reason keeps up his defense, until Presence manages to get close enough to throw a powder in his eyes that blinds him. The meaning of the allegory is obviously that even the most rational man cannot resist the very presence of the female, and Reason is sent staggering off to be made a fool of by these dangerous Amazons.

Dunbar is now captured and becomes Beautee's prisoner— that is, he has fallen in love, if love is the word for the aggression to which he has fallen prey and for his entirely passive response to it. He rapidly becomes more deeply beguiled by the pretense of female favor, but as soon as "New Acquyntance" (220) has embraced him she disappears for ever, and then with equal rapidity Dangere (standoffishness and rejection, just as in the *Roman de la Rose*) makes her appearance, regarding him with hostility. She too disappears (that is, presumably, the lady ceases to pay any attention at all to her lover, even to show ill will), and Dunbar is left prey to Hevynesse (depression). But at this moment, fortunately, Aeolus the god of winds blows every sign of the dangerous season of spring from the landscape (this is a Scottish allegory, after all), the dream-figures re-embark on the ship, it sails away firing its cannon, and Dunbar leaps up in fear and wakes in relief from his nightmare.

   The Goldyn Targe is a poem which shows voyeurism as the only possible role for a male poet in a courtly dream-world pervaded with his fantasies of female aggression; but even the voyeur's role is perilous, because these terrifying women are not content to be watched—they are determined to destroy their impotent male observer. On one level *The Goldyn Targe* can be read as a fictional production script for the kind of allegorical masque that was really performed at the court of James IV, with the elaborate artifice of the masque's setting and machinery turned into a short narrative poem.[23] It might then be interpreted as a warning to the king not to let the attraction of women (to which he was notoriously susceptible) overcome his reason. But on another level it is William Dunbar's dream, and it is made out of just the kind of anxieties and fears that might haunt a celibate cleric's unconscious mind and find expression, distorted by allegory, in his dreams. To stick to poetry might seem the wiser course, and indeed *The Goldyn Targe* ends, after Dunbar wakes, with some flowery stanzas in praise of Chaucer, Gower, and Lydgate (representing the courtly and learned tradition of poetry in English); but alas, that poetic tradition too is haunted, as we have seen, by sexual voyeurism. There is no escape from sex into poetry when the predominant poetic tradition is one that assumes that sex is what poetry is about. Another poem of Dunbar's, *The Tretis of the Tua Mariit Wemen and the Wedo*, about which I have written elsewhere,[24] shows him in an even more degraded role, as the secret overhearer of what women say about men when men are not there; needless to say, it displays the utmost contempt for men, and especially for their pretensions to sexual potency and sexual dominance. Dunbar, as a priest committed to celibacy, writing for a king and court notorious for their sexual license, was well placed to take the conception of the medieval poet as voyeur to its extreme limit; but I hope it has emerged from my discussion that the connection between love-narrative and voyeurism had its roots far back in the medieval courtly tradition.

5

Love and Power in the Twelfth Century, with Special Reference to Chrétien de Troyes and Marie de France

My concerns in this essay are love and power in twelfth-century Europe. By power, I refer not only to the power inherent in love in many twelfth-century narratives, but also to two other kinds of power with which love coexisted in the fiction—and, I suspect, to a great extent in the cultural imagination—of this exciting, innovative age: the power inherent in the exercise of armed force and the shaping, creative power of the verbal artist. My aim is to contribute to an adequate assessment of the twelfth century's fascination with love by showing how two of its greatest narrative poets, Chrétien de Troyes and Marie de France, create linkages and confrontations between the varied manifestations of love, prowess, and art. Before turning to the passages I have selected from Chrétien and Marie, however, I must offer some initial remarks about how their cultural moment shaped their understanding of love and power.

Stated most broadly, the background for the achievement of Chrétien and Marie is nothing less than twelfth-century Europe's rediscovery of the centrality, and the power, of love and creativity in the functioning of a civilization. The rediscovery was part of a radical reorientation of cultural priorities, away from investing maximum energy and resources in the cultivation (and hence the dominance) of martial prowess and toward the exploration of the potential for personal and social empowerment inherent in the more private sphere of human feelings, emotions, and intellectual capacities. The religious background (and analogue) of this reorientation was the Church's attempt, during the eleventh and twelfth centuries, to bring under control the aggressive energies of a feudal, warrior aristocracy insufficiently restrained by centralized secular authority. The Church-sponsored Peace of God and Truce of God movements, and from the end of the eleventh century onward, the preaching of Crusades can also be seen as political strategies aimed at liberating an increasingly stable, commerce-oriented and town-centered northern European society from the potentially disruptive presence within it of a stratum or caste dedicated to (and all too often acting upon) ideals of martial prowess.

Within this cultural context, fraught as it was with new possibilities for peaceful mobility and for the exchange of goods and ideas as well as blows, other vocations besides that of the warrior began to attract able and ambitious young men, and thus to become endowed with an analogous aura of power. A famous evocation of what might be called the twelfth-century *translatio potentiae* occurs at the beginning of Peter Abelard's autobiographical (or pseudo-autobiographical) "letter to a friend," the so-called *Historia calamitatum*. The age's most controversial linguistic philosopher opens his account of the crises of his public and personal careers by offering a compact, highly stylized account of the basic vocational decision that changed his life:

> To begin, then, I was born in a town called Le Pallet in Brittanny near the border about eight miles I would say east of Nantes. I was light-hearted and had talent for letters, characteristics derived from my country and family. My father was a man who had acquired some literary knowledge before he donned the uniform of a soldier and he retained such a liking for learning that he intended to procure for whatever sons he was to have a training in letters before their military service. And he carried out his purpose. As he loved me the more, being his first-born, so he saw to it that I was carefully instructed. The further I went in my studies and the more easily I made progress, the more I became attached to them and came to possess such a love of them that, giving up in favor of my brothers the pomp of military glory along with my right of inheritance and the other prerogatives of primogeniture, I renounced the field of Mars to be brought up at the knee of Minerva. Since I preferred the armor of logic to all the teaching of philosophy, I exchanged all other arms for it and chose the contests of disputation above the trophies of warfare. And so, practicing logic I wandered about the various provinces wherever I heard the pursuit of this art was vigorous and became thereby like the peripatetics.[1]

Abelard's self-consciously artful prose contrasts the life he would be expected to follow as the eldest son of a member of the warrior aristocracy and the career he in fact chose to pursue. Yet he also assimilates the two options by the metaphors in which he recounts his decision. The field of Mars opposes the knee of Minerva; the armor of logic outstrips the teachings of philosophy; the contests of disputation please him more than the trophies of warfare. In effect, Abelard has opted for one type of aggression, one kind of power, above another. As Mary Martin McLaughlin pointed out some years ago in a perceptive essay on the *Historia calamitatum*, he depicts the opening phase of his life as a logician on the model of the *juvenes*, the young warriors who travelled from lord to lord and battle to battle during the twelfth century, seeking repute and fortune.[2] The most striking implication of this passage is precisely that it presents the intellectual life in terms of aggression and potential power, in order to suggest to its age that the life of the mind, because of its innately heroic qualities, deserves the cultural status hitherto accorded to the life of armed combat.

Abelard stands before us, then, at the beginning of his autobiographical account not so much as a first-born, prodigal son who has refused the inheritance (and the power) offered him by his father and run away from home to seek his fortune, but rather as the heir in a larger, more symbolic, sense to the authority and power that northern European society had hitherto (and of necessity) accorded to the military class of which his father was a member. Abelard seeks a new world of adventure in words rather than deeds: a sphere of grammar, logic, and rhetoric in which strong men compete for glittering prizes—repute, students, even beautiful mistresses—and risk the disgrace and harm (both professional and, in Abelard's case, physical) that come with the territory. In short, this passage endows the verbal combat of the professional intellectual with a panache, a centrality, and above all a cultural power that had for centuries been the exclusive province (at least in northern Europe) of the intrepid warrior, and of his religious analogue, the heroic saint.

The *Historia calamitatum* exemplifies one twelfth-century strategy of dealing with the phenomenon of an entrenched warrior class, a strategy we may call cultural diversification: the transference of competitive, aggressive energies from one field of endeavor to another, with the consequent appropriation by the new vocation—scholar—of some of the social approbation, and notoriety, hitherto reserved by secular society for the old, established vocation: man of arms. A more complicated and, I believe we may say, more advanced strategy of cultural *transformation* finds a fanciful but, I would suggest, nonetheless genuine embodiment in some of the vernacular fictions written later in the century by men (and, as the example of Marie shows, even women) who were in many ways the beneficiaries of Abelard's vocational choice and the purveyors of its discipline and outlook, modified by the needs of both author and audience, to the great courts of northern Europe. As my first example of such cultural transformation, I offer Chrétien de Troyes's great romance, *Yvain, or the Knight of the Lion.* The overall intent and outlook of *Yvain* are by no means clear to me—its male and female protagonists have many problematic aspects, and Chrétien frequently submits them to considerable irony—but I am convinced that its climax and denouement constitute a meditation on the personal resources available to neutralize, and the socio-political resources available to replace, violence as a culturally sanctioned mode of solving problems.

The latter part of *Yvain* is organized around a conflict between two sisters, the heirs of the recently defunct Lord of Noire Espine. The older sister seeks (unjustly, the text makes clear) to keep all the father's lands, but her younger sibling, resisting this aggression, seeks redress at Arthur's court in the form of a knight who will undertake trial by combat on her behalf with any knight chosen by her sister for the same purpose. Unfortunately, the unjust sister, learning of this plan, hastens secretly to the court and enlists the aid of the best knight, Gawain, as *her* champion, thus (it would seem) thwarting the younger sister's attempt to retain her rightful share of the inheritance. Gawain agrees to fight for the older sister, but only on condition that his identity be kept secret—a condition strongly suggesting his awareness that he is in fact dedicating his formidable prowess to an iniquitous cause. When he subsequently rejects, as he now must, the younger sister's plea for aid, the desperate damsel declares to Arthur, "My lord, I came to you and to your court to seek help, yet have found none, and I am surprised that I cannot find any here. . . . Moreover, I would like my sister to know that she could have what is mine out of love, if she wished it; but I will never surrender my inheritance by force, if I can obtain help and counsel" (4777–87).[3] This *cri de coeur* links two equally damning indictments of force as an instrument of problem solving: first, it is essentially amoral, in that it pretends to be a weapon of justice, but under this disguise is equally ready to fight for injustice; and second, it is self-defeating,

and much inferior to love as an instrument of policy, for antagonism creates resistance to goals that reconciliation can achieve.

King Arthur sees where justice lies in this dispute, but can
only urge, not order, the older sister to act equitably, given the superior problem-solving status of the trial by combat. Thus royal
wisdom and benevolence are also held hostage to a system that
legitimates and privileges violence. Arthur's only power lies in resisting the older sister's demand that the younger furnish a champion at once or forfeit her lands; instead, he offers the latter a forty
day delay, which she immediately accepts, hoping in that inter-
val to find the Knight of the Lion who, she had heard, "devoted
himself to helping women in need of aid" (4821–22). She goes off
in quest of her potential champion, encountering fear and hard-
ship but also eliciting sympathy and cooperation at every turn, as
Chrétien deliberately inverts, and subverts, the male adventure
quest which seeks, and finds, armed hostility in its encounters
with strangers.

In the nick of time, on day forty, the younger sister returns
to Arthur's court with Yvain, who has assumed the guise of the
Knight of the Lion as part of his penance for having abandoned his
new wife to seek honor through prowess. This concealment, added
to Gawain's unwillingness to defend an unjust cause *in propria
persona*, prevents the two champions from recognizing each other
and thus, as best friends, refusing to do battle. Nor is there, Chrétien tells us, even the minimal verbal communication between
them that would also have led to recognition and reconciliation:
"Neither spoke to the other, for had they spoken to one another
their meeting would have been different! There would have been
no lance or sword blows struck at that encounter: they would have
run to embrace and kiss each other rather than attacking, but
now they were assailing and injuring one another" (6114–21). So
the two knights—hidden from each other, we recall, by the armor
that obscures their features and thus their personal identity—
pummel each other mercilessly for hours, inflicting near-fatal
wounds while Chrétien virtuosically rings rhetorical changes on
the paradox of two men who can simultaneously love and hate
each other so strongly. Finally, when the warriors have been reduced to a state of mutual fear and exhaustion, they get around to
asking each other's name. The resultant discovery of true identi-
ties leads at once to an insistence on the part of each friend that
he will make amends for this terrible mistake by declaring himself
defeated by the other. Chrétien's tableau of violence is transformed
to an iconography of love and self-sacrifice: "Thus speaking they

dismounted; each threw his arms around the other's neck, and they embraced; but even this did not prevent each claiming to have been defeated" (6315–19).

The newly reunited Yvain and Gawain bring before King Arthur their love-inspired mutual claims of defeat, and the monarch seizes upon their subversion of the normal expectations of a system of violent competition in order to resolve the dispute between the sisters without further recourse to force: "My lords," says the king, "you clearly show your great love for one another when each claims to have been defeated. But now rely on me, for I believe that I can effect a reconciliation that will bring honor to you both, and for which everyone will praise me" (6378–84). He thereupon traps the unjust sister by a verbal trick into admitting, against her intention, that she has "forcibly and maliciously disinherited" her sibling, and threatens (untruthfully, Chrétien assures us) to declare her champion the loser unless she voluntarily agrees to his judgment. Having thus obtained her acquiescence out of fear of defeat—i.e., by capitalizing on her adherence to a concept of justice grounded in violent antagonism—Arthur makes the following determination about the disputed land: "Restore it to her outright, and let her be your vassal woman and hold it from you; love her as your vassal woman, and let her love you as her liege lady and as her blood-born sister" (6444–49).

Chrétien's presentation of the dispute between the sisters of Noire Espine, and of its resolution, amounts to a major ideological statement about the limits of violence in solving problems and establishing equity, about the primacy of love as a human value over the pursuit of victory through prowess, and about how the abandonment of force will make possible the empowerment of a justice based on mutual love and well-wishing. In effect, the exercise of prowess in this episode is a consequence of the willed (by greed) or unwilled (by disguise) obscuring of relationships—kinship, friendship—that should issue in love and reconciliation, not hatred and confrontation. Put differently, a system based on the obtaining of judgments through combat marginalizes situations or feelings conducive of harmony and integration, while privileging a posture of acquisitive combativeness that allows its adherents, as they seek wealth or honor, to ignore and dismiss aspects of those with whom they interact that could encourage sympathy and reconciliation. Once combatants recognize in the Opponent something, and someone, to love, the whole system of antagonistic prowess grinds to a halt, unleashing and empowering forces of reconciliation that can transform a system of justice based on force and fear into a system of justice founded upon mutual respect and love.

Of course, Arthur's recasting of the system of justice does require trickiness, the use of language to trap malefactors into confession. Arthur, in effect, becomes the first criminal lawyer of Arthurian legend. And this use of ingenuity and verbal resources to gain what force cannot suggests an allegiance between love and ingenious eloquence in opposing and dismantling a system of victory through prowess. That this is the case is underscored in the final episode of Chrétien's romance.

Once the case of the two sisters is closed and Yvain has had his battle wounds healed, he can turn his full attention to the crisis at the center of his life, namely his continuing estrangement from his wife, Laudine, who repudiated him after he broke his promise to return to her at the end of a year spent pursuing, with Gawain, the life of honor through prowess. Thoroughly penitent and convinced that he will die if Laudine does not take pity on him, Yvain resolves "to leave the court all alone and go to do battle at her spring; and there he'd cause so much thunder and wind and rain that she would be compelled to make her peace with him, or else there would be no end to the storm at her spring . . . " (6524–31). The spring in question is located at the edge of Laudine's lands and has the magical property that if a passing knight pours water from it onto a large precious stone set in the ground beside it, a ferocious storm will spring up to devastate the surrounding country, and, by ancient custom, a knight charged to defend the spring will then ride out from town to do battle with the stranger.

The spring is the central symbolic landmark of Chrétien's romance. Yvain first discovers it when on quest to avenge a kinsman who had, years before, created a storm there and then been soundly thrashed by the spring's guardian. Yvain, by contrast, kills the guardian, who turns out to be the local lord of the territory, and then falls in love with the widow, Laudine, as she mourns disconsolately for her dead husband and cries for vengeance on his murderer. Chrétien thus establishes a highly paradoxical and ironic situation in which his protagonist's exercise of prowess has made him most hated by the woman he most loves. The spring is the pivotal feature of this dilemma and of its resolution. As the trigger mechanism for both storms and bloody combat—the former unleashed by a wandering aggressor, the latter by the resident defender—the spring functions as a powerful (and bizarre) metaphor for the disruptive potential of culturally sanctioned violence. Because Laudine needs a new defender for the spring, she is convinced of the logic of accepting as the new champion (and as her husband!) the man who has demonstrated his worthiness to assume both roles by destroying his predecessor in them. The creator of this clever, rational, and troublingly amoral denouement for what had seemed an insoluble problem is Laudine's damsel and confidante, Lunete, who schemes to save Yvain from frustration—and from probable death at the hands of Laudine's followers—out of gratitude for the hospitality he had once shown her at Arthur's court.

Yvain's career as Knight of the Lion after his banishment by Laudine involves putting his prowess to better use than the random, ritual violence of the magic spring. (Basically, he rescues women from situations of injustice that recall his treatment of his wife, and is aided by a grateful lion whom he has saved from destruction by a serpent.) But his desperate plan to activate the spring as a way of making peace with his lady provides Chrétien with another way of showing, as he has just done in the episode of the two sisters and their champions, the limits and counterproductiveness of prowess as a problem-solving mechanism. The "peace" which Yvain hopes to obtain from Laudine is basically the peace of unconditional surrender to his aggression at the spring. These are bully tactics, constituting both a symbolic form of wife-beating in the interests of domestic tranquility and a bitter parody of the chivalric convention whereby a knight performs deeds of prowess in order to inspire and win the love of a beautiful woman. Indeed, I would argue that the curse laid by Laudine's knights on their ancestors when Yvain re-activates the spring represents, in however fictionalized a form, Chrétien's awareness of his real contemporaries' reaction against a tradition of armed prowess that holds them and their civilization hostage: "The boldest of [Laudine's] knights were so afraid that they cursed their forefathers, saying: 'a curse upon the first man to build a manor in this country, and upon those who built this town! In all the world they couldn't find a more hateful place, for a single man can invade and torment and beleaguer it" (6550–61).

In this moment of crisis, it is Lunete, still motivated by gratitude to Yvain—he has recently saved her life—who brings about the reunion he so desires. She convinces Laudine to let her seek the Knight of the Lion as a new defender of the spring, and wins from her mistress the promise to do everything she, Laudine, can to effect a reconciliation between the knight and his estranged lady. (Laudine is, of course, unaware that the Knight of the Lion is her husband, and thus does not know what she is promising.) Lunete now rides to the spring "merrily and with a smile on her face" (6670), unexpectedly finds Yvain close at hand, and leads him to Laudine, who is forced, by the promise she has just made, to make peace (*la pes faire*, 6804) with him. And on this note of reconciliation—"Or a mes sire Yvains sa pes" (6805)—the romance ends.

Lunete's witty manipulation of situations and characters—her artfulness, in short, which makes her a surrogate of Chrétien himself—here replaces prowess as the agent of both narrative closure and the fulfilment of Yvain's desire for love and peace. Gratitude and a desire to serve her benefactor—both forms of love in its subset *caritas*—prompt Lunete's trickery, and just as, in the preceding scene, Chrétien dramatized the triumph of love over prowess by describing Yvain and Gawain embracing instead of fighting, so here he creates an iconography of the primacy of love-inspired ingenuity over desperate violence: instead of a knight on a charger riding out to do battle with Yvain when he agitates the spring, a smiling Lunete appears on her "gently paced palfrey" to lead him to his beloved.

It is, I hope, clear from this recapitulation of the last part of *Yvain* that love and artfulness—the latter encompassing plotmaking and tricky language—confront and replace prowess as the effective impulses in Chrétien's fictional world, both at Arthur's court and in Laudine's land. Furthermore, these two alternative forms of power must work together if they are to bring about the peace and reconciliation unobtainable by force. We can read this alliance at two levels, one social and experiential, the other literary and fictional. At the social level, Chrétien appears to applaud his age's cultivation of emotional and intellectual faculties to supplement or replace the martial virtues. At the level of art, *Yvain* celebrates the incorporation of love, the lyric subject par excellence, and of eloquence and compositional skill, the fruits of literacy and learning, into the vernacular narrative of *res gestae*.

Whereas Chrétien's romances take as their starting point, and then complicate or subvert, the narrative of armed adventure, the *Lais* of Marie de France, which challenge Chrétien's *oeuvre* as the pinnacle of twelfth-century vernacular narrative, have as their common denominator love in its many guises: married and adulterous, young and mature, successful and unsuccessful, idealized and degraded, comic and tragic.

Marie considers the connection between love and eloquence or art in several of the lais. I have chosen two of these to examine in the remainder of this paper, one—the lai of *Guigemar*—in which Marie's approach is witty and tinged with comedy, and the other—the lai of *Yonec*—in which she strikes a more earnest note.

In connection with the latter story, I shall also attempt to sharpen our understanding of how Marie assimilates the power of love to the power of the imagination by contrasting her presentation of a crucial development in *Yonec* with the treatment of a closely analogous turning point in two narratives from very different cultural milieux.

In the lai of *Guigemar*, Marie's young protagonist discovers the joy and pain of love in seeking a woman who can cure a wound he has inflicted upon himself while hunting. (The wound is clearly a metaphor for newly experienced sexuality and desire.) When Guigemar comes to the point where he must reveal his love to the woman who is its object, Marie describes the fear of rejection that makes him hesitate to do so, and then continues,

> Guigemar was deeply in love;
> he must either get help quickly
> or live in misery.
> So love inspires bravery in him;
> he reveals his desires to the lady.
> [496–500]

The joke of this passage is that, according to the literary traditions of chivalry, when love inspires bravery in a knight he normally goes off to fight an enemy, whereas here he must do the even harder thing: speak out, use his God-given eloquence. Furthermore, Guigemar's obligation to speak if he is to prosper establishes a parallel between this young lover and Marie the artist, who tells us in the opening lines of her Prologue to the *Lais* that those given eloquence by God must not hide it if their gift is to flourish.

A bit later, after Guigemar has confessed his passion, his beloved seems to put him off, saying, "I'm not accustomed to such a request," and this demurral evokes from the young knight a casuistical response worthy (and reminiscent) of one of the rhetorically facile wooers in the first book of the neo-Ovidian treatise, *De amore*, by Marie's contemporary, Andreas Capellanus. Guigemar argues,

> My lady . . . it's appropriate for an inconstant woman
> to make some one plead with her for a long time
> to enhance her worth; that way he won't think
> she's used to such sport.
> But a woman of good character,
> sensible as well as virtuous,
> if she finds a man to her liking,

> oughtn't to treat him too disdainfully.
> Rather she should love and enjoy him;
> this way, before anyone knows or hears of it,
> they'll have done a lot that's to their advantage.
>
> [513–25]

In other words, the best sign of a woman's virtue is her readiness to go to bed with a would-be lover!

Guigemar's eloquence has the desired effect, and he and the lady retire to bed. And now, in another slyly comic manoeuvre, Marie subtly intertwines her protagonists' full enjoyment of love's power with her audience's full use of its powers of imagination and intellect. As the lovers hug and kiss, Marie interjects, "I hope they also enjoy the *surplus*/that others are accustomed to on such occasions" (533–34). Now, in the Prologue to the *Lais*, there is a famous (and much argued over) passage in which Marie describes how modern readers must "gloss the letter" of ancient texts and appropriate them by adding a *surplus* of contemporary meaning to them. Here in *Guigemar*, Marie coyly applies this technical term, *surplus*, to a sexual, rather than a textual, transaction; by means of this ostensible euphemism, she in fact invites her audience to gloss the letter of her story and supply the erotic *surplus* either from its own sexual experience or from its familiarity with other, less reticent fictions. In either case, we become co-creators of Marie's fiction at this point, and simultaneously co-creators (and completers) of the protagonists' relationship. Finally, as one last joke, Marie arranges that the happy reunion of the lovers, after long separation by marital and feudal obstacles, will depend upon each being able to untie a knot he or she has previously made in the other's garment. Surely this device, besides being a version of the birthmark that establishes the identity of hero or heroine in romance, constitutes a quibbling reference to Marie's activities in managing the improbable denouement of her love story.

A more serious equation of love and art animates the lai of *Yonec*. Its heroine is both the protagonist in a story of tragic but finally triumphant love and a portrait of the artist at work. The young wife of an impotent but jealous old husband who keeps her locked in a tower, she utters one day a passionate lament for her own sorry state, then muses:

> I've often heard
> that one could once find
> adventures in this land
> that brought relief to the unhappy.

> Knights might find young girls
> to their desire, noble and lovely;
> and ladies find lovers
> so handsome, courtly, brave, and valiant
> that they could not be blamed,
> and no one else would see them.
> If that might be or ever was,
> if that has ever happened to anyone,
> God, who has power over everything,
> grant me my wish in this.
>
> [91–104]

Immediately, a bird flies into her tower and turns into a handsome knight who announces he has long loved her, but could not appear until she summoned him. To calm her fears that he is the devil, he takes her form in order to receive communion from a priest. He also professes his faith in God the creator-redeemer, and thereby reminds us that, in fact, the creator of this moment is the lady herself, who has undertaken to make her own love story on the pattern of others she has heard, and thereby brings about her close encounter of the bird kind.

Inevitably, the husband discovers the lovers and arranges to kill the bird-knight, but not before the lady has become pregnant. The son she bears grows up believing that the jealous husband is his father, and only discovers the truth at a moment prearranged by the real father before his death. When the son, Yonec, arrives at his father's tomb, accompanied by his mother and stepfather, the woman at last reveals the secret of his paternity, gives him his true father's sword, and dies. Yonec kills the stepfather and is declared lord over his real father's land.

The lai of *Yonec* invites interpretation as a story about each of the three kinds of power that has concerned us here. From one perspective, it turns out to be a conspicuously Oedipal tale of a young warrior-aristocrat's arrival at maturity, symbolized by the handing on of the paternal sword, which he can now use to destroy the man whom he thought, until that moment, to be his father: "Thus with his father's sword he avenged his mother's sorrow" (543–44). Yonec is empowered by this act of violence to assume the lands and authority rightfully his by descent, but until now denied him. A second reading of *Yonec* sees it celebrating the ultimate triumph of love over jealousy and tyranny, a triumph possible because of love's generative power—the next generation grows up to redeem its predecessor. (Such a multigenerational model of loss and recovery or estrangement and reconciliation occurs often in romance, and is perhaps most familiar to us from Shakespeare's last plays.)

And from yet another angle, *Yonec* offers, in the career of its female protagonist, an allegory of the artist's travails and ultimate triumph. First of all, the imprisoned, wretchedly unhappy wife begins her story through an exercise of the imagination, and thereby undertakes a "grevos ovre" which will deliver her from her "grant dolur." (The French terminology comes from the Prologue, where Marie uses it to describe the nature of and motivation for her self-imposed task of writing her *Lais*.) Next, the artist-surrogate succeeds in giving birth to a new idea (Yonec) that will save the plot just when it seems headed for collapse. Finally, she is able to marshall her creative skills so that she can arrange a discovery and reversal, thanks to the eloquence with which she communicates her special knowledge to her chosen audience. (Once again, I am paraphrasing the Prologue to the *Lais*, in which Marie argues that those possessing eloquence and knowledge—*eloquence* and *escience*—must use rather than hide them.)

To validate this reading of *Yonec* as a poem containing a significant linkage between love and art, I wish to close my discussion with a brief comparison between a key moment in Marie's lai and two analogues to it: one from a Welsh tale of early but uncertain date, *Pwyll, the Prince of Dyfed*, and the other from a nineteenth-century novella, Henry James's *The Europeans*. Bringing into play two works so different from each other and from Marie will, I hope, further define, by contrast, the intimate relationship between love's power and art's in Marie's fictions.

The moment in question is the pivotal one where Marie's heroine, alone in the locked chamber that represents her loveless, confining marriage, bitterly laments her fate, and curses her family for having thus given her to a rich, jealous old man who needs a wife in order to have heirs. In her despair, the young woman suddenly crosses the boundary that separates harsh reality from mythic fantasy, as she exclaims,

He'll never die—
when he should have been baptized
he was plunged instead in the river of hell; his sinews are hard,
his veins are hard,
filled with living blood.

[86–90]

Her extreme physical and emotional constraints seem to have prompted a compensatory liberation of her imagination, and she reinvents her husband as the grotesque parody of a classical hero rendered invulnerable by immersion in the Styx. Thus engaged, the wife's imaginative capacities now begin to articulate possibilities of relieving, as opposed to intensifying, her grief, as she recalls, in the lines I quoted earlier, old stories of knights and ladies offering secret solace to each other in distress. The immediate appearance of a hawk, and its metamorphosis into a knight who has long loved her but can not come until she summoned him, constitute, in the terms of Marie's Prologue, the wife's gloss on the stories she has heard, a salutary *surplus* supplied from her desperate *sens* of her plight.

In the branch of the Mabinogion that transmits adventures of Pwyll, the prince of Dyfed, the second adventure concerns Pwyll's taking to wife the beautiful and resourceful Rhiannon. Once, the tale tells us, after a great feast at his court, Pwyll went to sit on the top of a nearby mound. A retainer tells him, "it is the peculiarity of the mound that whatever high-born man sits upon it will not go thence without one of two things: wounds or blows, or else his seeing a wonder."[5] Hoping to see a wonder, Pwyll sits on the mound; soon, a beautiful woman comes by riding a white horse. All attempts to intercept or overtake her prove futile, for the faster the pursuit, the farther she appears out of reach. Finally Pwyll attempts the chase, and experiences the same frustration. At last he calls out to the woman, " 'Maiden, for his sake whom thou lovest best, stay for me.' 'I will, gladly,' said she, 'and it had been better for the horse hadst thou asked this long since'" (p. 11). When the prince asks her errand, she tells him she is seeking him, identifies herself as Rhiannon, and says that she is about to be married against her will, that she loves only Pwyll, and that she has come to find out if he will marry her instead. Pwyll immediately agrees to do so, and the rest of the tale is taken up with a battle of wits between Rhiannon—who must constantly propose strategems to her naive lover—and the other man who wants her as his wife.

In this tradition-based Welsh tale, it is the woman who appears suddenly to the man she loves, but not because he has asked for her. There is in fact a logical discrepancy between Rhiannon's seeking Pwyll because she wishes to marry him rather than another—a motivation quite analogous to that of Marie's protagonist, wishing relief from an already accomplished, loveless marriage—and the necessity for Pwyll to sit on the magic mound, and then to call after Rhiannon when he cannot ride her down, if the future spouses are to meet. The discrepancy results, I believe, from the fact that the tale of Pwyll combines the didactic and commemorative functions common to much tradition-based art. Thus the episode of Rhiannon's appearance not only transmits a marvellous story about the career of a legendary hero; it also incorporates a lesson about how one can sometimes accomplish one's desires more effectively with courtesy than with force. Establishing a link between love and art seems far from the tale's concerns.

Henry James's tale of the encounter between a provincial American family and its distant European relatives may seem an odd place to seek an instructive analogue to Marie's Breton lai, but the analogue is present, nonetheless. Early in the novella, James recounts Gertrude Wentworth's first meeting with her European cousin Felix, whom she will later marry. Felix has been sent by his sister, the Baroness Eugenia, on a scouting mission to the Wentworth home outside Boston, a strategic preliminary to Eugenia's own visit. The Baroness charges her brother to "observe everything [and] be ready to describe to me the locality, the accessories—how shall I say it?—the *mise en scène.*" When Felix asks what message he should bring from his sister, she replies, "Say what you please. Tell my story in the way that seems to you most—natural."[6] In short, Felix sets out to fulfill responsibilities of full description and natural narration that bear a suspicious similarity to the mimetic techniques of his creator—a similarity underscored by the fact that James begins the chapter that immediately follows this exchange between brother and sister with precisely the kind of circumstantial account, to us, of the Wentworth *mise en scène* that Felix is to bring back to his sister.

It is Sunday morning in the country, and all the Wentworths are off to church except Gertrude, whom James presents in a vaguely restless and rebellious mood that, we are led to believe, is not unusual for her. James defines Gertrude's situation and its discontents by means of her brief conversations with her gently admonitory, repressed sister, Charlotte—"'I don't think one should ever try to look pretty,' [Charlotte] rejoined earnestly" (p. 21)—and with her somewhat stout, somewhat importunate, and obviously approved suitor, Mr. Brand, whom she clearly does not fancy. Alone at last, Gertrude wanders through the house, feeling "an agreeable sense of solitude" that "always excited [her] imagination" (pp. 23–24). Not quite knowing what to do, she begins to read a romance from the *Arabian Nights*: "There, for a quarter of an hour, she read the history of the loves of the Prince Camaralzaman and the Princess Badoura. At last, looking up, she beheld, as it seemed to her, the Prince Camaralzaman standing before her. A beautiful young man was making her a very low bow; . . . he appeared to have dropped from the clouds; he was wonderfully handsome; he smiled. . . . Extreme surprise, for a moment, kept Gertrude sitting still; then she rose, without even keeping her finger in her book. . . . 'Will you kindly tell me,' said the mysterious visitor at last, 'whether I have the honour of speaking to Miss Wentworth?' 'My name is Gertrude Wentworth,' murmured the young woman. 'Then—then—I have the honour—the pleasure—of being your cousin.' "

The relationship of this moment to the appearance of the hawk-lover in *Yonec* is clear and indubitable. But just as Marie has (in Northrop Frye's term) displaced a traditional tale about the magic onset of love into a metaphoric fiction concerned with the relative power of love, imagination, and social constraint, so Henry James has further displaced the tale in conformity to the canons of mimetic, or realist, fiction. The notion that the scene has something to do with the power of art and imagination is present in the suggestion, already mentioned, that Felix's responsibilities resemble those of the novelist, and in his appearance to Gertrude as she reads the *Arabian Nights* story. Indeed, James teases his readers with the possibility that Gertrude has indeed brought her exotic visitor into existence: "The young man had so much the character of an apparition that his announcement seemed to complete his unreality. . . . Gertrude had been wondering with a quick intensity which brought its result; and the result seemed an answer—a wondrous, delightful answer—to her vague wish that something would befall her. . . . She had never in her life spoken to a foreigner, and she had often thought it would be delightful to do so. Here was one who had suddenly been engendered by the Sabbath stillness for her private use" (pp. 24–26). But this possibility that Gertrude's dissatisfaction with her constrained existence—her unwanted suitor, her family's puritanical lack of appreciation for her fanciful, we might say artistic temperament—has in some supernatural way elicited the arrival from afar of a suitor who will rescue her is, of course, denied by the depiction, in the preceding chapter, of Felix, his sister, and their motives for being in America. James in effect toys with our desire that such miracles could happen, smiling at our—and Gertrude's—romantic susceptibilities even as he nourishes them.

By mounting Marie's imprisoned wife and her hawk-knight lover in a literary tryptych, flanked on one side by Pwyll and Rhiannon and on the other by Gertrude and Felix, and by showing how only the twelfth-century Anglo-French poet uses the shared fictional motif of the suddenly appearing beloved to establish a profound metaphorical connection between the power of love and the power of the imagination, I hope to have contributed to our understanding of the heightened cultural importance, as well as the close relationship, of these areas of human experience and achievement. Chrétien de Troyes and Marie de France embody in their works a new impatience with, and skepticism about, the efficacy, and therefore the real power, of physical force; they exalt instead the efficacy of wit, creativity, eloquence, and love in all its guises. Theirs is a vision we would do well to embrace in our own age of misplaced reliance on the saving power of an armed might that threatens instead to destroy us all.

6

Chastity and Love in
the Decameron

The story of Nastagio degli Onesti (*Decameron* 5.8) is one of Boccaccio's most remarkable tales, both for its theme and for the figurative substance in which the theme is developed. In the tale, Nastagio squanders the immense wealth he has inherited in a vain attempt to court a daughter of Messer Paolo Traversari. His friends and relatives finally prevail on him to leave Ravenna, and he retires to Chiassi, where one day he sees a beautiful, naked young woman fleeing through the woods pursued by two hounds and a knight. Challenged by Nastagio, the knight explains the cause of his action, then slays the woman and feeds her heart to the dogs. Nastagio decides to use this marvel to his own purposes and invites the Traversari to join him a week hence. When the scene is reenacted before the guests, the daughter accepts Nastagio's love, and he goes further to propose marrying her.

The figurative substance of the tale results from the rather violent juxtaposition of two representational dimensions: one, cast in a realistic frame reflecting everyday life, is constituted by romantic elements taken from the tradition of courtly love, while the other, eschatological in nature, is constituted by sadistic rituals taken from the tradition of religious literature. The theme consists in the opposition of love and chastity, which at the beginning of the story are seen as incompatible elements.

This thematic opposition seems to be part of a more comprehensive polarity of nature and social conventions, or, homologously, love and social conventions, which is one of the most important polarities organizing the figurative substance of the *Decameron*.[1] However, if love and chastity had remained incompatible throughout the narrative, the thematic course that develops their opposition would run from the affirmation of chastity as a negation of love in the beginning, to the affirmation of love as a negation of chastity at the end. Indeed, this would be hardly surprising within the axiological structure of the *Decameron*, and it would be warranted even by the development of the story itself. For after witnessing the bloody ritual in the pine woods of Chiassi, the girl sends a message to Nastagio stating that "she was ready to do anything he pleased." In other words, she was ready to undertake an illicit relation with him.[2]

Nastagio brings this imminent development of the thematic course to a different turn, however, by opting to marry the girl. Here Boccaccio chooses, as he does elsewhere,[3] to bring the thematic course of the story not to the reversal of the opposition, but rather to a reconciliation.[4] In our story, it is not a question of nature or love (intended as an overpowering natural force) that necessarily subverts social conventions or institutions, since the final choice of the two youths reaffirms the validity of marriage. The thematic opposition in our story runs from the affirmation that the reasons of chastity must prevail over the reasons of love, with which they are irreconcilable, to the affirmation that the reasons of love and those of chastity may coexist.

The reasons of chastity are both religious and social: chastity is necessary for the salvation of the soul in the other world just as it is necessary in this world for the preservation of social honor. To yield to the call of love would mean to jeopardize those reasons. To defeat the reasons of chastity, Nastagio has to prove that, on the contrary, love is a dynamic force that has the power of achieving both the preservation of honor and the salvation of the soul, a power that chastity by itself does not possess. From the girl's behavior, it appears that chastity is conceived as a static attitude manifested as lofty indifference to passion and the revelries of love rather than as an active moral fortitude. It is "that hard cold heart, wherein love and pity could never enter," as Guido degli Anastagi, the Knight–huntsman, complains. Boccaccio thus questions whether the social and religious value we place on chastity is in effect justified; whether chastity is really a virtue or rather an antisocial behavior; whether it actually leads to salvation or is simply the cause of grief and death.

Boccaccio was well aware that the question was an old one, which through the ages had been posed and developed sometimes in ways similar to his, sometimes differently. When we analyze the figurative substance of the story of Nastagio, we are amazed to find that all its figurative components can be traced back to a good number of stories developing the same thematic course.

These stories can be grouped into Eastern, Western, and classical traditions, and all of them seem to be connected, in their origin, with a religious cult or milieu.

The motif of the chaste woman tempted through the portrayal of punishment for chastity is developed in a story already contained in the *Kathâ-sarît-sâgara* written by Somadeva in the eleventh century.[5] Devasmitâ is an incorruptible wife. During her husband's absence, she is approached by four merchants through a female ascetic who lives in a sanctuary of Buddha who has consented to oblige the young men. The "reverend madam" manages first to gain the confidence of Devasmitâ and then, one day, feeds a chunk of meat soaked with pepper dust to a small female dog chained at the entrance of the wife's private rooms. Soon after, the little dog starts to shed tears, arousing the astonished curiosity of Devasmitâ, who wonders what could be the cause of the strange phenomenon. The ascetic go-between is ready with an interesting explanation:

> In a former birth I and that bitch were the two wives of a certain Brahman. And our husband frequently went about to other countries on embassies by order of the king. Now while he was away from home I lived with other men at my pleasure, and so did not cheat the elements of which I was composed, and my senses, of their lawful enjoyment. For considerate treatment of the elements and senses is held to be the highest duty. Therefore I have been born in this birth with a recollection of my former existence. But she in her former life, through ignorance, confined all her attention to the preservation of her character; therefore she has been degraded and born again as one of the canine race; however, she too remembers her former birth. . . . This creature recognized me today as having been its companion in a former birth and began to weep.

Besides being chaste Devasmitâ is also clever, and she becomes suspicious of this novel conception of duties towards nature. Curious about the reverend madam's aims, she asks her to help her avoid the risk of a degradation in her next birth. The ascetic promises to allay her worries by sending four rich and handsome merchants to her house that night. Waiting for the night, Devasmitâ has the opportunity to devise a plan. She commands one of her chambermaids to impersonate her, and when each of the four lovers arrives, he is drugged, stripped of his clothes, branded on the forehead as a slave, and finally thrown into a filthy ditch. When the maladroit lovers awake the next morning, they think they are in "the hell *Avîchi* assigned to *them* by *their* sins." After she punishes the go-between in an even crueler way, Devasmitâ goes before the king claiming the four merchants as her slaves, thus demonstrating, as the author says, that "women of good family ever worship their husbands with chaste and resolute behaviour and never think of any other man, for to virtuous wives the husband is the highest deity."

Somadeva's story shares several interesting features with Boccaccio's tale: the thematic question and the oppositions on which it is built are similar. In Somadeva's story we also find that the narration of the punishment of chastity aims at influencing the chaste lady to affirm the value of unchastity. Actually, the apologue told by the sanctimonious go-between contains two stories with opposite denouements: one concerning the chaste wife punished by being changed into a bitch, the other concerning the unchaste wife rewarded by being upgraded to a woman of religion. So chastity in this life is punished in the next, whereas unchastity in this life is rewarded in the next. Furthermore, the story of Devasmitâ and the go-between's apologue are connected through the juxtaposition of two incompatible dimensions, one mimetically real, the other eschatological.

In the Indian story, chastity triumphs over a law of nature according to which, in the words of the Buddhist ascetic, the "considerate treatment of the elements and senses" represents "the highest duty"; observance of this law is duly rewarded in metempsychosis. But at this point we cannot help wondering why such a law of nature and the hatching of such an obvious deceit are placed in the mouth and mind of a religious woman. The religious attributions of the go-between are quite clear: she lives in the sanctuary of Buddha, she has devoted disciples, the merchants treat her with great respect, calling her "reverend madam," she easily gains access to the private rooms of Devasmitâ. Therefore she must be a *dêva-dâsî*, a "handmaid of the god" or "woman of the temple," of high rank. On the other hand, the role she plays in the story does not seem to require any religious rank or habit.

If one assumes that there are no antireligious or anticlerical intentions in Somadeva's *Kathâ-sarît-sâgara*, one must conclude that the go-between represents the remnant of a previous stage of the story in which the religious character of the question and the religious milieu in which it originated must have had some importance. It is legitimate to suspect that the story originally dealt with hieropornia, or sacred prostitution, and more precisely with the recruitment of honorable ladies to the service of the temple.[6] We shall later see how this hypothesis fits well with the significance of the Greek myth we are going to examine. I should like to point out here that the first books of Somadeva's collection, which include Devasmitâ's story, represent a re-elaboration of what remained of a larger and much more ancient work, the *Brihat-Kathâ*, dated around the fifth century A.D. This work is lost, but we know from a table of contents found in Kashmir that it did contain our story.[7]

According to our hypothesis, in the *Brihat-Kathâ* version the thematic course of the story imposed the renunciation of chastity in the name of a more fundamental law of nature or in the name of service to the god. However, at about the time when Somadeva was writing, after Northern India had been devastated by Moslem invasions and sacred prostitution was being persecuted as part of the Hindu religion,[8] the change in axiological values imposed a radical mutation in the denouement of the story. Similarly, the eschatological dimension represented by the allusion to the "hell *Avîchi*" into which the four lovers believe they have been thrown, probably had a meaningful function in the original story which now escapes us.

The story of the bitch, which the go-between tells in order to seduce the chaste wife, appears in an abridged form and severed from all other events constituting the story of Devasmitâ in other Eastern collections—namely the *Sukasaptati*[9] and the collection that goes under the name of *Book of Sindibâd*,[10] which is related to the tradition of the *Seven Sages of Rome* and represented by various redactions. To these we can add the twelfth-century *Disciplina clericalis* by Petrus Alfonsi, which introduces the story to the Western world (the Spanish translation of the *Book of Sindibâd, Libro de los engannos,* was to remain unknown until the nineteenth century). The date of composition of the *Sukasaptati* is unknown; the parent version of the *Book of Sindibâd* seems to go back to the eighth century. This proves that the story of the bitch was already in circulation before and independently from Somadeva's collection, but probably not from his source. Severed from the ideological matrix that had generated it, the story undergoes important transformations: the eschatological dimension provided by the metempsychosis is lost and so is the contrasting behavior of the two women; there is only one woman, changed to a bitch because she refused to accept a lover. The transformation from woman to bitch is brought about by the disappointed lover's curse or by magic (no cause is mentioned in the *Disciplina*). Similarly, the lovers of the woman whose chastity is being tempted are reduced to one.

We do not know whether these collections derive the story from a common source, though that is rather unlikely. It is interesting to note, however, that in the *Disciplina* the go-between appears "religionis habitu decorata," a detail that has no narrative function or ideological meaning in the text, but somehow links Alfonsi's version to the form of the story known to Somadeva.

In the *Sukasaptati* a mother uses the story in order to induce the wife of a prince to accept the love of her son, who had desperately fallen in love with her. In the case of the *Disciplina* and *Sindibâd*, the story is narrated as an *exemplum*, in order to admonish against the deceptions of women. And as before, the denouement imposed upon the story varies according to the axiological disposition of values in the dominant ideology. Thus in the *Disciplina*, written after the author's conversion to Christianity in 1106, the chastity test has negative results: the chaste woman tempted by the go-between with the story of the bitch is actually seduced, as in the *Sukasaptati*. Unlike Somadeva, who was interested in portraying the ideal of a chaste wife, Petrus Alfonsi intends to show how easy it is to corrupt an honest woman by means of a well-wrought lie.

Somewhat more complex is the denouement in *Sindibâd*: the chaste woman is persuaded to accept the lover, but the adultery does not take place, since the man that the go-between brings to her house is actually the husband. According to some versions, he has disguised himself in order to test his wife's fidelity; in other versions, he has replaced the original lover, who has suddenly disappeared. The solution is interesting in that it probably manifests the tension created between the dominant axiological values, which impose the affirmation of chastity, and the values of the author, who tries to avoid that imposition by presenting the adultery as a hypothesis rather than as a fact.

The *Sindibâd* version of the second type later reappears, in a form much more developed but with few substantial variants, in two of the redactions of the *Arabian Nights*,[11] but it has no followers in Western literature. The *Disciplina* version, due to the enormous popularity enjoyed by the book throughout the Middle Ages, reappears very often in various collections of sermons and *exempla*. It is found in the *Exempla* by Jacques de Vitry (CCL), in the

Promptuarium of Johannes Herolt (V. 12), in the *Summa predican-tium* of John Bromyard (*Latin Stories*, XIII), in the *Gesta Romano-rum* (ed. Oesterley XXVIII), in the fifteenth-century *Scala Celi* of Jean de Gobi (fol. 87), and in the Middle English romance *Dame Sirith*. All these texts present very few variants in the figurative details.

Boccaccio certainly knew one or more versions of this story. But he also knew other stories about adulteresses punished in the other world. Among these, the closest one to the figurative sub-stance of his novella is a story narrated in the *De cognitione sui* (XIII) by Helinandus de Froidmont (who lived between the end of the twelfth century and the beginning of the thirteenth century),[12] and reproduced immediately after with few linguistic variants by his editor Vincent of Beauvais in his *Speculum historiale*.[13] The story proceeds as follows:

One night, while watching his charcoal kiln, a poor but pious coalman suddenly sees a naked woman running, chased by a man mounted on a black horse and brandishing a sword. The knight reaches the woman on the edge of the kiln: he plunges his sword into her body, and then, dismounting, throws her on the burning coals. After a while he takes her from the kiln half-burned, puts her on the horse in front of him, and gallops away. In each of the following nights, at the very same time, the scene is punctually repeated before the terrorized coalman. The coalman's master, the count of Nivers, seeing him perturbed, asks the reason for his dis-tress. The coalman describes to him what he has witnessed during the previous nights. The count wants to see for himself the "vi-sionem magnam." He prepares himself spiritually, takes commu-nion, and goes with the coalman to the wood where the kiln is located. Around midnight, preceded by hair-raising noises, the woman is hunted again by the implacable knight: the horrid ritual is once more repeated. Before the horseman has time to disappear with his victim, the count asks him to stop in the name of God and tell him the reason for such cruel pursuit. The horseman stops and says: "I used to be one of your knights and this woman is such and such lady, who was married to such and such knight, whom she killed so that she could lay with me more often and conve-niently. We both died in this sin and now share the same punish-ment, for every single night, stabbing and burning this woman, I inflict upon her the torments she did not suffer at the moment of her death." The count asks again: "What about that horse you mount? Who is he?" "A devil," answers the knight, "which incites us with undescribable torments."

Helinandus's story was well known: in addition to being reproduced by Vincent of Beauvais, it was succinctly retold in the *Alphabetum narrationum* (DCXIII),[14] by John Bromyard (*Summa predicantium* XVII, 12), in the *Scala Celi* (fol. 110v), in *Schimpf und Ernst* by Johannes Pauli (CCXXVIII), and in three manuscript versions indicated by the *Catalogue of Romances* (III, 134, 432, 574).

In Italy, Helinandus's story reappears in the *Specchio della vera penitenza* of Jacopo Passavanti (V),[15] who elaborates on some of the figurative details, gives a name to the lovers (who are anonymous in the source), and takes great care to offer a justification for Helinandus's location of the chase in Purgatory by interpolating the sinners' confession *in extremis*. L. Di Francia,[16] after collating several linguistic elements, believed that Boccaccio's direct source was Helinandus's or Vincent of Beauvais's copy. Later, on the basis of no less convincing evidence, Angelo Monteverdi held instead that Boccaccio must have somehow known Passavanti's text, the only difficulty being that, according to the evidence we have, it appears that the *Specchio della vera penitenza* was composed by Passavanti after the *Decameron*.

This difficulty can be solved, however, if we take into account another *exemplum*, already noted by Toldo and by Monteverdi, narrated by Cesarius of Heisterbach in his *Dialogus miraculorum* (XII, 20).[17] Cesarius was a contemporary of Helinandus and belonged, like him, to the Cistercian Order. According to Cesarius, one night a man saw a terrified woman in her shirt and shoes run towards him crying for help. The man realized she was the priest's concubine, who had died the day before. At the point of death, she had insisted on wearing that particular pair of shoes, saying she badly needed them. The woman was chased by a hunter mounted on a horse and accompanied by fierce dogs. The man, trying to help her, seized the woman by her hair with his left hand and brandished his sword with his right hand in order to defend her from her persecutor. But as the hunter was approaching, the woman shook herself loose from her defender, leaving her hair in his hand and running away. The hunter soon caught up with her, threw her on his horse, and disappeared from sight.

Cesarius's text reappears almost *verbatim* in the *Alphabetum narrationum* (CCCCLVI), in the *Exemples moraulx* by Mansel, and in the *Scala Celi* (fol. 111). Jean de Gobi must have noticed the affinities between the text of Cesarius and that of Helinandus, since he places them one after the other under the same title of "De luxuria."

Now, if it is true—as Monteverdi maintains and as it actually seems from a collation of the two texts—that Passavanti took his story not directly from Helinandus but from the *Alphabetum narrationum*, this would suggest that the variations between the *Specchio di vera penitenza* and the *De cognitione sui* can be explained as the result of a *contaminatio* of the two versions of the Cistercian monks. The same could explain, in turn, the coincidences between the text of the *Decameron* and that of the *Specchio di vera penitenza*. In other words, Boccaccio, like Passavanti, could have read the two *exempla* in the *Alphabetum* and effected the same type of *contaminatio*. This would also explain the figure of the mastiffs in Boccaccio's story, which more likely descends from Cesarius's dogs rather than from the "black bitches, eager and swift" of *Inferno* XIII, 125, which, although more poetically suggestive, are figuratively more distant. It would also explain the witness's intervention in defense of the pursued woman, a detail which is present in Cesarius and in Boccaccio, but is absent from the texts of Helinandus and Passavanti.

We do not have historical or philological elements to decide whether the texts of the two Cistercian monks are diachronically dependent on one another or have been derived from a common source. It is in fact clear that the versions of Helinandus and Cesarius represent two variations on the thematic opposition of chastity vs. non-chastity, which remains implicit in the latter but is made explicit in the former. For our present purposes, however, rather than establishing diachronic dependences among the various texts, we are interested in emphasizing their synchronic affinities. It was on the basis of these affinities that Boccaccio conceived the idea of re-organizing their respective figurative elements into a structure which, while preserving them, could regenerate them from within and present itself as an original narrative unit.

Now, from the synchronic standpoint, do we find affinities between the story of the pursued adulteress and that of the woman degraded to bitch? Not, perhaps, if we look at the figurative substance. But once we look at the structures of the bitch story, especially in the text of the *Kathâ-sarît-sâgara*, affinities begin to emerge. Helinandus's legend can be reconstructed as the story of the chaste-bitch with inverted characters and ideological values. Instead of the incorruptible wife who refuses the lovers' advances in order to remain faithful to her husband, we find in Helinandus' story the corrupted wife who, in order to satisfy her lust, kills her husband and induces her lover to a life of sin. The lover's death in the latter story assumes the symbolic value of the spiritual death of a man who, in his turn, becomes the executioner of the woman who had caused his death. Thus, the inversion of ethical values is accompanied by a concomitant inversion of figurative elements. Helinandus's legend is also formed as a story within a story, a story which explains itself.

The two juxtaposed narrative units are no longer related reflexively, as in the story of the chaste-bitch, but in a mirror-like reflection, as in Dante's *contrapasso*, in which victim and persecutor exchange their respective roles in this and the other world. The eschatological dimension, which had disappeared from the later versions of the chaste-bitch, reappears in the legend, because the punishment of the unchaste woman takes place in Purgatory, though it is visible to the eyes of living witnesses. The narrative functions of the character of the lover are also inverted. In the story of the chaste-bitch he functions as antagonist, whereas in the fiendish chase he appears as proto-antagonist (first victim, then executioner) in the order of the *fabula* (i.e., in the chronological succession of events), and as protagonist in the order of the plot. Thus he becomes the point of projection of the narration as well as of the axiological values which are syncretized to it.

Finally, the demonic elements which in the Cistercian legend are manifested by the horse are also present in the story of the chaste-bitch, both explicitly and implicitly: explicitly in the figure of the hell *Avîchi* into which the four pretenders are thrown, implicitly in the degradation of the chaste wife to bitch. In the *Disciplina*, in fact, the disciple to whom the story is narrated, remarks: "Nunquam audivi tam mirabile quid, et hoc puto fieri arte diaboli." Therefore, at this end of our analysis, the religious matrix of the thematic opposition and the figurative substance we are concerned with seem to re-emerge again.

Now, is the fiendish chase an original development of the medieval mind or is it rather a transformation of more ancient figurative substance? The persecution of the adulteress had already been connected to the figure of Wotan chasing a woman (his wife or lover, according to some scholars) in Germanic mythology. Doubtless, the suggestion is interesting insofar as it greatly extends the diachronic dimension of our figurative material. The indication, however, has little functional value for our research, for two basic reasons: first, it concerns only one isolated element in the complex substance we are here analyzing; second, it has no bearing on the thematic opposition on which our research is focused.

It seems to me, instead, that the figurative substance of the fiendish chase in all its complexity can be traced back to the Maenadic rituals practiced within the cult of Dionysus, who soon annexed, among other attributions, that of Zagreus ("the great hunter") the *nuctipolos* ("night-wanderer"), and who was venerated at the *Agrionia* in Boeotia (hence the attribution of *agrionios*, again "the hunter").[19] We cannot here discuss the various Dionysiac rituals, which are the subject of a vast specialized bibliography. We must, however, dwell on some of the mythologic material connected with that cult, for it constitutes the third figurative tradition that concerns Boccaccio's story.

Not all women, when called upon by the god, were ready to follow his rites and become his Maenads. Some of them resisted the call, either because they did not believe in the divinity of Dionysus (like the daughters of Cadmus, whose story is narrated in Euripides's *Bacchae*), or because they despised the god's cult (like the daughters of Proetus),[20] or simply because they wanted to keep to their homes and domestic work, like the daughters of Minyas of Orchomenos. The stories of the daughters of Proetus and that of the Minyads seem to be two variants of the same myth, and this was probably also true, at the original stage of the myth, of the story concerning the daughters of Cadmus. The story of the Minyads, which interests us directly, is narrated by Ovid and less succinctly by Antoninus Liberalis and Claudius Aelianus, both of whom belong to the end of the second century A.D.[21] The story is definitely more ancient: Liberalis' source (and probably also Ovid's) is certainly Nicander (second century B.C.),[22] who took it from Pindar's teacher, Korinna.[23]

According to Aelianus, the three daughters of Minyas, wishing to attend to their looms and other domestic work in preparation for legitimate marriage, refuse to become the god's Maenads. In order to divert them, Dionysus causes a series of miracles: snakes or ivy vines clasp onto the loom, while wine or milk drops from the ceiling. The three girls are finally seized by the Dionysiac mania, under the influence of which they rend to pieces Hippasos, the son of one of them, taking him for a fawn, and then join the other Maenads on the Citheron mountain. But the Maenads, angered by their crime, pursue them until they are changed into crows and owls.

Antoninus Liberalis's story is very similar: the three "very hard working" sisters despise and mock girls who abandon the city in order to go to the mountain as Maenads. Dionysus appears to them disguised as a girl and then as a lion, a bull, and a leopard, warning them not to neglect his initiation rituals. At the same time, nectar and honey drop on their loom. Finally, seized by the god's mania, they rend to pieces the child Hippasos, chosen by lot, leave their father's house, and join the Maenads on the mountain, where Hermes changes them into a bat and owls. The rending of the child, which represents the *diaspàragmos*, the ritual dismemberment of the human victim and the ritual homophagy, is absent from Ovid's poetic rendition.

The names of the three Minyads are, in Aelianus, Leukippe, Aristippe, and Alkithoe; in Antoninus, Leukippe, Arsippe and Alkathoe; in Ovid, Alcitoe and Leukonoe, while the name of the third is not given. In Ovid, the three sisters, while attending to their domestic work, also tell in turns stories of tragic or unfortunate love. Jeanmaire (285) notices the peculiar recurrence of the suffix -*ippe* in most of the Minyads' names: Leukippe ("the white mare"), Arsippe ("the pawing mare"), and Aristippe ("the best mare"); also Alkitoe or Alkatoe ("the valiant runner"). In the analogous myth of the daughters of Proetus, the names are Lysippe ("the unrestrained mare"), Chrysippe ("the golden mare"), and Hipponoe ("mare's heart"). To these we should add the name of the child, Hippasos ("the one that can be mounted"). The mythologist suggests that they have to be connected with the demonic powers attributed to the horse in ancient mythology and to its symbolic meaning as messenger of the other world, incarnation of the spirit of the dead and of infernal divinities.[24]

The myth of the Minyads enjoyed great popularity in the Greek world. It was thought they were among the first and most effective propagators of the cult of Dionysus in Greece.[25] It seems that their myth formed the argument of Euripides's lost tragedy *Xantriai*.[26] But most interesting of all is that their ritual was still symbolically celebrated in the annual *Agrionia* in Boeotia at the time of Plutarch, who gives us a very important detail for our search. In his *Greek Questions* 38, Plutarch gives the following answer to the question, "Who are the Psoloeis and who the Oleiai among the Boeotians?":

> They say that the daughters of Minyas, Leukippe and Arsinoe and Alkatoe, became frenzied and craved for human flesh, and drew lots about their children. The lot fell upon Leukippe and she gave her son Hippasos to be torn in pieces. And their husbands who, through mourning and grief donned ill-favoured raiment, were called Sooty (Psoloeis), but the women themselves Oleiai, as it were Murderesses. And up to

the present time the people of Orchomenos give this name to the women of the family descended from them. And once a year in the Agrionia there takes place a flight and pursuit of them by the priest of Dionysus holding a sword. And when he catches one of them he may kill her. And in our own time Zoilos the priest killed her.[27]

The infernal chase, therefore, does not seem to be a creation of medieval imagination, but rather a transformation of much more ancient rituals. How and when such rituals reached medieval Christian writers I cannot say. We know, however, that Dionysiac cults and rituals, among them the *diaspàragmos* and homophagy, were still discussed by men like Porphyry at the end of the third century and Photius in the ninth century.[28]

It is interesting to note that the crime imputed to the Minyads is that of refusing to answer the call of Dionysus and of maintaining a disdainful indifference towards the revelries and mysteries of his Maenads (Jeanmaire, 8). The refusal to answer the god's call would seem to suggest a similarity between the myth and what might have been the situation in the original story of Devasmitâ in the *Brihat-Kathâ*. In the absence of the latter text, such similarity cannot be established, yet the fascination of the hypothesis is inescapable. The Minyads' disdainful indifference has the same quality we have already attributed to the "chastity" of the daughter of Paolo Traversari in Boccaccio's story. It is identical to the point of departure for the conceptual opposition between chastity and love on which the story of Nastagio degli Onesti is built.

Did Boccaccio know the story of the Minyads? There can be little doubt that he knew Ovid's version of it. Whether or not he knew Plutarch's text is a moot question. It should be noted, however, that during the fourteenth century Plutarch's *Moralia* (which contain the *Greek Questions*) circulated in Italy in no fewer than six manuscripts, the oldest of which dates from the end of the thirteenth century.[29]

The material we have discussed above constitutes the figurative tradition handed down to Boccaccio. While it is difficult to say whether he was directly acquainted with all the details we have presented, it is certain that he was acquainted with a substantial part of them. Scholars are usually ill at ease with the question of sources, because sources are generally studied for two purposes: to establish an antecedent for the figurative substance used in a certain work, or to reconstruct the cultural background of a certain author. In either case, scholars tend to assume an apologetical attitude. Especially when it comes to establishing the antecedents of figurative substance, they usually fear that the uncovering of sources may detract from the originality of their author, since originality is commonly equated with inventiveness, creation *ex nihilo*.

But, as we know, artists, especially great ones, work on material which tradition hands down to them. Their greatness lies in the degree to which they succeed in changing the figurative or conceptual endowment they receive from tradition, and in giving it, in the process, new meaning. Lesser artists limit themselves to handing down to new generations the patrimony they received, with minor alterations. This is why the study of sources represents an important analytical tool in literary criticism.

In restructuring the figurative material received from tradition, Boccaccio takes as the point of departure for his thematic opposition not the unfaltering chastity of Devasmitâ or the lust of Helinandus's adulteress, but rather the disdainful indifference of the Minyads. Similarly, he transforms the lust of the lovers into sincere love. He then resumes the alternation of the two thematic courses developed in the apologue of the Indian go-between: the punished chastity in the story of Guido degli Anastagi, the rewarded loss of chastity in the story of Nastagio degli Onesti. He maintains the eschatological dimension already present in the Indian as well as the medieval tradition, specifically adopting the double level from Helinandus's type. The point of projection of the whole narration is thus no longer synchretized to the female, but to the male character, Nastagio. This substitution allows him to achieve a higher degree of tension between *fabula* and *plot* and therefore a very interesting narrative structure. The chrono-topological order of the *fabula*, in fact, is the following:

Guido degli Anastagi from Ravenna loves a girl who remains indifferent to his love. Seized by desperation, the young man kills himself and is sentenced to hell. Soon after, the girl he loved also dies and, because of her insensitivity, she is sentenced to be daily persecuted and dismembered by the man who had loved her in life for as many years as there were months when she persisted in her cruel indifference. Another young man from Ravenna, Nastagio, later finds himself in a similar situation to Guido's. One day he happens to witness the tragic chase, and, seized by an impulse of generosity, rushes to the aid of the victim. But he is dissuaded by the persecutor, who tells his own story. Nastagio then conceives the idea to have the girl he loves witness the infernal vision, which takes place every Friday at the same place. The girl and her family witness the fiendish chase; some of them attempt to help the victim, but they too are stopped by the knight who tells everyone his sad story. Following this vision, the girl whom Nastagio loves has a change of heart and decides to accept his love and become his wife.

Boccaccio was obviously free to follow the order of the *fabula*, as he actually does in other cases. The result would have been an altogether different story with a different meaning. In narration, though, plot cannot be considered an arbitrary re-organization of the componential elements of the *fabula*, or as simply responding to an undefined creative freedom; rather, it constitutes the very basis of signification. Plot structures must therefore be considered as the fundamental structures of a narrative text, to which all other elements are subordinate.

In radically restructuring the components of the *fabula*, Boccaccio obtains three narrative units inserted one within the other, like Chinese boxes. We have the story of Nastagio degli Onesti, which contains the story of the girl's punishment, which in turn contains the story of the unhappy love of Guido degli Anastagi. The relationships among these three units maintain the reflexivity of the relations between the two levels of the chaste-bitch story and the mirror-like reflection of the two levels in the Helinandus type. The third unit (the story of Guido degli Anastagi) is developed as a reflexive structure of the first unit (the story of Nastagio): the two women and the two men are built on identical ethical characters and figures.[30] Guido degli Anastagi kills himself; Nastagio conceives the determination to kill himself; the first name Nastagio becomes the family name of Guido degli Anastagi.[31] By the alteration in the denouement (which Boccaccio takes from the story of the chaste-bitch), Nastagio will marry the girl he loves, whereas Guido can never marry his.

The second unit, telling the chase of the hated-beloved by the lover-hater, is structured as a mirror-like reflection of the two other units through the transformation of the opposition "love generating hope" into a contradictory one, "desperation generating hatred." In the concomitant transformation, the conquest of the heart of the beloved as symbol of love turns into the conquest of the heart of the beloved as flesh to be fed to the mastiffs. This mirror-like reflection is reiterated in the tale's spatial movement. Guido degli Anastagi's ritual moves from its own eschatological dimension to the pine woods of Chiassi, while the story of Nastagio moves from the urban dimension of Ravenna to the woods of Chiassi, a place favorable to visions[32] and closer to the eschatological dimension, as Dante (*Purgatorio* XXVII, 1–28) reminded Boccaccio.[33] Indeed, what other meaning could there be for the movement of Nastagio, who leaves Ravenna "accompanied by a multitude of friends and great equipment, as if he intended to go to France or Spain or to any other distant country," and stops instead three miles from the city?

What we have here is then a "chase of love" and of its contrary, narrated in three modalities which reflect each other in a progressive "mise en abîme" of an identical figurative motif. Since the infernal interlude occurs twice in the narration, it would seem that the story of Nastagio's love is divided into three parts. During the first occurrence, the vision is represented in detail as an autonomous unit interrupting Nastagio's own story; in the second, it is incorporated into the basic narrative texture, which is not interrupted. Nastagio's narrative unit is therefore split in two parts: the first one, disphoric in intonation, narrating the events leading to the crumbling of his hopes; the second, euphoric, narrating his renewed hopes and the measure he takes to prepare for his final success.

Between these two parts we find the second unit, narrating the pursuit of the girl. The narration of the fierce ritual in which the insensitive heart is transformed into feed for dogs is also broken into two parts: the generous but naive intervention of Nastagio stops the sword already lifted against the victim. Each young man recognizes his own image in the face of the other: "I am of the same city as yourself, and you were still a little child when I . . . was more deeply in love with this woman than you are now with your Traversari." The interruption breaks the story further into two distinct parts: in the first we find the euphoric chasing after the prey until she is seized, while in the second we see Nastagio witness the cruel laceration of the once beloved. Here again, between the two parts, the third unit is inserted, narrating the defeat of Guido in the first person. The two parts of this third unit—the disphoric desperation of the lover and the euphoric revenge—are mediated, at their very center, by the suicide of Guido. His death explains the revenge, while his story in its entirety explains and gives sense to the macabre chase among the pines. The chase, in turn, mediates and connects the two broken parts of Nastagio's story.

Therefore death, self-destruction, conceived by Nastagio *in pectore* and contemplated by him among the pine woods of Chiassi, is the central mediating element of the entire novella, the element that changes Nastagio's love story by inspiring him with the solution that will regenerate his feelings and those of his beloved. It is the ultimate transformation, by which death becomes the source of life.

To each of these three narrative units a different temporal value is attached: the story of Nastagio is immersed in the historical present; the chase is atemporal, like the eschatological dimension in which it takes place; the unfortunate story of Guido is immersed in a past so remote that the memory of the bystanders can hardly reach it.[34] This past, however, like the suicide at its center, acquires a symbolic value and an exemplary validity which extend over the totality of the future. It is this exemplary validity that finally convinces the daughter of Paolo Traversari to change heart and accept Nastagio's love.

The acceptance of love represents, then, the point of arrival for the thematic course. The negation of chastity is therefore not advocated in the name of a sensual law of nature, nor in the name of the god, nor yet as submission to his will. Mediated as it is by the negation of death, the negation of chastity is brought about by the affirmation of human love which is, simultaneously, an affirmation of life. Moreover, since such an affirmation can hardly be conceived within the axiological values of the medieval mind, it also signals the dawn of a new age.[35] At the end of the story, the return to Ravenna, leaving behind the indefinite green space of the pine woods, means for Nastagio the victory of sentiment over indifference. But such a victory could not have been possible without the celebration of the ritual of hatred and death among the pines and could not have been conceived without the celebration of the death and resurrection of love. Thus it also means the victory of life over death.

7

From Fin Amour to Friendship: Dante's Transformation

Early in the *Commedia*, Dante rejects *fin amour* to the extent that it involves adultery. His persona meets Paolo and Francesca da Rimini in Hell among other carnal sinners. The couple has been damned presumably for having indulged in extramarital love. Their action resulted, as Francesca relates, from their having imitated a version of the Old French *Lancelot du Lac*. Married by proxy to a cruel and deformed husband, she had sought to replace the ugliness that she saw with the beauty of art. Her language in relating the experience is reflective of good breeding, courtesy, wide reading, and graciousness. Her answers to the persona's various requests and summons are generous, even though for her to answer "is to remember past happiness in present grief" (*Inferno* 5:122–23). Vital to "the very root" and course of their love are three tercets which begin with the word "Amor":

> "Amor, che al cor gentil ratto s'apprende,
> Prese costui della bella persona
> Che mi fu tolta, e il modo ancor m'offende.
> Amor, che a nullo amato amar perdona,
> Mi prese del costui piacer sì forte,
> Che, come vedi, ancor non mi abbandona.
> Amor condusse noi ad una morte:
> Caino attende chi vita ci spense."
> Queste parole da lor ci fur porte.
> [5:100–09]

The first tercet reveals Paolo's initial reaction to Francesca and, with its inclusion of "cor gentil," evokes the poetry of Guido Guinizelli: "Amor, che al cor gentil ratto s'apprende" ("Love, which is quickly caught in the noble heart"). It establishes Paolo's worth and indicates that, instead of responding to virtue as lovers do in Guinizelli's verse, he responds to her person ("bella persona"). Francesca's own response, which occupies the next tercet, is similarly directed to physical appearance, a delight in his person that yet moves her. Fused, the couple is then led by Love into the "one death" at her husband's hand that sets them in Hell. Her explanation is not their misperception or misunderstanding of true love, but their having been swayed by the fictional Lancelot's kissing Guinivere into betrayal. Couched in moral as well as literary allusion, the episode warns jointly of literature's ability to corrupt, the inability of Hell's inhabitants to know really why they are there, and, in the persona's response, the poet's lingering attachment to aspects of courtly love.[1]

This attachment to the Provençal lyric and aspects of courtly love has been especially noted by scholars of Dante's early lyrics and *The Vita Nuova*. They have seen the attachment in the poems' sensitive appeals, in the recourses to common phrases, scenes, and reactions, and in the figure of Love which appears in *The Vita Nuova* to assist the action. However, they point out that adultery changes in Dante's hand into moral reformation and the external progress of love that occurs in Provençal lyrics becomes internal.[2] From this perspective, *The Vita Nuova* begins in troubadour fashion with the address of the work's first sonnet to "every captive soul and gentle lover." The address takes the meeting with Beatrice out of the solitude of the bedchamber into the arena of social discussion that typifies troubadour behavior. This behavior extends with the work's "screen ladies" into a troubadour "rule of secrecy" that ends with gossip and Beatrice's eventual snub (Chapter X). The work then moves to Guinizellian concepts of the lover and a debate between Cavalcantian and Guinizellian positions of Love's harmful and beneficial nature. The "debate" lasts through Chapters XVII and XVIII and Dante's decision to "take up a new and nobler theme than before" and the revelation that "many people had guessed from [his] appearance the secret of [his] heart." No longer having to keep a rule of secrecy, he composes the canzone that Bonagiunta identifies in the *Purgatorio* as the beginning of the *dolce stil novo* (24:49–51) and which moves the abode of Love from *mente* to *intelletto* and makes possible the "rational" religious turn on which the book ends. This turn forces Dante to write no more on Beatrice until he can do so "more worthily" in the hope of then composing "concerning her what has never been written in rhyme on any woman" (Chapter XLII). If the Beatrice of the book is, in fact, Beatrice dei Portinari, she would have been married, and in courtly love fashion, the poet through much of the work is weighing sin.

This attachment to aspects of courtly love and the Provençal lyric is also part of Dante's early prose study on language, *De Vulgari Eloquentia*. Concurring with statements in *The Vita Nuova* that composition in one's native language "was invented from the beginning for the purpose of writing of love" and that his writing in the vernacular was part of a wish "to make his verses intelligible to a lady who found it difficult to understand Latin" (Chapter XXV), Dante uses love and the Provençal lyric to support and illustrate a division of late Latin into the poetries of *oc, sì,* and *oïl* (1.9.3). Thibaut de Champagne announces that out of *fin amour* arise "wisdom and goodness" ("De fin'amour si vient sèn et bonté"), and Guinizelli makes love and the noble heart one and inseparable ("Nè fe'amor prima che gentil core, / nè gentil cor prima che amor"). Dante goes on to cite other examples of love from the works of Guido della Colonne, Giacomo da Lentini, Rinaldo d'Aquino, Guido Ghisilieri, Fabruzzo, Onesto degli Onesti, and Guido Cavalcanti and to single out Arnaut Daniel and Cino da Pistoia in particular as poets who appeal to man's animal soul by writing on love (2.2.9). One learns from the citations of Rinaldo and Guinizelli that, in addition to "wisdom and goodness," *fin amour* brings about "joy" ("Per fino amore vo si letamente") and "joy and happiness" ("gioia ed allegranza"). But the subsequent allusion to Guinizelli by Francesca (*Inferno* 5:100) and his inclusion with Daniel among the penitent lustful in Purgatory (Canto 26) lead one again to feel a discouragement with and evolution beyond the doctrines of *fin amour*. The placement of Guinizelli and Daniel among the bestial seems to occur because Dante decides that, in seeking consummation outside the laws of marriage, their love severs men from reason and leaves them in use only of their sensitive natures (*Convivio* 2.7.3–4).

Indeed, the dispositions of Paolo and Francesca and Guinizelli and Daniel suggest an implicit attitude toward marriage critically at odds with that of the Provençal lyric and courtly love. As part of an emphasis on freedom, both the Provençal lyric and courtly love had distinguished love from *maritalis affectio*, arguing—as Cicero had for friendship and blood kinship—that love not be obligatory but personal and subject to choice and, hence, conducive to virtue. By the end of the twelfth century, the widespread beliefs that *maritalis affectio* did not necessarily exclude love and could also further virtue and salvation helped in turning marriage into a sacrament, and it seems that in the *Convivio* and the *Purgatorio* the beliefs are part of Dante's mature view. In the *Convivio*, he does not see marriage's domestic tie as an obstacle to the true religious life, "for God does not require us to be professed save in heart" (4.28.65–74), and in the *Purgatorio*, he numbers "women and husbands" among the chaste, "as virtue and marriage require of us" (25.134–35). Moreover, it is clear that, if the events of the *Commedia* are meant to be autobiographical, Dante sees his own spiritual development in terms of a constant bond with the memory of Beatrice which, however initially close to violating the sixth and ninth commandments, comes to resemble a "mystical marriage." Rather than God, memory of her provides an almost continual presence, transforms his higher faculties in respect to their mode of operation, and supplies the habitual mental image of virtue. It furnishes the rational force that Nino de' Visconti finds lacking in the sensitive leanings of his wife who, after his death, is not able to preserve the fire of love, "if eye and touch do not often rekindle it" (8:70–78). Based like the Provençal lyric and courtly love on man's sensitive nature (*De Vulgari Eloquentia* 2.2.6), her reaction cannot support his climb up Purgatory and seems resistant to any help that he may be able to provide from a vantage place in eternity.

The positive elements of the Provençal lyric and courtly love that Dante subscribes to in these early works are their beliefs in the ennobling force of human love, the beloved's superiority to the lover, and love's emergence as an unsatiated, ever increasing desire. Supporting these elements are other ancillary features which, although present in Provençal poetry and courtly love, have parallels and analogues in classical literature, medical lore, and medieval Latin and Arabic love traditions. Love, for example, continues to appear as he does in Roman literature as an irresistible god whom lovers serve and obey and who aids them in their efforts. The cause of love remains beauty, which passes through the eye into the heart and there inflicts its wound. Its occurrence is sudden, and it is followed by the lover's total preoccupation with the lady. Physically afflicted, the lover grows pallid and weak and lapses into sighs and fits of weeping. The lady's initial coolness increases his suffering, and any signs of warmth fall on him like a blessing. She becomes the source of his joy and efforts toward improvement. Often, as an aspect of Love, her beauty elevates all who approach her and, at times, overwhelms the lover. Nonetheless, her identity must be protected, prompting, when necessary, the pretense of loving others (screen ladies). Indeed, it is courtly love's sensitive response to human qualities that enlists Beatrice's complaint of inconstancy in *The Vita Nuova*. After her death, human beauty prompts the poet's love for a "donna gentile" (Chapters XXXV–XXXVIII) that in Chapter XXXIX Beatrice returns "in glory" to stop. She redirects the young poet away from "the desire by which [his heart] had so basely allowed itself to be possessed . . . against the constancy of reason."

In *The Heresy of Courtly Love* (1947), A. J. Denomy argues the amorality of courtly love and its inappropriateness for Christian culture. He sees Andreas Capellanus's exposition of it in the first two books of *De Amore* on natural grounds and his moral rejection of it in the third book—the *De Reprobatione Amoris*—as contradictory. For Denomy, they anticipate Beatrice's complaint and Dante's treatment of Paolo and Francesca. It simply will not work, he says, to assign "to the lower soul a role of partnership with the rational soul whereby love of external beauty, sexual love, serve[s] as an aid in approaching the divine" and to require the "submission of the animal soul to the rational soul" and "the domination of the rational soul over the animal soul." Francesca is so overwhelmed by emotion and delight in Paolo's person that "the King of the Universe" is not her friend and her delight in Paolo "even now" persists. The division, which Denomy likens to later expositions of Aristotle and Averroes, leads to a view of "double truth," or the existence of two simultaneous different truths: one supported by reason (philosophy), the other supported by revelation (religion). While Dante may have known Andreas's treatise, there is no indication that he ever accepted a view of "double truth" or "as rationally necessary a single philosophical conclusion at variance with Christian dogma or revelation." On March 7, 1277, Bishop Stephen Tempier of Paris condemned such "double truths" along with Andreas's treatise. Dante places one of its practitioners, Siger of Brabant (1235?–c. 1281–84) "in the fourth heaven of the Sun, together with St. Albert the Great and St. Thomas Aquinas" (*Paradiso* 10:136–38). He does not do so for any statements on "double truth" or love, however, but rather because Siger contributed to *De Monarchia* by his having proposed "that theology has no authority over natural morality nor on politics which are founded on natural morality."[3]

Kenelm Foster is more specific about these issues in "Courtly Love and Christianity" (1977). He asserts that "the *emotional* atmosphere of the *De Amore* . . . is quite different . . . from that which Dante evokes in the Francesca episode." Francesca may claim helplessness, but love in *De Amore* "is desire carefully controlled and directed by reason; [the] ideal lover, man or woman, is a *sapiens amator*, one who uses his or her brains all the time." In this regard, Foster sees Andreas's treatise as "a representative document" and "in part an assertion of personal values against a social and juridical order which in some respects had come to appear excessively impersonal." It was "an attempt to vindicate for the sexual impulse an intrinsic value, a potential moral worth apart from its procreative purpose" that was denied by a theology that insisted that "whatever pleasure married people give to and receive from one another, apart from the desire for children, cannot be free from sin." Its frankly "sexual attraction, elevated and refined by reason . . . was not exactly Platonic" and certainly not mystical. Nor was it, as Dante makes love in the *Commedia*, "somehow *dispositive* toward divine love or . . . an *image*, an analogy, of that love." Andreas "has only the paltriest conception of grace—even . . . when he speaks as a theologian" in the "stereotyped and conventional" *De Reprobatione Amoris*.[4] Clearly, Dante's having to deal with different circumstances—notably love which could include a woman already dead—enters in. Coition could no longer be an end or a possible ingredient in denial. Something was needed that would permit constancy and salvation by revealing one's self and making one's soul more like God and, therefore, more like itself.

Étienne Gilson approaches the necessity of this "association of human love with charity" in his discussion of *The Mystical Theology of Saint Bernard* (1940). Noting that Dante chooses Bernard "as his supreme guide toward ecstasy" in the *Paradiso*, he concludes that in the *Commedia* Dante is "evidently under the influence" of Bernard's "sharp opposition to every kind of carnal love" and, hence, to both the concupiscence and the unrequited desire of courtly love. For Bernard, "love belongs to the order of friendship, and friendship essentially implies mutual goodwill," not denial. Gilson finds that what is common to both Cistercian mysticism and courtly love, namely that "the beatifying love goes to the beatifying object itself and for itself, rather than to the joy it gives," has an antecedent in Cicero's *De Amicitia* (44 B.C.). And it seems no accident that friendship dominates the *Convivio*, which acts as Dante's bridge from the *fin amour* in the early lyrics and *The Vita Nuova* to the "disposition toward a certain mystical mode of feeling" that readers later encounter.[5] In Tractates 1 and 3 of the *Convivio*, friendship is used metaphorically to explain how language and philosophy relate to an individual, allowing for a discovery of self and implicitly through that discovery—since man is created in God's likeness—to behavior that is constant and will assist salvation. Although his discussion is based primarily on Aristotle's treatment of friendship in Books 8 and 9 of the *Nicomachean Ethics*, Dante acknowledges having read Cicero's *De Amicitia* after having completed *The Vita Nuova* (2.13.17–22). Cicero, he says, is "in harmony with the opinion of the Philosopher [Aristotle, as it is] set forth in the eighth and ninth books of the *Ethics*" (1.12.19–21).

The qualities of friendship which Dante singles out in the *Convivio* are its universality, its origin in proximity, similarity, and attraction, its link to reciprocal and mutually defining characteristics, and the means of its lasting. Like Aristotle, he acknowledges its natural base (1.1.55–56) and the impossibility of one's having a perfect life without friends (4.25.6–7). He, likewise, agrees that, in uniting opposites, its root lies in utility and, in uniting similars, in pleasure or virtue. However, he does not—as Aristotle does—distinguish friendship from love. In the *Nicomachean Ethics*, love does not always involve mutual affection. It can be one-sided and involve inanimate objects like wine and gold and, therefore, not be called friendship (1155b). By accepting a universe permeated by love and virtue as a gift of God and the root of true friendship, Dante can, like Cicero—for whom virtue is more civic and bred—extend friendship's powers to imaginative abstractions (philosophy) if not to memories of the dead (*De Amicitia* 6.29; 27.102). Dante can also be less concerned than Aristotle with what Aristotle calls unequal friendships, namely those between father and son, husband and wife, man and woman, and master and servant (1158b). He recognizes that in these friendships love is proportional. The better or more useful member receives more love than he gives and, at times, receives differently from what he gives. But by concentrating on virtue, Dante like Cicero believes that "by familiar association," the difference can be lessened (3.1.60–61): the lesser "may enjoy [the greater's] character, equal him in affection, become readier to deserve than to demand his favors, and vie with him in a rivalry of virtue" (*De Amicitia* 9.32). On the part of the lesser—often Dante—unequal friendships lead to advances in virtue and clarifications of will that have implicit in their growths an ideal friendship with God.

Thus, in Canto 2 of the *Inferno*, when Beatrice mentions Dante to Virgil as her "friend, and no friend of fortune" ("l'amico mio, e non della ventura"), and Virgil responds by addressing her

as "O lady of virtue" (2:61 and 76), she sets up a series of references not only to the *Convivio* but to a library of statements on
friendship; besides those in Aristotle and Cicero, these include
statements in the Bible, St. Augustine's *Confessions* (c. 400), and
St. Thomas Aquinas's *Commentary on the Nicomachean Ethics*
(c. 1269). In so doing, she establishes the proper love relationship
against which the improper relations of courtly love and Paolo and
Francesca can be set.

Especially important for understanding the relationship are
statements in Augustine, the Mass, the Bible, Thomas, and the
works of other Church spokesmen. John C. Moore finds in the
Confessions "an order of love, *ordo amoris*," an "idea that creatures should be loved in proportion to their position in the hierarchy of existence." Essential to this order are the view that "created
goodness and beauty help lift one's mind to the creator" and the
second great commandment: that one love one's neighbor as oneself (Matthew 22:39). The death of one of Augustine's friends
echoes in the *Confessions* (4.6.11) Cicero's notion of "true friendship" as "one soul in two bodies." And although he, too, finds
friendship in this world rare, transitory, and insecure, and does not
mention its existence between men and women, Augustine does
make friendship and male and female relationships part of the
peace of the City of God. In this City "self-love and self-will have
no place, but a ministering love that rejoices in the common joy of
all, of hearts makes one, that is to say, secures a perfect concord"
(*The City of God* 15:3).[6] It is this "perfect concord" which the
Christian community invokes at Mass with its *Communicantes*
and *Nobis quoque* prayers, linking it to all the living and the dead,
and which Dante insinuates with Beatrice's identification.

She is in death, as she was in life, superior to Dante. In so
being, she presents the superiority of the beloved in courtly love,
and also evokes Dante's example of disparity in friendship in his
"Letter to Can Grande," namely "friendship with God." Unlike
Francesca and Vanni Fucci, Beatrice is not excluded in the *Inferno*
from the friendship of God (5:91 and 25:4). Nor is she said, like
Ovid's Myrrha (*Metamorphoses* 10:298 sqq.), to have transgressed
the bonds of friendship and rightful love (30:38–39), or to have
proved traitor to friends and guests like the denizens of Dante's
third ring of Hell's final circle (Canto 33). She is, in addition, not
so much desired and denied as initiating the corrective that will
get Dante out of the "woods" in which he finds himself, and that
will allow his eventual accommodation to eternity. In embodying
"exception," Beatrice embodies the Old Testament use of "friend-

ship with God" to identify men who have wisdom and perfectly observe God's laws (Wisdom 7:14 and 27; Judith 8:22; and Exodus 33:11). In the New Testament, their number had been extended by Christ to include his disciples (John 15:14–15), and the Fathers of the Church extended the title "friends of God" to all Christians. Her high status also gains from Dante's subsequent use of disparity in station to explain in the "Letter to Can Grande" the dedication of the *Paradiso* to him in return for his goodwill and gifts. In courtly love as in classical literature, this disparity is compensated for by the lover's promise of a similar immortality through art for the beloved in return for her favors. Dante's having promised to write of Beatrice "what has never been written in rhyme on any woman" at the close of *The Vita Nuova* leads one to suspect at first that this may be what he is doing in the *Commedia*. But only the inhabitants of Hell want fame or obscurity in the world. Those of Purgatory want prayers, and those of Paradise, shared joy in their condition.

A summary of Thomas Aquinas's remarks on friendship in "friendship with God" is useful here. Thomas begins his argument with a review of Aristotle's requisites of "mutual benevolence, mutually known, and based on an honest good." He considers beforehand, however, "accord" and "community." Arguing from things better known "to arrive at a knowledge of things less known," he extends Aristotle's rejection of friendship between man and inanimate objects to animate but irrational creatures. Just as a man cannot be friends with wine or gold, so, too, he cannot be friends with a horse. Accord in friendship means similarity of form. Accord with God is established in man's being created in God's image and likeness (Genesis 1:26–27) and his ability to become assimilated to God through knowledge and love "formally achieved by Grace." Community means "common interests, common life, [and] the participation of common goods." Natural reason, revelation, faith, and prayer provide its means. The mutual benevolence or goodwill "must be habitual and efficacious." It cannot be one-sided or have as its principal motive advantage to oneself. It must, likewise, be mutually known and have goodness as its object. In terms of friendship with God, charity defines the basis of love and divine beatitude defines its object. In loving God, man seeks happiness in that he wishes not happiness for himself but to refer himself and his happiness to God. In desiring and striving to promote God's external glory, he gives to God things which God Himself does not possess. God's gifts to man are many, and grace is what God loves most in man; it constitutes the communication upon which God's friendship is based.[7] Though not "friendship with God," friendship with one already in Paradise takes on aspects and reflections of these qualities.

In using "friend" to identify Beatrice's feelings, Dante would have known as well the views on friendship expressed by Ambrose, Jerome, Cassian, and Aelred of Rievaulx. Early on, Ambrose had redefined virtue in friendship from Cicero's natural aristocratic attribute into something that "humble men and women who embrace poverty and chastity" could acquire. He had made its pursuit accessible to all. It was available to whoever would accept the Gospel and be perfected by God's grace. By example, Jerome had extended the reaches of friendship to male-female associations, and in this extension, he was supported by the model of Christ's friendship with Martha and Mary. The purely male-male bonding that one associates with Cicero was thus muted, though it was argued that male-female friendships were even rarer and more difficult, and were best kept through exchanges of letters. In dealing primarily with cloistered individuals, Cassian turned the idea of friendship's mutual goodwill being rooted in virtue to virtue's inevitably bringing about the mutual goodwill of friendship. If individuals are alike in virtue, said Cassian, friendship results from the affinity, virtue again being the product not of nature but of God's grace. He proposed that obedience and humility promote virtue, and whenever virtue appears, there is love. Behind these modifications and redefinitions are often the same negative reaction to erotic love and bias toward rational friendship that Dante comes to express. Almost in anticipation of Beatrice, Aelred argued in *On Spiritual Friendship* (1160) against those who fear friendship's distracting man from the love of God and his neighbor. Rather than distract, true friendship, he said, is a way to reach God: "The friend, adhering to his friend in the spirit of Christ, is made one heart and one soul with him and so rising up through the stages of love to the friendship of Christ, he is, in one kiss, made one spirit with him."[8]

It is clear that true friendship does not exist in Dante's Hell. Despite the occurrences of paired and grouped souls, accord and virtue are lacking in its inhabitants. As if to underscore their lack, Dante has Hell's souls violate one common tenet of friendship by having companions repeatedly publicize each other's names and faults. The practice is so widespread that in Canto 25, on encountering a group of three Florentines, Dante's persona remarks that "it happened, as usually it happens by some chance, that one had to name another" (25:40–42). The violation points up the discord which is Hell and which its inhabitants endure as part of their discord from God. Nor, one might add, is friendship permitted between Hell's inhabitants and Dante. Such friendship would violate the principle of Aristotelian community in two ways. First, for Christians like Dante, it violates the important community of believers in and servants of God (Augustine's City of God). Hell's inhabitants are not friends of God. Second (and less significant because its rule can be broken) is the community of being. Dante's difference in not being dead is continually singled out. Whereas he may by changing his ways avoid their damnation, Hell's inhabitants are forever damned and consequently without hope. Their lack of hope eliminates mutual benevolence, for mutual benevolence presupposes a hope of change. And however much Dante's persona would like things to be different with Paolo and Francesca or Ser Brunetto or Count Ugolino, their natures will not allow change. Lesser communities like those among poets are possible (4:94–102), but however consoling these communities are for the sense of one's craft, they are no replacement for God. It is no wonder, then, that the word "amico/-ca" occurs only four times in the canticle, and except for Beatrice's use of "amico" to identify her relationship to Dante, it occurs consistently to identify a lack or violation of friendship.

Purgatory is different. It allows the appearance of friendship to occur among its inhabitants and between them and Dante. Accord is conveyed in the group singing that goes on among its inhabitants and in union with Dante's live persona. Goodwill between the living and the dead is, likewise, conveyed in their mutual prayers for one another to amend each other's errors (4:133–36; 6:28–42). Virtue is apparent not only in Cato, who exemplifies it in its classical sense, but as Dante and Virgil climb higher, in the various, increasingly Christian sense of Ambrose. In Canto 11, for example, Provenzan Salvani, in keeping with a classical ideal of sacrifice (*De Amicitia* 7.24), dons the clothes and manner of a beggar to get money to ransom a friend held prisoner by Charles of Anjou (133–38). Again, the basis of community, as the exchange between Cato and Virgil in Canto 1 concerning Marcia affirms, is an acceptance of God. Cato indicates that however pleasing Marcia was to him on earth, now that she dwells "beyond the evil stream," she no longer *by law* moves him (1:85–90). Mutual goodwill and friendship cannot occur. Nor, given honesty's key role in friendship, can Cato accept as friendly Virgil's violation of honesty with flattery (1:92; see also *Inferno* 18:100–36 and *De Amicitia* 26.98–99). Reaffirming this difficulty of friendship with one in

Hell, Virgil later asks of Statius only "the appearance of friendship" (22:19–21). Again, as with Dante's numbering himself among the great writers in the *Inferno*, their basis for community is craft, not virtue. Still, one may argue that Virgil is a special case. His being singled out for the task of guiding Dante through Hell and most of Purgatory suggests special talents, including an ability to get the job done. The bases of these special talents could be his presumed ability to foresee and celebrate Christ's coming in Eclogue 4, his familiarity with Hell in Book 6 of the *Aeneid*, and the high regard in which the Middle Ages held both works.

Purgatory also contains Dante's account of natural love on which both erotic love and friendship are based. The account centers the *Commedia* and serves as a prelude to the persona's encounter with Beatrice in Canto 30. As in *De Amicitia, amicitia* (friendship) derives from *amor* (love) (8.26). Virgil tells Dante that love "responds to everything that is pleasing and awakens by pleasure into activity." One apprehends and inclines toward what is apprehended. Desire results, and it continues until the object inclined to makes one rejoice. Virgil cautions his companion that not everything apprehended and inclined to is necessarily good. Man is aided in determining what is good and directing his desire by "a specific virtue contained within himself" and which is not seen except in its action. Thus, even if an inclination arises from necessity, man has within him the power to arrest its course (*Purgatorio* 18:19–72). In friendship, this desire is toward goodness and what is honorable and comprises man's affection for truth and virtue (*Convivio* 1.12.89–102; 3.3.86–89). Divided into natural and artificial movements, love accorded with one's nature (i.e., natural) cannot be wrong, whereas that accorded with reason can err either through one's choice of what love rationalizes toward or the speed at which it proceeds (*Purgatorio* 17:91–139). The movements do not automatically bring about, as in friendship, the mutuality of a countermovement by the object (*Convivio* 3.11.74–78), since objects of love can be inanimate and irrational. If those involved are similar and virtuous, friendship results in the manner of Cassian by means of virtue's natural appeal. Though he has yet to set aside completely his erotic feelings, the persona has, by traveling through Hell and three terraces of Purgatory, moved significantly toward understanding what friendship requires.

The meeting with Beatrice that occurs in the Earthly Paradise (Canto 30) locates the persona and his object in a place to which neither can lay claim. He is still alive and she resides in Paradise. The meeting climaxes a series of references that confound a desire for her image with a desire for the knowledge that the persona is repeatedly told that she will provide. From his initial reaction, it is clear that a meeting later in some other place would be troubling. However much he recognizes that it was not her physical beauty but her lofty virtue that pierced him when he was younger, his blood trembles and he experiences "signs of the ancient flame" (30:46–48). Coming as the reaction does after the persona's meetings with Guinizelli and Daniel in Canto 26, it indicates the continuing, strong appeal of sensitive memory and *fin amour*. Beatrice's response is to shame him "sternly like a mother her child."

In supplying truths upon which self-discovery and correction can be made, the move is properly within the duties of a friend (*Convivio* 1.2.29–30; 3.10.54–55). Put into the context of the persona's failed potential and possible damnation, her account refocuses on sensitive memory. Her rising from flesh to spirit and undergoing, thereby, an increase in beauty and virtue meet with depreciation, neglect, and a pursuit like Nino's widow of "false visions of good." Nor do efforts like those in Chapter XXXIX of *The Vita Nuova* to call him back succeed. In contrast to his interested trembling, her action is disinterested and concerned with him, not anything that he can give her (30:115–45). She will go further and soon surpass for him her ancient self and reflect Christ's Griffon (31:83 and 112–18), and he will gaze too fixedly at her and again be reproved (32:9). Soon, too, as he rises with her heavenward, he will experience, as Gilson notes, not the denial of *fin amour* but a different and better way to accept her presence.

Affection in Paradise is essentially Thomas's "friendship with God." In Canto 12, the Franciscans Illuminato and Augustine are described as having made themselves friends of God (12:132), and in Canto 25, Dante's persona pronounces hope of redemption in "the souls which God has made his friends" (25:90). To reach this stage of friendship, one passes like Cunizza, Folquet of Marseilles, and others, like Dante, born of amorous temperament and ardent affections, through *fin amour*. As Cunizza tells Dante, she sees the effect of the passage as gain not loss (9:35–36). Her love affair with the troubadour Sordello has been expanded beyond an exclusive association into the broad acts of charity with which she filled her later life and about which Dante may have personally known. So, too, the poet Folquet exchanges the *fin amour* of troubadour poetry for the charity of a Cistercian monk. He, likewise, does not repent his sensitive life and remembers the work that it ultimately brings about (9:103–05).

Their states of recollecting error in present happiness contrast to that of Francesca, who remembers *fin amour* as past happiness in present grief. The meetings act as a reminder that, however inclined toward bestiality or amorous and ardent one's nature is, one also has within him a "specific virtue" which can arrest the excesses of emotion and direct him toward God. This is precisely the intent in permitting Dante's persona to travel through Hell, Purgatory, and Paradise: that he, too, should discover the greater happiness of disinterested rational love and become "a friend of God." Toward this end *fin amour*, as it pertains to his early affection for Beatrice and the "donna gentile," is a gain not a loss, provided that it prompts the penitence of Guinizelli and Daniel and leads beyond the good works of Cunizza and Folquet to real love of God. For this end even Beatrice's memory proves distracting, as she gives way to Saint Bernard. The persona must cease following her beauty in poetry (30:28–33) and, to quiet his sensitive nature, accept her return to "the circle third from the highest rank" (31:67–69).

The function of Beatrice in the *Commedia* is thus made clear. As a friend, she reflects the truth of Dante's persona, and in doing so, she assists him in knowing himself (*De Amicitia* 6.23). She is intimate ("distinto") and being intimate, part of their one will (*Convivio* 1.6.35 and 46). Her goodness begets love and inspires in him the love of others. This prompts his will and pleasure to so attend her that unlikeness is reduced to likeness; and as likeness to one's self emerges through likeness to her, so, too, does a likeness to God (*Convivio* 1.12.100–02; 2.2.21–22; and 3.1.60–61). Her superior morality and beauty command constancy and his proper behavior before her death (*Purgatorio* 30:121–23), and guide his song both in life and death (*Paradiso* 30:28–30). Her loyalty in not abandoning him after his fall provides hope for his capacity to reform. As an element in and instrument of God's purpose, she is part of the Communion of Saints, and as such, she is part of one mystical body with Christ as its head. She intercedes for penitent Christians on earth because what is of interest to one part of this body is of interest to the rest, and each helps the rest. She acts in the poem initially as a messenger of the Virgin Mary to Virgil to aid in Dante's reformation, and then as the persona's guide to the Earthly and the Celestial Paradise. It is through her that he acknowledges remorse and then comes to perceive the Celestial Paradise, just as it is through her that he sees the truth of his nature. Both are seen by him as reflections. She thus comes to represent the light of grace (*lumen gratiae*) to Virgil's natural light (*lumen naturale*) and God's light and Glory (*lumen gloriae*). She is the image of rational love by which the persona comes to understand the love of God, and which he must attain for salvation. As such, she is both a desensitizing example of how to view the universe through the love of God and also a memory token awakening the desire for such vision.

Moreover, just as the love that Beatrice embodies in the *Commedia* is different from the *fin amour* on which Dante's ideas of love begin, so, too, the friendship which she represents is different from the friendships that he writes of in regard to Cavalcanti, the addressee of Epistle 9, Can Grande, and Philosophy. The first three of these friends are live people and the friendships involved are based variously on pleasure and utility. In *The Vita Nuova* (Chapters III, XXIV, XXV, and XXX), Dante calls Cavalcanti his "closest friend" ("il principio dell'amistà" and "il mio primo amico"); it appears that they enjoyed each other's company and that Dante learned much about writing and life from the wealthier Cavalcanti. Still, during Dante's priorate, when it was decided to send the leaders of both the White and Black factions of the Guelf Party into exile, Dante did not prevent Cavalcanti's being exiled to Sarzana where he contracted the malaria from which he died shortly afterward. It is true that the actual exile was only a few weeks and that there was no foreknowing that he would contract malaria; nonetheless, the models of friendship in Cicero's *De Amicitia* (7.24) and his own *Purgatorio* (11:133–38) suggest that he should have taken some action to prevent the exile. The addressee of Epistle 9 is unknown, though it appears that he and Dante were related and that he was a priest. In it, Dante thanks him for his help but rejects the conditions of the pardon upon which he himself may return to Florence. Can Grande's gifts and assistance have already been mentioned. Dante considers the friendship utilitarian, though his admiration for Can Grande is apparent in Canto 17 of the *Paradiso*, where he celebrates Can Grande's warlike exploits, indifference to money and work, and magnificent bounty (17:78–86). Can Grande is also thought by scholars to be the greyhound of the *Inferno* (1:101–11) and possibly the DXV of the *Purgatorio* (33:43–45).

Philosophy poses special problems for the question of friendship. Dante identifies her origin in the *Convivio* as a real woman and the same woman that he mentions in *The Vita Nuova* (*Convivio* 2.2.8–45). Scholars are skeptical, however, especially since Dante also says in the *Convivio* (2.13.40) that she is Philosophy "made in the likeness of a gentle Lady" ("fatta come una Donna gentile"). There are differences between these fictional women. The woman of *The Vita Nuova* inspires base reactions and is the adversary of reason. She incurs the poet's scorn. The woman of the *Convivio* is noble and, although not superior to Beatrice, she does represent wisdom. This wisdom makes possible the love of Divine Wisdom and tends toward true happiness. But Dante makes clear in *De Monarchia* that its end is "the bliss of this life" as opposed to the revelation which attains "the bliss of eternal life" (3.16). As a real woman, she is capable of friendship; as a symbol, she is inanimate. Although capable of evoking metaphors of friendship, she is incapable, according to Aristotle and Thomas, of true friendship.

Problems of community and mutual goodwill, mutually known, abound. Being an invention of man, Philosophy differs as well from Beatrice, who as a creature of God has a life in eternity beyond her time on earth. Being an active member of the Communion of Saints, Beatrice has the potential for community and mutual goodwill, mutually known, despite whatever symbolic significance she may also assume.[9] So, when Dante says in the *Convivio* that he has become the friend of Philosophy ("amico di questa donna"), he means that he began "to love and hate in accordance with her love and hatred," i.e., "to love the followers of truth and to hate the followers of error and falsehood" (4.1.13–24). He participates in what Aristotle would—because of its onesidedness—call love, although in the *Convivio* (3.11.126–27) Dante argues an all-consuming "friendly" goodwill on the part of philosophy toward its practitioners that in the *Purgatorio* he has Beatrice condemn as "false visions of good" (30:131).

Scholars have seized too upon the rhetorical antithesis of Beatrice's pronouncement of friendship to suggest an antithesis between what she symbolizes and "ventura" or Fortune. In his notes to the *Inferno*, Charles Singleton reprints a medieval illumination of a world ruled by Sapience and Fortune, as if Beatrice in death were, indeed, Dante's version of *sapientia creata*. Howard R. Patch cites Virtue as a Roman alternative to Wisdom in controlling Fortune, and Virgil's addressing Beatrice as "O lady of virtue" (*Inferno* 2:76) lends weight to it as an alternate possibility. Dante's Fortune proper, however, as readers of the *Inferno* know, is like Beatrice, part of a divine order (7:67–96). She is "in bliss . . . with the other primal creatures" and "entirely subservient to the Christian God."[10] One suspects, then, that however much "ventura" and "fortuna" are interchangeable in the Middle Ages, Dante means them to be different in Beatrice's statement. "Ventura" appears to mean "chance," either as a real possibility in a God-ordered universe or as a misperception of divine order. As such, it approximates philosophical truth at odds with revelation in an instance of "double truth" like that advanced by critics for Andreas's *De Amore* and proposed by Siger. In these circumstances, there is no question of Beatrice's being an opposite. But, again, as with Philosophy, can Fortune really engage in friendship? Does one not have again friendship used metaphorically, based on the presence of a few personified characteristics? How does Fortune, for example, relate to rationality or community and mutual goodwill, mutually known? And, since Beatrice's statement is in the negative, how is one to regard a person's not being friendly with an agent with whom it is in fact impossible to be friends? Indeed, what does not being Fortune's friend mean; except again to convey significance and the importance of Dante's being Beatrice's friend in the work's unfolding?

There are other friends, for example the relative of the lady for whom Dante writes the sonnet of Chapter XXXII of *The Vita Nuova*, Cino da Pistoia, the unspecified *amici*. But it is safe to say that Dante's dominant friendship is with Beatrice because it assists him in knowing himself and achieving friendship with God. It is clear, especially in Chapter XXIX of *The Vita Nuova*, that for this purpose she is endowed with qualities others do not have. Still, if, as critics claim, the *fin amour* which is so much a part of the early stages of Dante's knowledge is also part of a move surfacing in the twelfth century to expand the existing world view to include nature, then Dante's final emphasis on friendship can be taken as part of a further expansion. Moves toward it can be seen in the rebuffs of *The Vita Nuova* (Chapters X and XXXIX) and the *Purgatorio* (Canto 30) and in the persona's acknowledgments before being bathed in the waters of Lethe of his persisting sensitive memory and fault in turning from Beatrice. Support for it can be seen not only in a clerical distrust of erotic emotion and the mysticism of Bernard but also in the writings of the Cistercian Joachim of Fiore (*Paradiso* 12:140) who, in foreseeing imminent world end, saw also man's spirit being regenerated by the appearance of two new religious orders in the thirteenth century. Much as Christ's birth had required a special worldly order associated with Virgil and the *pax Romana* of Augustus, so, too, a special worldly order associated with a new Virgil and emperor was needed for Christ's return. To the extent that this new order aimed for "friendship with God," it would transcend rationality for the direct vision which, with the help of Bernard, the persona begins to exercise in the closing cantos of the *Paradiso*. That the new order never came about is history. Nonetheless, it represents Dante's last answer to *fin amour*.

8

Faithful Translations:
Love and the Question of Poetry in Chaucer

In the Prologue to *The Legend of Good Women*, Chaucer makes one of the most important statements about his art and his poetic materials. Like his other critical statements, this one is embedded in characterization, rhetorical address, poetic themes, and narrative action. The poet dreams that he lies in a meadow on a May morning, contemplating the daisy, when the God of Love approaches, leading Queen Alceste and nineteen attending ladies. As Cupid passes, he notices the poet observing his regal court and leaves him anticipating the "drede of Loves wordes and his chere."[1] Cupid's procession enters the meadow, kneels on the soft grass, and honors the daisy as a figure of the "trouthe of womanhede" (297). The noble company seats itself in a circle, arranged according to the decorum of social rank, but it soon transforms from a love court to a law court in which Chaucer's poetry is subject to judgment. The god charges the poet as "thow my foo" (G: "my mortal fo"), and says, "al my folk werreyest, / And of myn olde servauntes thow mysseyest, / And hynderest hem with thy translacioun" (322–24).[2] In the logic of the analogy between the love court and the law court, Chaucer stands accused of two related ecclesiastical offenses—"heresye ayeins my lawe (330)" and apostasy: "thou reneyed hast my lay" (336).

The instrument of the poet's alleged disloyalty is translation. The etymology of *translation* is rich in meanings, and the term carried rhetorical, ecclesiastical, and doctrinal significations in Chaucer's day. Two primary meanings are evidently intended in this scene—"the action or process of turning from one language to another" and "transformation, alteration, change."[3] It was for translation in both these senses that the French poet Eustache Deschamps had lavishly praised Chaucer in a balade sent to the poet in 1386.[4] Cupid contends, however, that by the act of poetic rendering Chaucer has carried transformation and adaptation to the point of trespass.[5] The poet, he says, has betrayed his service to love by translating the *Roman de la Rose* "in pleyn text, withouten nede of glose" (328) and by writing of Criseyde "as the lyste" (332). Translating the *Rose*, he goes on to say, has made "wise folk" withdraw from love; translating Boccaccio has made men trust women less.

This confrontation with Cupid is a scene of dramatized aesthetic assessment, and scholars like Robert O. Payne and Robert Worth Frank, Jr., have taught us to read it as a self-conscious summation of the early and middle phases of Chaucer's poetic career.[6] The scene gives a special prominence to the motifs of disclosure and scandal. Chaucer's persona is the author of his own accusatory dream which begins with an elaborately contrived specular moment: he has Cupid discover him observing the court "to knowen what this peple mente" (309). The dreamer seeks to learn their intentions; ironically, his intentions have become the legal issue. At a conceptual and thematic level, then, the social and literary texts are related symbolically, for the aims of Love's court are revealed and displayed as openly as the meaning of the texts that Chaucer has done into English from French and Italian writers. The G text accentuates this sense of disclosure: "Hast thow nat mad in Englysh ek the book / How that Crisseyde Troylus forsok, / In shewynge how that wemen han don mis?" (264–66). By focusing on translation as the poet's act of disaffection, Cupid defines one of Chaucer's essential creative activities as a model of betrayal—indeed, a double betrayal, of love and the materials of the poet's art. He reduces Deschamps's estimate ("Grant translateur, noble Geffroy Chaucier") to the formula *traduttore-traditore*, and he means by this reduction to subordinate poetry to love as a determining social value.

The poet-dreamer finds in Queen Alceste a capable and forceful advocate in this trial; she sues for mercy and reminds Cupid that the poet, "Al be hit that he kan nat wel endite" (414), has nonetheless made "lewed folk delyte / To serve yow, in preysinge of your name" (415–16). As evidence of this dedicated service she adduces the corpus of early dream poems (*Book of the Duchess, House of Fame, Parliament of Fowls*) and the "little known" story of "the love of Palamon and Arcite / of Thebes," which is usually taken to mean an early version of the *Knight's Tale*, if not the actual text in the *Canterbury Tales*. Alceste's defense does nothing, of course, to refute Cupid's charges; it seeks "grace" rather than exculpation.[7] Alceste asserts the dreamer's good intentions or at least his absence of malice. But in doing so, she allows translation to remain an ambiguous and problematic form of poetic discourse: "he useth thynges [G: bokes] for to make; / Hym rekketh noght of what matere he take" (F 364–65).

This disavowal of responsibility, which is at the same time a negation of authorship and reading, presents two crucial oppositions within which Chaucer writes about love and its subsidiary themes of marriage, sexuality, and friendship. From a compositional standpoint, *making* (fashioning verse in a technical sense) stands opposed to *enditing* (creating an original poem), while the audience for Chaucer's poetry divides between the "wise folk" who withdraw from Cupid because of the translations and the "lewed folk" who are drawn to serve love by means of poetic fabrication.[8] In the judicial debate between Cupid and Alceste, an implied proportion seems to govern the way in which Chaucer's main poetic works should be read: "making" is directed to "wise folk" as "enditing" is directed to "lewed folk."

I have begun with this Prologue because it represents the social and artistic contexts of Chaucer's writing. All his poetry before the *Canterbury Tales* is directed to the court. The Prologue dramatizes a reading of Chaucer's poems that seems to privilege their social over their artistic meaning. Cupid argues the primacy of the social text. On this view, love is an ideology and social practice that necessarily defines the meaning of poetic works; it informs those "thynges" that a poet "makes." At a semantic level, the social text, poetic making, and "wise folk" are all connected. The defense of his artistry that Chaucer reflexively marshals in the Prologue is more oblique than Cupid's formulation—and at the same time truer, I think, to its aesthetic commitments. Chaucer defends the poetic text by representing and subverting the appropriation of poetry to social purposes.[9] Cupid charges the poet with heresy and apostasy, but, as Lisa Kiser remarks, "He has badly misread the *Troilus* and the *Romaunt of the Rose*" (p. 77). The dreamer distinguishes "what so myn auctour mente" (470) from his own "menynge" (474), which ostensibly furthers love in more ample terms than the God of Love envisions:

> . . . yt was myn entente
> To forthren trouthe in love and yt cheryce,
> And to ben war fro falsnesse and fro vice
> By swich ensample; this was my menynge.
> [471–74]

Even Alceste's precisely delineated taxonomy of the poet's works subverts the social appropriation of poetry. She proposes that the narrative love poems remain apart from the offending translations, on the one hand, and, on the other, from the lyrics and "other holynesse" (424), which consists of doctrinal works that Chaucer had translated from Latin. Yet the love poems, too, are works of translation, drawing freely from the French and Italian authors whom Cupid rejects and using these sources to "make the bookes" that supposedly praise Cupid's name.

Thus we find an alternative to Cupid's formulation. If the social text "makes" for the benefit of "wise folk," the poetic text "endites" for "lewed folk." And it operates, as my title suggests, through faithful translations. By way of example, I want to examine two specimens of such writing from the list Alceste enumerates and then return briefly to the kind of writing Cupid presumably expects in the *Legend*. A careful reading of all three may reveal the wisdom directed to the "lewed folk."

In the *Book of the Duchess*, Chaucer gives a normative view of love which is shaped by retrospect and designed to idealize sentiment, social values, and the virtue of love. The poem, as John Lawlor says, portrays the "attainment of the highest earthly good."[10] The general occasion is the death of Blanche, the wife of Chaucer's patron John of Gaunt, the Duke of Lancaster. John is represented by the grieving figure of a man in black, whom the poet-dreamer stumbles on while following an allegorical "herthuntyng" (1313). It is a much-debated issue whether the dreamer is aware of Blanche's death and consequently whether he is simple-minded and obtuse or cunningly therapeutic in leading the man in black to explain his sorrow and recount the history of his love affair with "goode fair White." For our purpose, though, the issue is not Chaucer's persona, but the formulation given to what many informed readers have regarded as a paradigm of late medieval "courtly love."

How, then, does the man in black construct his love affair? He recounts a tale that shows his realization of his innate capacities within the protocols and norms of courtly service to a lady. His history unfolds over three defining elements—his subjective experience as a lover, the lady's position as an object of desire, and the social codes that bring the two of them into relation. Furthermore, his account locates his history as a lover within a framework of philosophical and aesthetic terms. Describing himself "in my firste youthe" (799), the man in black connects erotic self-definition to questions of knowledge. He has been a "tributarye"

and the "thral" to love ever since he has had "any maner wyt" or
"kyndely understondyng / To comprehende, in any thyng, / What
love was" (761–63). His "servage" to Love entails the organization
of all his faculties—"good wille, body, hert, and al" (768). And yet
we are told this wilful dedication is a kind of erotic preconscious,
an indeterminate period ("longe, and many a yer," 775) given over
to pleasing Love and worshipping a "lady dere" who remains
unidentified and undifferentiated, a generic courtly lady. Throughout this phase of his service the lover himself remains unshaped
and unaware:

> Paraunter I was therto most able,
> As a whit wal or a table,
> For hit ys redy to cacche and take
> Al that men wil theryn make,
> Whethir so men wil portreye or peynte,
> Be the werkes never so queynte.
>
> [779–84]

His description of himself here as a *tabula rasa* draws on the imagery of memory developed in Plato (*Theaetetus* 191 D,E) and Aristotle (*On Memory and Recollection* 450 a1–b15). It is related as
well to Stoic conceptions of the soul.[11] In its poetic effect, Chaucer's use of the imagery conveys the absence of purpose and specific intention in love. Action is insubstantial, thought unstable
and capricious: "al my werkes were flyttynge / That tyme, and al
my thoght varyinge" (801–2). Consequently, there is no principle
of ethical discrimination to guide the lover and inform his knowledge of erotic experience: "Al were to me ylyche good" (803).

It has been noted that the lover's description of himself in
this condition is "thoroughly conventional," amalgamating passages from the *Roman de la Rose* and Guillaume de Machaut's
Remede de Fortune and *Le Jugement dou Roy de Behaingne*.[12]
Machaut is the proximate source, for example, for the imagery of
the *tabula rasa* incorporated in the black knight's self-portrait.
Nonetheless, there are new emphases in Chaucer's translation of
the sources. Unlike the dreamer in the *Roman de la Rose* who asserts Love's domination of him and restricts the effects of individual will, the black knight focuses on his own volition in serving
love. Chaucer concentrates on one of the two images (mirror and
wax seal) used by Machaut to describe cognitive processes.

> Car le droit estaat d'innocence
> Rassamble proprement la table

Blanche, polie, qui est able
A recevoir, sans nul contraire,
Ce qu'on y vuet pendre et portraire;
Et est aussi comme la cire
Qui sueffre dedens li escrire,
Ou qui retient fourme ou empreinte,
Si comme on l'a en li empreinte.[13]

The prominence assigned to will and the structure given to the philosophical terms represent Chaucer's additions in translating the received materials. The man in black also speaks of love in explicitly aesthetic terms: "I ches love to my firste craft" (791). His portrayal of himself as a painting that awaits execution is also the description of a text that awaits writing, hence a "tale" to be created and told or retold from antecedent models. Reading back from the language Alceste gives us in the *Legend of Good Women*, we might surmise that such a story—"redy to cacche and take / Al that men wil theryn make"—would likely be a translation that induces men to praise love.

The point of the knight's self-portrait, it seems, is to define his initial experience of love as only the potential of love. His account is formalistic rather than substantive, necessary but not sufficient; and much like the lyric poets of the Dolce Stil Nuovo and the younger Dante, he suggests that the full experience of love will unfold according to the model of potency and act.[14] What he lacks at this point is the ethical substance of love, the informing power which allows him to realize what is latent and indwelling in his inclination and which makes it possible thereby to isolate the singular good from all the other goods that are merely like each other. This power is conferred through the "accident" ("Shal I clepe hyt hap other grace," 810) of his seeing the woman whose absence the poem now laments, and it is worth observing that, although the rhetoric of praise for Blanche is commonplace, within the thematic economy of the poem this discovery constitutes the lover's first gesture of discrimination: "y sawgh oon / That was lyk noon of the route" (818–819).[15]

Much of the scholarship on the *Book of the Duchess* has dealt with the idealized role that Blanche plays. She is a paragon of courtly beauty, the social objectification of virtue, an analogue to the Virgin. Her qualities, as D. W. Robertson, Jr. remarks, "belong to the realm of the intelligible."[16] While claiming that her value is absolute, the knight nonetheless describes her through a perspectival technique, for she exists coevally in his perception and in the moral climate of a courtly social environment. Thus he surrounds her with attributes not only of intrinsic beauty but moral presence, and his vocabulary spans the distance from the individual to the political level, associating "goode faire White" with "mesure" (872), "resoun" (922), "trouthe" (1003), "grace" (1006), "stedefast perseveraunce, / And esy, atempre governaunce" (1007–8). Appropriately, it is the knight's own ethical plea ("I ne wilned thyng but god," 1262) that begins finally to persuade Blanche to grant him mercy and take him "in hir governaunce" (1286).[17]

In its manifest content, this account embodies an ideology of love, Cupid's social text, that we are tempted to abstract from the dramatic situation of the knight's speech. As the knight sees her in society, Blanche enacts a principle of charity: "She loved as man may do hys brother" (892). As he looks back on her, she subsumes the disparate qualities of his own being, and makes possible within marriage a model of erotic and moral reciprocity:

> For certes she was, that swete wif,
> My suffisaunce, my lust, my lyf,
> Myn hap, myn hele, and al my blesse,
> My worldes welfare, and my goddesse,
> And I hooly hires and everydel.
>
> [1037–41]

Surely here, if anywhere, Chaucer comes close to expressing a notion of marital love and friendship: "Esteem enlivened by desire," as the eighteenth-century poet James Thomson described the ideal. And yet there are, I think, sound reasons for regarding this formulation as profoundly complex and not simply reflective of an ideal, not reduced merely to praising love as a value that determines meaning.

The passage I have just quoted contains an interesting word play that points up some of the tensions residing in this normative portrait of Blanche. The knight calls her "My suffisaunce, my lust." The first term is not in Machaut, where, incidentally, the speaker is a lady lamenting her dead lover. The second—"lust"— concentrates several senses in Chaucer's rendering that are enumerated loosely in Machaut's original as "pleasure, desire, wish, object of delight or desire."

> Et je l'amoie
> Si loiaument que tout mon cuer mettoie

En li amer, n'autre entente n'avoie;
Qu'en li estoit m'esperance, ma joie
Et mon plair,
Mon cuer, m'amour, mon penser, mon desir.[18]

In Chaucer's dense translation, Blanche is at once the completion and object of desire, the source of fulfillment and the absence that makes fulfillment possible—"My suffisaunce, my lust." This is the paradox of desire and, as the knight makes clear, it is also the mechanism of reciprocity and mutual exchange.

But the sense of completion, celebrated here in the absolute, refers us as well to what I have called the story's erotic preconscious—that is, back to the knight as "a whit wal or a table, / For hit ys redy to cacche and take / Al that men wil theryn make." It is precisely this potential for love that Blanche fulfills. When she first appears before the knight's imagination ("in my thoght," 837), she completes the erotic transcription that has been prepared by the man's inclination and will. Chaucer makes this connection explicit by having the knight echo the language used earlier to convey the potential of love in his "firste youthe":

And Love, that had wel herd my boone,
Had espyed me thus soone,
That she ful sone in my thoght,
As helpe me God, so was *ykaught*
So sodenly that I ne *tok*
No maner counseyl but at hir lok
And at myn herte. . . .
                                    [835–41; italics mine]

As these words reverberate in the text, the repetition makes us reconsider in some measure the nature of the erotic bond that the black knight describes from retrospect. Whatever the ideology of love expressed through Blanche, the relation is not simply reflective of a set of marital values, but is embedded in subjectivity and aesthetic creation; it is the product of the man in black's "firste craft," an art that elsewhere in the poem stands as an analogue to the poet's capacity for imagination and invention.

I am suggesting, then, that the social text of love, which Cupid wants to regulate in the Prologue to the *Legend of Good Women* as service to him alone, is enriched and complicated by the poetic text of the *Book of the Duchess*—by the affinities between the man in black and the poet, by the enlargement of love's scope from social practice to psychological and moral definition. Chaucer's translation of the French poets serves Cupid better—more copiously—than he would have himself served. But the price of Chaucer's devotion is that the narrow definition of service to love gives way to disclosure. By its very nature, the poetic text reveals contradiction and makes accessible to wise and lewed folk alike what lies beneath the doctrine of service to love.

The second text I want to consider, the *Knight's Tale* from the *Canterbury Tales*, furnishes an example in larger dimensions of the ways in which Chaucer's faithful translation uncovers and interrogates the social text of love. In the Prologue to the *Legend of Good Women*, Alceste indicates that the *Knight's Tale* may be a problematic work within that group of narratives which make "lewed folk" delight to serve Cupid. Chaucer's translation of Boccaccio, taking the term in a large sense, presents a story that is, she says, "knowen lyte." Even more interesting than the ostensible novelty of the story is the phrasing she gives the title: "al the love of Palamon and Arcite / Of Thebes." The construction, somewhat awkward but not unique in Chaucer, yields several meanings. On the surface, it refers to the love of the two protagonists for Emily, which is the main action of the poem and the source of tragic conflict. But at a deeper level, it suggests that this parallel desire for the same object may transform somehow into a form of mutual desire. In Boccaccio, the title makes Emily a focal point ("il libro del Teseida delle nozze d'Emilia"), and the author's gloss (*chiosa*) explains the triangulation of desire. Boccaccio says, "Con ciò sia cosa che la principale intenzione dell'autore di questo libretto sia di trattare dell'amore e delle cose avvenute per quello, da due giovani tebani, cioè Arcita e Palemone, ad Emilia amazona" ("the main purpose of this little book's author is, as his prologue shows, to deal with the love of the two young Thebans Arcita and Palemone for the Amazon Emilia, and with the events that followed as a result of it").[19] In Alceste's account of Chaucer's translation, Emily drops out of the title, and the protagonists remain bound to each other by love and their origin in tragic, incestuous, internecine Thebes.

Palamon and Arcite enter Chaucer's poem as indistinct, undifferentiated figures.[20] In the aftermath of Theseus's righteous (if only too eager) battle with Creon, the pillagers discover the Theban princes in a "taas of bodyes dede," severely wounded, "liggynge by and by, / Bothe in oon armes, wroght ful richely" (1.1011–12). The figures can be distinguished by name, but everything in the scene points to their identification with each other; their armor, the narrator notes, is identical, and their mothers are royal sisters. In writing the original scene, Boccaccio had emphasized Arcita and Palemone's royal bearing and may have modelled their haughtiness and disdain on Dante's Farinata (*Inferno* 10. 35–36), the figure who questions Dante about his lineage and remarks that he scattered his forebears twice.[21] Chaucer makes the characters more sympathetic, and he rewrites the scene so that the bodies originally lying not far from each other ("E' non eran da sé guari lontani," 2.86.1) now lie side by side and the armor simply mentioned in the original ("armati tutti ancora," 2.86.2) now carries the same heraldic device. From Boccaccio's account, Chaucer has composed a scene that depicts a mythic rebirth in which the Theban princes emerge as two versions of a single figure.

This shared identity operates in the preconscious of erotic desire in the *Knight's Tale*. It has antecedents in medieval romance (Yvain and Gauvain in Chrétien de Troyes's *Yvain*), and it endures in the *Knight's Tale* until the two find the same object of desire— that is, find someone different from themselves as they are mirrored in the other and identified by the same sign ("oon armes"). But despite the sign conferred by their dual lineage as kinsmen and royal heirs, the two Theban knights are like the "whit wal" in the *Book of the Duchess* before Emily appears on the scene to write on them by striking through the eye and reaching the heart.

Chaucer is careful, moreover, to plot the exact moment when their single identity splits into adversarial opposition. When Palamon sees Emily and sighs, Arcite comforts him ("Cosyn myn, what eyleth thee," 1.1081), and mistakenly consoles him over their imprisonment; in fact, he offers a proleptic version of the Boethian wisdom that Theseus will announce after the poem's tragic reversal. But when Arcite suffers the same effect from beholding Emily, Palamon regards him "dispitously" and asks whether he speaks of her "in ernest or in pley" (1.1125). This sharp differentiation revises Boccaccio's account in several significant ways. Chaucer has given Palamon priority in seeing Emily, and he has intensified the reversal of feeling in the two princes by marking it as a sudden shift from friendship to enmity. By contrast, Boccaccio protracts the scene and has the two lovers comfort one another with words: "Così ragionan li due nuovi amanti, / e l'un l'altro conforta nel parlare" (3.26.1–2). It is not until after Arcita returns disguised as Penteo and is overheard by Palemone's servant complaining of his love that Palemone gives in to jealousy. And even then Boccaccio distances their enmity by subsuming it within the bloody pattern of Theban history.

Chaucer's difference from Boccaccio might be described as a preference for immediate effect and dramatic economy over psychological process and mythographic amplitude. By condensing Boccaccio's richly nuanced account, Chaucer has placed "al the love of Palamon and Arcite" in the foreground of the tale. Consequently, the terms that designate their relationship—"the seurete and the bond" (1.1604), "trouthe" (1.1610), and "felaweshipe" (1.1626)—operate under the pressure of profound contradiction. The pressure intensifies, moreover, beyond the scope of mutual obligations. Arcite, pressing his claim to love Emily despite Palamon's seeing her first, associates love with natural law and asserts its power to supersede human conventions: "And therfore positif lawe and swich decree / Is broken al day for love in ech degree" (1.1167–68). Love thus works a series of changes unforeseeable from the vantage point of courtly values. Palamon and Arcite transform themselves into mediators of each other's desire. Exiled, Arcite imagines that the prison is a "paradys" (1.1237) that may eventually allow Palamon to win Emily; Palamon concedes the advantage to Arcite whom he thinks may be able to take Emily by arms or force a settlement that leads to marriage. Though they proclaim the spontaneity of their love, each operates through the agency of the other. They dwell not on the ostensible object of desire but on their rivalry.[22] At the same time love binds them in competition, it ruptures the formal protocols that regulate social life. Arcite may believe love is a form of natural law, but the effects it produces are narrow determinism at the personal level and the disruption of social covenants that allow societies to escape their history.

Chaucer makes a second and equally important revision in his portrayal of Emily. Boccaccio's Emilia is a figure of erotic ambivalence, both in her actions and the motives ascribed to her by the narrator. She initially goes to the garden out of her own inclinations ("di propria natura"), but the narrator hastens to assure us that she is not impelled by love: "non che d'amore alcun fosse constretta" (3.8.3). She hears Palemone's sigh, knows what it means, and delights in being desired, though the narrator asserts she is unready for complete love (3.19). Taking pains to adorn herself, she returns to the garden time and again alone or in company, and so becomes a conscious actor in a pageant of display, surveillance, and seduction. Chaucer is careful, however, to suppress the erotic texture of Boccaccio's portrayal and the limited, though still real, autonomy it confers. Emily is unaware of the Theban knights who watch her in the garden from their adjacent prison.[23] And when Theseus discovers Arcite and Palamon battling in the grove, he makes this point an ironic reproof of their love:

> But this is yet the beste game of alle,
> That she for whom they han this jolitee
> Kan hem therfore as muche thank as me.
> She woot namoore of al this hoote fare,
> By God, than woot a cokkow or an hare!
> [1.1806–10]

In the first half of the *Knight's Tale*, then, Emily exists chiefly as an object of desire, captured first by Theseus as part of the Amazonian booty and now waiting her final disposition according to the outcome of a tournament, featuring Arcite, Palamon, and two hundred knights, whose major cultural anxiety is to avoid "destruccioun / To gentil blood" (1.2538–39), that is, the interruption of male genealogy. At issue is not the intrinsic quality of love but the mechanism of exchange. How shall the domesticated younger sister be paired off with the survivors of Thebes's shattered dynasty? In this context service to love only mystifies the tragic history behind the tale and obscures the forms of political control that the tale incorporates.

Chaucer's ending to the *Knight's Tale* modifies the exclusive focus on mediated desire and thereby rescues some portion of an idealized, though highly ideological, view of heterosexual love. It also situates the Theban princes in an order of chivalry whose scale and uniformity presumably cancel out the troublesome specificity of their history. The wounded Arcite commends Palamon to Emily with words of exalted praise—"trouthe, honour, knyghthede, / Wysdom, humblesse, estaat, and heigh kynrede" (1.2789–90). The language better describes Theseus, if anyone, than Arcite's "cosyn deere." Chaucer changes Arcite's final words from Boccaccio's "A Dio, Emilia" (10.113.7) to a more enigmatic "Mercy, Emelye" (1.2808), a cry for pity and perhaps a bitter word of thanks.[24] Nonetheless, his final account of Palamon and Emily suggests that there is a satisfactory realization of desire in marriage:

> Bitwixen hem was maad anon the bond
> That highte matrimoigne or mariage,
> By al the conseil and the baronage.
> And thus with alle blisse and melodye
> Hath Palamon ywedded Emelye.
> And God, that al this wyde world hath wroght,

Sende hym his love that hath it deere aboght;
For now is Palamon in alle wele,
Lyvynge in blisse, in richesse, and in heele,
And Emelye hym loveth so tendrely,
And he hire serveth so gentilly,
That nevere was ther no word hem bitwene
Of jalousie or any oother teene.

[1.3094–3106]

Chaucer greatly elaborates Boccaccio's scene in which the various kings return home and leave Palemone "in gioia e in diporto" (12.83.4). The point to be grasped, however, is not that the bonds of desire and violence that join the chivalric heroes are superseded by marriage, in which love requites service and produces well-being. Rather, it is that the normative values of marriage achieved at the end of the poem rest on conflicts which are not resolved, despite Theseus's imposition of an ending and his appeals to a First Mover.[25] As David Aers points out, Theseus's efforts to impose order elsewhere in the poem rest on violence.[26] Here the admonition to "make of sorwes two / O parfit joye, lastynge everemo" (1.3071–72) is punctuated by an appeal to pragmatic social reality, for Theseus reminds Emily, "He is a kynges brother sone, pardee" (1.3084). As V. A. Kolve observes, Theseus "does not stand outside the suffering and confusion he attempts to declare rational and purposive" (p. 145).

In a sense the *Knight's Tale* serves as a practical commentary on Chaucer's earlier poems about love, and Alceste is right to list it last—and emphatically—among Chaucer's early love poems. The tale qualifies the man in black's idea of marriage as complete reciprocity by pointing up the contradictory imperatives at work within chivalric culture, the tension between erotic and homosocial bonds, the permutations of service to love and political control. By representing the social text of courtly values in pagan antiquity, Chaucer's translation of Boccaccio offers a mature wisdom to balance the delight that makes "lewed folk" serve love.

We might turn now from those texts that ostensibly serve Cupid by praising his name to the task given Chaucer to expiate his sins against love by composing the *Legend of Good Women*. Alceste proposes a "penance" (479) to compensate for the poet's trespass. He is to "make" tales of true women and thereby to "forthren yow [Cupid] as much as he mysseyde / Or in the Rose or elles in Creseyde" (440–41). The full charge and its implications are given in the following lines:

Thow shalt, while that thou lyvest, yer by yere,
The most partye of thy tyme spende
In makyng of a glorious legende
Of goode wymmen, maydenes and wyves,
That weren trewe in lovyng al hire lyves;
And telle of false men that hem bytraien,
That al hir lyf ne don nat but assayen
How many women they may doon a shame;
For in youre world that is now holde a game.
And thogh the lyke nat a lovere bee,
Speke wel of love; this penance yive I thee.

[481–91]

The formula good women-false men defines the ideological polarity of the work Chaucer has been assigned, and Alceste makes it
clear that the formula represents a social text: betrayal, she tells
the poet, "in youre world . . . is now holde a game" (489). The
proper values, as Cupid remarks, center on Alceste herself: "For
she taught al the craft of fyn lovynge, / And namely of wyfhod the
lyvynge, / And al the boundes that she oghte kepe" (544–46).

But it is the poetic rather than the social text that seems to
concern Chaucer. Cupid wants to invest Chaucer with the office of
the courtly maker. Ironically echoing his charge that Chaucer has
spoken of Criseyde according to his own wish ("as the lyste," 332),
he tells him, "Make the metres of hem [the good women] as the
lest" (562). Thus he assigns him a task of translation, ordering
"That thou reherce of al hir lyf the grete, / After thise olde
auctours lysten for to trete" (574–75). It is no doubt fitting that
translation should repair the damage that translation has caused,
but in setting the task Cupid unwittingly magnifies the distance
between his expectations and Chaucer's office.

This is not the place to review all the transformations that
Chaucer makes in his sources. Robert Frank's and Lisa Kiser's
studies of the *Legend* provide insightful readings of the stories and
their literary sources. We might note briefly, though, that throughout the *Legend*, Chaucer asserts the authority of his poetry over
and against the kind of making that Cupid associates with the
ideological agenda of praising love. Chaucer claims the "storyal
soth" (702) of Cleopatra's legend and cites Ovid as his source for
the legend of Thisbe (725), which incidentally he makes an example of men and women being "trewe and kynde" (921). With Dido's
story he says he will "take / The tenor, and the grete effectes
make" (928–29) from Virgil and Ovid; in other words, he will

amplify and adorn according to his own sense of the materials. The consequence is that he rejects the substitution of Cupid for Ascanius as it is reported by Virgil, and he is later so overcome with pity for Dido that he cannot continue to *endite*.

In succeeding episodes this sense of poetic authority serves to call into question the courtly values associated with Cupid and his folk. Though Theseus may be the ethical center of the *Knight's Tale*, he is reproached in the *Legend* for his "grete untrouthe of love" (1890), and his betrayal of Ariadne is repeated in his son Demophon's abuse of Phyllis. Jason is presented as a distortion of the courtly lover, yet he is seen in Pelleus's kingdom as "a famous knyght of gentilesse, / Of fredom, and of strengthe and lustynesse" (1404–5). His betrayal of Hypsipyle takes place in a courtly world of *pley*, natural courtesy, social codes, and reputation. Hypsipyle's concern for the visitors whom she sees arrive on the coast is part of her courtly bearing; it was "hire usaunce / To fortheren every wight, and don plesaunce / Of verrey bounte and of curteysye" (1476–78). She recognizes Hercules and Jason's standing from the customary signs of the court: "And she tok hed, and knew by hyre manere, / By hire aray, by wordes, and by chere, / That it were gentil-men of gret degre" (1504–06). Her exhortation to Hercules that he be "Sad, wys, and trewe, of wordes avyse, / Withouten any other affeccioun / Of love, or evyl ymagynacyoun" (1521–23) reflects the conviction that social gestures and courtly language can be determinate in their meaning, that the social text of the noble life is to be accepted without reservation.

Chaucer invents the scene in which Hercules inflames Hypsipyle's desire by his praise of Jason as a "lusty knyght" (1542) who embodies the ideals of the courtly world. Hercules, the poet tells us, has planned this "shrewed lees" (1545) with Jason, and he perpetrates it so that Hypsipyle's natural affections transform to desire. The deception depends precisely on observing the conventions of courtly manners and "fyn lovynge," for Jason, "coy as is a mayde" (1548), remains silent but casts his look "pitously" and shows his largesse to the counselors and officers of the court. Hercules and Jason's collusion is an ironic inversion of the rivalry between Arcite and Palamon in the *Knight's Tale*, and it relies on the elements of sight and language that Jason will employ again in his betrayal of Medea, to whom he appears "of his lok as real as a leoun / And goodly of his speche, and famler" (1605–6).

The deception engineered by Hercules and Jason no less than the rivalry that joins Palamon and Arcite in the *Knight's Tale* reveals how mediation can structure erotic conduct in ways that go beyond the protocols that Cupid confidently assumes. Mediated desire is what leads to Tarquin's rape of Lucrece and the subsequent deposition of kingship in Rome, for it is Colatyn's speech and his complicity in spying on his wife that cause Tarquin to conceive his mad desire. Tarquin proposes to wile away the tedium of a protracted siege. "With oure speche lat us ese oure herte" (1704), he says, but Colatyn quickly substitutes the clandestine demonstration of his wife's virtue for mere words. In the action that follows from Tarquin's obsessive rumination on her beauty, Lucrece in fact suffers a double rape. Violence against her person leads to violence against her name, when Brutus "openly" (1865) tells her tale to the Romans and displays her corpse as proof of the deed. His object is to overthrow tyranny and establish a political system that properly regulates the relations between free males.

What I am suggesting is that, as Chaucer translates the authors who preserve a culture's memory, he also uncovers what the culture would suppress. Cupid charges him to compose a two-dimensional exemplary history illustrating values that can be designated but not examined closely. The importance of the poetry he writes despite Cupid's charge is that it establishes a realm of moral speculation related to but independent from the social text of "fyn lovynge." The legends, like the early narratives that supposedly praise Cupid, complicate and add thematic resonance to the representation of love. Chaucer's faithful translations remain true, in the end, to the complexity of an artistic vision. That is the "pleyn text" of the *Rose* and the *Troilus* and what the *Canterbury Tales* will disclose in their own ways.

9

Man, Men, and Women in Chaucer's Poetry

One of the most provocative arguments of modern feminism has been that language itself carries buried within it the elements of invidious sexual discrimination—in particular, that the word "man," when used to describe the species *homo sapiens*, inherently dismisses half of the human race.[1] This argument has had a number of recent effects, reactions, and counterreactions. It has led to revisions in nomenclature, with some substitutions of "person" for "man" more universally accepted than others. It has affected even the bromides of politicians, for whom saying "he" without "she" or "men" without "women" is becoming—and properly so—as much a taboo as using racial epithets in public. The new attention to this particular linguistic nuance may also alter our responses to the past—not least, by giving us the ability to perceive with a greater clarity what is already there.[2] My argument in this essay is that Chaucer—drawing on a long tradition of Biblical commentary—is well aware of the sexual dimensions of word choice, even of the double meaning of "man," and that he plays on the relationship between naming and sexual differentiation. His reasons for doing so are several, but stem above all from the fact that, in Gavin Douglas's memorable phrase, Chaucer "was evir—God wait—al womanis frend."[3] What this "friendship" meant in practice, beyond a generalized sympathy with women, appears when he explores the issues of sexual politics, even as they are embedded in more or less unconscious uses of language. Chaucer wittily reveals the ideological dimensions of courtly game-playing; and he subjects all the conventional literary treatments of women by men, critical or adulatory, to a debunking examination of motive.

The issue of naming and sexuality is hardly new. It has its origin in the most famous book of origins, the text of Genesis; and its potential divisiveness is apparent in the differences between the creation narratives of the Jahwist and Priestly scribes.[4] The Jahwist account, the earlier of the two, describes the creation of Eve and her naming in the context of the naming of the animals and birds (Gen. 2.18–24): in part because of this context, the account implies that Eve is subordinate to Adam, and sufficiently differentiated from him that he can assign her a name different from his own. The Priestly account, by contrast, appears to suggest, or can at least be taken to suggest, that male and female, both subsumed under the term "homo" or "adam," are coeval. In St. Jerome's Vulgate translation of the Bible: "Et creavit Deus hominem ad imaginem suam: ad imaginem Dei creavit illum, masculum et feminam creavit eos" (Gen. 1.27) [And God created man to his own image; in the image of God he created him. Male and female he created them]. The abrupt shift in number and gender—"man" to "male and female," "him" to "them"—is perhaps less startling here than it would be in later contexts: in classical Latin "homo" is the normal word for the species, differentiating the human from the non-human (though certainly with a masculine bias), and "vir" the normal word for a male human being, "man" in contrast to "woman." In medieval Latin, Old French, and Old and Middle English, on the other hand, the words "homo," "ome," and "man" describe both human beings and males specifically (and in French and English become the indefinite pronoun as well). Sometimes the results may be jarring only to modern ears, as when in the *Anglo-Saxon Chronicle* for 639, Eormengota is praised as "hali femne and wundorlic man," or when the late twelfth-century *Bodley Homilies* describe Adam and Eve as "þa ereste men."[5] And this passage in Genesis—"in the image of God he created him. Male and female he created them"—has inspired some wishful readings recently, arguing that a patriarchal tradition of commentary has corrupted what was originally an argument for sexual equality.[6] Nonetheless, the inclusion of two sexes within one term is a matter for comment beginning with Jesus himself, who uses this passage from Genesis as an argument against divorce: "Have ye not read that he who made man [hominem] from the beginning made them male and female? And he said: For this cause shall a man [homo] leave father and mother and shall cleave to his wife; and they two shall be in one flesh. Therefore, now they are not two, but one flesh. What therefore God hath joined together, let not man [homo] put asunder" (Matt. 19.4–6). Jerome uses "homo" to translate the *anthropos* of the Greek New Testament here, preserving its ambiguity; by contrast, he almost always translates the sex–marked *aner* with "vir."[7] St. Augustine points out that the word "homo" can be either generic or gender–specific, and argues that the potential sexual difference within it must be noticed or ignored according to context. He says (*De Civ. Dei* 15.17) that the name of Seth's son, Enos, "means 'man' [homo] but not in the same sense as Adam. For although Adam means 'man' [homo], we are told that in Hebrew it is common to male and female [here Augustine quotes Gen. 5.2: "He created them male and female; and blessed them; and called their name Adam, in the day when they were created"]. This makes it clear that although the woman was called Eve, and that was her personal [i.e., proper] name, the name Adam, which means 'man,' belonged to them both. Enos, on the other hand, means 'man' [homo] in the sense which makes it impossible for it to be used as a woman's name."[8] Elsewhere, commenting on Jerome's translation of Isaiah 66.24, which substitutes "the carcasses of men" [cadavera virorum] for the Vetus Latina "limbs of human beings" [membra hominum], he argues that the words "homo" and "vir" are to be understood as synonymous, both of them in this passage applying to male and female alike. (The passage reads: "And they shall go out and see the carcasses of the men that have transgressed against me.") "For no one is likely to assert that women who transgress will not incur that punishment! The fact is that both sexes are included under the more important sex, especially as that was the sex from which woman was created" (*De Civ. Dei* 20.21).[9] And when Augustine comments on Ephesians 4.13, which uses the word *vir* to describe Christ as "a perfect man," he states: "If . . . this passage is to be referred to the form of the resurrected body, what is there to prevent our supposing that the mention of 'man' implies 'woman' also, *vir* being used here for *homo* . . . ? There is a similar sense in the verse, 'Blessed is the man (*vir*) who fears the Lord,' [Ps. 112.1] which obviously includes the women who fear him."[10]

The differences between the Jahwist and Priestly narratives are, for patristic and medieval commentators, merely apparent differences, since the two accounts are, of course, a single one, the work of Moses; and Pope John Paul II's 1988 apostolic letter *Mulieris Dignitatem* itself argues that there is no "essential contradiction between the two texts."[11] This harmonizing impulse in Biblical commentary accords with the text it comments on; for the Genesis narrative insists on similitude, likeness bridging a gap of difference, in God's creation of man: "Faciamus hominem ad imaginem et similitudinem nostram" (Gen. 1.26) [Let us make man to our image and likeness]. The question of similitude also dominates the account of man's relationship to the rest of Creation. For, most interestingly, the search for a mate for Adam "like unto himself" [*simile sibi*] provokes Adam's first use of language:

> Dixit quoque Dominus Deus: Non est bonum esse hominem solum: faciamus ei adiutorium simile sibi. Formatis igitur, Dominus Deus, de humo cunctis animantibus terrae, et universis volatilibus caeli, adduxit ea ad Adam, ut videret quid vocaret ea: omne enim quod vocavit Adam animae viventis, ipsum est nomen eius. Appellavitque Adam nominibus suis cuncta animantia, et universa volatilia caeli, et omnes bestias terrae: Adae vero non inveniebatur adiutor similis eius. (Gen. 2.18–20)

And the Lord God said: It is not good for man to be alone; let us make him a help like unto himself. And the Lord God having formed out of the ground all the beasts of the earth, and all the fowls of the air, brought them to Adam to see what he would call them: for whatsoever Adam called any living creature the same is its name. And Adam called all the beasts by their names, and all the fowls of the air, and all the cattle of the field: but for Adam there was not found a helper like himself.

Modern critics have remarked on the "extraordinary naiveté" of this passage, which implies that "the whole animal creation is the result of an unsuccessful experiment to find a mate" for Adam.[12] But for earlier commentators, Adam realizes here his superiority to the other creatures (so argue Augustine, Bede, and Peter Comestor)[13] or becomes aware, when he sees that they are all sexually differentiated and paired, of his own solitariness (Ambrose and Rashi).[14] As the *Golden Legend* puts it—quoting Genesis 2.18, "It is not good for man to be alone"—man was "not perfect till the woman was made";[15] and Chaucer's *Tale of Melibee*, quoting the same Biblical text, adds: "Heere may ye se that if that wommen were nat goode, and hir conseils goode and profitable,/ oure Lord God of hevene wolde nevere han wroght hem, ne called hem help of man, but rather confusioun of man" (VII.1104–05).[16] In this context of Adam's search for his similitude, his naming the birds and animals involves a complicated interplay between his intuitive understanding of their natures and his rational awareness that they are different from him, and not possible mates "like unto himself." The act of naming itself requires the articulation of difference: just as God divided light from darkness and "called the light Day, and the darkness Night," Augustine argues (*De Gen. contra Man.* 1.9; *PL* 34:180), so He "thus divided and arranged all things so that they might both be discerned and receive their names." And in some commentaries, the fact of division is by itself a forecast of the Fall: Jerome argues that the omission of "And God saw that it was good" on the second day of creation, the summation that appears on each of the other days, is intended to show us that "a double number is not good, because it divides from union" (*Adv. Jov.* 1.16; *PL* 23:246);[17] and Guibert of Nogent, commenting on the singular "man" and plural "male and female" of Gen. 1.27, compares the division between the sexes to that between the spirit and the flesh: "Primo in homine quaedam fuit identitas, sed ex peccati poena accidit demum diversitas, ut in duo divideretur humanitas" [At first there was a kind of identity in man, but from the punishment of sin resulted at length diversity, as humanity was divided in two] (*PL* 156:57).

The names Adam gives to his helpmate, one name before and one after the Fall, play on similitude and difference: they in fact register a shift first from unity to multiplicity—mirroring God's own act of creation—and then in moral terms, from integral connection to alienation. Adam copies God's verbal economy and assertion of similitude when he names his mate *isha* (Gen. 2.23), for the name itself shows her near–identity with the man, *ish*, from whom she was made, "woman" from "man," "os ex ossibus meis, et caro de carne mea" [bone of my bones, and flesh of my flesh].[18] According to Rashi, this Adamic wordplay on *ish/isha* in fact proves that the world was created in Hebrew. If so, English may have a better claim than Greek or Latin to be a sacred language, because *man/woman* translates this wordplay so easily. Augustine notes that the "mulier" in the Vetus Latina translation of Genesis loses the effect of this similitude [*similitudinem*], which "virago" or "virgo" would preserve;[19] and Jerome's Vulgate in fact uses "virago" to copy the verbal mirroring in the Hebrew text.[20] Eve may be so called, Peter Comestor says, because "virago" means "a viro acta" ["brought forth from man"] (*PL* 198:1071); and this etymology is widely disseminated by his *Historia Scholastica* and by the standard dictionaries of Guilelmus Brito and Johannes Balbi de Janua.[21] (The *Golden Legend* likewise explains *virago* as "made of a man, and . . . a name taken of a man" [1:172]; and there is a reminiscence of this argument in *Paradise Lost*: "woman is her name, of man/ Extracted" [8.496–97].) The *OED* notes that "virago" in this sense appears in the Middle English *Cursor Mundi* and in the Wycliffite translation of Genesis. The first *OED* listing of the word in its pejorative sense, interestingly, is Chaucer's *Man of Law's Tale*: "Virago, thou Semyrame the secounde!" (II.359)—though a pejorative sense is evident in Isidore's etymology "virum agit, hoc est opera virilia facit" [she acts the man, that is does masculine works], and his use of the term to describe "corruptae mulieres" [corrupted women] (*PL* 83:68). Nicholas of Lyra in fact argues that "virago" is the wrong word to use to translate "isha," "quia uirago non significat mulierem de uiro sumptam uel deriuatam: sed magis significat mulierem uiriliter agentem" [because "virago" does not signify a woman taken or derived from man, but more a woman acting manfully]; "vira," he says, would be a better choice, if Latin permitted it.[22] (Isidore argues in fact that "vira," following the pattern of "serva" and "famula," was the ancient word for "femina" [*Etym.* 11.2.23].)

Up to the point of the Fall, God's injunction "Increase and multiply" (Gen. 1.22) has a wholly benign effect, for the Creation, mirroring the original act of its Creator, divides and subdivides, but with the bond of virtuous similitude holding together its disparate, multiple parts. Or so we must infer, following the commentators, since there is hardly time for this benign process to advance very far before the Fall turns its play of likeness and difference into a cancerous multiplication—first, to the two genealogies from Adam, those of Seth and of Cain; then, to the division at Babel of the one true tongue into seventy-two languages. Peter Comestor notes that "Adam" and "virago" or "isha" were proper names at first, but are now common nouns (*PL* 198:1071); the otherwise innocent implications of a change from singular to plural, the need to give the first woman a name to differentiate her from her progeny, has a darker significance because Adam renames his mate after the Fall, giving her the proper name Eve. The similitudes of Eden quickly become demonic: Satan disguises himself as a serpent with "virgineum vultum . . . , quia similia similibus applaudunt" [a maiden's face, because like applauds like] (*PL* 198:1072);[23] and Chaucer's Merchant uses Genesis 2.18—" 'Lat us now make an helpe unto this man/ Lyk to hymself' " (*CT* IV.1328–29)—only ironically: January gets what he deserves as his similitude when he marries May. The name Eve implicitly plays on a dissimilitude within itself, in effect a kind of punning, which mirrors the dissimilitude the Fall brings to Adam and Eve separately, in their division from God, and together, in their division from each other.[24] Its positive meaning, "Living" or "Life," appears in the immediate explanation "because she was the mother of all the living" (Gen. 3.20).[25] But there are more sinister connotations within her name: Augustine discusses the paradoxes in Adam's renaming her (*PL* 34:212), and Jerome glosses "Eva, calamitas, aut vae, vel vita" [Eva, calamity, or else woe, or life] (*PL* 23:778). As the Middle English *Genesis and Exodus* summarizes the change:

> Adam abraid, and sag that wif;
> Name he gaf hire dat is ful rif:
> Issa was hire firste name,
> Thor of thurtc hire thinken no same;
> Mayden, for sche was mad of man,
> Hire first name thor bi-gan.
> Sithen ghe brocte us to woa,
> Adam gaf hire name eua.
>
> [231–38][26]

(According to Martin Luther, Adam's renaming Eve is part of her punishment, a further token that she must be subjected to the power of her husband; and this punishment, he says, survives in women's loss of their surnames when they marry.)[27]

Jerome's gloss, with its alternative and contradictory possibilities, ushers in a number of etymological or verbal examinations of the doubleness within Eve's name and self. Isidore of Seville states:

> Eve interpretatur vita sive calamitas sive vae. Vita, quia origo fuit nascendi: calamitas et vae, quia prevaricatione causa extitit moriendi. A cadendo enim nomen sumpsit calamitas. Alii autem dicunt: ob hoc Eva vita et calamitas appellata, quia saepe mulier viro causa salutis est, saepe calamitatis et mortis, quod est vae.

> [Eva is explained as life or calamity or woe. Life, because she was the source of what was to be born; calamity and woe, because by her transgression the cause of dying sprang into being. For the noun "calamity" derived from the word "falling" [or, calamity assumed Eve's name because of the Fall; or, assumed her name because of its ending]. Some say, moreover: Eva is called life and calamity, because often woman is

the cause of well-being for man, often the cause of calamity and death, which is woe.][28]

This simultaneous reading of Eve's name *in bono* and *in malo* is worthy of Chauntecleer, for whom the "sentence" of "mulier est hominis confusio" is its contradiction (*CT* VII. 3163–66). Isidore's wordplay on *a cadendo*, on grammatical ending and another kind of Fall, is copied word-for-word by Rabanus Maurus (*PL* 111:31), and leads to the kind of grammatical punning Paul Lehmann and others have noted, in which "declining" takes on a double meaning as Adam and Eve become "oblique" nouns after their Fall or "declension."[29] The name "Eva" opens itself to various kinds of deconstruction: the most famous is the "Eva"/"Ave" reversal, in which the three letters of the angel Gabriel's first word to the Virgin, the linguistic prelude to the Redemption, signal a cosmic peripeteia.[30] But in the context of merely fallen language, there are more acerbic possibilities, as in Innocent III's division of Eve's name into syllables of woe:

> Omnes nascimur eiulantes ut nature miseriam exprimamus. Masculus enim recenter natus dicit "A," femina "E." "Dicentes 'E' vel 'A' quotquot nascuntur ab Eva." Quid est igitur "Eva"? Utrum dolentis est interiectio, doloris exprimens magnitudinem. Hinc enim ante peccatum virago, post peccatum "Eva" meruit appellari, ex quo sibi dictum audivit: "In dolore paries."

> [All are born crying in order to express the misery of nature. For the newly born male says "Ah," the female "E". "All are born of Eve saying 'E' or 'Ah'." What is "Eve" therefore? Either syllable is the interjection of one in pain, expressing the magnitude of the pain. Hence she deserved to be called virago ("made from man") before sin, "Eve" after sin, because of which she heard said to her: "In sorrow shalt thou bring forth children."][31]

In his versified Bible, the *Aurora*, Peter Riga sums up our fall and redemption in the letters of Eve's name:

> Dicta *virago* fuit mulier prius; *Eua* uocatur
> Post culpam, quasi *ue* parturit iste sonus.

Eua necem mundo dedit; hoc nomen retrouerte,
  Fiet *aue*, per quod fulsit in orbe salus,
Nam Gabrielis "aue" totum ue diluit Eue,
  Dum Sacra Virgo suum concipit aure Patrem.
Omnis masculus .a. nascens, .e. femina profert;
  .A. dat Adam genitor, .e. parit Eua parens.

[The woman was previously named *virago*; after the Fall she
is called *Eva*, as if that sound gives birth to *woe*. Eva gave
death to the world; this name reversed will become *ave*,
through which deliverance shone in the world. For the "ave"
of Gabriel dissolves the whole woe of Eva, when the Holy
Virgin conceives her own Father through her ear. Every male
brings forth "a" when he is born, every female "e." Adam the
father bestows "a," Eve the mother creates "e."][32]

Here we have an acrostic of original sin. Dante is almost certainly
thinking of the earlier commentators on the "Eva" in babies' cries
when he measures the loss from Adam's first sound, which, he
says, must have been "El," the name of God: "Nam sicut post pre-
varicationem humani generis quilibet exordium sue locutionis in-
cipit ab 'heu,' rationabile est quod ante qui fuit inciperet a gaudio"
[for just as after the transgression of the human race, anyone's first
venture in speech is "alas!" ["heu"], it is reasonable that whoever
existed before this transgression would have started out in joy].[33]
The slip of the tongue from "El" to "eu" marks the fall of human
language and humankind.

This line of thought has its peculiarly English variant in late medieval and Renaissance texts. In *Paradise Lost*, Adam's first bad
pun after his Fall finds significance in the sound of his wife's
name: " 'O Eve, in evil hour thou didst give ear/ To that false
worm' " (9.1067–68). Eve's first, wholly innocent name is also
tainted, for Renaissance English writers, when "woman" is derived by pseudo-etymology from "woe." (It in fact comes from Old
English "wif-mann," though it is impossible to resist mentioning
Richard Verstegan's characteristically zany suggestion "womb-
man.")[34] In the Chester *Drapers' Play* Adam complains:

Yea, sooth sayde I in prophecye
when thou was taken of my bodye—

mans woe thou would bee witterlye;
Therfore thou was soe named.
[269–72][35]

Milton's Adam too remarks: "But still I see the tenor of man's
woe/ Holds on the same, from woman to begin" (*Paradise Lost*
11.632–33). But in *Paradise Lost* the angel immediately puts him
in his place: "From man's effeminate slackness it begins" (11.634).
That is to say, Adam's complaint risks being merely male self-pity,
of the sort that Robert Southey expresses in his derivation of the
word "lass" from "alas!"—a sigh, he says, "breathed sorrowfully
forth at the thought the girl, the lovely and innocent creature upon
whom the beholder has fixed his meditative eye, would in time
become a woman, a woe to man!"[36]

The closest approach in Chaucer to the later pseudo–etymology is in the *Nun's Priest's Tale*: "Wommannes conseil broghte us
first to wo" [VII.3257]. Elsewhere "woe" is something that women
characteristically suffer, not cause: "Ther made nevere womman
moore wo" than Criseyde (*Tr.* 5.1052). Chaucer's linking of "wo"
and "womman" may be in part the effect of alliterative attraction:
he habitually puts "wo" in alliterative patterns with other words,
especially "wele," and he also describes "womman" by such allit-
erating adjectives as "worthy" (*CT* I.459) and "wys" (*CT* III.209,
524). Any wordplay on "wo" and "womman" is basically visual,
not aural, so one would be pressing hard to find it in such a passage as this:

Therto we wrecched wommen nothing konne,
Whan us is wo, but wepe and sitte and thinke;
Oure wrecche is this, oure owen wo to drynke.
[*Tr.* 2.782–84]

Yet such alliteration is so conspicuous in the *Man of Law's Tale*—
where "womman" is "wrecche" (II.285), "wery" (514), "woful"
(522), "wrecched" (918), "wayke" (932), "worldly" (1026; also see
III.1033), and "wikke" (1028)—that some phrases strongly appear
to reflect not simply alliterative attraction, but a conscious wordplay. The most startling example of this wordplay opposes Constance, the "woful womman" (II.522) who is the paragon of
feminine virtue, to the mannish "virago" the Sultaness. Constance herself invokes the Virgin Mary as her exemplar:

"Mooder," quod she, "and mayde bright, Marie,
Sooth is that thurgh wommanes eggement

Mankynde was lorn, and damned ay to dye,
For which thy child was on a croys yrent.
Thy blisful eyen sawe al his torment;
Thanne is ther no comparison bitwene
Thy wo and any wo man may sustene."

[841–47]

The final line, in which the word "man" can be construed equally
well as "human being," as the indefinite pronoun, or as "male,"
invites us to meditate on the sexually determined gradations of
suffering, as "woman" and the "wo man" may sustain, separate or
merge together. (The *OED* notes a similar version of this wordplay in Thomas More's *Comfort against Tribulation*: "Man him-
selfe borne of a woman, is indeede a wo man, that is, ful of wo
and miserie.")

Chaucer thus opposes later practice by presenting sympathetically the relation of women to woe; but he also often subjects
such sympathy for women to a searching irony, by examining the
motives of the men who praise them. He repeatedly shows, first of
all, that certain ways of praising women are inherently antifeminist. In the *Man of Law's Tale* and *Physician's Tale*, he noticeably
alters his sources, to make Constance and Virginia much weaker
and more passive than their prototypes. The Man of Law and Physician use their heroines as vehicles for conventional laments
about female martyrdom; but their sentimental tales are in fact
the work of moral hypocrites, concerned primarily to establish
their own piety. In the *Franklin's Tale*, when Dorigen is faced with
an apparent choice between suicide and dishonor, her first response is to recite a long list of the virtuous ancient women in her
situation who chose to kill themselves. The list comes from the
most notorious antifeminist document in the Middle Ages, St. Jerome's *Against Jovinian*, which praises these women as exceptions
to the norm of female behavior. The *Franklin's Tale* implicitly
points out that there are some inconsistencies here: suicide would
be exactly the wrong thing for Dorigen to do (since she is able to
avoid both death and dishonor); and in a Christian context, Jerome's praising pagan women for committing a mortal sin is hardly
useful. The catalogue Dorigen recites, moreover, is comically te-
dious on purpose, in large part because Chaucer—like someone
cribbing a book report from the *Encyclopaedia Britannica*—takes
his flurry of examples from Jerome's text in order.[37] The effect is
an unconvincing recital of rote knowledge—and a lack of what we
might call suitable role models. Dorigen's list is simply the reverse

of Jankin's Book of Wicked Wives, in the *Wife of Bath's Prologue*, which is also much indebted to St. Jerome: Chaucer shows that antifeminism and an unworldly standard of female virtue are opposite sides of the same coin. In this context of male readings of women, it is especially interesting that the tale of St. Cecilia, who is the one forceful, actively heroic woman in the *Canterbury Tales*, should be assigned to the Second Nun (who, in a notorious crux, refers to herself as a "sone of Eve" [VIII.62]).[38] The Second Nun proves that the Wife of Bath is correct: if lions, the Wife says, could paint, their pictures of lion-hunts would look rather different from human ones; so too, a woman's description of womanly virtue, or of the battle between the sexes, would not be the same as a clerk's. And the Clerk's tale of patient Griselda, despite what he claims (IV.932–38), hardly disproves the Wife's contention that clerks are hostile to women.

Chaucer makes his point first by being unusually attentive to the tonal register of gender-defining adjectives. "Womanly" and "manly" are both almost always complimentary, "womannish" and "mannish"—both used to describe or define women—generally not so. But these adjectives all become open to deflection according to the particular speaker who uses them. The straightforward uses of "manly" often add the qualities of being "noble" or "heroic" to maleness: Lygurgus, in the *Knight's Tale*, has a "manly . . . face" (I.2130), and Julius Caesar, in the *Monk's Tale*, a "manly . . . herte" (VII.2711). Troilus is "a manly knyght" when he rides by Criseyde's window (2.1263); Pandarus exhorts him to "manly sette the world on six and sevene" (4.622); and when Criseyde leaves Troy, "He gan his wo ful manly for to hide" (5.30). The Monk in the *Shipman's Tale* is "manly of dispence" (VII.43), i.e., "generous." Yet in other contexts the virility defined by such manliness is inappropriate or suspect: the Monk should be a Godly, not a "manly man" (I.167); and the forthright courage in the rapist's "manly voys" when he says "What thyng that worldly wommen loven best" (III.1033–36) quickly gives way to his sullenly churlish response to the hag who has saved his life, a response much in contrast to Gawain's unfailing courtesy in the analogues to the *Wife of Bath's Tale*. Theseus calls on Emelye's "wommanly pitee" at the end of the *Knight's Tale* (I.3083), the quality also ascribed to dame Prudence as a political mediator (VII.1750) and hoped for in the lover's lady ("Complaint to His Lady" 101); it is closely akin to the "verray wommanly benignytee/ That Nature in youre principles hath set" that the sorrowing falcon finds in Canacee (V.486–87). When the Physician praises

Virginia for her speech, "ful wommanly and pleyn" (VI.50), he means that she is properly shamefast and humble; but the word, used as an adverb, elsewhere describes livelier skills, in the playfulness of Blanche (*BD* 850), the singing of Criseyde (5.577), and the solicitude of Helen of Troy (2.1668). It describes the paradigmatic femininity of Alceste (*LGW* F 243) and Criseyde's "noblesse" (1.287). Troilus in fact twice invokes Criseyde's virtuous qualities as a "wommanliche wif" (3.106 and 1296): in the first of these instances, the narrator notes Troilus's own "manly sorwe" (3.113).

"Wommanysshe," on the other hand, describes the disagreeable visitors to Criseyde (4.694), whose banal condolences vex her mightily.[39] And "mannysh," though it simply means "human" at one point in *The Tale of Melibee* (VII.1264), is elsewhere what a woman is not or should not be. Criseyde's "lymes so wel answerynge/ Weren to wommanhod, that creature/ Was nevere lasse mannyssh in semynge" (1.282–84). The two other appearances of the word are in contexts narrowed by a speaker's misogyny, attacking the Amazonian forcefulness which Boccaccio praises in *De mulieribus claris*. Justinus warns, in the *Merchant's Tale*, that a wife may turn out to be "mannyssh wood" (IV.1536): despite some recent arguments that the phrase means "man-crazy," i.e., "lustful" or "mad for men," the older reading "a fierce virago," "mad like a man" is, I think, more likely to be correct.[40] The Man of Law, likewise, proclaims in an apostrophe:

> O Donegild, I ne have noon Englissh digne
> Unto thy malice and thy tirannye!
> And therfore to the feend I thee resigne;
> Lat hym enditen of thy traitorie!
> Fy, mannysh, fy!—o nay, by God, I lye—
> Fy, feendlych spirit, for I dar wel telle,
> Thogh thou heere walke, thy spirit is in helle!
>
> [II.778–84]

In this tale, where the word "virago" is entirely pejorative, the improperly "mannysh," even "feendlych" Donegild contrasts with the passive, feminine Constance. In the Man of Law's source, Nicholas Trevet's *Chronicle*, Constance is ingenious, self-reliant, and forcefully active in her own defense; the Man of Law praises feminine virtue by enervating it.

The nouns from which these adjectives derive offer more complex possibilities of wordplay, precisely because the definition of "man," as "human being" or simply as "male," depends so much on whether "woman," either named or conspicuously unnamed, intervenes to limit its range of reference. The connotations of the word "womman" itself can be either neutral, pejorative, or favorable: Chaucer is unusual in the number of times he uses it in a favorable context. Most strikingly, Criseyde reflects on her own independence, free from the bonds of marriage or love: "I am myn owene womman, wel at ese" (2.750). Later in the poem, Criseyde defines her womanhood as sudden resolution and headlong speech:

> "I am a womman, as ful wel ye woot,
> And as I am avysed sodeynly,
> So wol I telle yow, whil it is hoot."
> [4.1261–63]

In the *Merchant's Tale*, May uses the word as a marker of social class: she avows, as she is about to trick January, "I am a gentil womman and no wenche" (IV.2202). The most interesting examples for my present purposes are those, especially in the polemical context of the *Legend of Good Women*, when "woman" as a generic marker distinguishes her sex from that of "man." Pandarus, describing male perfidy, laments: "No wonder is, so God me sende hele,/ Though wommen dreden with us men to dele" (3.321–22). The narrator proclaims at the end of the *Legend of Thisbe*: "But God forbede but a woman can/ Ben as trewe in lovynge as a man!" (910–11), and adds:

> Of trewe men I fynde but fewe mo
> In alle my bokes, save this Piramus,
> And therfore have I spoken of hym thus.
> For it is deynte to us men to fynde
> A man that can in love been trewe and kynde.
> Here may ye se, what lovere so he be,
> A woman dar and can as wel as he.
> [917–923]

The sexual polemic that sets "woman" against "man" prepares us for a double reference within the word "man" itself. Thomas Usk's *The Testament of Love* gives us warrant for finding such ambiguities even in the word "mankind," because he twice uses it to refer only to men: "thus for the more parte fareth al mankynde, to praye and to crye after womans grace, and fayne many fantasyes to make hertes enclyne to your desyres"; and, quoting "goddes wordes . . . " in Genesis: 'It is good to mankynde that we make to him an helper.' "[41] In Chaucer, we feel no jarring effect when the Prioress praises Mary as the "honour of mankynde" (VII.619). But in the *Prologue* to the *Legend of Good Women*, there is some ambiguity when the word appears: after the procession of the nineteen exemplary women, there

>   . . . coome of wymen swich a traas
> That, syn that God Adam hadde mad of erthe,
> The thridde part, of mankynde, or the ferthe,
> Ne wende I not by possibilitee
> Had ever in this wide world ybee;
> And trewe of love thise women were echon.
>   [F 285–90]

Given the insistent propaganda of the *Legend*, it is hard not to read in a sexual distinction between "mankynde" and these faithful women—especially because these lines are emphatically difficult to paraphrase. Are there more true women here than a third or a fourth of all the human beings who ever lived (implying that they represent half or two–thirds of all the women)? Or are all the men who have ever lived only a third or a fourth of their number? Or are they merely a third or a fourth of all the men who have ever lived? The confusing ambiguities of gender and of mathematical fractions in this passage suggests that it is unsupported and ill-considered hyperbole: at any rate, the very next line "Now wheither was that a wonder thing or non" (F 291), like the narrator's earlier request that we "honouren and beleve/ These bokes, there we han noon other preve" (F 27–28), appears to suggest a lack of modern exemplars of female virtue—something that Boccaccio explicitly laments in *De mulieribus claris*.

In the *Wife of Bath's Prologue*, which answers clerical antifeminism by not only admitting but exulting in all the faults commonly attributed to women, the words "mankynde" and "man" comically hover between generic inclusiveness and reference to men alone, as when Jankyn reads his nightly lesson from his "book of wikked wyves":

> Upon a nyght Jankyn, that was oure sire,
> Redde on his book, as he sat by the fire,
> Of Eva first, that for hir wikkednesse
> Was al mankynde broght to wrecchednesse,
> For which that Jhesu Crist hymself was slayn,

That boghte us with his herte blood agayn.
Lo, heere expres of womman may ye fynde
That womman was the los of al mankynde.

                                        [III.713–20]

In the first appearance of the word here, the human race is what is
"broght to wrecchednesse," and Jesus saves "us," male and female
alike; in the second, when "womman" is blamed twice in quick
succession, "mankynde" becomes more or less exclusively male.
As the Nun's Priest puts it, tongue-in-cheek:

Wommannes conseil broghte us first to wo
And made Adam fro Paradys to go,
Ther as he was ful myrie and wel at ese.

                                        [VII.3257–59]

In this male idyll, the loss of Eden for mankind is its loss for men.
The Wife of Bath turns such thinking on its head, for her discourse
gives a special pungency and limited sexual reference to moral
maxims with a normally general application. "Of alle men his
wysdom is the hyeste/ That rekketh nevere who hath the world in
honde" (III.326–27): this good advice about forgoing jealousy and
envy becomes a counsel that husbands give up the fight; as for its
source, Ptolemy, she says, "Of alle men yblessed moot he be"
(III.323), for showing an uncharacteristically male good sense. In
her most wonderful example, the Wife outrageously misappropri-
ates the Gospel to let "Jhesus, God and man," describe her own
situation. St. Jerome had compared virgins to wheat bread, and the
incontinent to barley bread; the Wife accepts his distinction, but
adds: "And yet with barly-breed, Mark telle kan,/ Oure Lord Jhesu
refresshed many a man" (145–46). The miracle of the loaves and
fishes becomes a bawdier, and more specifically male-directed,
form of divine largesse:

In swich estaat as God hath cleped us
I wol persevere; I nam nat precius.
In wyfhod I wol use myn instrument
As frely as my Makere hath it sent.

                                        [III.147–50]

The Wife's exuberant response to antifeminism contrasts
with some other, more sober ones. The task Christine de Pisan
will set herself—answering the antifeminists with historical accounts of female virtue—is one that had been previously taken up

by men. Boccaccio's *De mulieribus claris* uses ancient women to browbeat their degenerate descendants, much as St. Jerome does; and in this work at least, most of us would agree with the comment in Castiglione's *Book of the Courtier*, that Boccaccio shows himself to be "a very great enemy of women."[42] In the *Canterbury Tales* as well, when male narrators praise women, Chaucer almost always casts doubt on the sincerity or disinterestedness that the narrator professes to have, and uses the wordplay to disclose hypocrisy or hidden self–interest, whether conscious or not. In the *Man of Law's Tale*, in which the narrator's hypocritical praise of women depends on defining female virtue as passivity, against a background of general misogyny, the neutral meaning of "men" continually shades over into the specifically male, the center of value in the tale:

> Now wolde some men waiten, as I gesse,
> That I sholde tellen al the purveiance
> That th' Emperour, of his grete noblesse,
> Hath shapen for his doghter, dame Custance.
> Wel may men knowen that so greet ordinance
> May no man tellen in a litel clause
> As was arrayed for so heigh a cause.
>
> [II.246–52]

When, in a passage I have quoted already, Constance sets Mary's woe against any "wo man" may sustain, Mary may contrast with the merely human, with the indefinite "one," or with the purely male. To the degree that her suffering is specifically female instead of superhuman, it fits within the Man of Law's inclination—which the Wife of Bath points out in clerks and the Clerk himself reveals—to divide women into virtuous martyrs and the unredeemable corrupters of men. When he comments, "Men myghten asken why she was nat slayn?" (II.470), there is a particular aptness in reading "men" as "males," and taking the question with some seriousness: in St. Jerome's account of virtuous female suicides (recounted by Dorigen in the *Franklin's Tale*), as in the Physician's story of Appius and Virginia, Chaucer shows us a male propensity to kill off virtuous women as a means of proclaiming self-congratulatory male piety.

Chaucer's own case, in the *Legend of Good Women*, is more complex. The god of Love accuses the narrator of being a heretic against Love's religion; and orders him, as penance for having kept

alive the story of Criseyde, to spend the rest of his days writing
saints' lives of women who were martyrs for the religion of love.
As I have argued at length elsewhere, the result is a wonderful exercise in comic censorship and distortion, in which the narrator is
apparently under orders to say nothing bad about any woman.[43] As
part of this continuing joke, the indefinite meaning of "man" always shades over into the particular, usually with a polemical implication. In the hagiographer's account of Lucrece—"What, shal
she fyghte with an hardy knyght?/ Wel wot men that a woman
hath no myght" (1800–01)—what is general human knowledge is
also of particular benefit to potential imitators of Tarquin. In the
G version of the Prologue, the narrator praises ancient female virtue with the following summation:

> And this thing was nat kept for holynesse,
> But al for verray vertu and clennesse,
> And for men schulde sette on hem no lak;
> And yit they were hethene, al the pak,
> That were so sore adrad of alle shame.
> These olde wemen kepte so here name
> That in this world I trowe men shal nat fynde
> A man that coude be so trewe and kynde
> As was the leste woman in that tyde.
>
> [G 296–304]

The first two appearances of "men" here, apparently referring to
people in general or serving as the indefinite pronoun, take on an
added charge when the "man" in line 303 suggests that we should
have been understanding "males" throughout.

The point of Chaucer's joke is not that we should substitute
an antifeminist moral for feminist propaganda: what he shows is
that a newly chastened devotee of Cupid's religion has motives
that are not entirely trustworthy. Chaucer's procedure here comments on a range of courtly game-playing in the later fourteenth
century, and points out the problematic nature of male motives in
a courtly context. In 1399, the marshal Boucicaut and several of
the highest nobles of the French court established a chivalric society, the Order of the Green Shield with the White Lady, dedicated
to defending "the honor, estate, reputation and praise of all women
and damsels of noble lineage."[44] And in 1400 a Cour Amoureuse
with formal rules and an annual poetry contest was established
at the French court to the same purpose—founded "a l'honneur,

loenge, recommandacion et service de toutes dames et demoi-
selles," and with a special injunction against poetry with antifeminist sentiments:

> ... qu'ilz ne facent ou par autre facent faire dittierz, com-
> plaintes, rondeaux, virelays, balades, lays ou autres quel-
> conques façon et taille de rethorique, rimee ou en proze, au
> deshonneur, reproche, amenrissement ou blame de dame ou
> dames, damoiselle ou damoiselles, ensemble quelconques
> femmes, religieuses ou autres, trespassees ou vivans, pour
> quelconques cause que ce soit, tant soit grieve dolereuse ou
> desplaisant.[45]

What are we to make of these gallant enterprises? Chaucer's
own skepticism about them becomes most evident in his treatment of the Squire, who is distinguished from his father the
Knight by his attention to personal appearance, his courtly manners, and a martial skill exercised "In hope to stonden in his lady
grace": "So hoote he lovede that by nyghtertale/ He sleep namoore
than dooth a nyghtyngale" (I.88; 97–98). The Squire's expressed
sympathies in his tale are entirely with the plight of women in
love, and with women's virtue more generally: while all the Tar-
tar men get drunk and stay up all night, he tells us, Canacee goes
to bed early and sober, because she is "ful mesurable, as wommen
be" (V.362). But, as I have argued more extensively in a recent
essay,[46] Chaucer undermines the Squire's effort to identify with
women by showing it to be part of his larger effort to assert identity in place of otherness: the tale shows, despite the Squire's best
efforts, that Mongols are not like Europeans, birds not like humans, and women not like men. Chaucer makes some jokes, of the
sort he makes in the *Nun's Priest's Tale* and the *Parliament of
Fowls*, on the incompatibility of human and avian frames of reference, undercutting the narrative's claim that birds can be called
"men," and that male birds and male human beings are alike in
their maleness, that is to say, their capacity for perfidy. The falcon,
describing her treacherous lover, proclaims:

> Ne nevere, syn the firste man was born,
> Ne koude man, by twenty thousand part,
> Countrefete the sophymes of his art.
> [V.552–54]

Here the uncertainty of reference is compounded by the possible
meanings of "man," first "human being" as well as "male," then

indefinite pronoun, human, and male—with special emphasis on the last—all at once.

These questions of gender and species come up with special force when the falcon, using a Boethian commonplace, berates her lover for abandoning her:

> That "alle thyng, repeirynge to his kynde,
> Gladeth hymself"; thus seyn men, as I gesse.
> Men loven of propre kynde newefangelnesse,
> As briddes doon that men in cages fede.
>
> [608–11]

In the phrase "thus seyn men, as I gesse" or "briddes . . . that men in cages fede," "men" must, or at least may, refer to both men and women; in the single verse that separates these two phrases, "Men loven of propre kynde newefangelnesse," "men" are males, and they suffer the obloquy directed against all amorous males in the *Squire's Tale*.[47] The fracture here between "men" and "men," that is to say between men and women, in the end leads us to ask about the Squire's own motives in identifying so completely with a woman's point of view: if no man is to be trusted, why should he be? The Squire presents himself as a male sympathetic to women, and tries to distinguish himself from all other men by thinking as a "man," i.e., a human being, instead of as a "man." But his sympathy and unremitting praise of women may be seen as at heart, however unconsciously, another seduction ploy. For as Ovid and the *Roman de la Rose* suggest, one of the best deceptions for a lover to employ is the unremitting blind praise of all women (see *Romaunt* 2229–38).

My final examples of Chaucer's play on the word "man" in effect return my argument to the Biblical examples with which it began, for they at once prophesy an escape from sexual division and divisive categories, and yet reveal the impossibility of our making such an escape, unless in soteriological expectation. In *Troilus and Criseyde*, one of the paradoxes we are confronted with from the start is that the narrator of the poem is not a lover, has no experience or hope of experience in love, and yet is love's poet, indeed, as he comically suggests, the Pope of love's religion—the *servus servorum dei Amoris* (1.15). His audience of lovers includes both men and women, as the frontispiece to the Corpus Christi *Troilus* forcefully reminds us, and his task of helping lovers is presumably directed at both sexes. But from the beginning of the poem, it is apparent that his primary duty, as he conceives it, is to the male initiators of love, the lovers at first sight who seek womanly pity—"if this may don gladnesse/ Unto any lovere, and his cause availle" (1.19–20); "sende hem myght hire ladies so to plese" (1.45). And from the moment of Pandarus's first appearance—with the repeated reminders that Pandarus is, like the narrator, a poet and fiction-maker—we are aware that the narrator's sympathies, when choices are necessary, are male sympathies: when discomfort arises about the morality of deceiving and seducing Criseyde, the best he can suggest is that love is a good, and that a happy love is in Criseyde's own best interest, if only she knew it. This bias appears most noticeably, and most comically, in the narrator's rhapsodic injunction at the crucial moment in Book Three: "For love of God, take every womman hccdc/ To wcrkcn thus, if it comth to the neede" (3.1224–25). But when Criseyde's betrayal of Troilus is imminent, the narrator's growing anxiety about issues of sexual politics—is Criseyde's action an accusation of all women?—appears in the wavering reference of the word "man":

> And trewely, as men in bokes rede,
> Men wiste nevere womman han the care,
> Ne was so loth out of a town to fare.
>   [5.19–21]

The thought that general human knowledge is of particular interest to men, as they search out notable examples of female faith or perfidy, is even more conspicuously evident later. "Men seyn—I not—that she yaf hym hire herte" (5.1050).

> But trewely, how longe it was bytwene
> That she forsok hym for this Diomede,
> Ther is non auctour telleth it, I wene.
> Take every man now to his bokes heede,
> He shal no terme fynden, out of drede.
>   [5.1086–90]

At the very end of the poem, however, after Troilus's sister Cassandra tells him the unwelcome truth about Criseyde's deceit, the narrator remembers rather nervously that his audience includes women as well. Having mollified them, by speaking against the treachery of men (5.1772–85), he copies Troilus's detached, heavenly perspective on our earthly blindnesses and limitations with his own condemnation. The last stanza of the poem, which quotes Dante's great invocation of the Trinity—three in one, and one in three—as the resolution of all paradox and division, ends with the figures of Jesus and Mary, sexually identified but beyond the world of sexual difference. This final resolution is presaged by an earlier, more limitedly human one. St. Paul tells us that in Christ's promise "There is neither Jew nor Greek; there is neither bond nor free; there is neither male nor female" (Gal. 3.28). Chaucer, with an allusion to the Genesis text about which so much commentary is concerned (is woman too created in the image of God?), answers its questions by including both sexes,[48] as he moves beyond sexual difference to the spiritual lesson that the poem gives us all:

> O yonge, fresshe folkes, he or she,
> In which that love up groweth with youre age,
> Repeyreth hom fro worldly vanyte,
> And of youre herte up casteth the visage
> To thilke God that after his ymage
> Yow made.
>
> [5.1835–40]

Even so, this restoration of equal status, first in the equal possibility for betrayal, then for an achievement of understanding that surpasses sexual difference, coexists at the end of the poem—and beyond, since Chaucer gestures to his palinode *The Legend of Good Women* (5.1777–78)—with an Ovidian point-counterpoint that reminds us with a vengeance of the persistence of such difference, even as we talk of its transcendence. One of Chaucer's great jokes in the *Legend of Good Women* (once again playing on the two meanings of the word "man") appears when his narrator's attacks on his own sex establish his credentials as the woman's man who is alone to be trusted:

> Be war, ye wemen, of youre subtyl fo,
> Syn yit this day men may ensaumple se;
> And trusteth, as in love, no man but me.
>
> [2559–61]

Even today, "we," or "people," can see examples; in love, Chaucer advises, trust no "man" but me. (There is another joke here, as Lee Patterson points out, if we read "men" not as "people" but as "males": "men, the line disturbingly claims, are a subtle foe precisely *because* ['syn'] they continually see examples of male tyranny. Far from dissuading men from treachery, the legendary form provides them with models. . . . ")[49] At the end of *Troilus and Criseyde*, the narrator apologizes for the subject of his poem, a woman's faithlessness, and makes an abrupt change of course:

> Bysechyng every lady bright of hewe,
> And every gentil womman, what she be,
> That al be that Criseyde was untrewe,
> That for that gilt she be nat wroth with me.
> Ye may hire gilt in other bokes se;
> And gladlier I wol write, yif yow leste,
> Penopeës trouthe and good Alceste.
>
> N'y sey nat this al oonly for thise men,
> But moost for wommen that bitraised be
> Thorugh false folk—God yeve hem sorwe, amen!—
> That with hire grete wit and subtilte
> Bytraise yow. And this commeveth me
> To speke, and in effect yow alle I preye,
> Beth war of men, and herkneth what I seye!
>
> [5.1779–86][50]

Is it possible to be wary of men, and take a man's advice? Is it possible to trust no men, and yet trust a male narrator? Only if we grant wholeheartedly that the poem's ending has moved us irrevocably beyond the terms of earthly experience; and that is precisely what we are unable to grant.[51] In these instances, Chaucer shows himself to be well aware of the confining effects of gender, of the many respects in which—both for our own ulterior motives and against our best disinterested efforts—none of us can escape the sexual implications of his voice.

10

From Dorigen to the Vavasour: Reading Backwards

The franklin's conception of gentilesse is thus consistent with the entirely superficial nobility of a wealthy man of the middle class who is "Epicurus owene sone" and is, hence, like the summoner in the friar's tale, blind to anything beneath surface appearances.

D. W. Robertson, Jr.

. . . Chaucer meant the Franklin to be admired, emulated—and loved?—rather than derided and scoffed at.

Henrik Specht

The problems of the Franklin's Tale . . . do not reside in the Franklin.

Derek Pearsall[1]

I am in favor of companionate and reciprocal love; and affection, friendship, and mutuality between committed lovers and marital partners seem like very good things, indeed. Furthermore, I am sure that those earnest readers who wish to find such values illustrated and celebrated in the *Franklin's Tale* are honorable men and women. But I am not sure they are the best of readers. This is an essay about reading, and about two distinct approaches to the tale and its portrayal of marital partnership.

One of the curious features of critical debate about the *Franklin's Tale* is the tendency it has shown to become fixated on the question of the moral intelligence of the narrator. To be sure, the influence of "the dramatic principle" in discussing Chaucer's pilgrims, along with midcentury interest in irony, rhetoric, and unreliable narrators, has encouraged a forensic approach to the persona of the Franklin. But it is nonetheless remarkable that so much energy has been spent on praising or blaming him, as if Kittredge's dictum that "the tales exist for the sake of the tellers" here received its fullest confirmation.[2] I would seem to have been part of that process myself, in that my 1964 essay on "The Promises in the Franklin's Tale" promulgated the thesis that "a whole tale can be turned back against its teller to comment satirically on his character and the values he represents."[3] And so a summary of debate tends to turn into a list of those who "attack" the Franklin and those who "defend" him.

What gets lost in the process is much account of the experience of reading the tale which could lead to a mapping of its poetic terrain. *Franklin's Tale* criticism is overcharged with preachments for or against "pleyn delit," based on extracts and paraphrases from the poem. That it is in rime and meter seems not to signify; that it has a poetic structure and a complex literary plan seems to matter not much more. The Franklin campaigns for our approval and we vote for or against his principles, without too much attention to his methods. Perhaps Nicolas Jacobs has it right when he says that "among the better-known *Canterbury Tales* the Franklin's is commonly more admired than enjoyed."[4]

I am persuaded that this tendency of so much of the criticism to stay general rises not from mass folly (surely an unthinkable condition among Chaucerians), but from an understandable reaction to the way the story is told—where poetic beauties stand in separated splendor, like Follies at the ends of lawns (to be admired at a distance and then passed by), and where the conception of a Teller is a function of the prosiness of the tale, concerned to deal with ideas and ideals in a palatable way, pleasing every taste without obtrusive art.

But I am also persuaded that the story most richly apprehended invites several kinds of reading at once, in a contradictory yet complementary manner. I am going to distinguish these kinds as "reading forwards" and "reading backwards," two discardable terms that do not deserve immortality. But in the present argument they will help me discuss the way the Franklin comes to inhabit our imaginations, the way his tale gets told, and the way we might try to characterize "his" discourse.

To illustrate each kind of reading I will examine first two passages in which one or the other can be described as peculiarly called for. The first, "reading forwards," will be seen as unscrolling a text as if it were being complacently listened to. The second, "reading backwards," will be seen as an activity of resistance: handling the book, re-leaving the progress of the narrative.

I. READING FORWARDS

Let us begin, then, by considering a passage near the end of the work which offers the assurance that everything will be happily resolved. It is like reaching the summit after a grand hike up a mountain, where the narrative lets us look out over the miles of well ordered landscape as a reward for our having pressed on and followed the trail:

> My trouthe I plighte, I shal yow never repreve
> Of no biheste, and heere I take my leve,
> As of the treweste and the beste wyf
> That evere yet I knew in al my lyf.   1540
> But every wyf be war of hire biheeste!
> On Dorigen remembreth, atte leeste.
> Thus kan a squier doon a gentil dede
> As wel as kan a knyght, withouten drede.
>   She thonketh hym upon hir knees al bare,   1545
> And hoom unto hir housbonde is she fare,
> And tolde hym al, as ye han herd me sayd;
> And be ye siker, he was so weel apayd
> That it were impossible me to wryte.
> What sholde I lenger of this cas endyte?   1550
>   Arveragus and Dorigen his wyf
> In sovereyn blisse leden forth hir lyf.[5]

The editors are not certain about the attribution of lines 1541–44: who is speaking? If close-quotes are put at the end of 1540, it would be the Franklin who is then moralizing; but if they are placed at the end of 1544 (as in *The Riverside Chaucer*), it would be Aurelius who is concluding his speech with such a warning. However, because quotation marks are an invention of modern printing and appear in none of the Chaucerian manuscripts, the answer can only be pursued in a larger context. Line 1540 is definitely the Squire speaking, with his "that evere yet I knew"; while line 1545 is clearly not reported speech but a narrative of action: "she thonketh hym," etc. Although lines 1543–44 are paralleled by the Clerk's at 1610–12, and use the same *dede/drede* rime, the syntax is not as similar as the thought: it is awkward to have Aurelius speaking *to* Dorigen and at the same time speaking *about* her. Thus John M. Manly would transfer the lines to follow 1550, though without textual authority.[6]

If the lines are from Aurelius, they are a trivializing of morality—like the exchanges of cock and fox at the end of the *Nun's Priest's Tale*—from one whose authority is suspect (since he had won Dorigen by a trick rather than his own labors). The couplet at 1541–42 even seems a bit mean, acting as if Dorigen's promise had been carelessly constructed instead of (as was the actual case) misconstrued, tainting the more generous praise of Dorigen as "the treweste and the beste wyf."

If the lines are from the Franklin, we recognize yet another "intrusion" from him into the narrative, drawing our attention to its meaning and its exemplary force; and this would be added to those other places where he speaks to us about what is happening, as we build up a sense of his special voice, a distinctive medium for the story. But since it is not a very profound observation, and has very little to do with larger themes of *fredom* and *gentilesse*, it can be taken as a sign of the Franklin's simplicity and with his concern for plain speaking, not to mention his *besynesse* as he fiddles with the elements of his tale.

Notice also lines 1547–50, which modulate from "ye han herd me sayd" to "it were impossible me to wryte" or "lenger of this cas endyte." How can the Franklin, riding on his horse to Canterbury, say he will "write" anything? Even if these collocations are taken generally, one is at liberty to look past the persona-debate touched on above and conclude that the real "I" of the whole passage is the author, i.e., Chaucer himself in some shape or fashion (but not the teller of *Thopas*, not on horseback). In which case, the attempt to distinguish a moralizing Aurelius from a moralizing Franklin can be laid aside: both are verbal constructs in a tale whose shape and distinctive features are, quite simply, Chaucerian.

My point has to do with the process of reading. For a reader who is "reading forwards," as I will call it, the experience is a model of listening to an oral performance. Quotation marks do not exist within this dimension. Someone actually reading aloud might try to devise an accent for Aurelius distinguishable from the Franklin's, from which it would be clear who was saying lines 1541–44; but normally the ear would be aware that the tale flowed first into Aurelius's renunciation, then briefly paused for the exemplary exclamation, and then flowed on with the recital of events.

The moralizing couplet about *gentil* emulation (1543–44) would be felt primarily as a marker of the pleasing reversals in the story occasioned by Arveragus's surprising decision, one which led the reader on with interest to see whether the clerk would respond in a similar way. Which character said what would be less important; the *tale* said it.

It follows that the "character" of the Franklin, the realization of that persona we deduced from the portrait in the *General Prologue*, is only intermittently encountered. When the poetry deals with his person and that person talks about himself, most notably in the prefatory sections, we hear the Franklin; but once the tale is under way it is hard to keep in mind a special set of characteristics that foreground a narrator-"character." The soul of the Franklin cannot dominate our attention; the story must be allowed to proceed on its own. Here, recent theory can help in restoring our awareness of what David Lawton has called "the standard high-style" narrator.[7]

I have spoken of a "model of listening," for I take oral performance as the context of this "reading forwards." It is a practice of attention eager to learn what is to happen next, and immediate juxtaposition and contiguity are of greatest importance, along with narrative pace. Hence, Aurelius's "quit claim" in lines 1533–40 is built out of two quickly flowing four-line sentences, the first without marked pauses at line-ends, the second with strong enjambment at 1537. The problematic lines at 1541–44 are shaped not only as riming, but as chiming couplets, especially "hire biheeste / atte leeste"; and with the conjunctions of "But" followed by "Thus," the narrative is briefly arrested while a moralizing spotlight plays over the meaning of events. The resumption of the narrative is marked by renewed parataxis with a succession of parallel clauses linked with *and*'s. Within this prosody of presentation, the "hearer" does not have a chance to remark on subtleties of indirect discourse or distinctions of voice and persona: Dorigen is safe; Aurelius has done the right thing; now, what about the Clerk?

Furthermore, this prosody does not require the kind of analysis I have just provided, for its effects are meant to be felt, not seen, directing our attention to what is said, not how something is expressed.

We are not expected to say to ourselves, "how fluent this fellow is, how cunningly he uses rime to join or divide the flow of sense!" Nor are we reminded of the Teller who so colorfully told us he knew nothing of *colours*. Thus, paradoxically, even the appearance of the verb, "write," becomes an aspect of the image of oral discourse, ignoring the Franklin and carrying on like that "writer," Chaucer, who talks the way he writes and writes the way he talks.[8]

II. READING BACKWARDS

They take hir leve, and on hir wey they gon,   1490
But they ne wiste why she thider wente.
He nolde no wight tellen his entente.
        Paraventure an heep of yow, ywis,
Wol holden hym a lewed man in this
That he wol putte his wyf in jupartie.   1495
Herkneth the tale er ye upon hire crie.
She may have bettre fortune than yow semeth;
And whan that ye han herd the tale, demeth.
        This squier, which that highte Aurelius,
On Dorigen that was so amorus,   1500
Of aventure happed hire to meete
Amydde the toun. . . .

This passage addressed to "an heep of yow" takes us into yet more complicated textual matters. The authoritative early manuscript, Peniarth 392 D, National Library of Wales (the "Hengwrt" ms.) lacks lines 1493–98, as do all other manuscripts except the related cousins, Huntington Library 26.C.9 (the "Ellesmere"), and British Library Additional 35286. The absence of a manuscript tradition for what seems a lively and interesting set of lines permits almost any kind of speculation, since there can be no possibility of proving their authorship. Yet they are thoroughly Chaucerian, both in their craft and their cunning.[9]

Without these lines, the story changes not a whit; and it is hardly likely that any in the audience would need relief from the suspense, for Dorigen will gain her release only twenty-seven lines later. What, then, do they contribute? A retrograde gesture. There is another paradox at work here, but moving in a direction opposite to the one discussed above. Even though these remarks seem to point apologetically forwards and are couched as an address to a group of listeners, the self-regarding form of the apology draws our attention to the process and authority of the narration. We are thus encouraged to read "backwards."

The lines reveal a Franklin at work at his wheels and levers, like the Wizard of Oz exposed behind his curtain. They invite us to contemplate his anxiety, and to think about the tale not just as a story unfolding in time, but as a set of motives whose consequences require justification. This is a little different from what Germaine Dempster once described as "the soothing influence spreading over the whole of the tale from an anticipation of its charming end."[10] That "influence" was part of the prosody of presentation, a matter of vague generic gestures, conventional diction, and genial characters; this remark from the Franklin, even though partaking of the attitude of oral delivery, turns us into readers more than listeners. It requires a kind of self-consciousness, and directs us to the mechanisms of this fiction; and in so doing, it momentarily pushes us outside of the fictional continuum of time and turns us into contemplators of the narrative process.

I think it likely that any scribe or editor other than Chaucer would try to improve the sense of the story as something told forwards; only the author with his authorial "entente" (that is, one who has a vision of how he wants his text to "play") would construct additions that worked "backwards," and that is the reason I am so sure these lines are genuine, even though I cannot tell if they stand as late additions or accidentally preserved deletions.

It is not necessary here to join debate with those critics who use these lines to emphasize the sincerity of the Franklin, towards defending Arveragus's command to Dorigen as a daring act of faith in the power of goodness and truth to draw forth truth and goodness from others. It is enough to draw attention to the Janus-like quality of the passage: for even as it looks forwards to a happy ending, it stresses the necessity of attention, of contemplating the plot of the tale and the manner of its unfolding. By foregrounding the issue of performance, and by linking it, even jocularly, with moral judgments, it encourages a consideration in which ethics and aesthetics can come together. "Reading backwards," then, is reading with a certain kind of memory, employing a sifting that requires comparisons and contrasts, re-reading, and reflection. None of these activities is congenial to the act of listening. To be sure, listeners can develop a powerful attentiveness and draw upon a lively memory, but they cannot "turne over the leef," nor can they control the pace and timing of what they are hearing. To read backwards is to catch the author at his game, and to enter into play with him, back and forth through the pages of a book.[11] I will elaborate on these ideas before I finish, but it is time now to put my definitions to work on three passages I have selected.

I have not chosen to discuss Arveragus's mighty words about keeping *trouthe* (1479), nor the activities of Aurelius in dealing with the rocks of Brittany, nor the fateful "rash promise" of

Dorigen. These topics have been discussed at length in my 1964
essay on the promises, whose logic I stand by, especially as source-
comparisons are concerned.[12] What I am trying to sketch out here
is a somewhat larger theory of reading that can avoid the excesses
of "the dramatic principle." Thus I return to passages that intro-
duce the philosophical themes the tale is supposed to exemplify
and bring to our attention the attitudes and values of the presumed teller of the tale.

III. THE LADY AND THE VAVASOUR

The first passage for analysis features the complaint of Dorigen concerning the black rocks of Brittany (which are not black). It
is central to the story and to the unfolding of her personality. It
rises out of her desolation at her husband's absence and fear for his
safety, and shows us the height of her sensibilities:

> "Eterne God, that thurgh thy purveiaunce   865
> Ledest the world by certein governaunce,
> In ydel, as men seyn, ye no thyng make.
> But, Lord, thise grisly feendly rokkes blake,
> That semen rather a foul confusion
> Of werk than any fair creacion   870
> Of swich a parfit wys God and a stable,
> Why han ye wroght this werk unresonable?
> For by this werk, south, north, ne west, ne eest,
> Ther nys yfostred man, ne bryd, ne beest;
> It dooth no good, to my wit, but anoyeth.   875
> Se ye nat, Lord, how mankynde it destroyeth?
> An hundred thousand bodyes of mankynde
> Han rokkes slayn, al be they nat in mynde,
> Which mankynde is so fair part of thy werk
> That thou it madest lyk to thyn owene merk.   880
> Thanne semed it ye hadde a greet chiertee
> Toward mankynde; but how thanne may it bee
> That ye swiche meenes make it to destroyen,
> Whiche meenes do no good, but evere anoyen?
> I woot wel clerkes wol seyn as hem leste,   885
> By argumentz, that al is for the beste,
> Though I ne kan the causes nat yknowe.
> But thilke God that made wynd to blowe
> As kepe my lord! This my conclusion.

To clerkes lete I al disputison.
But wolde God that alle thise rokkes blake
Were sonken into helle for his sake!
Thise rokkes sleen myn herte for the feere."   890

The passage is elaborately prepared for, beginning at 814, and is the lamenting aria that follows a recitative reacting to her sight of the "grisly rokkes blake" by the seacoast. The passage in effect builds the rocks as personal terror and philosophical problem so hugely into the story that their presence influences all subsequent action. Even though Dorigen complains about the role of the rocks in the scheme of things, the impact of the passage on one who reads forwards will be emotional rather than intellectual, concluding with the pagan/Christian appeal at lines 888–89. Dorigen looks for her husband's safety more than she seeks philosophical instruction; and, indeed, she poses no question here that the story will answer: she is not to discover why God made the rocks. But the story does show us her single-minded devotion to her husband and his safe return, and introduces a sign of peril—"an hundred thousand bodyes of mankynde / Han rokkes slayn"—which will reverberate at that moment in the garden when she refuses Aurelius, as it were, in the name of the rocks.

It is her helplessness that is her help: she shares with Griselda a deep faith in what she loves, a large capacity for suffering, and a passivity that is the feminine version of strong deeds. Like Griselda's, her predicament intensifies the strains in the story and engages our active sympathy. There can be no question of mockery, reading forwards. Dorigen is the good woman who is the good wife, and her complaint is a swirl of emotional colors—"grisly feendly rokkes," "foul confusion," "sleen myn herte for the feere"—that paint her true feelings.

To read the same complaint "backwards" only means with a wider sense of context (so, "sideways," too!) and a closer attention to its movements. It still does not require one to turn on Dorigen and call her names, because in the process the evaluation of her character is not an issue. We are required to learn how the poetry thinks. Here is where a comparison with the *Knight's Tale* can help:

Thanne seyde he, "O crueel goddes that governe
This world with byndyng of youre word eterne,
And writen in the table of atthamaunt   1305
Youre parlement and youre eterne graunt,
What is mankynde moore unto you holde

Than is the sheep that rouketh in the folde?
For slayn is man right as another beest,
And dwelleth eek in prison and arreest,   1310
And hath siknesse and greet adversitee,
And ofte tymes giltelees, pardee.
    "What governance is in this prescience,
That giltelees tormenteth innocence?
And yet encresseth this al my penaunce,   1315
That man is bounden to his observaunce,
For Goddes sake, to letten of his wille,
Ther as a beest may al his lust fulfille.
And whan a beest is deed he hath no peyne;
But man after his deeth moot wepe and pleyne,   1320
Though in this world he have care and wo.
Withouten doute it may stonden so.
The answere of this lete I to dyvynys,
But wel I woot that in this world greet pyne ys."

I have put Dorigen's complaint next to a somewhat similar complaint from the *Knight's Tale*, for it is the Knight and his presumed world that the Franklin most deeply admires, even though he dares only to address the Knight's son. The vast epic-romance with which the Knight led off has become a black rock in the Franklin's creative unconscious. I say, "the Franklin," but wish it understood now that the term is a convenience, for we are not so much thinking of an old gentleman with an unruly son who speaks out his story, as we are coming to grips with what I shall call "the vavasorial mind." What this vavasorial mind can be, I will explain by making some contrasts between the two passages here.

    The substance of them both is the same, deriving from complaints against Fortune and God's Providence which are discovered early on in Boethius' *Consolation of Philosophy:*

> "We men, that ben noght a foul partie, but a fair partie of so greet a werk, we ben turmented in this see of fortune. Thow governour, withdraughe and restreyne the ravysschynge flodes . . ." [Book 1, Metrum 5]

    I take this passage to be the philosophical seed that grew into the *Franklin's Tale,* and which explains the shift from the winter-blooming garden in Boccaccio's *Filocolo* to the rocks of Brittany.

But that is not yet the whole point. A careful reading of Boethius's meter will show that sea images are part of the metaphorical vocabulary of philosophy, and that Boethius is not stopping to question the rightness of rocks—indeed, takes their rightness as a *donnée* for his argument—but is rather complaining against "folk of wikkide maneres" who "sitten in heie chayeres." In other words, Dorigen broods over a literal sea of fortune, and complains against geology, not wicked men.

Note the different salutations: "O crueel goddes," etc., and "Eterne God," etc. Palamon is more bitter and closer to the Boethian concern; Dorigen is politer and more plaintive. With her, Boethius (at least, in terms of medieval stereotypes) has been feminized.

Dorigen observes that God ("as men seyn") makes no thing without purpose, and seeks to point out an apparent inconsistency to the Deity. Palamon runs through imagery of restriction and hard necessity ("byndyng of youre word eterne," "table of atthamaunt") in asserting that God is less inconsistent than heedless: men are worth no more in his sight than sheep. Palamon does not speak of accidents like shipwrecks, but of the horrors of life: prison, sickness, "greet adversitee," and innocent suffering. This is the iron string of Boethius. Again, Dorigen uses a feminine word for the parallel point: "Ther nys *yfostred* man, ne bryd, ne beest." And she focuses exclusively on the catastrophes of navigation: her vision of evil is expressed in the hyperbolic "an hundred thousand bodyes"—dreadful enough, to be sure, yet so much narrower than the universe of unmerited pain Palamon cries out against. And then, the juxtaposition of that unintentionally comic phrase, "al be they nat in mynde," has the effect of deflecting the force of the huge number so that tragedy is converted into bathos. This way of thinking takes iteration for argument, and its brief concession looks forward to the later attempt to catalog good wives who died for virtue.

Both complaints confess their inability to work out a satisfactory answer, and invoke the authorities—at once acknowledging them and passing them by:

> The answere of this lete I to dyvynys,
> But wel I woot that in this world greet pyne ys.

Palamon asserts the pain which will not be dispersed with arguments. Dorigen has a more "womanly" response (whereas the Wife of Bath will draw on her Martian qualities to offer a spirited defiance to male authorities):

> I woot wel clerkes wol seyn as hem leste,
> By argumentz that al is for the beste,

and so forth, not ending with a gesture towards a coast of corpses, but turning it all back to her wifely concern: "as kepe my lord!"

I do not mean to hold up the "male" Palamon for approval as being more realistic, nor is Dorigen to be blamed for narrowing her focus (Palamon's pain, after all, is self-regarding, while hers is not). The backwards-reading I am trying to practice does not need to confine itself to imagined personalities. Rather, what this comparison reveals is the nature of the questions asked, the depth and breadth of the view explored. Notice that the reader never sees the rocks apart from the account of Dorigen's emotions. They are realized only in her mind, and not even there does Dorigen actually count up 100,000 bodies littering the beaches.

The complaint invokes a Boethian vocabulary ("purveiaunce," "certein governaunce," "confusion," "stable," "unresonable") in order to sing a Boethian tune, yet the function of the speech goes no farther than detailing a state of anxiety and, even more important, the obsessive devotion of a wife who yearns for her lord. This is the vavasorial temper, to gesture towards philosophy on the way to comforts untested by any fire or true pain. (My unanchored "this" in the previous sentence intends to reach out past the character of Dorigen to perceive the behavior, or set of values, that these fictions allegorize.[13])

IV. THE ETHICS OF PROSPERITY

The second passage for analysis will again be set next to a comparative passage from the *Knight's Tale:*

> Heere may men seen an humble, wys accord;
> Thus hath she take hir servant and hir lord—
> Servant in love, and lord in mariage.
> Servage? Nay, but in lordshipe above,   795
> Sith he hath bothe his lady and his love;
> His lady, certes, and his wyf also,
> The which that lawe of love acordeth to.
> And whan he was in this prosperitee,

Hoom with his wyf he gooth to his contree,   800
Nat fer fro Pedmark, ther his dwellyng was,
Where as he lyveth in blisse and in solas.
        Who koude telle, but he hadde wedded be,
The joye, the ese, and the prosperitee
That is bitwixe an housbonde and his wyf?   805

❖❖❖

"Suster," quod he, "this is my fulle assent,   3075
With al th'avys heere of my parlement,
That gentil Palamon, youre owene knyght,
That serveth yow with wille, herte, and myght,
And ever hath doon syn ye first hym knewe,
That ye shul of youre grace upon hym rewe,   3080
And taken hym for housbonde and for lord.
Lene me youre hond, for this is oure accord.
Lat se now of youre wommanly pitee.
He is a kynges brother sone, pardee;
And though he were a povre bacheler,   3085
Syn he hath served yow so many a yeer,
And had for yow so greet adversitee,
It moste been considered, leeveth me,
For gentil mercy oghte to passen right."
        Thanne seyde he thus to Palamon the knight: 3090
"I trowe ther nedeth litel sermonyng
To make yow assente to this thyng.
Com neer, and taak youre lady by the hond."
        Bitwixen hem was maad anon the bond
That highte matrimoigne or mariage,   3095
By al the conseil and the baronage.
And thus with alle blisse and melodye
Hath Palamon ywedded Emelye.
And God, that al this wyde world hath wroght,
Sende hym his love that hath it deere aboght;   4000
For now is Palamon in alle wele,
Lyvynge in blisse, in richesse, and in heele,
And Emelye hym loveth so tendrely,
And he hire serveth so gentilly,
That nevere was ther no word hem bitwene   4005
Of jalousie or any oother teene.

In the first passage above, the Franklin is in the process of
getting started, and pauses in his exposition to become richly

intra-textual. That is to say, he is not here citing authorities or alluding to other books or sources, or even drawing unconsciously from the larger book of Culture, but is drawing together issues and vocabulary prominent in other pilgrims' uses. If we take his "For o thyng *sires*" (761) as more precise than a general formula, he ignores the Wife of Bath, yet as everyone realizes it is her discourse he is re-arranging with his remarks on love and *maistrie*. He repudiates the idea of dominance, draws upon the virtue of *pacience,* nodding to the Clerk but avoiding the servility of Griselda's obedience, and praises mutual trust and forbearance, thus healing the condition of jealousy and betrayal the Merchant had described (803–5 are essentially a repetition of 1337–41 in the Merchant's mock-encomium of marriage).

I have placed next to this passage part of the conclusion from the *Knight's Tale* as a reminder that the intratextuality of this disquisition from the Franklin involves more tales than those of the Wife, Clerk, and Merchant, for here is yet another place where the arbiter of true nobility serves as an original.

And here is a vocabulary the Franklin will mimic: "that gentil Palamon . . . that serveth yow," "ye shul of youre grace upon hym rewe," "taken hym for housbonde and for lord." And there is more: Theseus appeals to Emily's "wommanly pitee," and says that even if Palamon were "a povre bacheler" he would still deserve her, "syn he hath served yow so many a yeer." (The hypothetical case in the *Knight's Tale* was transferred to the actual situation in the Franklin's.) Then follows the solemn elaboration of "the bond / That highte matrimoigne or mariage," and the glowing clause, "with all blisse and melodye / Hath . . . ywedded." The description of their happy life, 3101–6, uses the concepts of tender love from the woman and service from the man which are reiterated by the Franklin at 793, etc. So it will be seen that, rather than coming up with a new concept of love and marriage, the Franklin reaffirms what the Knight had already described (cf. Donald Howard: "The Franklin presents his ideas with a buoyancy which makes them sound like a breakthrough . . . ").[14]

In terms of the *Knight's Tale,* the virtue of *suffrance* did not need stressing, for the relationship between husband and wife was not made problematic—it lay over the horizon in the happy-ever-after of romance. The Franklin wishes to concentrate on that relationship, and his summary is affirmative, polite, persuasive. The paradoxes of the lines quoted here are part of a program of inclusion—both/and rather than either/or: "His lady, certes, and his wyf also"; and again:

Wommen, of kynde, desiren libertee,
And nat to been constreyned as a thral;
And so doon men, if I sooth seyen shal.
768–70

But we are now at a critical flashpoint. Jill Mann (warmly seconded by Derek Pearsall, pp. 158–60) finds that "Chaucer's own comments constitute an unhesitating endorsement of the wisdom of this situation and of the participants in it," and then throws down this challenge:

> . . . any reader who wishes to dissociate him- or herself from the warm approval in these lines will face the same difficulty—and that is the difficulty of finding a location in the tale for true wisdom and worthiness, if both characters and narrator offer only false images of these qualities.[15]

It is just at this point that "reading backwards" offers a reply, perhaps even a solution. It begins with a wider reference: this ideal marriage that the Franklin expounds is not necessarily one that *any* member of the Marriage Debate would disapprove. How could they? All principles are mixed together, with no sense of strain. Although Arveragus says he will take the sovereignty except in name, Dorigen swears to be obedient. He will continue to serve her, but so did Palamon continue to serve Emily after their wedding.

Much will depend upon where one takes hold of the disquisition. The beginning sounds most radical, when Arveragus swears that he will never "upon hym take no maistrie / Agayn hir wyl . . . / But hire obeye, and folwe hir wyl in al" (747–49). This resembles the end of the *Wife of Bath's Tale*, and the Franklin warms to his commendation of their mutual surrender of wills. Yet a little further on, without repudiating the earlier conditions, the knight is promising "suffrance" and she is swearing there will be no "defaute in here." Now, forbearance does not necessarily contradict obedience to one's lover, yet it is not quite the same thing. One can evince great condescension and restraint in dealing with another without necessarily treating her as an equal.

As he addresses the company, the Franklin seeks to act as a judge-mediator, reconciling what had been alienated. His technique is to incorporate value-loaded words from the marriage discourse and balance them in a harmony of affirmation. Notice that the disquisition ends on a twice-repeated word: "in this prosperitee" (799), and "the joye, the ese, and the prosperitee / That is bitwixe an housbonde and his wyf" (804–5). No contradiction is felt too keenly, and neither griefs nor grievances are admitted. His glance is so benevolent and impartial that a great many modern readers have been convinced that Kittredge was right:

> Marriage is an affair of practical life. . . . To the Franklin . . . we lend a credent ear. He is no cloistered rhetorician, but a ruddy, white-bearded vavasour, a great man in his neighborhood, fond of the good things of life and famous for his lavish hospitality. . . . Such a man lies under no suspicion of transcendental theorism or vague heroics. When *he* speaks of mutual forbearance and perfect gentle love between husband and wife, we listen with conviction. The thing is possible. The problem need puzzle us no longer. [p. 210]

So the Franklin carries us forward by the strength of his wishing it so. The story lies ahead, not behind, and we anticipate an exemplum that will parallel, while correcting, the *Wife of Bath's Tale*. There is thus no time here to ask for details, or to inquire whether "servage" in lines 794 and 795 means courteous attentions or domestic thralldom. Many critics are sure they know, however, and the *Franklin's Tale*, more than any other, has generated approving homilies based on its matrimonial themes.[16] It is the triumph of vavasorial optimism and the ethics of prosperity.

The Franklin's way is to press forward and not look back. Hence only the backwards-reading critic feels much discomfort over the consequent news that Arveragus has gone off to England to seek honor in arms, leaving his wife utterly distraught. One obviously cannot even think of asking why, after more than a year, she isn't pregnant; but one is certainly free to wonder how the decision to leave was arrived at. If Dorigen is so grief-stricken, how can it be imagined that Arveragus acted only in obedience to her will? If she did give full assent, what did their discussion sound like? There is no way to know. And, in fact, there will be no opportunity to see how their special "humble, wys accord" (791) worked out in detail. D. W. Robertson, Jr., has intensely aggravated those who approve of the Franklin's ideal of marriage by claiming that what he actually wants "is a marriage which avoids the image of the sacrament" (*Preface to Chaucer*, p. 472); and yet the only time we see the couple making a decision together the knight is absolutely in command, and acts with such unchallenged authority that it is hard to see how even a traditionalist could find fault.[17]

So our backwards-answer to Mann is this: there is no reason to "disapprove" of the lines she finds so commendable since, like the Tale's resolution, they are designed to evoke the best from us. And yet, what will that be? A warm feeling, at best. They teach nothing except well-wishing, which is not a vice yet hardly a strong virtue. In fact, strength is the missing element here, because there is no significant resistance from the world to be overcome. Alfred David's wry formulation is good backwards-reading: "Perhaps a better solution never has been devised or imagined, but this is not the same thing as saying that it works."[18]

The way it works is to make the story come out right, as the Franklin promises it will. Fortunately, Arveragus is not Walter, Aurelius is not Damian, and Dorigen is not Alysoun. If one of those pairs should change places with the other, the world would not seem so gentle. Paul Olson has summarized such an arrangement with devastating accuracy:

> His tale celebrates a group of people who can act decisively without imposing tyranny or sorrow, who eliminate suffering and evil through a tolerance, a generosity, and an insouciance that fulfill the dream of the Epicurus in Dante's *Convivio*, namely delight without pain.[19]

Donald Howard has called this a "country-squire version" of *gentilesse* (p. 270), but I would prefer to call it GENTLENICENESS. We can all "approve" of gentleniceness, but where does that get us? Perhaps to that sanguine, post-prandial haze of good will so well described by Paul Ruggiers: "It is . . . this repeated action of generosity which rouses in us a sense of approbation, of mellow feeling, of almost-laughter touched by reflection" (p. 234).

I would submit that the comparative passage from the *Knight's Tale* shows us these same elements put together with much more cohesion and strength. Theseus is commanding a wedding that will reconcile two city-states, but he does so with courteous condescension, alluding to his wardship of Emily as her brother-in-law, and also to the consensus by which his rule is supported (3075–76). The decision, unrolled in complex syntax ("that . . . that"), actually tells her that they have decided she is to take pity upon Palamon and show him "grace." So here is a strong contradiction: the imperatives of state *versus* the promptings of the heart. Yet they are gracefully put in order, partly because Emelye had not ruled out what is proposed, and so has no reason to resist, and partly because the union is set within a hierarchy of passion and duty which accords with the philosophical overview Theseus has just finished giving.

After announcing his decision, he prays her to give her own hand in agreement and show "wommanly pitee," concluding "For gentil mercy oghte to passen right" (3089). In that line I find the strongest formulation of true nobility, *gentilesse*, which I take to be the thematic core of the tale. And at this point it is richly significant, since it brings together the movements of Theseus's rule with the inclinations of Emelye's virginal will, and caps the preceding reference to "greet adversitee." Within the poem, adversity has proved more than frustrated love and heart-sick yearning: it has meant jealousy and discord, prison, painful exile, and death. Mere gentleniceness could not survive in this environment. At a solemn moment of state, after great loss and sorrow, the personal will is put back in fruitful harmony with common profit. Note that such an ending encourages looking back, since it is memory of the adversity all have endured that gives such sharpness and sweetness to the prosperity about to be achieved. "Adversity" and "prosperity" are, of course, resonant Boethian terms, so that the foregrounding of "prosperity" at the end of the Franklin's disquisition invites the backwards reader to contemplate the validity of such a description, structured only by a refusal to accept difference or opposition as problems. The most telling comment on the Franklin's version would seem to be this by Alfred David: "The weakness of the Franklin's 'fredom,' whether we look at it as a Christian or a courtly virtue, is that no one has to pay" (p.192). Not even twenty pounds (see line 683), let alone a thousand.

V. DE-AUTHORIZING THE FRANKLIN

Those anxious to defend the Franklin will have become suspicious of the previous remarks, since it seems he is once again under attack for heedless superficiality, or for having the presumption to wish everyone well. How can one say that "the Franklin" is not the subject of the backwards-reader's amused contempt when he is the author of the special pleading just analyzed?

To meet this objection, we must turn at last to the point where this character/*persona*/author is introducing himself:

> But, sires, by cause I am a burel man,
> At my bigynnyng first I yow biseche,
> Have me excused of my rude speche.

I lerned nevere rethorik, certeyn;
Thyng that I speke, it moot be bare and pleyn.   720
I sleep nevere on the Mount of Pernaso,
Ne lerned Marcus Tullius Scithero.
Colours ne knowe I none, withouten drede,
But swiche colours as growen in the mede,
Or elles swiche as men dye or peynte.   725
Colours of rethoryk been to me queynte;
My spirit feeleth noght of swich mateere.
But if yow list, my tale shul ye heere.

If we keep the fiction of oral performance in mind and ignore the editorial rubrics that box off various parts of the beginning in printed editions, we can appreciate how long the Franklin has been positioning himself before us with his flow of friendly talk. The pilgrims have not to this point shown themselves very courteous to each other, so his compliments to the Squire mark him as a congenial fellow; and even when he is cut off by the Host, he replies in good temper, illustrating his "suffrance." The old tale he proposes to say sounds safely remote and recreative, and he now promises to go nice and easy. He is a "burel man," not a fancy-talker. Naturally we understand him to say he won't put on airs, even though he knows a thing or two.

There is nothing foolishly naive about such a forwards-reaction. The humility-*topos* the Franklin elaborates is as obvious and familiar as an old shoe, and Benjamin Harrison got critics off on the wrong foot when he called it "rhetorical inconsistency."[20] No one could be fooled into thinking the Franklin would be drably plain through his "rude speche" (135). It is the attitude towards his material that is important, as he displays a non-pedantic agility that invites us to share an unintimidated pleasure in the game. And it *is* a game. The *traductio* on *colores* is, as Constance Wright has made clear, an unsurprising trope, so widely known and used that one need not imagine either the Franklin or Chaucer a student of Persius.[21] But still, the little chain of puns is a feat of dexterity for us to admire, all the more for its deference. Again, a cry of derision over the ignoramus-spelling of "Marcus Tullius Scithero" may be misplaced, for this is a jaw-breaker of a line and a mischievous piece of riming. The presumed misspelling is less important than the comically controlled polysyllables.

After all, as Russell Peck has reminded us, the Franklin is hardly dressed in homespun (p. 257). The man who says his speech is "bare and pleyn" could be expected to welcome his dinner guests with the announcement that he has planned "just a simple little meal"—as he calls forth a blizzard of meat and drink, and plies his unsurprised but delighted guests with dainties.

Perhaps the reason so many critics have thought the Franklin was foolishly posturing sprang from their conviction that he was a *parvenu*, reaching towards a higher tone than he could convincingly manage. But the attempt to place him exactly rather misses the point. In his shire he has power and prestige enough; yet he is not a knight, and if he can be thought of as a squire, he still looks over a country mile at the knight's son, a squire in quite a different system.[22] That gives us the necessary relationships, and leaves him all the authority he needs to get started. And it is authority he is seeking, first leading his audience to trust him as a disinterested but congenial speaker. His next step will be to expatiate on the good marriage, demonstrating his power to integrate what had threatened to fly apart. In this he will act as a literary Justice of the Peace, superseding Harry the Bailiff.

We have reached a self-consciousness about narrative and narrator here that surely has turned into backwards-reading, but the moment of transition should not pass without insisting that a forwards-reading can go a long way with the Franklin in understanding and accepting his rhetorical play. These mock-disavowals encourage fellowship by inviting the audience, with a wink, to feel included in the game. But let there be no mistake: the Franklin plays to win, and under rules that he invents. His aim is total control. His behavior seems deferential and permissive, but the tale is an absolutely authoritarian structure. It is as a reflex against the loss of freedom as a reader that one begins to de-authorize the Franklin by reading contrariwise.

At what point does forwards-complaisance begin to erode? Although it is not necessary to argue that everyone reaches the same point at the same time, it is obvious enough that clues are set out in the Franklin's portrait in the *General Prologue*—and I refer to clues to the art of reading a-right (and a-left), not to some abstract summing up and judging. For the portraits teach us how to read the tale to come, how to deal with its ideas and its language—a formulation which begins to contradict Kittredge absolutely;[23] in fact, I suspect that many, if not all, of the portraits were composed after a tale had been completed and its attribution determined. But when do the clues arrange themselves into a pattern? It is not hard to imagine a fairly untroubled forwards-reading, in which one gains a serene sense of a hearty old fellow, well known and generous, who loves playing the role of St. Julian.

There is no reason why the allusion to Epicurus and "pleyn delit" should cause all alarms to sound—the subject seems to be variety and refinement, not grossness and gluttony. Backwards-reading surely is a function of coming back for another look, perhaps stimulated by the Franklin's self-presentation at the start of his tale. What is so "burel" about his ever-ready hall? And how does one bridge the gap between that repellent Epicurus, old Januarie, and this sanguine dispenser to all and sundry of "pleyn delit"? (For it simply cannot be that the Epicurus allusion works the same way for the Merchant as for the Franklin.) The backwards-reader, I should think, will find the very notion of "delyt" being problematized.

Also, the same reader, bemused by the Franklin's apparent eagerness, under Harry, to do exactly what he is told, might review the clear signs of the Franklin's officiousness: as it is suffered by his cook (351–52), shown by his ostentatious dagger and purse (357–58), and inventoried in the listing of the roles he played as "lord and sire" (355). But most remarkable of all, in coming back to the sequence of observations in the portrait, should be the discovery of the last words, in the last line: "was nowher swich a worthy *vavasour*" (360). For this alerts the reader at once to several ongoing aspects of Chaucer's poetry that belong to a bookish world and a reader's reflections.

First, it makes the portrait part of the game of ringing the changes on the outer/inner value-word, "worthy." To call the Franklin worthy is not necessarily to advance him as a model of virtue—the Merchant was the last to be called worthy (279) as part of a sentence describing his shrewdness in shady business dealings, "his chevyssaunce" (279–82), and Chaucer repeats the "worthy" in a disdainful closing couplet (283–84). And then, of course, before this we were told of the brilliantly unscrupulous Friar, that "ful wel biloved and famulier was he / With frankeleyns over al in his contree, / And eek with worthy wommen of the toun" (215–17).

Then, in a coup of couplet-writing and portrait construction, Chaucer drops into place that final word, "vavasour." The associations would have been primarily to a literary universe, and would foreground the Franklin's fictionality, as Roy Pearcy has demonstrated (see also Coss, p. 148). The effect is to heighten the reader's awareness of the poetic process and of the problem of interpretation. To say that this literary complex has become a vavasour in addition to a Franklin is to suggest two levels of response to the details that have been assembled, and hence to make the character an image that is to be seen through. It does not necessarily follow that "see through" means we strain to detect the Franklin in a deception; it may mean, instead, that we catch sight of a larger *entente* behind him which will complicate—interestingly, enjoyably—our relationship to our reading.

For what is a vavasour, held up against the light as a painting on glass? He is some manifestation of Chaucer, and of ourselves. The delicious resemblances of the first part are easily discovered: Chaucer had been a Justice of the Peace and a Knight of the Shire, did buy land, did live in the country, and evidently gave portly evidence that he was addicted to the pleasures of the table. Of all the characters on the pilgrimage, the Franklin's comes the closest to approximating Chaucer's social position and life-style (a term most appropriate for a Franklin); and of course the Franklin's apology for his homespun speech is not far from what Chaucer says at the end of his Prologue: "My wit is short, ye may wel understonde" (746).

The resemblances of the second part are broader and somewhat more speculative, yet no less important to assert. First, among the wealthy London burghers and prominent civil servants Chaucer knew as friends, the Franklin would stand as a country cousin in wealth, duties, and rank; and like Chaucer, they all would be turning their wealth into property whenever it came to hand. The Franklin would seem removed from them and yet uncomfortably alike. Second, the Franklin is an epitome of Ricardian features: interested in the display and forms of gentility, not interested in the affairs of bloody war or in grand heroic gestures, affecting a personal style of some culture or at least "refinement," and putting together a public personality gathered from various aspects of fashionable Europe, including fine clothes, fine talk, and fine emotions.

When I said the Franklin was "ourselves," however, I intended the reference to apply as well to modern as to medieval audiences. For the Franklin, of all the characters on the pilgrimage, is closest to the citizens of the New World: uneasily fallen out of the feudal order, emulous of European culture, anxious to please, anxious to do well, at once distrustful and admiring of old gentility, ingenious, complacent, warmhearted, platitudinous. It was not such a long trip to Philadelphia.[24]

These resemblances do not mean that we are constrained to admire Chaucer's Franklin any more than we necessarily admire ourselves. But because our readership is so deeply involved in his identity, and because that identity is so peculiarly bound up in the reading process, we are invited to enter the text with a metapoetical awareness I have (not very elegantly) called reading backwards. Because the Franklin is a version of Chaucer, we must pay attention to him in the process of composition; because he is a version of us, we must catch ourselves in the act of reading. We shall be deconstructing the Franklin, then, and reconstructing—both identifying from the text and drawing out of ourselves—a master image of the Vavasour, lord and sire of our sessions.

I should think that backwards readers upon reaching the Franklin's account of his "burel" qualities would return to the portrait for guidance as to the aspects of performance one must assess. As in his household, so in his tale: the way a thing is done is extremely important, possibly to win approval, certainly to provide pleasure. But to what end? The resistance a backwards reading generates is to being overcomfited with dainties and swept along in the current of events, taken irresistably to a point entirely within the Franklin's power. The attention a backwards reading requires focuses on the coherence of narrative and the moral logic of cause and event. An analysis of the Franklin's speaking develops into the study of a particular relationship proposed between words and things. The inquiry is into the true worth of a vavasorial conception of the world.

I have spoken of the "de-authorizing" of the Franklin, as if there were to be some kind of struggle in the reading process, and as if the reader's freedom were at stake. In speaking of the backwards reading process, and of the way we look at the Franklin and then through him, I have been aiming to respond to a major objection by Derek Pearsall to the "systematic ironisation" of the Franklin's character: "it simplifies the text in an intolerably reductive manner" (p. 148). That is true (and to be avoided) only if one reverses every sign and changes positive to negative, white to black, and virtue to vice. It certainly can become a dangerous practice when the Franklin is treated like the prisoner in the dock for whom one prepares a final verdict. And it hovers as a mischievous possibility when the Franklin's character is treated like a figure on the stage or in a (nineteenth–century) novel, rather than as a sequence of gestures, tones, and events. Attacking and defending "the Franklin" prevents building up a critical understanding of The Vavasour, and fails to engage in the time-and-space-defying game of reading. One can always read *both* forwards and backwards—neither kind requires erasing the other, and both are a larger number, taken together, than two.

What may seem "systematic ironisation" is the challenging process of following the Franklin—without losing one's independence. It should be possible to enjoy the depiction of his characters, even to shiver at their dilemmas, and possibly even to warm to his idealism. But it should also be possible to demur at answering his loaded question at the end, and to demand a more liberating concept of "fredom" than he exemplifies.

In so doing, the reader is released into uncertainty—not about the vital importance of love, courtesy, and integrity, but about the way these names can be realized. Assertion is not proof; slogans are not philosophy; wishes are not horses; beggars cannot ride. The vavasorial vision of life asks for credit on the basis of a smile and a shoeshine. Those whose reading is too exclusively forwards must be prepared to share the blame for the inevitable bankruptcy of this insupportable fiction of prosperity.

11

Reason, Machaut, and the Franklin

That Uncle Pandarus counts Lady Philosophy among his immediate ancestors is well recognized. When in Book I of *Troilus* the love-struck hero sits Boethius-like in his chamber lamenting his fate and composing poetic complaints, and Pandarus appears to "parten" his pain, to scold and to advise, then situation, sentiment, and diction suggest the *Consolation of Philosophy* as a subtext, or perhaps a super-text.[1] At the same time there are obvious references here besides those to the *Consolation*, other works which mediate importantly in the adaptation of Boethius to the drama and dialectic of Chaucer's "litel tragedie." These are the *Roman de la Rose*, both parts, and the *Remede de Fortune* of Guillaume de Machaut.[2] In this paper, I want first to explore the paradigm of consoler-consolation-consolee as it appears in the four successive works (*Consolation, Roman, Remede, Troilus*) in order particularly to establish the centrality of the *Remede* in the development, and then I want to examine at more length another literary nexus for which *Remede* acts as intermediary between the *Roman* and a work of Chaucer. This involves the Franklin's suggestion that friendship may provide a basis for the relationship of marital partners, and suggests a reconsideration of the Franklin's contribution to the marriage debate.

It was the idea of Guillaume de Lorris to adapt the Boethian topics and dramatic situation to a love narrative. In his work the counterparts of Philosophy, Boethius, and the cosmic lament are Reason, Amant, and the lover's complaint. Jean de Meun subsequently employs the same elements in his part of the *Roman*, enriching the character of Guillaume's Reason with features originating with St. Augustine and Cicero.[3] The overriding difference between the French poem and the Latin works is that the subject has become human love instead of God and Providence. Because of this difference some of the Boethian materials found in

Jean de Meun's *Roman* seem less than completely assimilated, in a manner in line with his customary procedure.

Obviously inspired by the model of the *Roman*, in the *Remede de Fortune* Guillaume de Machaut creates another Boethian situation when his Amant experiences a lover's desperation. But it is no Wisdom figure who appears in Machaut's poem; rather, it is one of the comforts personified which the God of Love promised the lover in the *Roman*, Esperance—Hope. In place of the more or less dependable rational advisor, whose proper locale is in part the mind of man and in part the divine mind, Machaut gives us an objectification of an emotion or feeling clearly based in the Lover's head and heart.[4] Consequently, the relationship of advisor to advisee is quite changed, and whereas the Lover of the *Roman* feels compelled to reject the measured counsels of Reason, who would forbid him to love, Machaut's Amant finds just the help he wants in Hope, who encourages his love.

The long interview between Hope and the Lover, which at length emboldens him to search out the lady and declare his love, occupies 1700 of the 4400 lines of *Remede* (1481–3180) and is pivotal in it. A great deal of the comfort which Hope offers is drawn directly from Boethius. Obviously, substantial measures of adaptation were required since the philosophical preoccupations of Philosophy and Reason, who are trying to lead their pupils to right thinking, are replaced by the more practical aims of Esperance, whose aspirations are for the success of the Lover. Esperance does not egregiously misapply the lessons of Boethius, but rather she is selective, drawing her materials mainly from the first two books of the *Consolation*.

Chaucer is following the *Roman* and the *Remede de Fortune*, then, in creating the Boethian parallel in his love story. His close familiarity with the *Roman* and his ubiquitous use of it in his poetry ensure that it is part of the context, and there are specific echoes of the *Remede* in Troilus's complaint against Fortune and Pandarus's response that guarantee the presence of Machaut's poem.[5] Pandarus reflects all three of his predecessors. He is a comic version of Lady Philosophy and Lady Reason, physicians of the soul mimicked by an unprincipled procurer:

> For whoso list have helyng of his leche,
> To hym byhoveth first unwre his wownde.
> To Cerberus yn helle ay be I bounde,
> Were it for my suster, al thy sorwe,
> By my wil she sholde al be thyn to-morwe.
>   [1.857–61]

At the same time, he is a genuine representative of Hope. For all you know, he tells Troilus, as Esperance tells the Lover (2531–35), Fortune's mutability may make things turn out just as you wish (1. 851–54). In contrast to Pandarus, any moral defect in the advice of Machaut's counsellor is excused by the fact that she acts simply according to her nature, and furthermore that the affair which she promotes in the *Remede* has no evident immorality. In *Troilus*, as in the *Remede*, the advisor is a cheerleader for the lover; as in the *Roman* (but not the *Remede*), an illicit affair is in question.

Philosophy and Reason are very nearly related, but Machaut's ageless *consolatrice* Esperance has an entirely different intrinsic character,[6] and in Chaucer's *Troilus* the essential nature of Pandarus is radically different from those of his ancestresses. Nevertheless, other features remain constant in the family history of the works, as for instance certain personality traits of the counsellors. From Philosophy to Pandarus, they are garrulous and rather disdainful of their pupils' lack of acuity. The pupils, moreover, are comparably full of self-pity. Certain topics also recur, the most notable being that of Fortune. Book II of the *Consolation* is wholly devoted to Fortune. In the *Roman* subsequently Reason treats the subject of Fortune in two substantial passages, once in contrasting true friends to the friends of Fortune (4807–4944), and the second time at great length in encouraging the lover to choose to love her instead of following Fortune (5812–6913). Jean makes the Boethian origins of his treatment of Fortune quite clear, and again the intertextual chain that he establishes is lengthened by Machaut and Chaucer with modifications appropriate to their poems. In Machaut's *Remede* Amant's long complaint against Fortune (905–1208) and Hope's extensive defense of the goddess's behavior (2378–2772) recall both the *Roman* and the *Consolation*, while the words about Fortune in the *Book of the Duchess* and *Troilus* derive from these two plus Machaut's poem.

The chain of borrowing, the passing on of literary as well as philosophical features, and modifications effected from one text to the next are of interest for various aspects of analysis. They can show us much about the relationship of Chaucer's work to the *Roman de la Rose*: we see Chaucer learning from the procedures followed in the *Roman*, reacting to the work's content and artistry, and also filtering his uses of it through Machaut. The last has not been much attended to, yet it is of substantial importance for understanding the effect of the *Roman*. I would generalize that when Chaucer's text contains simultaneous reference to the *Roman* and to Machaut, Chaucer's sense will be closer to that of his contemporary. This is true, for example, of the characters of

Esperance and Pandarus, not alike, but closer to each other than to Reason.

The generalization is illustrated in numerous other cases when Machaut acts as intermediary between the *Roman* and Chaucer. An important instance which I wish to elaborate now has a bearing on the whole Marriage Group in the *Canterbury Tales*. It involves the Franklin's words on mastery at the beginning of his tale, when he states, in approving Dorigen's and Arveragus's mutual agreement to obey each other in their marriage,

> For o thyng, sires, saufly dar I seye,
> That freendes everych oother moot obeye,
> If they wol longe holden compaignye.
> Love wol nat been constreyned by maistrye.
> Whan maistrie comth, the God of Love anon
> Beteth his wynges, and farewel, he is gon!
>
> [V 761–66]

He goes on to elaborate these sentiments for another thirty lines.

The agreement between the two lovers and the commentary of the Franklin, while once hailed by critics as a solution to the discussion of marriage in the *Canterbury Tales*, have more recently been criticized as inappropriate to a medieval marital situation. In his wishing to preserve the name of lordship while giving up the right to it, Arveragus is seen as both devious and uxorious, while the Franklin in subscribing to the lovers' actions is viewed as shallow and crass. Nevertheless, substantial justification for the Franklin's attitude, and perhaps complete vindication of it, may be found in the medieval tradition of friendship. One aspect of his statement about the marital relationship that has not been sufficiently attended to is his claim that friends ought to obey each other. By this statement he invokes the medieval tradition of friendship and makes it part of the context. The Franklin's words raise at least two questions that the tradition can shed light upon: Is it true that friends ought to obey each other? And is it appropriate to apply the term "friend" to medieval marriage partners? If the answer to these questions is positive then there seems to be a basis for the Franklin's characterization of proper marital concord.

The best-known vernacular discussion of friendship in the Middle Ages is probably that of Jean de Meun. When the lover asks Reason to tell him of the kinds of love he might experience, the first kind she names is friendship (4655). In developing the theme she utilizes the standard Latin discussions, Cicero's *De amicitia* and Aelred of Rievaulx's *De spirituali amicitia*, eventually arriving at Boethius's treatise in distinguishing between true friends and the friends who follow Fortune. Among these four antecedent texts (*Roman*, Cicero, Aelred, Boethius), Boethius alone has nothing to say about the obedience of friends, about how far one should submit to the friend's requests; Jean, Aelred, and Cicero all provide a good basis for the Franklin's statement that they should obey each other. All three agree that one ought to do whatever a friend asks so long as it is not immoral.[7]

As for the question of friendship between the sexes, the discussion of friendship in the *Consolation* gives no indication that Boethius considered the relationship of friends applicable to marriage partners or any association of man and woman. And Cicero's *De amicitia*, which would have carried considerable authority for Boethius, consistently treats friendship as a masculine affair. Nevertheless, in the discussions of friendship in the *Roman*, where the overriding topic is the love of a man for a woman, we find the patent implication that a man and woman can be friends to each other. And Aelred's treatise, though addressed to monks and largely based on Cicero, corroborates such an inference; it finds a lesson in equality and friendship between man and woman in an apparently unlikely place, the story of woman's creation. One might assume that a medieval thinker like Aelred would find in woman's emergence from man's side a lesson in the natural lordship of the male; instead, however, he sees the story as instructing mankind in the natural fellowship of human beings:

> Finally, when God created man, in order to commend more highly the goods of society, he said: "It is not good for man to be alone: let us make him a helper like unto himself." It was from no similar, nor even from the same, material [i.e., clay] that divine Might formed this help mate, but as a clearer inspiration to charity and friendship he produced the woman from the very substance of the man. How beautiful it is that the second human being was taken from the side of the first, so that nature might teach that *human beings are equal and, as it were, collateral, and that there is in human affairs neither a superior nor an inferior, a characteristic of true friendship*. Hence, nature from the very beginning implanted the desire for friendship and charity in the heart of man. [1:57–58, italics mine]

Here it seems that there is presented a full precedent for the Franklin's imputing the relation of friendship to the marital partnership of Dorigen and Arveragus and for their treating each other as equals.[8]

Notwithstanding, it might be asserted that in their courtship the Franklin's couple has gone through the rituals associated with carnal love relationships such as the lovers have in the *Roman*, and that Jean de Meun is careful to differentiate the love of true friends, indifferent to Fortune, from that which his Amant practices, which is under the aegis of the goddess.[9] Here is where the mediation of Machaut between the *Roman* and Chaucer is instructive. In the *Remede de Fortune* Hope answers the Lover's complaint against Fortune in several ways: she points out to him that he has put himself in the power of Fortune of his own free will so that he should not blame Fortune for showing her true nature; that also he should comfort himself that since Fortune always changes, his present bad situation is bound to change; and finally that if he loves loyally he will place himself out of the power of Fortune, "Qu'amy vrai ne sont pas en compte / Des biens Fortune, qui bien compte, / Mais entre les biens de vertu" (2801–03) ("For in proper reckoning true lovers are not accounted among the goods of Fortune, but among the goods of Virtue"). This last claim echoes the Boethian sentiment that friendship belongs to "the goods of virtue, not of Fortune,"[10] which Hope sees as applicable—at least *in potentia*—to the love affair in *Remede de Fortune*. She clearly believes that Amant can go through the sufferings of the conventional lover and yet arrive at a wholly virtuous relationship with the lady, which she implicitly equates with friendship.

In the *Remede* the affair is consummated ceremonially with an exchange of rings presided over by Esperance, a quasi-marriage which the lady talks about in terms which foreshadow—and no doubt helped inspire—the Franklin's discussion. The lady states,

> "Mes chiers amis,
> Puis qu'Amours ad ce nous a mis
> Que nos deus cuers ensemble joindre
> Vuet sans partire et sans desjoindre,
> Et que faire vuet un de deus,
> Pour Dieu, ne faisons paire d'euls;
> Car il sont perdu et honni,
> Se si pareil et si onni
> Ne sont qu'en bien et mal commun

Soient, et en tous cas comme un,
Sans pensee avoir de maistrie,
De haussage, et de signeurie,
Qu'adès a tençon et rumour
Entre signourie et amour.
Et seurtout que chascuns regarde
Qu'onneur et pais a l'autre garde."

[4039–54]

My dear friend,
since Love has brought us
to join our two hearts together
completely and inseparably,
and wishes to make two into one,
in God's name, let us make them equal;
for they will be lost and shamed
if they are not kept alike and united
in both good times and bad,
always equal, with no thought of mastery,
supremacy, or lordship.
For there are always quarrels and disputes
between mastery and love.
And above all each of us must keep
honor and peace with the other.

Whether we take these words as applicable to a courtship or to a virtual marriage, the sentiments seem unexceptionable. And when the Franklin uses them to characterize an unambiguous marriage they appear equally valid.

Behind both Machaut's and Chaucer's words on the incompatibility of love and mastery are the words of Friend in the *Roman*, in a passage contrasting the behavior of people in the Golden Age, when all were content to be equal, with that of the tyrannical husband making his wife miserable:

Trestuit pareill estre soloient
ne riens propre avoir ne voloient.
Bien savoient cele parole,
qui n'est mençongerie ne fole,
qu'onques amor et seigneurie

ne s'entrefirent compaignie
ne ne demorerent ensemble:
cil qui mestroie les dessemble.
Por ce voit l'en des mariages,
quant li mariz cuide estre sages
et chastie sa fame et bat. . . .

[8417–28]

[They (of the Golden Age) were accustomed to be completely equal,
nor did they wish to own property.
They knew well the saying,
which is neither a lie nor folly,
that Love and Lordship never kept company
nor lived together:
he who asserts mastery divides.
Thus one sees in marriages,
when the husband thinks himself clever
and scolds and beats his wife. . . .]

Machaut's poem disengages the opposition of Love and Mastery from the historical-philosophical ambience of Friend's presentation, which treats the husband's assumption of mastery and his consequent abuse of his wife as simply one more consequence of the world's decay, and applies the opposition to an entirely different situation.[11] In referring to the incompatibility of Love and Lordship, the lady of *Remede* is advocating openness and equality between herself and the lover in their recently declared love. She essentially is setting forth a basis for nuptial accord. Chaucer's Franklin in turn applies the same principles to the marital agreement of two noble lovers. Golden Age harmony and wife-beating, the poles in Jean de Meun's opposition, are comparably inappropriate in Machaut's and Chaucer's contexts, which both concern questions of courtly relationships.

I do not claim (or believe) that the tale the Franklin subsequently tells represents an ideal answer to the marriage problem, but his characterization of Dorigen's and Arveragus's agreement as "an humble, wys accord" is a sound one in the context of the standard medieval discussions of friendship. In the round table discussion of marriage that forms the Marriage Group of tales, it does provide a supportable solution. Aelred says that friendship extends beyond, and entails a relationship superior to the ties of charity itself: "For we are compelled by the law of charity to receive in the embrace of love not only our friends but also our enemies. But only those do we call friends to whom we can fearlessly entrust our heart and all its secrets" (1:32). The relationship described here surely agrees with the spirit of the sacrament of marriage, whether medieval or modern.

Kittredge's original formulation of the much-discussed "Marriage Group" in the *Canterbury Tales* simply states that in the sequence beginning with the *Wife of Bath's Prologue* and ending with the *Franklin's Tale*, "the subject is Marriage, which is discussed from several points of view."[12] His description of the marital discussion is dominated by the imagery of drama. "Nowhere is the dramatic spirit of the Canterbury Pilgrimage more evident than in the Marriage group of tales" (pp.185–86). They form an "act" in a "Human Comedy" (p.185) featured particularly by the interplay of character; e.g., the Clerk's Envoy "is completely dramatic" in its response to the Wife of Bath (pp. 198–202). It was later critics rather than Kittredge who talked about how the individual stories provide implicit installments in the marriage discussion. Such extension of Kittredge's notion naturally led to widespread disagreement, for what distinguishes this part of the *Canterbury Tales* is not that the narratives make points about marriage. Numerous others implicitly comment on the subject: *Miller's Tale, Nun's Priest's Tale, Melibee*, etc. And at the same time, none of the *stories* in the Marriage Group is primarily about marriage: the *Wife of Bath's Tale* is about what women want, the Clerk's about patience or obedience, the Merchant's about foolish senility, and the Franklin's about true "franchise." What especially characterizes and makes coherent this act in the Human Comedy is, as Kittredge essentially said, the *discussions* of marriage which pervade it, and which conclude with the Franklin's introductory remarks about the agreement between Dorigen and Arveragus. The tale of the Franklin, Kittredge himself states, "throws no light on the problem of sovereignty in marriage" (p.206). Accordingly, he concludes his words about this "act" of the *Tales* with a characterization of the Franklin's introduction, which he believes should be regarded "as summarizing the whole [marital] debate and bringing it to a definitive conclusion which we are to accept as a perfect rule of faith and practice" (pp.209–10).

The idea that the Franklin's *dicta* represent a "perfect rule" seems extreme. It does not accord at all with the image of the Franklin that critics have created in the past twenty or thirty years. Notwithstanding, some of what the foolish Polonius says is wise, much of what the wicked Pardoner says is moral, and the pragmatic Friend sometimes speaks to noble purposes. Even if we grant the worst of what is said about the Franklin, he may still enunciate the final wisdom about marriage. That marriage partners should treat each other as friends, and that neither should assert lordship agrees with the greatest medieval authorities on friendship and marriage, and certainly appeals to common sense. If the Franklin is no consistent counterpart to the wisdom figures of the *Roman* and the *Consolation*, he nevertheless is one in this one passage, and he thereby provides a basis for comparing the Mirror of Love which is constructed by Jean with the Mirror of Marriage devised by Chaucer.

In the *Roman* Reason inaugurates the major discussion of love and provides the frame for the discourse, to which Friend, Faus Semblant, La Vieille, Nature, and Genius contribute. If there is a touchstone, as I am inclined to believe there is, it is Reason.[13] The frame of discourse for Chaucer's Marriage Group, however, is set by the Wife; as subsequent echoes of her presentation and references to her by name indicate, she dictates the terms of the discourse. But of course she is no touchstone; rather, it is the last contributor, the Franklin, who speaks with most authority. This difference in presentation leads to a rather different effect. In the *Roman* all that follows Reason's words stands in their shadow and becomes an ironic illustration of their cogency. In the Marriage Group—more accurately the Marriage Discussion—all of the ironic commentary on love and marriage which the Wife, the Clerk, the Merchant, and the Host supply is undercut by the wise accord of the partners, as expatiated upon by the Franklin. For all of Jean's good comedy, in the light that Reason casts over the whole, love between the sexes appears disordered and ill-fated, and for all of the heavy irony of Chaucer's marital discussion, the Franklin's remarks provide for it a benign and optimistic denouement.

12

Empathy and Enmity in the Prioress's Tale

Midway through the impassioned prayer that precedes her tale, Chaucer's Prioress alludes to the Incarnation in terms of joined contraries conveying sublime paradox:

> O mooder Mayde, O mayde Mooder free!
> O bussh unbrent, brennynge in Moyses sighte,
> That ravyshedest doun fro the Deitee,
> Thurgh thyn humblesse, the Goost that in th'alighte,
> Of whos vertu, whan he thyn herte lighte,
> Conceyved was the Fadres sapience. . . .[1]

The force and economy with which these contradictions are joined are rhetorically heightened by the chiastic structure of the first of these lines, "O mother Virgin, O virgin Mother noble." The following line too is structurally compressed, juxtaposing contraries in the "unburnt, burning" bush, a familiar type of Mary, who "was fyred brente not, for she was moder without losse of maydenhod."[2] In the next two lines, the Prioress astonishingly transforms the Gospel account of the Incarnation, in which Gabriel tells Mary that the Holy Spirit will come upon her, and the power of the Most High will overshadow her (Luke 1.35). In the nun's fervent reworking, it is instead the Virgin who ravishes the Holy Ghost down from the Deity! Yet the heat and energy suggested in the word *ravyshedest* are paradoxically contained, like the flames of the burning bush, within the chastity of the Conception.[3] And the fact that Mary ravishes the Holy Ghost through her humility, compelling or possessing through acquiescence, further extends the paradox in this prayer. The joining of contraries in paradox is thus as crucial to the Prioress's prayer as the joining of contradictions in irony is to her *General Prologue* portrait. But there is still another contradiction here: that the Prioress, whose faith and emotion seem so shallow and misplaced in the *General Prologue*, should utter so ardent a prayer at all.

Much of the mystery and delight of Chaucer's poetry issues from the marriage of such contraries, the reconciliation of the apparently irreconcilable, often in wonder and surprise, if not in peace. As much as any of Chaucer's pilgrims, the Prioress embodies a juxtaposition of such polarized qualities. A bride of Christ, she is nonetheless described as if she had stepped out of an Old French romance. Her ecclesiastical authority seems subverted in the *General Prologue* by her spiritual superficiality. Yet this shallowness is later shown, in her prayer, to conceal a burning religious fervor. And her genteel spotlessness in the *General Prologue* is shockingly contrasted in her tale by the bloody child cast in a dungpit. She is undeniably a creature of love, however compromised, and yet she embeds in her tale an animosity, directed toward Jews, that is as passionate as her prayer. Wordsworth observed that her tender-hearted sympathies are set off against her fierce bigotry, and D. S. Brewer says that the Prioress is the gentlest of the pilgrims who tells the only cruel and fanatical tale.[4] Talbot Donaldson notes in her tale a "strange mixture of delicacy and horror."[5] "Jewels and jakes," says Alan Gaylord, "charm and depravity," says Ian Robinson.[6] And, we must add, love and hate.

This essay is an exploration of the intersection of love and hate, and of the unresolved play between these and other contradictions in Chaucer's presentation of the Prioress. I attempt here to discover the connectedness in her contraries, and to deconstruct the moral dichotomy in her depiction of Christian and Jew. In the process, I review historical scholarship on Christian-Jewish relations in the late medieval period in order to challenge the assertion that Chaucer himself necessarily participated in a universal intolerance toward Jews.

Long before the advent of post-structuralism, critics detected the subversions that pervade the Prioress's description and problematize her tale. The Prioress's intention is not complex: she attempts to illustrate the simple beauty of her faith by offering a beautiful and simple Miracle of the Virgin. In so doing, she valorizes innocent faith while rejecting the cursed Jews, whom she presents as the enemies of naive devotion. Her tale is thus intended to represent and vindicate her own qualities. For most of this century, however, critics have observed the ways in which the Prioress's qualities differ from themselves. And in recent decades, they have debated the degree to which these differences complicate and undermine her simple intention. In consequence, the profound conflicts in so shallow a pilgrim have been reproduced as conflicts in readings of the text.

Chaucer's description of the Prioress is itself a matter of spirited debate. Despite nearly general critical agreement that he wrote this portrait with restraint and even affection, virtually every line has provoked conflict among readers. The Prioress's age and appearance are an extreme case: some critics regard her as young and beautiful, others as old and overgrown. True, beautiful medieval foreheads were large, but D. W. Robertson, Jr., says that the Prioress's signified stupidity or lack of discretion.[7] Gordon Harper says that a forehead a span broad would scarcely conform to any notion of beauty.[8] And F. N. Robinson's note on this line questions whether a nun's forehead shouldn't have been covered in any case. Harper, in an essay titled "Chaucer's Big Prioress," takes the fact that the Prioress "was nat undergrowe" to mean that she was unusually large, even fat, and he makes a dastardly reference to her as bulbous. But Muriel Bowden says that being "nat undergrowe" means that she is well proportioned, and Talbot Donaldson and John Block Friedman assume that the Prioress's figure is good.[9] The gentle Prioress threatens to become a different creature for each reader, so that for Sister M. Madeleva, a sensible, mature nun, the Prioress is one too.[10] And for G. K. Chesterton, the Prioress is a spinster, but particularly English, with a special kindness to animals so much valued by the English gentry today.[11] The Prioress's tale has, as we shall see, undergone similar shapeshifting.

John Livingston Lowes gave classic expression to the contradictions and subversions in the Prioress's portrait by observing that she is a religious who is described by language appropriate to a romance heroine. The manner of her smile, the choice of her name, and indeed her entire description, are, said Lowes, "steeped in reminiscences of the poetry of courtly love," creating a "delightfully imperfect submergence of the woman in the nun."[12] The *General Prologue* portrait, in fact, is constituted of qualities that seem mislocated and misdirected. The Prioress's concern for physical spotlessness, for example, parodies the true interest of a religious, the safeguarding of spiritual spotlessness. Worse, this passage is modelled on the advice of the sinful figure La Vieille in the *Roman de la Rose*, who recommends such table manners among women's wiles to attract men. Sister Madeleva, one of the staunchest defenders of the Prioress, denies irony in the portrait,

arguing that her table manners, for instance, reflect the nun's natural desire to keep her habit clean.[13] Arguments of this kind are
valid in themselves, but they fail to consider the context of the
passage, both in the portrait and its source. And they account neither for the manner of presentation, the language employed, nor
what is left unsaid.

There is further misdirection and mislocation in the Prioress's *conscience and tendre herte*. The irony is conveyed, as Bowden points out, by the fact that it is a mouse that calls forth the
Prioress's sympathy, not the suffering of her fellow man.[14] God and
neighbor are the true objects of charity, adds John Steadman, who
observes that the falseness of the Prioress's choice of objects is
made obvious by contrast with the Plowman.[15] Robertson notes
that this passage, like much of the portrait, proceeds by anticli-
max, raising expectations by referring to conscience, charity, and
pity, and then descending to the trapped mouse that benefits from
those qualitites.[16] And Chauncey Wood, developing Stanley Fish's
idea that readers make anticipatory judgments, or partial closures,
says that the reference to conscience is one of many instances in
this portrait in which the reader is teased into a false expectation,
only to be surprised by what follows.[17]

The reader's expectations are similarly misled by the portrait
as a whole. It does not, for instance, prepare us for the passion of
Eglentyne's prayer, which is presumably concealed beneath the
"chere of court." We are similarly surprised by her tale. Critics
have often found the Prioress of the *General Prologue* to be charming, possibly beautiful, but spiritually superficial, oversentimental,
conflicted, and, to some scholars, stupid. Yet there is no hint
within the portrait of the outburst of intolerance that will follow.
Quite the contrary, the focus is on love. This love is misdirected
and made pathetic, as in the Prioress's tears for suffering mice.
And sacred and profane love are conflated, as emblematized in the
Prioress's motto. But the central theme remains love, not hate, and
the newcomer to Chaucer, having read the *General Prologue* description, may well expect the Prioress's tale to speak of love, however confused, and perhaps of the rescue of nuns in distress.

In fact, the Prioress does tell a tale of love, and of rescue, a
Miracle of the Virgin. The story begins with a *litel clergeon*. This
litel child attends a *litel scole* where, while studying his primer
one day, he hears the older children singing the antiphon *Alma
redemptoris mater*. He does not understand the Latin, and fails
in his attempts to have it explained to him, but it is sufficient
for him to know that the song is in praise of Mary. This inno-

cent learns the song by rote, and sings it twice a day as he passes
through the city's Jewry, a place

> Sustened by a lord of that contree
> For foule usure and lucre of vileynye,
> Hateful to Crist and to his compaignye.
> [490–92]

The Jews are provoked, and the Prioress evokes both their traditional association with the devil and their assumed willingness to
kill in defense of their law:

> Oure firste foo, the serpent Sathanas,
> That hath in Jues herte his waspes nest,
> Up swal, and seide, "O Hebrayk peple, allas!
> Is this to yow a thyng that is honest,
> That swich a boy shal walken as hym lest
> In youre despit, and synge of swich sentence,
> Which is agayn youre lawes reverence?"
> [558–64]

With allusions recalling the conspiracy against Christ and the
Slaughter of the Innocents, the Prioress tells that the Jews hire a
murderer, another cursed Jew, who seizes the child, cuts his throat,
and casts him into a privy. Referring to Herod (another allusion to
the Slaughter of the Innocents), then to Cain's killing of Abel, the
nun reaches an emotional pitch reminiscent of her prayer:

> I seye that in a wardrobe they hym threwe
> Where as thise Jewes purgen hire entraille.
> O cursed folk of Herodes al newe,
> What may youre yvel entente yow availle?
> Mordre wol out, certeyn, it wol nat faille,
> And namely ther th'onour of God shal sprede;
> The blood out crieth on youre cursed dede.
> [572–78]

The Jews wickedly lie to the child's mother, denying that the boy
ever passed through the Jewry. But through the intercession of the
Virgin, the dead child, his throat cut, sings the *Alma redemptoris
mater.* The Christian folk hear the song, and send for the provost.
With torment and shameful death, the provost kills the Jews who
knew of the murder, dragging them by horses, then hanging them,

acts of which the gentle Prioress implicitly approves. The child then explains that Mary herself, the "welle of mercy," has brought about the miracle, placing a grain under his tongue, bidding him to sing the anthem, and then expressing a distinctly maternal consolation and assurance:

> My litel child, now wol I fecche thee,
> Whan that the greyn is fro thy tonge ytake.
> Be nat agast; I wol thee nat forsake.
>
> [667–69]

The martyr's "litel body sweete" is finally buried in a tomb of clear marble. The Prioress concludes by beseeching young Hugh of Lincoln, slain by "cursed Jewes" in a ritual blood slaughter, to intercede, so that merciful God, because of his mercy, will multiply his mercy on us "synful folk unstable." This juxtaposition of condemnation and mercy, the damned and the saved, the objects of hate and of sentimentality, crystallizes the contraries that inform her tale.

Many early critics took no notice of any such contraries. Instead, they spoke of the tale as a perfect illustration of the Miracle of the Virgin genre. George Lyman Kittredge, praising the Prioress's dignity and daintiness, speaks of the tale as "infinitely pathetic," never mentioning the Jews.[18] Chesterton says that the Prioress's tale is beautiful, and Nevill Coghill calls it one of the sweetest expressions of Chaucer's special feeling for the Blessed Virgin, conveying the beauty of holiness and of Christian triumph.[19] Wordsworth did speak of the bigotry set off against tenderness in the tale; but, as Florence Ridley notes, this did not stop him from rendering the tale in modern English.[20] Even Lowes, who so elegantly expressed the incongruities in the Prioress's portrait, speaks of her in ways that suggest affection and delight, betraying no sign of disturbance: he characterizes her description as "delicately ironical," "exquisitely sympathetic," "delightfully imperfect."[21]

The fact is that before the Holocaust much informed opinion about the *Prioress's Tale* was undisturbed by her treatment of the Jews, which was often not noticed at all.[22] Instead, her tale was praised for its beauty and perfection. This is significant and must be given full weight, for if it was so in our own century, one cannot expect Chaucer to have necessarily felt differently. For Kittredge and the others, and perhaps for Chaucer too, the Prioress's stereotyping of vicious Jews was no more serious a matter than the

Man of Law's treatment of the heathen Surryens, who also commit murder to defend their law, instigated by Satan's instrument, the Sowdanesse.

Since the Holocaust, by contrast, the question of anti-Semitism has been a central point of discussion about the Prioress. R. J. Schoeck argues that Chaucer presented the tale in order to denounce the ritual murder libel, and George K. Anderson calls the Prioress a vapid anti-Semite.[23] Several scholars, including Talbot Donaldson, Ian Robinson, Alfred David, and Donald R. Howard, have distinguished Chaucer's own views from the Prioress's, citing his greater awareness of Christianity and the posture of the Church, or his other personal qualities.[24] Others, notably Ridley and Albert B. Friedman, have refuted these assertions about the reputed tolerance of the Church, noting the ubiquity of anti-Jewishness at the time, and its pervasiveness in Christian piety.[25] Under such cultural circumstances, this line of argument suggests, the Prioress's bigotry loses significance. Her cruelty is manifest only from a point of view impossible to the Middle Ages, says Brewer, and David questions whether any medieval reader would have perceived the ironies in miracles of the Virgin that are apparent to the modern mind.[26] Ridley (p. 5) argues that the Prioress "and the rest of her credulous countrymen" regarded Jews "as strange, mysterious, and therefore sinister." Hardy Long Frank asserts that Jews were universally considered to be devils in late medieval Christendom.[27] And Friedman (p. 120) considers it foolish to expect Chaucer to have been above the narrow beliefs of his age when broadmindedness was impossible for Pascal, 250 years later.

This critical impasse over the horizons of Chaucer's possible attitude toward Jews illustrates with particular clarity the influence of history and ideology on critical perspective. Readers' responses, already divided by the contraries in the Prioress's portrait, have been further distanced by recent experience. Several post-Holocaust scholars, sensitized by the barbarism of the twentieth century, have looked for greater civility in the fourteenth, at least in the transcendent person of Chaucer. They implicitly view earlier assessments of the tale as naive and insensitive (like the Prioress herself) precisely because those views were conceived in innocence of the horrific consequences of intolerance that we have seen in our time. Other scholars have challenged the validity of applying such a modern sensibility to a medieval text. Their position is reinforced by more radical contemporary critical claims that broadly dismiss the notion of Chaucer as a man who transcended the influences of his period—who was in his time but not of it. The possibility that Chaucer escaped conventional prejudices will be rejected by some advocates of this view as a relic of a discredited Whig historiography.[28]

Both sides of this debate deserve reexamination. The assumption of an inescapable and constant medieval hatred of Jews in which Chaucer necessarily shared is drastically oversimplified. The actual historical picture across Europe over a period of centuries was far more complex. Many prominent medieval Jewish historians have concluded that enmity toward Jews, though widespread and often calamitous, was not universal. As the appendix below demonstrates, along with official oppression and popular hatred, there were many recorded gestures and declarations of respect and amity between individual Gentile and Jew. These interactions often occurred in spite of formal proscriptions, which themselves help document the behavior they were designed to suppress.

On the other hand, Chaucer's own attitude toward Jews is probably irretrievable. Beliefs and prejudices of this sort are often prelogical, and are not always discernible from an author's writing. This is particularly true of the portrayal of the Jews, which since the patristic period had typically been axiomatic rather than observed or deduced.[29] In the *Canterbury Tales*, the issue is further complicated, of course, by the fact that narratives are assigned to taletellers and often colored by irony. Moreover, to address the question of how Chaucer felt about Jews, one must interrogate the actions neither of Chaucer the pilgrim, nor even of Chaucer the poet, whose masked and fragmented qualities, to the extent that they can be inferred, are part of a posture offered to public view. Rather, one must investigate the inner life of Chaucer the private individual.[30] And there are reasons for skepticism that in issues of this kind a man's personal qualities are necessarily identical with the public ones suggested in his work. Barring new documentary discoveries, we cannot even establish that the issue was in any sense significant to Chaucer. What we can address, however, is the artistic function of the intolerance within the text.

The issue I wish to consider here, therefore, is not whether Chaucer was anti-Jewish, but rather how he transformed the conventional intolerance in a traditional Miracle of the Virgin in his presentation of the Prioress: why, in short, such an unexpected outburst of hatred is attributed to so gentle a nun.[31] The Parson's references to Jews are merely incidental. But the Jews of the Prioress's tale play, as I shall try to show, a particularized role that is specifically relevant to Eglentyne. Merely to assert that the Prioress participates in a general hostility toward Jews ignores the context in which they appear in her tale, and the function that they serve. Such an approach recalls the important but self-limiting work of the early critics of the *General Prologue* portrait, who documented historical practices and infractions resembling the Prioress's, but failed to account for the context and the manner of presentation of these elements in the Prioress's description. Moreover, this approach allows a divorce between the tale and the Prioress's character as it emerges in the *General Prologue* description. This, in fact, is precisely what John Lawlor recommends: he warns that attempting to fit the tale to the *General Prologue* description must call into play our modern suspicions, so that we will "view dourly any essay into that commonest of medieval modes, the pathetic."[32] But as Edward H. Kelly observes, in order to "more fully appreciate the poet's art of creation, it is necessary to see the description in the *General Prologue* as artistically functional in understanding the tale."[33]

Critics who have explored the unity of the *General Prologue* and the tale have in several instances emphasized the Prioress's unscrutinized sensibility or sentimentality, or the inherent association between these qualities and cruelty. Bowden (pp. 99–100) says that the implication of the Prioress's sympathy for mice rather than men is reinforced in her tale, in which she tells with perfect blandness of the tortures visited upon the Jews. Donaldson says that "Emotionalism that excludes the intellect—as it does in the *Prioress' Tale*—can be a dangerous thing, for the psychological transition from exquisite sensibility to bloodshed is an easy one."[34] Bertrand Bronson also puts the blame on the nun's "shallow sensibility," which, he says, is the obverse of cruelty.[35] Gaylord links sentimentality and brutality in describing the Prioress's actions, and Ian Robinson says that the Prioress's sentimentality is so thoughtless as to become wicked.[36] Ridley, taking a different approach, considers the tale a humorless display of naiveté, ignorance, blind vehement devotion, and (following Kittredge) suppressed maternal longing (p. 29).

Questions remain, however. Bowden's point about the Prioress's misplaced sympathy in the *General Prologue* does not explain the nun's explosion of enmity, or her abundant sympathy with the clergeon. And though sentimentality and shallow (or heightened) sensibility can accompany and conceal cruelty, they need not cause it, and are not invariably associated with it. The same is true of the naiveté, ignorance, and blind devotion that Ridley mentions. Current psychoanalytical thinking about intolerance proceeds, as we shall see, along very different lines. As for Kittredge's notion of thwarted motherhood, I think that it is mistaken, a "partial closure" inspired by the Prioress's sympathy for small animals and the little boy. For in her prayer, the Prioress emphatically adopts the perspective not of a mother, but of a child, with motherhood relegated to the nurturant Virgin Mother, whose guidance and strength Eglentyne beseeches.

The prayer, which serves as prologue to her tale, is the key to reconciling the Prioress's contraries. Beautiful and moving when considered in itself, this rarely examined prayer provides the missing elements that connect the portrait and the tale. And it reveals how the empathy and enmity in her tale are precisely suited to her character—or, rather, how her character is suited to the tale. The prayer begins with a versifying of Psalm 8:

> O Lord, oure Lord, thy name how merveillous
> Is in this large world ysprad—quod she—
> For noght oonly thy laude precious
> Parfourned is by men of dignitee,
> But by the mouth of children thy bountee
> Parfourned is, for on the brest soukynge
> Somtyme shewyn they thyn heriynge.
> [453–59]

This psalm, Sister Madeleva informs us (p. 30), is the first of several allusions in the prayer to the Little Office of the Blessed Virgin. The psalm also appears in the Mass for the Feast of the Holy Innocents, and so links the prayer to the liturgical and Scriptural reminiscences of the Slaughter of the Innocents in the tale.[37] Beyond that, the psalm serves as the text, as it were, for her tale, which illustrates praise from the mouth of a child. But, just as in our reading of the *General Prologue* portrait, we are surprised by what follows: the significance of these lines is transformed in light of the final stanza of this prayer, for the image of the nursing child refers not to the clergeon but to the Prioress herself:

> My konnyng is so wayk, O blisful Queene,
> For to declare thy grete worthynesse
> That I ne may the weighte nat susteene;

> But as a child of twelf month oold, or lesse,
> That kan unnethes any word expresse,
> Ryght so fare I, and therfore I yow preye,
> Gydeth my song that I shal of yow seye.
>
> [481–87]

The clergeon is seven years old, beyond infancy, but the Prioress images herself as still an infant. These lines display, in fact, the specificity with which the Prioress's qualities are reproduced in her tale. As a child of twelve months old or less, she places herself at the age of the Innocents to whose slaughter her tale refers. Moreover, she mirrors herself in that other innocent, the clergeon. The simple, faithful child becomes the repository of her own simple, childlike faith. Like her, he is *sowded to virginitee* "made fast in virginity," because he dies a virgin. His devotion, like hers in the *General Prologue*, is expressed only in song. And just as the clergeon is unaware of the meaning of his song, knowing only that it praises Mary, so we are told only of the *sound* of hers, and her manner of singing.[38] Both the nun and the child are filled with devotion for Mary, and for both, fervor substitutes for substantial understanding. Both are untutored in the suffering and compassion that inform Christianity. The child, after all, is only beginning to learn his Primer. And, significantly, the Primer is a source of the Prioress's prayer. For the Primer contains the Little Office of the Blessed Virgin, which the Prioress paraphrases in the prayer.[39]

The nun's frailty and vulnerability also reemerge in the child. In her prayer, Eglentyne stresses her childlike weakness, her frail inability to sustain her song.[40] And in her tale, the helpless child has his throat cut so that he can no longer sing. The treatment of his body also recalls the Prioress's portrait: she is obsessed with cleanliness, and the clergeon is killed by the forces of foulness and defilement, who cast his body in the uncleanest of places. Mary's intervention in the tale further identifies the Prioress with the clergeon, for he is saved by a miracle that answers the nun's own request of Mary: declaring that she is like a child, scarcely able to speak, Eglentyne prays that Mary will guide her song. In the tale, this actually happens to the child: he is rendered literally unable to speak, and Mary does guide his song. And the Prioress realizes her own desire for spotlessness through him by placing him among the 144,000 virgins of Apocalypse 14, who are *sine macula* "without spot," and who, as she says, follow the "white lamb celestial."

The function of the Jews in the tale lends specific meaning to the Prioress's outburst of enmity. By assigning this tale to the

Prioress, or, more correctly, by creating the Prioress and matching her so precisely with the tale, Chaucer introduced a detailed self-referentiality between teller and tale. In consequence, the Jews in the tale are not generalized bogeymen, as they may appear to be in the analogues, or in the tale considered in isolation. Rather, in signifying threats to childlike innocence, to virginal spotlessness, and to simple faith, the Jews are made to endanger the very qualities that Chaucer embodied in the nun. They are the foul representatives not only of spiritual stain, but also of physical defilement, which issues from their entrails. As such, they symbolize the most offensive possible contrary to the immaculate Eglentyne. The non-specific anti-Jewishness of the tale and its analogues is thus translated into the Prioress's revulsion at the qualities that constitute her own negation.[41]

This treatment of the Jews offers a striking parallel to the dominant psychoanalytical model of intolerance, in which the bigot localizes in the Jew the unwanted or threatening elements of his internal or external world.[42] A similar paradigm informs the cycle drama, in which the Jews represent precisely those qualities that the good figures must expel from themselves.[43] In terms of literary rather than psychological projection, the Jew in the Prioress's tale, as in the cycles, is a highly specific figure signifying a precise danger to the Christian. Deconstructed in this way, the conflict *between* faith and disbelief in these texts is seen as a conflict *within*, and the radically marginalized figure of the Jew emerges as central.[44]

Madame Eglentyne's enmity is aimed, then, at figures whose role is profoundly relevant to her. The same is true of her empathy. And this reveals the self-referentiality of the sentiment in which the Prioress bathes the clergeon: her loving approbation of the child with whom she shares so many qualities is, finally, love of self. Her love is thus misdirected, just as her pity and tenderness are in the *General Prologue*. But this does not negate her love of Mary, as is only fitting in a pilgrim so thoroughly composed of contraries, who reconciles in her nature such various expressions of love. In fact, this joining of personal and spiritual love recreates the ambiguity of the Prioress's love in the *General Prologue*, reenacting the imperfect submergence of the woman in the nun. In the end, though, it is Mary's perfect love that prevails in the tale, drawn down from heaven by the child's simple, unthinking, but ardent devotion. The nun thus vindicates her own qualities by having Mary reward them with the maternal love that the Prioress, in her spiritual infancy, requires.

Ultimately, much of the unresolved tension in the presentation of the Prioress centers on the question of love. The nun's love is confused, compromised. In the prayer and tale, by contrast, Mary's abundant love is unambiguous. And so in the tale Eglentyne, the humble, thorny, brier rose, has Mary, the noble "white lylye flour" of her prayer, bestow her love to redeem virginal innocence from the forces that endanger it.[45] In so doing, Mary redeems the Prioress too, and vanquishes ambiguity from the motto "*Amor vincit omnia.*" This is the triumph of love in the Prioress's tale. But it occurs only within the tale. In this regard, Eglentyne recalls the Wife of Bath, whose magical tale of marital peace and accord is incongruous with her own experience of marriage.[46] Similarly, the Prioress is assigned a tale that appears to miraculously transcend the misdirections and ambiguities in her portrait. The tale does not negate the contradictions in her makeup, however, but rather completes the restless Chaucerian marriage of contraries.

APPENDIX
THE HORIZONS OF TOLERANCE

Anti-Jewishness was inherent in Christian doctrine, and hostility toward Jews was widespread even a century after they had been expelled, as was the case in England when Chaucer wrote. Viewed telescopically, the official and popular intolerance toward Jews was generally progressive, and the principal events concerning them during the fourteenth century were marked by persecution, violence, and expulsion.[47] Having been expelled from England in 1290, they were evicted from all royal possessions in France in 1306. After returning to France in 1315, they were attacked in 1320 by the so-called Pastoureaux, or Shepherd crusaders, and were expelled again in 1322 after being accused of conspiring with lepers to poison wells. They were reinvited to France in 1359, but expelled definitively from most districts in 1394. In Germany at the time of the Black Death (1348–49), Jews were charged with well poisoning and burned *en masse*. Some cities, like Ratisbon and Vienna, successfully defended their Jews. But most German cities were emptied of Jews, many of whom went to Poland. Those who returned to their towns in Germany often did so under less favorable economic and political agreements than had previously obtained. And in 1391 in Spain, a pogrom movement accompanied by forced conversions anticipated events of a century later, when the Jews were expelled from that nation in 1492.

By Chaucer's lifetime (*ca.* 1343–1400), the European Jews had been widely abused and oppressed. Nationalist and economic pressures in concert with religious fervor, popular prejudice, and pogromist violence, had spurred many communities to degrade and ultimately expel the Jews.[48] Theologically, their guilt and spiritual infirmity had by then long been a commonplace. Chaucer would have been well aware that in both religious literature and popular belief, the Jews were traditional symbols of evil, perfidious and threatening allies of the devil.[49] Did he and all other Gentiles inevitably share this view? As recent criticism asserts, people are ineluctably affected by the ideology and social determinants of their time. But the specific responses to such influences are always individual and incalculable. The issue of intolerance provides a test case. Modern experience teaches that the reaction to highly propagandized prejudice can be contradictory, labile, even uncanny.[50] Medieval anti-Judaism differed in important ways from the racially-based anti-Semitism practiced in the twentieth century.[51] But along with that earlier hostility too, and despite the proscriptions and condemnations that it engendered, there are many signs of a crosscurrent of mutual tolerance between Christian and Jew. Moreover, the evidence suggests the existence of more than mere formal tolerance, which could, after all, be negotiated on the basis of self-interest, or purchased, or grudgingly conceded on theological grounds: there are in addition gestures and expressions of mutual respect and personal regard.[52] As Salo Baron (11:120–21) observes, Jews were often despised and haunted, especially at critical moments in history. But despite it all, Jews and Christians

> often maintained far closer social relations (even in the obscure realm of sex) than one might expect in the light of the stringent segregationist laws and preaching on both sides.
> [11:119–20]

Baron (11:187) adds that friendly daily exchanges often went unreported. But the closeness of relations between the groups can be inferred, as, for example, from the lavish efforts that had to be expended in order to cut off such contacts.

An explicit doctrine tolerating Jewish residence in Christian communities had been evolved in the patristic period and developed by Bernard of Clairvaux and Thomas Aquinas. From the thirteenth century, the Jews were technically *servi camerae*, or the king's serfs.[53] Jacob Katz notes that many Jews achieved high political standing, as evidenced by the fact that they were permitted to bear arms in France and Germany well into the thirteenth century.[54] Baron (11:114) adds that Jews were never prohibited from carrying arms in Italy or Spain. Katz asserts that despite oppressive rules and ideologies of separateness on both sides, neighborly and even friendly relations between Jews and Christians always occurred. The religious symbolism that permeated each community was a further barrier to social penetration, but, says Katz, Jews and Christians nevertheless often met in a friendly spirit.

Although the two communities remained socially unintegrated, common features marked their social life. Jews and Gentiles shared practices and beliefs and sometimes enjoyed common literary interests.[55] And in large measure, depending on the time and place, they dressed alike and spoke alike.[56] From the thirteenth century, Jews were required to wear a badge, undoubtedly an important step in their social degradation. The badge was not uniformly enforced during the medieval period, however.[57] And Baron (11:187) notes that it was imposed on Jews precisely because it was needed to distinguish them from Christians, with whom they had close relations.

Social interaction occurred in direct defiance of segregative laws. During the famous disputation in Paris in 1240, the Jewish spokesman is reported to have said that contrary to talmudic prescription,

> we do sell cattle to Gentiles, we enter into companionship with them, we stay with them alone, we entrust our infants to them to be suckled in their own homes, and we do teach *Torah* to a Gentile, for there are many clerics able to read Jewish books. [quoted from Katz, p. 108]

Despite formal prohibitions, Gentile and Jew gave gifts to one another until the end of the period.[58] Close personal ties appear to have developed. Israel Abrahams reports, for example, that Immanuel of Rome, Dante's Jewish imitator, required special consolation on Dante's death in 1321. Abrahams observes that no theological prejudice stood in the way of the mutual regard between the Christian poet and the Jew, and notes that Immanuel wrote in an Italian sonnet:

> Love has never read the *Ave Maria*, Love knows no law or creed. Love cannot be barred by a *Paternoster*, but to all who question his supreme power Love answers, "It is my will."[59]

Friendships between the groups, according to Abrahams (pp. 420, 426) were especially notable in Italy, where Jews and Christians played cards together and ate, drank, and danced together. Sentimental attachment is attested elsewhere in Europe as well during Chaucer's lifetime. Guido Kisch notes, for example, that German lawbooks reveal outspokenly friendly attitudes between individual Jews and Gentiles in the late fourteenth and the fifteenth centuries. Such utterances, Kisch concludes, gain weight because they were evidently free expressions, made openly in court, of popular sentiment in favor of Jews (*Germany*, p. 326). Abrahams (p. 426) cites the isolated but piquant instance of a Christian in Frankfurt who in 1377 applied the friendly epithet *selig* to a deceased Jew. Relationships between the sexes in this century often went well beyond friendship. Though formal marriage was not recognized unless one of the parties converted, affairs, common law marriage, and concubinage between Christian and Jew were frequent. So many Mediterranean Jews kept Christian concubines that this practice was often attacked by Jewish moralists.[60] Illicit relationships between Jews and Gentiles are also documented in France, Zurich, and Constance.[61] Each side tended to be more permissive if its own males had relations with females of the other religion, and Baron (11:82–84) observes that Christian popular literature in some cases sympathetically depicted the seduction of Jewish girls.

Expressions of personal respect and evidently of friendship—or at least of personal diplomacy—are documented from the fifteenth century as well. Despite longstanding warnings from both sides about defilement through exposure to the other's religious ceremonies, for example, social contact did occur at such events. A Sicilian Christian, to cite one instance, served as godfather at a Jewish circumcision in 1484. Baron observes that friendly acts of this sort were normally taken for granted, and so passed unnoticed by official documents.[62] In Germany, friendly exchanges of gifts in connection with religious rituals caused frequent problems. In Wiener Neustadt, for example, the eating of cakes that a Christian had brought to a Jewish wedding was officially permitted by R. Israel Isserlein. Isserlein also approved of Jews' giving gifts to Christians, including clerics, for New Year's, as well as on a Jewish holiday, the *Lag be–'omer*.[63] German Gentiles and Jews were sufficiently friendly, in fact, to provoke a Church council to forbid them to bathe, eat, or drink together.[64] Numerous similar prohibitions in German secular lawbooks further witness the amicable relationships that then existed (Kisch, *Germany*, p. 326). Sexual relations between Gentile and Jew are also documented from the fifteenth century: in the Orthodox German community of Ratisbon, for example, three Jews were prosecuted within the space of seven years (1460–67) on that charge, and several were reported awaiting trial.[65] In Italy in 1418, Jewish leaders complained about the sexual laxity of Italian Jews, many of whom considered Gentile women "permitted to them." And in Spain, personal associations with Gentiles were so close, and sexual relations so common, that some Jews attributed their downfall in that country to their excessive rapprochement with their Christian neighbors. A final illustration of trusting relationships between Christian and Jew in defiance of official regulation is the fact that fifteenth–century popes employed Jewish doctors in spite of papal decrees opposing such services.[66]

Most of the acts and gestures cited above were inspired by actual social contact between the groups. Whether Chaucer ever met Jews is purely speculative.[67] But even where personal interaction was unlikely, thoughtful people were capable of assessing Jews on their merits, rather than as a stereotypically damned and demonic people. In fourteenth-century England, for example, several religious and literary figures acknowledged the piety and ethicality in Jewish behavior.[68] Langland conceded, albeit grudgingly, that Jews were kinder to their needy fellows than were Christians.[69] The homilies of John Bromyard praise the Jews' piety, care for the poor, and heroic suffering for their faith, as well as their avoidance of swearing.[70] Thomas Brunton's printed sermons consider Jews superior to Christians in moral and religious practice.[71] Richard Rex notes that Wyclif and others argued that Jews, Saracens, and pagans could be saved on the basis of their virtuous acts.[72]

At least some fourteenth-century continental poets viewed the Jews more sympathetically than did religious polemic, treating them as human beings who were victimized by their historical circumstances. The German poet Heinrich der Teichner, who was active from about 1340 to 1375, wrote, for example, that "Many a man, who is himself much worse, bears an unjust grudge against the poor Jew." Jan van Boendale (de Clerk), a Flemish poet of the first half of the fourteenth century, wrote of the Jews:

> Want mi dunct emmer dat si
> also wel menschen syn als wi
> ende oec comen van Adame.

[It always seems to me that they are human beings like us and have also come from Adam].[73]

Respect toward Jews and the potential for friendship with them is prominently portrayed in the *Decameron,* the most suggestive analogue to the *Canterbury Tales.*[74] In the second tale of the first day, Neifile describes an intimate friendship between a Christian and a Jewish merchant named Abraham. The tale repeatedly emphasizes Abraham's integrity, goodness, learning, and modesty. It is his wisdom, in fact, that ultimately leads him to convert, for he realizes that a religion that can survive the spiritual decadence of its princes in Rome must be favored by God! The subsequent tale also portrays a wise Jew, Melchisedech, whose actions illustrate the declared lesson of the tale: that good sense can save a man from danger. In the process, Melchisedech compares Judaism, Christianity, and Islam to three rings. Originally there was only one ring, which signified that the son who was given it would inherit the wealth of his family. But in one generation a man had three virtuous and obedient sons whom he loved equally. So he had two more rings made, each virtually indistinguishable from the first. According to this parable, God gave the three religions to equally beloved peoples; each carries out God's commandments, and, says Melchisedech, the question of which is the true heir remains unsettled. These tales demonstrate the possibility of displaying Jews in a distinctly positive light. Melchisedech's contentions about the status of Judaism, though placed in a distant setting, are nonetheless remarkable. And the affection between the Christian and the Jew in Neifile's tale is represented emphatically and without apology, firmly suggesting that Boccaccio's audience would have regarded such a relationship as unexceptionable.

A caveat: though some of the instances cited here evidence longstanding patterns, others are isolated and possibly exceptional. At least some of them may belie private conviction. Their cumulative testimony demonstrates, however, that the historical position and experience of the Jews were far more complex than the simple assumptions of the *Prioress's Tale* and its literary and theological matrix suggest. The degradation of the Jews of medieval Europe was widespread and often agonizing. But there were other views and other voices than the Prioress's, and several of them indicate that the horizons of potential tolerance were less drastically constricted than has sometimes been supposed.

13

"Loves Hete" in the Prioress's Prologue and Tale

When, in Book I of *Troilus and Criseyde*, Pandarus encourages the despondent Troilus to try to win Criseyde's love, he cites, as is his wont, a number of general truths. Among them is something he has heard wise men say, to the effect that

> Was nevere man or womman yet bigete
> That was unapt to suffren loves hete,
> Celestial, or elles love of kynde.
> [1.977–79][1]

In view of Criseyde's beauty and youth, he continues, it is not appropriate that love in her case should be celestial "as yet," even if she were inclined toward that kind of love, or capable of it. Criseyde herself, however, seems at a later stage of the action to have a rather different opinion. After Pandarus, making his opening move in the conversation in which he plans to reveal to her that Troilus loves her, tells her to take off her wimple, dance, and observe the rites of May, she professes to be aghast. It would be more becoming for her, she says, to sit in a cave, praying and reading "holy seyntes lyves"; let maidens and young wives go to dances (2.110–19).

If we take our lead from the anachronistic "saints' lives" and translate Criseyde's cave into a fourteenth–century convent, we can think of the opposition between cave and dance as paralleling that between Pandarus's love celestial and "love of kynde," and of both pairs as representing two opposite modes of life available to women of gentle birth in Chaucer's time. A life based on natural love would manifest itself in social relationships with members of the opposite sex, leading to marital ties and in turn to the begetting and rearing of children; a life based on celestial love would be spent for the most part in cloistered isolation, in prayer and the contemplation of holy deeds.

Was the Prioress inclined to, or capable of, love celestial? To this question, the details making up her portrait in the *General Prologue* to the *Canterbury Tales* are, as everyone knows, wholly irrelevant—or, as regards the brooch inscribed "Amor vincit omnia," hopelessly ambiguous. We are probably right in inferring from them that, so far as outward appearances are concerned, she is a sentimental, snobbish, self-indulgent lady of some worldly pretensions. (Though it is true that she sings the divine service "well," it is also true that the Pardoner, the most morally reprehensible of the pilgrims, is "a noble ecclesiaste.") Yet nothing in her portrait rules out the possibility that she had an inner spiritual life suffused with devotional ardor, and it is this latent aspect of her that we see displayed when she reappears at the end of the *Shipman's Tale.*[2]

To the Host's elaborately deferential, indeed almost reverent, request that she be the next teller, she makes a gracious but brief and businesslike response which should perhaps remind us of the much-praised brevity of Mary's answers in Scripture: " 'Gladly,' quod she, and seyde as ye shal heere" (452). The Prologue that follows is in part an apologia or self-justification. Alluding to the "infants and sucklings" of Psalm 8, out of whose mouths God has perfected his praise, the Prioress implicitly distinguishes this miraculous activity (an infant [Latin *infans*] being literally "one incapable of speech") from that of the adult "men of dignitee" who are most fully qualified, by authority and learning, to "perform" God's praise in the natural order of things. She herself, a woman and therefore presumably lacking the qualifications of these male divines, resembles rather the inarticulate infants, and she invokes their praise of God as a precedent justifying her in her own attempt. Her story, she says, will be told in praise not only of God but of the Virgin Mary, who, though she is the mother of God and the "blisful queene" of heaven, was once a mortal woman like herself. After the Virgin has been invoked, she remains, though envisaged in meticulously correct subordination to the members of the Holy Trinity,[3] the center of the Prioress's rapt attention, contemplated with ardent veneration in all her transcendent power, glory, and goodness.

Given Mary's importance in the tale, it is appropriate that the Prioress should appeal to her in particular for help in telling it (473). In the sixth and last stanza of her Prologue, as she figuratively expresses her sense of her inadequacy to the task, this appeal takes a turn of some psychological interest:

> My konnyng is so wayk, O blisful Queene,
> For to declare thy grete worthynesse
> That I ne may the weighte nat sustene.
>
> [481–83]

The image of bearing a weight recalls one of the sources of *The Second Nun's Prologue*, a hymn by Venantius Fortunatus:

> Quem terra, pontus, aethera,
> Colunt, adorant, praedicant,
> Trinam regentem machinam,
> Claustrum Mariae bajulat.[4]

The verb *bajulat* in the last line is emphatic in meaning; *bajulare* is defined in Lewis and Short's *A Latin Dictionary* as "to carry a burden, to bear something heavy." In her miraculous parturition, Mary bore within her body and brought forth into the world nothing less than the divine ruler of the earth, the sea, and the heavens. The Prioress, too, is by analogy pregnant at this moment, but what she carries within her is not a child; it is the theme of her tale, the "great worthiness" of the Virgin which she feels herself too weak to "declare" or bring into the light.[5] The idea of weakness serves as a pivot, harking back to the image of the "children . . . on the brest soukynge" of the opening stanza. From the figurative pregnancy that overwhelms her, the Prioress imaginatively retreats or regresses to the condition of "a child of twelf month oold, or lesse, / That kan unnethes any word expresse" (484–85). She thus becomes one of the infants of the Psalm, and the Virgin, by implication, becomes the mother suckling the infant upon her breast. Insofar as her "declaring" of her story, despite this virtually inarticulate state, is made possible by the help and guidance of the divine mother, it is itself a miracle of the Virgin, spreading her praise through her own intercession, as does the miraculous singing of *O Alma redemptoris mater* by the martyred little boy in the story itself.[6]

Positioning herself thus in her Prologue in relation to the telling of her tale, the Prioress moves from the "real" world of the pilgrimage, and specifically that of the *Shipman's Tale*, to an imagined world existing far away in an unspecified past ("Ther was in

Asye, in a greet citee, / Amonges Cristene folk a Jewerye" [488–89]). As is true in medieval hagiographical literature generally, this world and the things that happen in it reflect the simplest and most reductive oppositions of adversary Christianity. Those who inhabit it are either faithful or infidel, labelled *a priori* and viewed as such beyond a shadow of a doubt; they are thus imbued either with a love of God, Jesus, and Mary which makes everything about them lovable and "good," or with a hatred which makes everything about them hateful and "evil." These identifications are confirmed, if confirmation were needed, by a series of direct interactions between natural and supernatural realms: in addition to the part the Virgin plays in the story, we see Satan inciting the Jews to do away with the boy and his singing (558–66), Jesus guiding the boy's mother to the pit in which the Jews have thrown him (603–6), and the Holy Trinity, invoked by the abbot, causing the boy to answer his question (645 ff.). This is a world, one might add, in which the Prioress herself, as Chaucer portrays her in the *General Prologue*, does not and indeed could not exist.

The events of the tale move, on the model of New Testament salvation history, from suffering through martyrdom to triumph; in the Prioress's narration of them, an emotional fervor associated with pathos and "affective piety" predominates over intellectuality, ruling out the possiblity of qualified moral judgment.[7] As, in her Prologue, she identifies herself both with the infant on the breast and the human mother of the infant Jesus, so in her tale she identifies herself both with the little boy and the Virgin, sharing equally in his devotion to her and her tender care for him. The love felt by infant and boy for the mother or mother-figure, and thus, implicitly, by the Prioress herself for the Virgin, is inarticulate, prerational, all-absorbing, wholly dependent on the unfailing reciprocal love and nurturance of the beloved, distanced from the adult world of "dignitee" and learning. Explaining to the abbot at the end of the story how it is that he can continue to sing even though his throat has been cut, the boy begins by telling of the emotion which is the first cause of the sequence of events in its entirety:

> This welle of mercy, Cristes mooder sweete,
> I loved alwey, as after my konnynge.
>
> [656–57]

(The phrase "as after my konnynge" significantly resembles the Prioress's "as I best kan or may" in the Prologue.) His immediate attraction toward the anthem praising Mary was caused by this love that had "always" possessed him, and was itself miraculous, in that he knew no Latin and therefore had no rational understanding of its content. He learned the anthem later not as a text set to music, but "by rote" (545), that is, as a sequence of discursively meaningless verbal sounds linked to the notes of a melody.

The pathetic simplicity of the tale, with its binary oppositions between goodness and evil, love and hate, is enhanced by complementary sets of images evoking the two emotions. The Virgin and the little boy are associated with the whiteness, respectively, of the emblematic lily and of the Lamb followed by the Holy Innocents in Revelation. The Lamb itself represents Christ in a sentimentally appealing aspect. Both Virgin and child are "sweet;" it was the "sweetness" of Christ's mother that had pierced the boy's heart from the beginning of his life on, and the Prioress refers to the martyred corpse as "his litel body sweete" (682). The boy is symbolized by two precious stones, the emerald of chastity and the ruby of martyrdom (609–10), and he is entombed at last in a sepulchre whose "marbul stones cleere" (681) would seem to derive from the liturgy of the Feast of Holy Innocents.[8] The attractiveness of these images is heightened by contrast with the repulsiveness of the "foule usure" practiced by the Jews, the Satanic serpent swollen with outraged pride, the wasp's nest, and the filth of the "ordure" in the Jews' privy (which last cannot do away with the sweetness of the body of the dead saint).[9]

The contrast between the inarticulate helplessness associated in the Prologue first with the infants sucking at the breast, then with the Prioress herself, and the articulate or discursive powers associated with worldly "men of dignitee," is symbolized by a pervasive opposition, in Prologue and tale alike, between song and speech. At the end of the Prologue, in the Prioress's final prayer to the Virgin, she refers to the tale that is to follow as a song: "Gydeth my song that I shal of yow seye" (487), that is, "Guide my song that I shall utter concerning you." A song, specifically, the anthem heard by the boy in school, is of course crucial to the tale's plot, and in learning it "by rote," the boy learns it, as I have said, primarily as music, including the sounds of words. This thematic distinction is made explicit at the end of the account of the anthem's meaning given the boy by his "felawe":"I kan namoore expounde in this mateere. / I lerne song; I kan but smal grammeere" (535–36). Song takes on an anagogical or otherworldly significance when, at the moment of the boy's murder, the Prioress suspends the telling of her story to address him directly, joyfully visualizing him in the company of 144,000 virgins whom John, in Revelation, saw following the Lamb:

> O martir, sowded to virginitee,
> Now maystow syngen, folwynge evere in oon
> The white Lamb celestial—quod she—
> Of which the grete evaungelist, Seint John,
> In Pathmos wroot, which seith that they that goon
> Biforn this Lamb and synge a song al newe,
> That nevere, flesshly, wommen they ne knew.
>
> [579–85]

We infer that, for the Prioress, an eternity of singing in the company of the Holy Innocents would represent the greatest imaginable joy.[10]

The *Prioress's Tale* is also songlike in that it is composed, not in the iambic pentameter couplets in which Chaucer wrote most of the tales, but in the seven-line stanza called *rime royal* which he seems to have thought appropriate to devotional stories. Since, by metrical convention, the end of each stanza of rime royal must also be the end of a sentence, the language of the tale is measured out in units of even length. It is in this sense, as well as by virtue of the elaborate rhyme-pattern of the stanza itself, more artificial, distanced from speech by one further remove, than the language of the *Shipman's Tale*, which precedes it. The language of the tale is also marked, as has often been noted, by the incantatory or songlike feature of reiteration. Phrases such as "Cristene folk" (489, 495, 614), "Cristes mooder" (506, 510, 538, 550, 597, 656, 678), and "litel child" (516, 552, 587, 596, 667), which occur again and again, become particularly conspicuous, and the words *singen* and *song* resound, appropriately, from beginning to end.

We see the unworldly innocence of a child taking precedence over the worldly experience of a "man of dignity" at the end of the poem in the effect of the boy's martyrdom on the abbot. It is he, as the person of highest authority in the scene, who takes upon himself the responsibility of finding out what has caused this supernatural event. Confidently invoking the Trinity in high formulaic language, he "conjures" the boy to explain how it is that he can continue to sing, though he should have died long since "by wey of kynde" (650). After he has been told about the grain placed by the Virgin on the boy's tongue, and has, by removing it, delivered him into her hands, he is overcome. He weeps copiously, and falls prostrate, lying "stille . . . as he had ben ybounde" (676), reduced to helplessness and silence.

Once the body has been entombed, the *Prioress's Tale* is at an end, and she closes as the Shipman had done, but to opposite effect, with a prayer on behalf of her fellow pilgrims: "Ther he is now, God leve us for to meete!" She prays, that is, that God may allow all of those present to meet in the company of the Holy Innocents, in which she had earlier visualized the martyred boy. But seven more lines follow, and in the space between the penultimate and final stanzas we are brought back from the faraway place and unspecified time of the tale to Lincoln, a city in England, and an event that occurred "but a litel while ago," in a historical past not far distant from the present. ("History is now and in England.") This is the "real world" of the *Canterbury Tales,* inhabited by the Prioress herself and her beloved little dogs, by the Monk of the pilgrimage, and by the Monk of the *Shipman's Tale.* Here, professed Christians, even members of the regular clergy, can also be "sinful folk unstable," desperately in need of the mercy of a merciful God, multiplied unstintingly in honor of the Virgin queen of heaven. The Prioress has enacted a withdrawal from this unstable "reality" to a realm where the truths of salvation history are self-evident and unquestioned. The relation of the mortal Christian to divine beneficence in this realm is modelled not on adult eroticism, the soul's recognition of and passionate response to its divine wooer, but on the thoughtless and instinctual bliss of the child surrounded by the loving care of its parents, exempt for the time being from all danger and doubt. This is celestial love as the Prioress knows it, and in reading her Prologue and tale we can, if we allow ourselves to be beguiled by Chaucer's consummate verbal and metrical artistry, experience it temporarily for ourselves.

Notes

INTRODUCTION

1. For a contrary view, see Lawrence Stone, *Family, Sex and Marriage in England: 1500–1800* (New York: Harper & Row, 1977).

2. Hagstrum gives a preliminary formulation of his project in "Is There An Ideal of Marital Friendship In Western Culture?" *National Humanities Center Newsletter* 7,2 (1985–86): 1–8.

3. The essays in this volume by Elizabeth A. Clark, Michael Sheehan, R. W. Hanning, Giovanni Sinicropi, Robert R. Edwards, and Stephen Spector were delivered in their original form as papers at the conference. Clark's essay was subsequently printed in *Recherches Augustiniennes* 21 (1986): 139–62; it is reprinted here by permission of the editors. An expanded, Italian version of Sinicropi's essay appeared in *Comunità* 42, nos. 189–90 (1988): 380–429.

4. Georges Duby, *The Knight, the Lady and the Priest: The Making of Modern Marriage in Medieval France,* trans. Barbara Bray (New York: Pantheon, 1983) and *Medieval Marriage: Two Models from Twelfth-Century France,* trans. Elborg Forster (Baltimore: Johns Hopkins University Press, 1978); David Herlihy, *Medieval Households* (Cambridge, Mass.: Harvard University Press, 1985).

5. Jean-Louis Flandrin and Philippe Ariès, *Western Sexuality: Practice and Precept in Past and Present Times,* ed. Philippe Ariès and André Béjin, trans. Anthony Forster (Oxford: Blackwell, 1985), chs. 10–12.

6. C. S. Lewis, *The Allegory of Love: A Study in Medieval Tradition* (Oxford: Clarendon Press, 1936), p. 2. For a review of the history of courtly love as a critical term, see Roger Boase, *The Origin and Meaning of Courtly Love: A Critical Study of European Scholarship* (Manchester: Manchester University Press, 1977).

7. Denis de Rougemont, *Love in the Western World,* trans. Montgomery Belgion, rev. ed. (New York: Pantheon, 1956). De Rougemont does not argue for the moral efficacy of "courtly love" but only suggests its historical persistence. Another view on the persistence of courtly love, again rejecting its moral efficacy, is set out by A. J. Denomy, *The Heresy of Courtly Love* (New York: D. X. McMullen, 1947).

8. E. Talbot Donaldson says that term "courtly love" was virtually unused in the medieval period and was popularized in the late nineteenth century by Gaston Paris ("The Myth of Courtly Love," in *Speaking of Chaucer* [New York: Norton, 1970], p. 154). Larry D. Benson notes, however, that *amor cortese* was in fairly common use in medieval Italian ("Courtly Love and Chivalry in the Later Middle Ages," in *Fifteenth-Century Studies*, ed. Robert F. Yeager (Hamden, Conn.: Archon, 1984), p. 239.

9. John F. Benton, "The Court of Champagne as a Literary Center," *Speculum* 36 (1961):551–91. See also his "Clio and Venus: An Historical View of Medieval Love," in *The Meaning of Courtly Love*, ed. Francis X. Newman (Albany: State University of New York Press, 1968), pp. 19–42.

10. Richard Firth Green, *Poets and Princepleasers: Literature and the English Court in the Late Middle Ages* (Toronto: University of Toronto Press, 1980).

11. D. W. Robertson, Jr., *A Preface to Chaucer: Studies in Medieval Perspectives* (Princeton, N.J.: Princeton University Press, 1962), pp. 391–503. R. E. Kaske, reviewing Robertson's *Preface*, says that the emphasis of Andreas's often satiric analysis falls elsewhere than on the moral aspects of sexual love: perhaps on the comedy created by differences in men's and women's attitudes, complicated by differences in social rank ("Chaucer and Medieval Allegory," *English Literary History* 30 [1963]: 175–92). For further views on Andreas, see Douglas Kelly, "Courtly Love in Perspective: The Hierarchy of Love in Andreas Capellanus," *Traditio* 24 (1968): 119–47; and John C. Moore, "Love in Twelfth-Century France: A Failure in Synthesis," *Traditio* 24 (1968): 429–43. Toril Moi, "Desire in Language: Andreas Capellanus and the Controversy of Courtly Love," in *Medieval Literature: Criticism, Ideology, and History*, ed. David Aers (Brighton, Sussex: The Harvester Press, 1986), pp. 11–33 anatomizes four styles of reading the *De amore*: a defense of courtly love, an exposition of the "double truth" of spiritual and secular love, an ironic condemnation of courtly love, and ironic treatment of both forms of love. Moi's own reading of the text emphasizes the ideological function of representing desire and the impossibility of knowing a beloved's intent, to which desire leads in a courtly context. She suggests, too, that the "historical" dimension of courtly love has to do with late medieval society rather than Andreas's immediate audience in the twelfth century.

12. Donaldson, "The Myth of Courtly Love," p. 161.

13. Henry Ansgar Kelly, *Love and Marriage in the Age of Chaucer* (Ithaca, N.Y.: Cornell University Press, 1975), Introduction. Kelly reviews early challenges to Lewis's definition of courtly love, beginning with Donnell Van de Voort's *Love and Marriage in the English Medieval Romance* (Nashville, Tenn.: privately printed, 1938).

14. Andreas Capellanus's view on the subject, adds Kelly (p. 39), was, as far as is known, not even heard of in England, and there was little or no reference to it in the literature of France, Italy, or Spain. But see P. G. Walsh, ed. and trans. *Andreas Capellanus on Love* (London: Duckworth, 1982), pp. 1–25 and Jerome Mazzaro's essay in this volume, p. 271 n.3.

15. Kelly, p. 60; D. S. Brewer, "Love and Marriage in Chaucer's Poetry," *Modern Language Review* 49 (1954): 461–64. Though Brewer sees the relationship between Troilus and Criseyde as something of an exception to this general practice, Kelly maintains that Chaucer made their relationship licit by maneuvering the lovers into a clandestine marriage (p. 61).

16. George Kane, "Chaucer, Love Poetry, and Romantic Love," in *Acts of Interpretation: The Text in Its Context 700–1600*, ed. Mary J. Carruthers and Elizabeth D. Kirk (Norman, Okla.: Pilgrim Books, 1982), pp. 237–55.

17. Peter Dronke, *Medieval Latin and the Rise of European Love-Lyric*, 2nd ed., 2 vols. (Oxford: Clarendon Press, 1968), I: 1–56. Kelly (p. 26) responds, however, that some so-called courtly characteristics were directly inspired by Ovid.

18. Paul Zumthor, *Essai de poétique médiévale* (Paris: Seuil, 1972), and *Langue et techniques poétiques à l'époque romane* (Paris: Klincksieck, 1963). Zumthor modifies his view to some extent in the remarks he makes in *Speaking of the Middle Ages*, trans. Sarah White (Lincoln: Univ. of Nebraska Press, 1986).

19. Robert Guiette, "D'une poésie formelle en France au Moyen Age," *Revue des sciences humaines* NS, fascicule 54 (1949): 61–69, and *Questions de littérature* (Ghent: Romanica Gandensia, 1960); and Pierre Guiraud, "Les structures étymologiques du 'Trobar,' " *Poétique* 2 (1971): 417–26.

20. Larry D. Benson, "Courtly Love and Chivalry in the Later Middle Ages," pp. 237–57. Cf. the earlier argument by Francis L. Utley in "Must We Abandon the Concept of Courtly Love?" *Medievalia et Humanistica* NS 3 (1972): 299–324.

21. Étienne Gilson, *The Mystical Theology of Saint Bernard*, trans. A. H. C. Downes (New York: Sheed & Ward, 1940).

22. George Lyman Kittredge, "Chaucer's Discussion of Marriage," *Modern Philology* 9 (1911–12): 435–67; rpt. in Edward Wagenknecht, ed. *Chaucer: Modern Essays in Criticism* (New York: Oxford University Press, 1959), pp. 188–215 and Richard J. Schoeck and Jerome Taylor, eds., *Chaucer Criticism*, 2 vols. (Notre Dame, Ind.: University of Notre Dame Press, 1960), I: 130–59.

CHAPTER 1

1. 418–419 A.D.: dating from Peter Brown, *Augustine of Hippo: A Biography* (Berkeley: University of California Press, 1969), p. 284. Although the necessity of distinguishing the varying periods in which Augustine developed his sexual and marital ethic seems an obvious necessity to the historian, many theological treatments of the topic fail to make this distinction and hence are of diminished value for an historian (e.g. the series of six articles on Augustine's sexual teaching by Davide Covi in *Augustinus* 16 (1971), 17 (1972), 18 (1973), and 19 (1974).

2. "And Adam was not deceived, but the woman was deceived and became a transgressor."

3. *De civitate Dei* 14.11 (*Corpus Christianorum, Series Latina* [hereafter *CCL*] 48.433): " ... *ille autem ab unico noluit consortio dirimi.* ... " For an overview of the Augustinian texts emphasizing the social view of marriage, see A. Brucculeri, *Il pensiero sociale di S. Agostino,* 2d ed. (Roma: Edizioni "La Civiltà Cattolica," 1945), pp. 145–63.

4. For example, Milton's campaign for the legalization of divorce in seventeenth-century England; see *The Doctrine and Discipline of Divorce,* Book 1.

5. On the three "goods" of marriage, see *De bono coniugali* 24.32 (*Corpus Scriptorum Ecclesiasticorum Latinorum* [hereafter *CSEL*] 41.227); *De nuptiis et concupiscentia* 1.17.19 (*CSEL* 42.231). The 1930 encyclical, *Casti Connubii,* is structured around Augustine's three "goods" of marriage; the pro-reproductive stance is upheld in the prohibition against birth control. Only in the post-World War II addresses, such as *The Apostolate of the Midwife* (1951), is even the "rhythm method" of contraception permitted.

6. *Confessiones* 4.6.11 (*CCL* 27.45); see Horace, *Odes,* 1.3.8; Ovid, *Tristia,* 4.4–72 for similar sentiments. For problems various Church Fathers experienced over the claims of friendship, see Elizabeth A. Clark, *Jerome, Chrysostom, and Friends: Essays and Translations,* Studies in Women and Religion 2 (New York and Toronto: Edwin Mellen Press, 1979), pp. 41–44, and references therein.

7. *Confessiones* 3.1.1. (*CCL* 27.27).

8. *Confessiones* 4.7.12 (*CCL* 27.46).

9. *Confessiones* 4.2.2 (*CCL* 27.41).

10. *Confessiones* 6.13.23, 15.25 (*CCL* 27.89, 90): she was nearly two years too young to marry. See M. K. Hopkins, "The Age of Roman Girls at Marriage," *Population Studies,* 18 (1965): 309–27. Calculating a fifteen year relationship of Augustine with his concubine, based on *Confessiones*

6.11.18 (*CCL* 27.86) is Emile Schmitt, *Le Mariage chrétien dans l'oeuvre de saint Augustin: Une théologie baptismale de la vie conjugale* (Paris: Études Augustiniennes, 1983), p. 26.

11. *Confessiones* 6.11.19 (*CCL* 27.87); although cf. 6.12.22 (*CCL* 27.88). Peter Brown wisely advises us to think that Augustine's relationship with his concubine crumbled "not through animal passion, but under the glacial weight of the late Roman caste system" (*Augustine and Sexuality* [Berkeley: The Center for Hermeneutical Studies in Hellenistic and Modern Culture, 1983], pp. 1–2). Brown's essay is a stimulating and sensitive treatment of the subject, a major advance on discussions found in older textbooks and monographs; the "social" dimensions of Augustine's teaching on sexuality are explored in new ways.

12. *Confessiones* 6.14.24 (*CCL* 27.89); cf. 6.12.21 (*CCL* 27.87).

13. *Confessiones* 6.3.5–4.12 (*CCL* 27.135–40). From the *Confessions* we learn scarcely anything about this period of retreat; Augustine claims here that he must "hasten on to tell of greater things" (cf. *Aeneid* 7.45). The dialogues composed at Cassiciacum reveal more. See Brown, *Augustine*, pp. 113–24, on the Cassiciacum period.

14. *Soliloquia* 1 (*Patrologia Latina* [hereafter *PL*] 32.869–84).

15. *De quantitate animae* (*PL* 32.1035–80).

16. *Confessiones* 9.4.8 (*CCL* 27.137).

17. Kenneth Burke, *The Rhetoric of Religion: Studies in Logology* (Boston: Beacon Press, 1961), p. 114.

18. *Confessiones* 8.11.26 (*CCL* 27.129). For possible negative influences on Augustine's views of sexuality exerted by Virgil, see John J. O'Meara, "Virgil and Saint Augustine: The Roman Background to Christian Sexuality," *Augustinus* 13 (1968), esp. 325–26.

19. *Confessiones* 8.7.17 (*CCL* 27.124).

20. *Confessiones* 8.11.27 (*CCL* 27.130).

21. *Confessiones* 4.8.13 (*CCL* 27.47).

22. Dating in Brown, *Augustine*, p. 74.

23. *Retractiones* 1.9.1 (*CCL* 57.30); cf. *De Genesi ad litteram* 8.2 (*CSEL* 28¹.232). For the Manichean mockery that the "image of God" might mean that God had nostrils, teeth, a beard, and internal organs, see *De Genesi contra Manichaeos* 1.17.27 (*PL* 34.186). For other Manichean complaints about Genesis and the Old Treatment, see (e.g.) *Contra Faustum* 4.1; 6.1; 10.1; 22.1, 3, 5 (*PL* 42.217, 227, 243, 401, 402, 403). Also see Gilles Pelland, *Cinq études d'Augustin sur le début de la Genèse* (Tournai: Desclée et Cie.; Montreal: Bellarmin, 1972), pp. 17–22.

24. See *Confessiones* 5.14.24 (*CCL* 27.71). On Ambrose's indebtedness to Philo and Basil of Caesarea for allegorical exegesis, see John J. Savage, "Introduction" in Saint Ambrose, *Hexameron, Paradise, and Cain and Abel*, Fathers of the Church 42 (New York: Fathers of the Church, 1961), pp. vi–viii; F. Homes Dudden, *The Life and Times of St. Ambrose* (Oxford: Clarendon Press, 1935), 2:680–1. For Augustine, see Michael Müller, *Die Lehre des hl. Augustinus von der Paradiesesehe und ihre Auswerkung in der Sexualethik des 12. und 13. Jahrhunderts bis Thomas von Aquin* (Regensburg: Verlag Friedrich Pustet, 1951), pp. 9–32; Yves M.-J. Congar, "Le Thème de Dieu-Créateur et les explications de l'Hexaméron dans la tradition chrétienne," in *L'Homme devant Dieu: Mélanges offerts au Père Henri de Lubac: Exégèse et patristique*, Théologie 56 (Lyon-Fourvière: Aubier, 1964), pp. 189–215.

25. *De Genesi contra Manichaeos* 2.7.9 (*PL* 34.200–1); see Kari Elisabeth Børresen, *Subordination and Equivalence: The Nature and Rôle of Woman in Augustine and Thomas Aquinas*, trans. Charles H. Talbot (Washington, D.C.: University Press of America, 1981), p. 16, for further discussion.

26. *De Genesi contra Manichaeos* 1.19.30 (*PL* 34.187).

27. *Ibid.*, Luke 20:34: "*Filii enim saeculi hujus generant et generantur. . . .*" See Bernard Alves Pereira, *La doctrine du mariage selon saint Augustin*, 2d ed. (Paris: Gabriel Beauchesne, 1930), pp. 10–11.

28. *Confessiones* 13.24.37 (*CCL* 27.264).

29. *Retractiones* 1.9.2. (*CCL* 57.30–31).

30. See Ambrose's treatises *De virginibus, De institutione virginis, Exhortatio virginitatis,* and *De virginitate* (*PL* 16.197–244, 279–380). For Mary, see, e.g., *De institutione virginis* 5.35; 5.37–9.62 (*PL* 16.328–29, 329–36). Ambrose on Mary's virginity *in partu:* Mary is the *hortus clausus* of Song of Songs 4:12 and the *porta clausus* of Ezekiel 44:1ff. (*De institutione virginis* 9.60–62; 8.52 [*PL* 16.335–36, 334]). On Ambrose's Mariology, see Charles W. Neumann, *The Virgin Birth in the Works of Saint Ambrose*, Paradosis 17 (Freiburg im Breisgau: Editions Universitaires, 1962). For an overview of patristic Mariology, see G. Joussard, "Marie à travers la patristique: Maternité divine, virginité, sainteté," in D'Hubert du Manoir, ed., *Maria: Études sur la sainte vierge* (Paris: Beauchesne et ses fils, 1949), 1:71–157.

31. *Epistula* 22.20 (*CSEL* 54.170).

32. See especially Jerome's catalogue in *Adversus Jovinianum* 1.47 (*PL* 23.288–91; also *Adversus Helvidium* 20 [*PL* 23.214]; *Epistula* 22.22 [*CSEL* 54.174–75]).

33. *Epistula* 54.4.1–2 (*CSEL* 54.469).

34. Jerome acknowledges Jovinian's asceticism, albeit grudgingly, in *Adversus Jovinianum* 1.40 *(PL* 23.280). The point should be underscored: the debate could take place even among members of the ascetic camp. On Jovinian, see Wilhelm Haller, *Iovinianus: Die Fragmente seiner Schriften, die Quellen zu seiner Geschichte, sein Leben und seine Lehre*, TU 17, 2 (Leipzig: J. C. Hinrichs, 1897); Ilona Opelt, *Hieronymus' Streitschriften* (Heidelberg: Carl Winter–Universitätsverlag, 1973), pp. 37–53; John Gavin Nolan, *Jerome and Jovinian*, The Catholic University of America, Studies in Sacred Theology, 2d series, 97 (Washington D.C.: The Catholic University of America Press, 1956).

35. *Adversus Jovinianum* 1.3 *(PL* 23.224).

36. *Adversus Jovinianum* 1.5 *(PL* 23.227).

37. *Adversus Jovinianum* 1.5 *(PL* 23.225–27).

38. *Adversus Jovinianum* 1.4, 16 *(PL* 23.225, 246).

39. *Adversus Jovinianum* 1.16, 24 *(PL* 23.246, 255), citing 1 Corinthians 7:29.

40. *Adversus Jovinianum* 1.27 *(PL* 23.260).

41. *Adversus Jovinianum* 1.16 *(PL* 23.246); cf. *Epistula* 22.19 *(CSEL* 54.169–70).

42. *Adversus Jovinianum* 1.3 *(PL* 23.223).

43. See Jerome, *Epistulae* 48–49 *(CSEL* 54, 347–87); esp. 49.2, 8, 9, 11, 14 *(CSEL* 54.352–53, 361–63, 364, 365–66, 374–75).

44. Dating from Brown, *Augustine*, p. 184.

45. So he states in *Retractiones* 2.48. [(=22).1] *(CCL* 57.107–8).

46. *Ibid.*

47. *De bono coniugali* passim *(CSEL* 41.187–231); *De sancta virginitate* 10.9, 12.12, 18.18, 21.21 *(CSEL* 41.243, 244, 251, 254–55). In addition to works already cited on Augustine's marital ethic, see Emanuele Samek Lodovici, "Sessualità, matrimonio e concupiscenza in Sant' Agostino," in R. Cantalamessa, ed., *Etica sessuale e matrimonio nel cristianesimo delle origini*, Studia Patristica Mediolanensia 5 (Milano: Vita e Pensiero [Università Cattolica del Sacro Cuore], 1976), pp. 212–72; François-Joseph Thonard, "La morale conjugale selon saint Augustin," *Revue des Études Augustiniennes* 15 (1969): 113–31.

48. *De bono coniugali* 2.2 *(CSEL* 41.188–90).

49. See above, on his earlier view in *De Genesi contra Manichaeos.* That Augustine's new view may owe something to Jovinian, see Jerome,

Adversus Jovinianum 1.29 (*PL* 23.262) where Jerome implies that Jovinian held the view, and my argument in "Heresy, Asceticism, Adam, and Eve: Interpretations of Genesis 1–3 in the Later Latin Fathers" in *Intrigue in the Garden: Genesis 1–3 in the History of Exegesis,* ed. Gregory Robbins (Toronto: The Edwin Mellen Press, 1989); also in my *Ascetic Piety and Women's Faith: Essays in Late Ancient Christianity* (Toronto: The Edwin Mellen Press, 1986).

50. As I have suggested elsewhere ("Heresy, Asceticism"), Augustine's report that he had "recently" (*nuper*) written *De bono coniugali* (*De Genesi ad litteram* 9.7 [*CSEL* 28¹.276]) gives a clue to the dating of *De Genesi ad litteram*. Although *nuper* can cover a variable amount of time, probably we need not stretch it to mean more than eight or nine years at most. For example, in *De sancta virginitate* 1.1 (*CSEL* 41.235) Augustine uses "*nuper*" to refer to the writing of *De bono coniugali*, which he had written in the very same year, 401 A.D. Books 10 and 11 of *De Genesi ad litteram* are usually dated to 412 A.D. or later, since they seem to involve discussion of Pelagian ideas: P. Agaësse and A. Solignac, "Introduction générale," *La Genèse au sens litteral I–VIII*, Oeuvres de saint Augustin, 7 ser. (Paris: Desclée de Brouwer, 1972), 48:28–31; Joseph Mausbach, *Die Ethik des hl. Augustinus*, 2d ed. (Freiburg im Breisgau: Herdersche Verlagshandlung, 1929), I:319; Book 9 dates to 410 A.D.

51. *De Genesi ad litteram* 9.3, 9, 10, 16–18 (*CSEL* 28¹.271–72, 277–80). Although Augustine allows for the possibility of sexual functioning in a sinless Eden, he still retains the notion that Genesis 1 describes the creation of the "causal reasons" and Genesis 2, the visible, physical creation: *De Genesi ad litteram* 6.5, 6, 14; 7.24; 9.1 (*CSEL* 28¹.175, 177–78, 189, 222–23, 268). For the change in Augustine's views, see Børresen, *Subordination*, pp. 36–40 (although I think factors other than the Pelagian dispute led to Augustine's changed view on the possibility of sexual relations in a sinless Eden).

52. *De Genesi ad litteram* 9.7 (*CSEL* 28¹.275). See Pereira, *Doctrine,* pp. 12–13.

53. *Confessiones* 3.11.20; 4.1.1 (*CCL* 27.38,40); *Contra epistolam fundamenti* 10 (*CSEL* 25¹.206); *De moribus Manichaeorum* 68 (19) (*PL* 32.1374); *De moribus ecclesiae catholicae* 18.34 (*PL* 32.1326). Pierre Courcelle (*Recherches sur les Confessions de Saint Augustin*, 2d ed. [Paris: Editions E. de Boccard, 1968], p. 78) has argued for a Manichean period of at least ten years.

54. On Jovinian's charges of "Manicheanism" directed against Ambrose and other ascetics, see Augustine, *De nuptiis* 2.15(5), 38(23) (*CSEL* 42.444–45, 458); *Contra Julianum* 1.2.4 (*PL* 44.643).

55. For overviews of Manicheanism, see Hans Jonas, *The Gnostic Religion: The Message of the Alien God and the Beginnings of Christian-*

ity, 2d ed., rev. ed. (Boston: Beacon Press, 1963), ch. 9; Henri Charles Puech, *Le Manichéisme: Son fondateur—sa doctrine,* Musée Guimet, Bibliothèque de Diffusion 56 (Paris: Civilisations du Sud, 1949); Geo Widengren, *Mani and Manichaeism* (New York: Holt, Rinehart and Winston, 1963); L. J. R. Ort, *Mani: A Religio-Historical Description of his Personality,* Supplementa ad Numen, Altera Series 1 (Leiden: E. J. Brill, 1967); H. J. Polotsky, "Manichäismus," *Paulys Real-Encyclopädie* Suppl. Bd. 6 (1935), 240–271; C. Colpe, "Mani-Manichäismus," *Die Religion in Geschichte und Gegenwart,* 3d ed. (Tübingen: Mohr, 1960), 4:714–22. For a discussion of Augustine's relations with Manicheanism, see now Samuel N. C. Lieu, *Manichaeism in the Later Roman Empire and Medieval China: A Historical Survey* (Manchester: Manchester University Press, 1985) ch. 5.

56. *De moribus Manichaeorum* 18.65 (*PL* 32.1373). See John Noonan, *Contraception: A History of Its Treatment by the Catholic Theologians and Canonists* (New York, Toronto: New American Library, 1967), pp. 151–54. According to Soranus's *Gynecology* 1.10.36, the woman's fertile period was thought to come at the end of menstruation.

57. So Noonan infers from *Contra Faustum* 22.30 (*CSEL* 25^1.624): in intercourse, the Manicheans "pour out their God by a shameful slip" (Noonan, *Contraception,* pp. 153–54). Recall Augustine's interpretation of the sin of Onan as *coitus interruptus.*

58. *De Moribus Manichaeorum* 18.65 (*PL* 32.1373): the Manicheans advised Augustine to refrain from sexual relations during the woman's fertile period. Cf. *Confessiones* 4.2.2 (*CCL* 27.41) (although we begrudge the birth of children, we love them after they arise) and *Contra Faustum* 20.23 (*CSEL* 25^1.567), on married Manichean Auditors who produce children, "albeit they beget them against their wills."

59. On Augustine's early sex life, see *Confessiones* 2.2.2, 4; 3.1.1; 6.11.20–15.25; 8.7 (*CCL* 27.18, 19, 27, 87–90). On a (probable) later reflection concerning his relationship with his concubine, see *De bono coniugali* 5.5 (*CSEL* 41.193–94). See note 11 above.

60. *De moribus ecclesiae catholicae* 63 (30) (*PL* 32.1336); cf. his later anti-Manichean treatise, *Contra Faustum* 30.6 (*CSEL* 25^1.755).

61. *Contra Faustum* 22.31–32, 43, 45, 47–50, 81 (*CSEL* 25^1.624–27, 635–36, 637, 639–44, 683). The theme is at the forefront in *De bono coniugali* 26–35 (*CSEL* 41.221–30). Augustine rejects the Manichean tendency to pit the asceticism of some New Testament passages against the pro-reproductive views of the Old Testament: *Contra Adimantum* 3, 23 (*CSEL* 25^1.118–22, 182); *Contra Secundinum* 21, 23 (*CSEL* 25^2 938–39, 941); *Contra Faustum* 14.1 (*CSEL* 25^1.401–4).

62. *Contra Faustum* 15.7 (*CSEL* 25^1.429–30); cf. *De moribus Manichaeorum* 65 (18) (*PL* 32.1373).

63. *Contra Faustum* 22.84 (*CSEL* 25¹.687); also later in *De adulterinis coniugiis* 2.12.12 (*CSEL* 41.396).

64. *Contra Faustum* 19.26 (*CSEL* 25¹.529).

65. *Contra Faustum* 15.7 (*CSEL* 25¹.429); *De moribus Manichaeorum* 18 (*PL* 32.1373). Pereira (*Doctrine*, pp. 45–50, 52–53) resolves the ambivalence of Augustine's teaching on marriage by distinguishing the "end," "goods," and "essence" of marriage; his distinctions seem overlyscholastic for Augustine, in my reading of the text. For references in Augustine to the reading of the *tabulae*, see Pereira, p. 153, and Marcello Marin, "Le *tabulae matrimoniales* in S. Agostino," *Siculorum Gymnasium* 29 (1976): 307–21, esp. 309–10.

66. *Confessiones* 2.2.3–4; 4.2.2 (*CCL* 27.18–19, 41).

67. *De peccatorum meritis et remissione* 1.57(29); 2(4), 39(25); 3.2(2) (*CSEL* 60.56, 73, 111, 130); *De natura et gratia* 3.3; 4.4 (*CSEL* 60.235–36); *De gratia Christi et de peccato originali* 43(38)–45(40) (*CSEL* 42.200–3); *De perfectione iustitiae hominis* 18.39; 21.44 (*CSEL* 42.40–41, 47–48). For Augustine's theory of original sin, see Pier Franco Beatrice, *Tradux Peccati: alle fonti della dottrina agostiniana del peccato originale*, Studia Mediolanensia 8 (Milan: Vita e Pensiero [Università Cattolica del Sacro Cuore], 1978); Beatrice's argument that Augustine derived his theory from the Encratites through Messalian teaching (pp. 222–59) seems dubious. Also see Mausbach, *Die Ethik*, vol. 2, ch. 3.

68. *De civitate Dei* 14.23, 26 (*CCL* 48.445–46, 449–50).

69. *De civitate Dei* 14.26 (*CCL* 48.449); cf. *De gratia Christi et peccato originali* 2.40.35–41.36 (*CSEL* 42.199).

70. *De civitate Dei* 14.23 (*CCL* 48.445); cf. *De gratia Christi et peccato originali* 2.40.35 (*CSEL* 42.199).

71. *De civitate Dei* 14.21 (*CCL* 48.443); cf. his spiritualized version in *De Genesi contra Manichaeos* 1.19.30 (*PL* 34.187).

72. E.g., *De nuptiis* 1.1, 6(5)–8(7), 23(21); 2.14(5), 19(8), 20(8), 42(16), 53(31) (*CSEL* 42.212, 216–20, 236, 265–66, 271, 272–73, 295–96, 309–10).

73. E.g., *Contra duas epistolas Pelagianorum* 1.9(5), 10(5); 2.9(5); 3.25(9); 4.9(5) (*CSEL* 60.430, 431, 469, 517–18, 529–30).

74. *Contra duas epistolas* 1.4(2); 10(5); (*CSEL* 60.425, 431); *De nuptiis* 2.15(15), 34(9), 38(23), 49(29), 50(29) (*CSEL* 42.266–68, 288, 291–92, 304, 305); *Contra secundam Juliani responsionem opus imperfectum* 1.24, 115 (*CSEL* 85¹.21, 132–33); and many other places.

75. *Contra Julianum* 3.15(7), 16(7), 30(16); 4.12(2); 6.59(19) (*PL* 44.709, 710, 717–18, 742, 858).

76. *Contra duas epistolas* 1.10(5), 31(15), 35(17) (*CSEL* 60.341, 448, 451–52); *Opus imperfectum* 1.68.5; 2.122; 5.14 (*CSEL* 88¹.75, 253; *PL* 45.1445); *Epistle* 6*.5.1; 7.2 (*CSEL* 88.34, 35–36). On the dating of the new *Epistle* 6*, see Marie-François Berrouard, "Les Lettres 6* et 19* de saint Augustin," *Revue des Études Augustiniennes* 27 (1981): 269–77, and Henry Chadwick, "New Letters of St. Augustine," *Journal of Theological Studies* 34 (1983): 429.

77. *Contra Secundinum* 23 (*CSEL* 25².940); *Contra Faustum* 20.11; 23.10 (*CSEL* 25¹.549–50, 716–17).

78. *De continentia* 23(9); 24(10) (*CSEL* 41.170); *Contra duas epistolas* 4.5(4) (*CSEL* 60.525).

79. *Contra Faustum* 2.1; 3.1; 7.1 (*CSEL* 25¹.253–54, 261–62, 302–3); also see *Sermo* 51.11(7)–16(10), 27(17) (*PL* 38.339–42, 348–49); *De consensu Evangelistarum* 2.2(1)–16(5) (*CSEL* 43.82–99); *Retractiones* 2.16, 55, 3 (*CCL* 57.103, 134).

80. *Confessiones* 7.19.25 (*CCL* 27.108–9); *De bono coniugali* 26(21) (*CSEL* 41.220–21), and numerous other places. On Augustine's Christology, see Tarsicius J. van Bavel, *Recherches sur la Christologie de saint Augustin: L'humain et le divin dans le Christ d'après Saint Augustin*, Paradosis 10 (Fribourg: Éditions Universitaires, 1954).

81. Jerome, *Adversus Helvidium* 4–16 (*PL* 23.195–211).

82. *Adversus Helvidium* 11–15 (*PL* 23.203–9).

83. *Protevangelium Jacobi* 8.3–9.1 (*Evangelia Apocrypha*, ed. K. von Tischendorf [Hildesheim: Georg Olms Verlagsbuchhandlung, 1966], pp. 17–18).

84. *Adversus Helvidium* 19 (*PL* 23.213).

85. *Adversus Helvidium* 4, 19 (*PL* 23.196, 213).

86. *Adversus Helvidium* 4 (*PL* 23.196); see Walter Delius, *Geschichte der Marienverehrung* (München, Basel: Ernst Reinhardt Verlag, 1963), 134–35.

87. Sexual intercourse is described as the *res nuptiarum* in *Adversus Helvidium* 4 (*PL* 23.196). Jerome describes the relationship as a *virginale coniugium* (*Adversus Helvidium* 19 [*PL* 23.213]). For a summary of Jerome's position (though pressing Jerome closer to Augustine's "correct" view), see Johannes Niessen, *Die Mariologie des heiligen Hieronymus: Ihre Quellen und ihre Kritik* (Münster in Westfalen: Aschendorffsche Verlagsbuchhandlung, 1913), pp. 88–96.

88. Ambrose, *De institutione virginis* 6.41 (*PL* 16.316). His ambivalence emerges in his early *Expositio Evangelii secundum Lucam* 2.7

(*CSEL* 32³.45): there he compares Mary to the Church in these words, *"Bene desponsata, sed virgo, quia est ecclesiae typus, quae est immaculata, sed nupta."* But against a true marriage of Joseph and Mary, see *Epistola de causa Bonosi* 4–5 (*PL* 16.1224) and *De institutione virginis* 7.47–48 (*PL* 16.332–33). See Neumann, *Virgin Mary,* pp. 85–86.

89. Dating in Brown, *Augustine,* p. 184.

90. *Contra Faustum* 7.1 (*CSEL* 25¹.302–3).

91. *Contra Faustum* 3.2, 3, 5 (*CSEL* 25¹.262–65, 266–67).

92. *Contra Faustum* 23.8 (*CSEL* 25¹.713).

93. *De consensu Evangelistarum* 2.1.2 (*CSEL* 43.82).

94. E.g., Luke 2:33, 40–41; 3:23.

95. *De consensu Evangelistarum* 2.1.3 (*CSEL* 43.83). See Delius, *Geschichte,* pp. 136–139.

96. *Sermo* 51.13, 21 (*PL* 38.344–45). Augustine believes that Mary had actually taken a vow of virginity: see *De sancta virginitate* 4.4 (*CSEL* 41.238) and discussion in Hilda Graef, *Mary: A History of Doctrine and Devotion, Vol. I: From the Beginnings to the Eve of the Reformation* (New York: Sheed and Ward, 1963), pp. 95–96; Delius, *Geschichte,* p. 139. This view is not present in Ambrose; see Neumann, *Virgin Mary,* p. 100. For other discussions of Augustine's views on the marriage of Joseph and Mary, see Schmitt, *Mariage,* p. 277, esp. n. 103 for contrast with Jerome and Ambrose; Joseph Huhn, "Ein Vergleich der Mariologie des Hl. Augustinus mit der Hl. Ambrosius in ihrer Abhängigkeit, Ahnlichkeit, in ihrem Unterschied," in *Augustinus Magister,* Congrès International Augustinien, Paris, 21–24 septembre 1954 (Paris: Études Augustiniennes, 1954), 1:221–39; Henri Frévin, *Le Mariage de saint Joseph et de la sainte Vierge: Étude de théologie positive de saint Irénée à saint Thomas,* Cahiers de Josephologie 15, 2 (Montreal: Centre de Recherche et de Documentation Oratoire Saint-Joseph, 1967), 239–67. For background, see Hugo Koch, *Virgo Eva-Virgo Maria: Neue Untersuchungen über die Lehre von der Jungfrauschaft und der Ehe Mariens in der ältesten Kirche,* Arbeiten zur Kirchengeschichte 25 (Berlin, Leipzig: Verlag Walter de Gruyter & Co., 1937).

97. *De bono coniugali* 1.1 (*CSEL* 41.187–88).

98. *De bono coniugali* 3.3 (*CSEL* 41.190).

99. *De bono coniugali* 7.6; 7.7 (*CSEL* 41.195–96); death alone can break the bond (15.17 [*CSEL* 41.209]).

100. *De bono coniugali* 8.7 (*CSEL* 41.197).

101. *De bono coniugali 9.9 (CSEL* 41.200–1).

102. *De bono coniugali* 16.18–19, 22; 20.24; 22.27–26, 34 *(CSEL* 41.210–17, 218, 221–29). The fact that Augustine raises and answers the questions Jovinian asked, e.g., "Do you think you are better than Abraham?" (22.27 [*CSEL* 41.222]), shows that Augustine is still dealing with the Jerome-Jovinian debate. See also *De sancta virginitate* 26.26; 45.46 *(CSEL* 41.262–63, 290–92) for more aftermaths of that debate.

103. *De bono coniugali* 18.21 *(CSEL* 41.215).

104. *De bono coniugali* 24.32 *(CSEL* 41.226–27).

105. *De bono coniugali* 24.32; 7.7; 8.7 *(CSEL* 41.227, 196–97).

106. On the history of the debate, see Albert Bruckner, *Julian von Eclanum: Sein Leben und Seine Lehre: Ein Beitrag zur Geschichte des Pelagianismus,* TU 15, 3 (Leipzig: J. C. Hinrichs, 1897); Yves de Montcheuil, "La Polémique de saint Augustin contre Julien d'Éclane d'après l'*Opus Imperfectum,*" *Recherches de Science Religieuse* 44 (1956): 193–218; François Refoulé, "Julien d'Éclane, théologien et philosophe," *Recherches de Science Religieuse* 52 (1964): 42–84, 233–47; shorter summaries in Michel Meslin, "Sainteté et mariage au cours de la seconde querelle pélagienne," *Mystique et Continence: Travaux scientifiques du VIIe Congrès International d'Avon,* Les Études Carmélitaines (Paris: Desclée de Brouwer, 1952), pp. 294–95; Brown, *Augustine,* ch. 42; Schmitt, *Le mariage chrétien,* pp. 56–61.

107. *De nuptiis* 1.12(11) *(CSEL* 42.224–25).

108. *De nuptiis* 1.13(11) *(CSEL* 42.225).

109. *De nuptiis* 1.12(11) *(CSEL* 42.224).

110. *De nuptiis* 1.23(21) *(CSEL* 42.236).

111. *De nuptiis* 1.11(10) *(CSEL* 42.222–23). On the indissolvability of the bond, see Giovanni Torti, *La stabilità del vincolo nuziale in Sant'-Agostino e in San Tommaso,* Università degli Studi di Parma, Istituto di Lingua e Letteratura Latina 4 (Firenze: La Nuova Italia Editrice, 1979), pp. 7–24, 33–49, 65–74.

112. *De nuptiis* 1.19(17) *(CSEL* 42.231).

113. *De nuptiis* 1.23(21) *(CSEL* 42.236).

114. *De nuptiis* 1.30(27) *(CSEL* 42.242).

115. *Contra Julianum* 5.62(16) *(PL* 44.818).

116. *Ibid.*

117. Tertullian, *De exhortatione castitatis* 9 (*CSEL* 70. 142).

118. *Contra Julianum* 5.46(12) (*PL* 44.810).

119. *Contra Julianum* 5.47(12), 48(12) (*PL* 44.810–11).

120. *Contra Julianum* 5.47(12)–48(12) (*PL* 44.811).

121. *Contra Julianum* 5.46(12) (*PL* 44.810).

122. *Contra Julianum* 3.43(21) (*PL* 44.724).

123. *Contra Julianum* 3.16(7) (*PL* 44.710).

124. *Opus imperfectum* 1.65 (*CSEL* 85^1.63).

125. *Opus imperfectum* 2.24.2 (*CSEL* 85^1.178). Augustine does not here answer Julian, but refers him back to his response in the *Contra Julianum* (3.25.57 [*PL* 44.731–32]). There Augustine agrees with Julian that the "activity of bodies" is part of the institution of marriage and asks rhetorically "Has anyone ever thought of marriage without the activity of bodies and the need of two sexes?" Marriage has a "contract of union," among its other goods. Augustine's response makes clear that he does not here consider marriage to exist *apart from* sexual activity, despite his earlier words on Joseph and Mary.

126. Matthew 22:30.

127. *Opus imperfectum* 6.30 (*PL* 45.1580, 1582).

128. *Contra Julianum* 5.48(12) (*PL* 44.811).

129. *Contra Julianum* 4.54(9) (*PL* 44.764).

130. *Contra Julianum* 5.48(12) (*PL* 44.811).

131. *Opus imperfectum* 5.14 (*PL* 45.1444–45); cf. *De civitate Dei* 14.23 (*CCL* 48.446), citing *Georgics* 3.136.

132. *Opus imperfectum* 5.15 (*PL* 45.1445).

133. *De Trinitate* 12.7.10 (*CCL* 50.364).

134. *De sermone Domini in monte* 15.41 (*CCL* 35.45).

135. *De nuptiis* 1.12(11) (*CSEL* 42.225); cf. *Contra Faustum* 23.8 (*CSEL* 25^1.713).

136. *Confessiones* 9.9.19 (*CCL* 27.145). For Augustine on the *tabulae matrimoniales*, see n. 65 above.

137. *Epistle* 262 to Ecdicia (*CSEL* 57.621–631).

138. See Clark, "Friendship Between the Sexes: Classical Theory and Christian Practice," in *Jerome*, pp. 35–106.

139. *Epistle* 211.4 (*CSEL* 57.358).

140. *Epistle* 211.1–4 (*CSEL* 57.356–59).

141. On women's education and the relation of education to class, see Clark, *Jerome*, pp. 70–78, with references to primary and secondary literature.

142. The factors must be inferred from legislation on, e.g., the return of dowries in cases of broken engagements, the status of concubines, captivity, and divorce. Useful discussions of Roman marriage law are contained in the following works: Riccardo Orestano, *La struttura giuridica del matrimonio romano dal diritto classico al diritto giustinianeo* (Milano: Antonio Giuffrè, 1951). vol. 1; idem, "Alcune considerazioni sui rapporti fra matrimonio cristiano e matrimonio romano nell' età postclassica," in Gian Gualberto Archi, ed., *Scritti di diritto romano in honore de Contardo Ferrini* (Milano: Ulrico Hoepli, 1946), pp. 345–82; Emilio Albertario, *Studi di diritto romano* (Milano: Antonio Giuffrè, 1933), vol. 1, esp. chps. 10–12; Percy Ellwood Corbett, *The Roman Law of Marriage* (Oxford: Clarendon Press, 1930); Jean Gaudemet, *Sociétés et Mariage* (Strasbourg: Cerdic-Publications, 1980) (Gaudemet's collected essays on the topic); (Wolfgang Kunkel), "Matrimonium," *Paulys Real-Encyclopädie* 14, 2 (1930): 2259–86; (Emilio Albertario), "Matrimonio," *Enciclopedia Italiana* 22 (1934): 580–81; Josef Huber, *Der Ehekonses im Römischen Recht, Studien zu seinem Begriffsgehalt im der Klassik und zur Frage seines Wandels in der Nachklassik*, Analecta Gregoriana 204 (Roma: Università Gregoriana Editrice, 1977); Hans Julius Wolff, "Doctrinal Trends in Postclassical Roman Marriage Law," *Zeitschrift der Savigny-Stiftung für Rechtsgeschichte*, Romanistiche Abteilung, 67 (1950): 261–319; Alan Watson, *The Law of Persons in the Later Roman Republic* (Oxford: Clarendon Press, 1967), esp. chps. 1–7; A. Esmein, *Le Mariage en droit canonique*, 2d ed. (Paris: Librairie du Recueil Sirey, 1929); Giuseppe d'Ercole, "Il consenso degli sposi e la perpetuità del matrimonio nel diritto romano e nei Padri della Chiesa," *Studia et documenta historiae et iuris* 5 (1939): 18–75. Helpful articles on non-legal aspects of Roman marriage in pre-Christian and Christian times include Gordon Williams, "Some Aspects of Roman Marriage Ceremonies and Ideals," *The Journal of Roman Studies* 48 (1958): 16–29; Marjorie Lightman and William Zeisel, "*Univira*: An Example of Continuity and Change in Roman Society," *Church History* 46 (1977): 19–32; Marin, "*Le Tabulae Matrimoniales.*" I wish to thank Professors Roger Bagnall and Charles Donahue, Jr., for their helpful comments on Roman marriage law.

143. See Watson, *Law*, pp. 44–46: did the daughter have to consent or not? If she did, when did her consent become required?

144. Corbett, *Roman Law*, pp. 2–3, 53–67, 86; Watson, *Law*, pp. 41, 44, 46, and esp. Orestano, *La struttura*, pp. 239–43.

145. Watson, *Law*, p. 41. Highlighting differences between law and practice is Susan Treggiari, "Consent to Roman Marriage: Some Aspects of Law and Reality," *Echos du Monde Classique/Classical Views* 26 (1982): 34–44. On the early age of marriage, especially for girls from aristocratic families, see Hopkins, "Age," 317, 321, 326. On a particular case of forced early marriage, see *Vita Melaniae Junioris* 1, trans. in Elizabeth A. Clark, *The Life of Melania the Younger: Introduction, Translation, and Commentary*, Studies in Women and Religion 14 (Toronto, New York: The Edwin Mellen Press, 1984), pp. 27–28; for a case presented to Augustine, see *Epistulae* 252–55 (*CSEL* 57.600–3).

146. *Digesta* 23.1.12 (*Corpus Iuris Civilis*, ed. Paul Krueger and Theodor Mommsen [Berlin: Weidmann, 1893], 1:295), discussed in Corbett, *Roman Law*, p. 3.

147. See especially the famous case in *Digesta* 23.2, 5, 5–7, discussed by Charles Donahue, Jr., "The Case of the Man Who Fell into the Tiber: The Roman Law of Marriage at the Time of the Glossators," *American Journal of Legal History* 22 (1978): esp. 1–2, 6–7; cf. Fritz Schulz, *Classical Roman Law* (Oxford: Clarendon Press, 1951), pp. 110–11; Orestano, *La struttura*; Albertario, *Studi*, p. 225.

148. (Ulpian), *Digesta* 50.17.30 (*Corpus Iuris Civilis* 1.869).

149. Wolff, "Doctrinal Trends," 228, 296–97, for a list of scholars who agree, including Kübler, Albertario, Pringsheim, Monier, Bidagor, Petropoulos, and Rasi. That Augustine's own works may have received interpolations in this regard is shown by the probable addition of the sentence "*Voluntas ista, non voluptas illa, nuptialis est,*" to the manuscripts of *De peccatorum meritis* 1.29.57; see *Nicene and Post-Nicene Fathers*, Series 1, vol. 5: *Saint Augustin: Anti-Pelagian Writings* (Grand Rapids: Wm. B. Eerdmans, 1978, reprint ed.), 37 n. 3; and *CSEL* 60.56 apparatus. Gaudemet, *Sociétés*, pp. 125–26, stresses that even if we agree that Roman marriage law was influenced by Christian teaching on the notion of consent, it upheld a different understanding of consent. For Roman law, he posits, consent was seen as ongoing (when the parties stopped giving consent, the bond was dissolved), while for Christian authors, the consent was understood as initially-given and as creative of a permanent, non–dissolvable bond. Also see d'Ercole, "Il consenso," 23–24, 28, for another expression of this view. Arguing to the contrary is Josef Huber, whose central thesis is that "initial consent" was always the meaning of consent from the third century B.C. to the post-classical period (*Ehekonsens*, passim, esp. pp. 28, 121–24, 146 and "Nachwort").

150. For criticisms of the earlier view, see especially Orestano, *La struttura*, pp. 73, 239–43, 260–63; "Alcune considerazioni," 349–50, 381–82.

151. Orestano, *La struttura,* pp. 239–43; "Alcune considerazioni," 382; Donahue, "The Case," 7–8.

152. As Donahue notes, " . . . in Roman law relatively few juridical consequences flow from a determination of the precise point at which marriage begins" ("The Case," 8).

153. Wolff, "Doctrinal Trends," 299, 291.

154. Wolff, "Doctrinal Trends," 291. Would they have considered it comparable to cases in which one partner was exiled? (On this point, the law changed from classical to post-classical times: see Albertario, *Studi,* pp. 219–21, 237–38). Gaudemet (*Sociétés,* pp. 53–4) argues that the physical possibility of union is implied by the classical laws on impuberty; only with Justinian does this regulation disappear. Huber (*Ehekonsens,* p. 28, n. 53) argues that the Fathers never thought of *copula carnis* as a constitutive element in marriage (he is proved wrong by Jerome's treatment of Joseph and Mary; also see Orestano, *La struttura,* pp. 274–78; idem, "Alcune considerazioni," 350–55).

155. Discussed in Wolff, "Doctrinal Trends," 291–92. On Theodosian marriage law, see Riccardo Orestano, "Consenso e solennità nella legislazione matrimoniale Teodosiana," in *Scritti in onore di Contardo Ferrini pubblicati in occasione della sua beatificazione,* Edizioni dell' Università Cattolica del sacro cuore, n.s. 18 (Milano: Società editrice "Vita e pensiero," 1947), 2:160–73.

156. Orestano, *La struttura,* pp. 260–76; idem, "Alcune considerazioni," 350–55.

157. See above; Esmein, *Le Mariage,* 1:194; Orestano, *La struttura,* p. 276.

158. Esmein, *Le Mariage* 1.89–90, 103: in early medieval canon law, consent was thought necessary to constitute marriage but not sufficient to perfect it as a sacrament; *copula carnis* was needed to make the union like that of Christ's with the Church. For a summary of some medieval debates, see Donahue, "The Case," 3–5, 11–53.

159. See above, and Wolff, "Doctrinal Trends," 268, 276; Huber, *Ehekonsens,* p. 146. The difference in pagan and Christian sentiment is summed up in Jerome's rhetorical phrase, *"Aliae sunt leges Caesarum, aliae Christi; aliud Papinianus, aliud Paulus noster praecipit"* (*Epistula* 77.3 [*CSEL* 55.39]). Arguing against a theory of strict "consent" and "contract" in Augustine's theory of marriage is R. Kuiters, "Saint Augustin et l'indissolubilité du mariage," *Augustiniana* 9 (1959): 5–11. That Augustine may have known some fine points of Roman marriage law is suggested by his reference to Antoninus Pius's decree that adulterous husbands could not accuse their wives of criminal adultery (*De adulterinis nuptiis*

2.8[7] [*CSEL* 41.389]]; cf. *Digesta* 48.5.14(13).3ff. For Augustine's views on divorce, see Henri Crouzel, *L'Église primitive face au divorce: du premier au cinquième siècle*, Théologie Historique 13 (Paris: Beauchesne, 1971), pp. 317–58. For an excellent new study of Roman divorce legislation, see Roger S. Bagnall, "Church, State and Divorce in Late Roman Egypt," in *Florilegium Columbianum: Essays in Honor of Paul Oskar Kristeller*, ed. Karl-Ludwig Selig and Robert Somerville (New York: Italica Press, 1987), pp. 41–61. On the slowness of Roman marriage law, including the notion of consent, to influence Celtic marriage law and practice, see Wendy Davies, "Celtic Women in the Early Middle Ages," in Averil Cameron and Amelie Kuhrt, eds., *Images of Women in Antiquity* (London, Canberra: Croom Helm, 1983), pp. 153–55. For particular cases of the effects of conversion on fourth–century Roman families, see André Chastagnol, "Le sénateur Volusien et la conversion d'une famille de l'aristocratie romaine au Bas-Empire," *Revue des Études Anciennes* 58 (1956): 241–53; Peter Brown, "Aspects of the Christianization of the Roman Aristocracy," *Journal of Roman Studies* 51 (1961): 1–11; Anne Yarbrough, "Christianization in the Fourth Century: The Example of Roman Women," *Church History* 45 (1976): 149–65.

160. *De civitate Dei* 26 (*CCL* 48.449): " . . . *inter se coniugum fida ex honesto amore societas*. . . . "

CHAPTER 2

1. Philippe Ariès, *Centuries of Childhood: A Social History of Family Life*, trans. R. Baldick (New York: Vintage, 1962), where the child is seen in relation to adults, is an example of this approach.

2. The importance of the development of social ideas is fundamental to Georges Duby, *The Medieval Marriage: Two Models from Twelfth-Century France*, The Johns Hopkins Symposia in Comparative History 11 (Baltimore: Johns Hopkins University Press, 1978) and Jack Goody, *The Development of the Family and Marriage in Europe* (Cambridge: Cambridge University Press, 1983). The common attitude of the social historian is different from that of the political scientist who traditionally has seen development of political theory as the usual prelude to political change. Cf. Michael Anderson, "The Relevance of Family History," in *The Sociology of The Family: New Directions for Britain*, ed. Christopher C. Harris, Sociological Review Monograph 28 (Keele: University of Keele, 1979), pp. 49–73, where the socio-economic impact on the formation of these ideas is stressed. For this reference and for other valued suggestions I thank Professor Judith M. Bennett.

3. See Michael M. Sheehan, "Marriage and Family in English Conciliar and Synodal Legislation," in *Essays in Honour of Anton Charles*

Pegis, ed. J. R. O'Donnell (Toronto: Pontifical Institute of Mediaeval Studies, 1974), pp. 211–14.

4. *Ibid.*, p. 205.

5. "Courtly Love and Christianity," in *The Two Dantes and Other Studies* (Berkeley: University of California Press, 1977), pp. 15–36. In this context it should be remembered that some canonists resisted the notion that marriage was a sacrament because the financial element involved in so many unions was redolent of simony.

6. *Le lien matrimonial*, ed. René Metz and Jean Schlick (Strasbourg: Centre de recherche et de documentation des institutions chrétiennes, 1970).

7. See Etienne Gilson, *History of Christian Philosophy in the Middle Ages* (New York: Random House, 1955), pp. 235–36.

8. Thus Aquinas in *Summa contra gentiles*, 3.123, in a discussion of the indissolubility of marriage, wrote: "Furthermore, the greater that friendship, the more solid and long lasting it will be. Now, there seems to be the greatest friendship between husband and wife, for they are united not only in the act of fleshly union, which produces a certain gentle association even among beasts, but also in the partnership of the whole range of domestic activity" (*On the Truth of the Catholic Faith: Summa contra gentiles*, 3.2, trans. Vernon J. Bourke [New York: Doubleday, 1956], p. 148).

9. Jean Leclercq, "The Development of a Topic in Medieval Studies in the Eighties: An Interdisciplinary Perspective on Love and Marriage," in *Literary and Historical Perspectives of the Middle Ages: Proceedings of the 1981 SEMA Meeting*, ed. Patricia W. Cummins, Patricia W. Conner, and Charles W. Connell (Morgantown, West Virginia: University of West Virginia Press, 1982), pp. 20–37; Leclercq, *Love in Marriage in Twelfth-Century Europe*, University of Tasmania Occasional Papers 13 (Hobart, Tasmania: University of Tasmania Press, 1978); "L'amour et le mariage vus par des clercs et des religieux, spécialement au XIIe siècle," in *Love and Marriage in the Twelfth Century*, ed. Willy Van Hoecke and Andries Welkenhuysen (Leuven: University Press, 1981), pp. 102–15; Leclercq, *Monks on Marriage: A Twelfth-Century View* (New York: Seabury Press, 1982). Professor Pierre Payer is well advanced on a study, "The Channelling of Desire: Ideas of Sex in the Later Middle Ages," in which the thinking of the theologians of the high Middle Ages will be analyzed in detail.

10. As was noted above, the canonical discussion of consent was of major importance in itself and from the point of view of social developments. This and the other requirements for establishing the bond were the aspects of marriage that received the most detailed development. For canonical thought and its regulations on sexuality and the living of the sexual life see James A. Brundage, *Law, Sex, and Christian Society in*

Medieval Europe (Chicago: University of Chicago Press, 1987); note the bibliography, pp. 621–34, for a valuable selection of earlier literature.

11. "Marital Affection in the Canonists," *Studia Gratiana* 12 (1967): pp. 479–509.

12. On the question as to whether this notion were a Christian interpolation, see Noonan, p. 482.

13. *Ibid.*, p. 488.

14. *Ibid.*, pp. 489–90.

15. "Ita illae quae in affectum ex Deo initum redeunt, merito sunt laundandae" (C.34, q.1, c.1); see Noonan, p. 492.

16. *Ibid.*, p. 499. Thus in his discussion (ca. 1213) of the relationship that caused a cleric to be bigamous, Robert of Flamborough insisted that it was marital affection (*Liber poenitentialis: A Critical Edition with Introduction and Notes*, ed. J. J. Francis Firth, Studies and Texts 18 [Toronto: Pontifical Institute of Mediaeval Studies, 1971], pp. 162–65); in a case of 1381 the official of Ely enquired about the marriage of Pobert Puf "super eo quod maritali affectione se invicem non pertractant" (Ely Consistory Court Register: Cambridge, University Library, Ely diocesan Records, D 2 (1), fol. 153ᵛ). In the Maddyngle case (1378) of the same register, marital affection is distinguished from other intentions of marriage: John's wife admitted their marriage but claimed that he was impotent. John countered: "iurati sunt cohabitare et se mutuo maritali affectione pertractare et operam carnalis copule prestare" (fol. 91ʳ).

17. C.32, q.2, c.5, *dict ad* IV. Pars. See the letter of 1205 from Innocent III regarding the wife who, under much pressure, had allowed her husband of about twenty years to enter a monastery, then, when he left religious life, demanded that he return to her. The Pope instructed his delegates that, if the woman were of an age that enforced continence might lead her to sin, then the husband was to be forced to receive her back as wife and treat her with conjugal affection ("ut eam recipiat eique affectum exhibeat conjugalem") (*PL* 215.593–94). Augustine tells us in his *Confessions* (2.3) that his mother wondered whether it would be possible for him to contain his sexual activity within the limits of conjugal affection: "cohercere termino coniugalis affectus" (*Sancti Augustini Confessionum libri XIII*, ed. Lucas Verheijen [*Corpus Christianorum, Series Latina* 27.21]).

18. Gen. 29:26–28; *Decretum dict. ad* C.29, q.1. See Noonan, pp. 486–87.

19. See the possibility suggested by Noonan, p. 499.

20. *Ibid.*, p. 501.

21. *Ibid.* pp. 503–4. See the letter of Innocent III, above, n. 17: in the Poynant case (Ely Register, 1378) the marriage of John Poynant and Joan Swan had been declared nul because of John's impotence. Joan married and John proved his sexual powers by less acceptable means, so the court declared the original marriage to be valid and John and Joan were "fore compellendos ut maritali affectione se invicem adhereant et pertractant" (fol. 142v). Joan at least seems to have been reluctant.

22. " . . . ut uxores viros, et viri uxores, qui leprae morbum incurrunt, sequantur, et eis conjugali affectione ministrent" (X:4.8.1); Noonan (pp. 502–3) points out that the recommendation was not concerned with intercourse, a question dealt with in X:4.8.2. Note that husband and wife are equally obliged.

23. Noonan also describes a different approach used in the time of Pope Gregory IX (1227–1241), namely, the evaluation of a marriage in terms of the three goods discussed by St. Augustine. (*De bono conjugale,* in *Corpus Scriptorum Ecclesiasticorum Latinorum* 41.185–231). He suggests that here, too, they were "objective touchstones,"; see pp. 508–9.

24. In this discussion of the *Summa confessorum*, I am indebted to the contributions of the members of my seminar, "Marriage and Family in Medieval Europe," especially to Jacqueline Murray, *The Perception of Sexuality, Marriage, and Family in Early English Pastoral Manuals* (Diss., University of Toronto, 1987).

25. See Pierre J. Payer, *Sex and the Penitentials* (Toronto: University of Toronto Press, 1984).

26. See Pierre Michaud-Quantin, *Sommes de casuistique et manuels de confession au moyen âge (XIIe–XVIe siècles).* Analecta Namurcensia 13 (Louvain: Nauwelaerts, 1962), and Josef G. Ziegler, *Die Ehelehre der Pönitentialsummen von 1200–1350: Eine Untersuchung zur Geschichte der Moral-und Pastoraltheologie,* Studien zur Geschichte der Katholischen Moraltheologie, ed. Michael Müller 4 (Regensburg: Pustet, 1956).

27. See Ziegler, *Die Ehelehre,* and Michael M. Sheehan, "Choice of Marriage Partner in the Middle Ages: Development and Mode of Application of a Theory of Marriage," *Studies in Medieval and Renaissance History,* 1 (Old Ser. 11) (1978): 19–25.

28. "Si non moveatur a concupiscentia, sed moveat concupiscentiam, majus peccatum est," 1.25: Alain de Lille, *Liber poenitentialis,* ed. Jean Longère, 2 vols., Analecta Namurcensia 17–18 (Louvain: Nauwelaerts, 1965), 2:33–34.

29. " . . . quia ille magis cogitur qui pulchram: ubi maior coactio, ibi minus peccatum" (*Liber poenitentialis,* 1.27; 2.34).

30. " . . . utrum uno aspecto in aliquam exarserit an paulatim in-flammatus fuerit. Ille enim magis peccat qui solo aspectu seducitur, quam qui ex convicto inflammatur" (*Liber poenitentialis*, 1.29; p. 34).

31. "Mulieribus tamen semper in penitentia iniungendum est quod sint predicatrices virorum suorum. Nullus enim sacerdos ita potest cor viri emollire sicut potest uxor. Unde peccatum viri sepe mulieri imputatur si per suis negligentiam vir eius non emmendatur. Debet enim in cubiculo et inter medios amplexus virum suum blande alloqui, et si durus est et immisericors et oppressor pauperum, debet eum invitare ad misericordiam; si raptor est, debet detestari rapinam. . . . ": *Thomae de Chobham Summa confessorum*, ed. F. Broomfield, Analecta Mediaevalia Namurcensia 25 (Louvain: Nauwelaerts, 1968), p. 375. The wider context of this instruction and the role of the treatise is discussed in detail in Sheehan, "Choice of Marriage Partner," 22–25 and Murray, *The Perceptions of Sexuality*, pp. 141–81.

32. On the author and the significance of his treatise, see Leonard E. Boyle, "The Summa Confessorum of John of Friburg and the Popularization of the Moral Teaching of St. Thomas and of Some His Contemporaries," in *St. Thomas Aquinas 1274–1974: Commemorative Studies*, 2 vols. (Toronto: Pontifical Institute of Mediaeval Studies, 1974), pp. 246–47. References to John of Friburg's *Summa* in what follows are to book, title and question, followed by the folio number of the Venice edition of 1568.

33. " . . . & mutuam exhibitionem, scilicet ut uterque reliquo in necessariis huiusmodi vitae, si possit, providere" (Bk.4 tit.2 q.1; fol. 217r). John had developed this statement earlier in his gloss to Raymund of Penafort's *Summa de poenitentia, et matrimonio, gl. ad* "matrimonium", Bk.4 tit.2 q.1 (Rome, 1603), p. 510. The care of the leprous spouse, urged by Alexander III in virtue of marital affection, would be included in this "mutua exhibitio".

34. "Cum in matrimonio requiratur consensus, queritur in quod sit ille consensus . . . " (Bk.4 tit.2 q.12; fol.218r).

35. Bk.4 tit.2 q.12; fol. 218r. The text is taken from the *Summa Raymundi*, Bk.4 tit.2 q.3, pp. 511–12; but, in this case, John refers it to the content of matrimonial consent, a point of view somewhat different from that of Raymond. [See Erik Kooper's discussion of the "rib-topos" in the present anthology, pp. 44–56—Ed.]

36. Bk.4 tit.2 q.23; fol. 219r. In these matters John closely follows Raymund, *Summa de poenitentia*. Bk.4 tit.2 q.6, p. 514.

37. " . . . non solum quando expresse petit debitum uxori vir tenetur reddere: sed etiam quando per signa apparet eam hoc velle. Non tamen idem iudicium est de petitionem viri: quia mulieres magis solent verecundari petendo debitum quam viri" (John of Friburg, Bk.4 tit.2 q.40; p. 439).

38. See Korbinian Ritzer, *Le mariage dans les églises chrétiennes du Ier au XIe siècle* (Paris: Éditions du Cerf, 1970); Jean-Baptiste Molin and Protais Mutembe, *Le rituel de mariage en France du XIIe au XVIe siècle,* Théologie historique 26 (Paris: Beauchesne, 1974), and Cyrille Vogel, "Les rites de la célébration du mariage: leur signification dans la formation du lien durant le haut moyen âge," in *Il matrimonio nella società altomedievale,* 2 vols., Settimane di studio del Centro italiano di studi sull'alto medioevo 24, (Spoleto: Centro italiano di studi sull'alto medioevo, 1977), 1:397–472.

39. In a late twelfth-century Cahors missal: " . . . et inquirat de parentela fortiter, et si est amor inter illos. Et si aliquam parentelam invenerit, non iungantur. Si autem amorem habent, et in parentela non inveniuntur, iungantur" (cited in Sheehan, "Choice of Marriage Partner," 29 and n. 74). On the source occurrences of this text, see Brian F. Bethune, *The Text of the Christian Rite of Marriage in Medieval Spain* (Diss., University of Toronto, 1987), pp. 102–21 et passim.

40. See the use of manuscript illustration by A. Melnikas, *The Corpus of Miniatures in the Manuscripts of Decretum Gratiani,* 3 vols, Studia Gratiana 16–18 (Rome: Libreria Ateneo Salesiano, 1975), 3:887–1058, 1085–1172. It is the nature of manuscript illumination, essentially private art as it is, to be an indication of understanding rather than a means of instruction.

41. The fundamental work is by J. B. Schneyer, whose *Reportorium der lateinischen sermones des mittelalters für die zeit von 1150–1350,* Beiträge zur Geschichte der Philosophie und Theologie des Mittelalters, Texte und Untersuchungen 43, 5 vols. (Münster: Aschendorff, 1969–73), awaits but an index for completion. Among recent studies of sermons dealing with marriage note especially: N. Berious and D. L. d'Avray, "Henry of Provins, O.P.'s Comparison of the Dominican and Franciscan Orders with the 'Order' of Matrimony," *Archivum fratrum praedicatorum,* 49 (1979): 513–17; D. L. d'Avray and M. Tausche, "Marriage Sermons in *Ad status* Collections of the Central Middle Ages," *Archives d'histoire doctrinale et littéraire du moyen âge,* 47 (1981): 71–119; David d'Avray, "The Gospel of the Marriage Feast of Cana and Marriage Preaching in France," *The Bible in the Medieval World: Essays in Memory of Beryl Smalley,* eds. Katherine Walsh and Diana Wood, Studies in Church History, Subsidia 4 (Oxford: Blackwell, 1985), pp. 207–24; idem, *The Preaching of the Friars: Sermons Diffused from Paris before 1300* (Oxford: Clarendon, 1985), especially pp. 69–70, 249–50, 257–58.

42. d'Avray and Tausche.

43. *Ibid.,* p. 77.

44. *PL* 172.867. The translation is from d'Avray and Tausche, 78. Note how Honorius has gone well beyond the instructions of St. Paul

(Eph. 5:22–25; Col. 3:18–19), where husbands were to love their wives ("Viri diligite uxores vestras") and wives were to be subject to their husbands ("Mulieres viris suis subditae sint").

45. d'Avray and Tausche, 74–75.

46. "Est enim dilectio socialis qua debent se coniuges diligere, quia pares sunt et socii" (d'Avray and Tausche, 114; the translation is drawn from the same source).

47. "Sit etiam inseparabilitas affectionis. Prov. xvii. Omni tempore diligit qui est amicus" (d'Avray and Tausche, 115 and n. 23).

48. "Sit etiam liberalitas correctionis ut libere possit vir uxorcm arguere, et ex dilectione illa recipiat, et e converso . . . " (d'Avray and Tausche, 116–117 and n. 25).

CHAPTER 3

1. Guillaume de Lorris and Jean de Meun, *Le Roman de la Rose*, ed. Félix Lecoy, 3 vols. Les Classiques Français du Moyen Age 92, 95, 98 (Paris: Champion, 1965–70), 2:36–37.

2. Guillaume de Lorris and Jean de Meun, *Le Roman de la Rose*, trans. Charles Dahlberg (Princeton: Princeton University Press, 1971), p. 169.

3. B. Hauréau, *Notices et extraits de quelques manuscrits latins de la Bibliothèque Nationale* (Paris: Librairie Klincksieck, 1890), 1:203.

4. Hauréau, 1:189.

5. D. L. d'Avray and M. L. Tausche, "Marriage Sermons in *Ad status* Collections of the Central Middle Ages," *Archives d'histoire doctrinale et littéraire du moyen âge* 47 (1980):71–119, especially 106.

6. Edward Schillebeeckx, O.P., *Het huwelijk: Aardse werkelijkheid en heilsmysterie*, 1 (all published) (Bilthoven: Nelissen, 1963), 1:18, trans. N. D. Smith as *Marriage: Secular Reality and Saving Mystery* (London: Sheed and Ward, 1965).

7. Beryl Smalley, *The Study of the Bible in the Middle Ages* (Notre Dame, Ind.: Notre Dame University Press, 1964), p. 89.

8. Michael Müller, *Die Lehre des hl. Augustinus von der Paradiesesehe und ihre Auswirkung in der Sexualethik des 12. und 13. Jahrhunderts bis Thomas von Aquin*, Studien zur Geschichte der katholischen Moraltheologie 1 (Regensburg: Pustet, 1954), p. 84. [cf. Elizabeth A. Clark's essay in the present collection—Ed.]

9. Augustine, *De bono coniugali* in *PL* 40.373–96, trans. Charles T. Wilcox as *The Good of Marriage* in *Saint Augustine: Treatises on Marriage and Other Subjects,* ed. Roy J. Deferrari (New York: Fathers of the Church, 1955), p. 12.

10. Hugh of St. Victor, *De Beatae Mariae virginitate,* in *PL* 176.863–64; cf. also Müller, *Die Lehre des hl. Augustinus,* p. 83.

11. Bernard of Clairvaux, *Sermones super Cantica Canticorum, 36–86,* trans. Kilian Walsh and Irene M. Edmonds as *On the Song of Songs,* vols. 1–4, Cistercian Father Series 4, 7, 31, and 40 (Kalamazoo: Cistercian Publications, 1971–1980). References in the text present the sermons first by number and section, then followed by the volume and page number of the translation.

12. Marcus Tullius Cicero, *De amicitia* in *De Senectute, De amicitia, De divinatione,* trans. William Armistead Falconer (Cambridge, Mass.: Harvard University Press: 1923), p. 131.

13. "Quia enim socia data est, non ancilla, aut domina; idcirco [nec de summo] nec de imo, sed de medio fuerat producenda. . . . Propterea de medio facta est, ut ad aequalitatem societatis facta probaretur. *In hoc tamen quodammodo inferior ipso* quod facta est de ipso, ut ad ipsum semper quasi ad principium suum respiceret, et ei individue adhaerendo, ab ea se (quae adinvicem constare debebat) societate non separaret" (Hugh of St. Victor, *De sacramentis Christianae fidei,* 11.11.4, in *PL* 176.485; trans. Roy J. Deferrari as *On the Sacraments of the Christian Faith,* The Mediaeval Academy of America, Publication 58 (Cambridge: The Mediaeval Academy of America, 1951), p. 329

14. Aelred of Rievaulx, *De spirituali amicitia,* in *Aelredi Rievallensis opera omnia: 1. Opera ascetica,* Corpus Christianorum, Continuatio Mediaevalis 1, ed. A Hoste et al. (Turnholt: Brepols, 1971).

15. Cf. the prefatory letter by Bernard and Aelred's own preface; see also Sir Maurice Powicke, ed., *The Life of Aelred of Rievaulx* (Oxford: Clarendon Press, 1950), pp. lvi–lxi.

16. Cf. Jean Leclercq, *Monks and Love in Twelfth-Century France: Psycho-Historical Essays* (Oxford: Clarendon Press, 1979), p. 64. This idea occurs in numerous other places, e.g., Cicero's *De amicitia,* 25.92; see Adele Fiske, "Aelred of Rievaulx's Idea of Friendship and Love," *Cîteaux* 13(1965):444–45.

17. The same distinction is found in Aristotle's *Ethics* and consequently in Thomas Aquinas's Commentary on that work (see Aristotle, *The Nicomachean Ethics,* trans. J. A. K. Thomson, rev. by Hugh Tredennick [Harmondsworth: Penguin Books, 1976], 8.3, and Thomas Aquinas, *Commentary on the Nicomachean Ethics,* trans. C. I. Litzinger, O.P., 2

vols. [Chicago: Henry Regnery, 1964], pp. 710–17], but not in Cicero, at least not explicitly (but cf. Cicero, *De amicitia*, 6.20, 22; 8.27).

18. References in the text are to the volume and page number in Aelred of Rievaulx, *De spirituali amicitia*, followed by a page number citation to Mary Eugenia Laker's translation as Aelred of Rievaulx, *Spiritual Friendship*, Cistercian Fathers Series 5 (Kalamazoo: Cistercian Publications, 1974). The idea of carnal friendship through sense attraction is also in Aristotle (*Ethics*, 9.5.1824) and Thomas (Litzinger, trans., *Commentary*, 810), and in Cicero (*De amicitia*, 19.68) and Bernard (*Sermones super Cantica Canticorum*, Sermon 67.3; 4.6).

19. Cf. Bernard's *De diligendo Deo*, 7.17, and his Sermon 83 (83.4; 4.184) as well as Cicero's *De amicitia*, 9.31.

20. Aelred may also have been inspired here by Ambrose, whose *De officiis ministrorum* he quotes frequently and who says that *amicitia* "was first placed by God in man and woman to make them one in spirit as well as body" (1.69). See also Fiske, 442, who translates *amicitia* here as 'benevolence'.

21. Lionel J. Friedman, "Jean de Meun and Ethelred of Rievaulx," *L'Esprit Créateur* 2 (1962): 135–41.

22. It was gratifying to discover that the research of June McCash into the twelfth century ideal of love, carried out simultaneously with but independently from mine, led to more or less the same conclusions: she too follows the line of Bernard, Hugh, Aelred, and likewise gives Hugh's passage in the *De sacramentis* as the source for the rib-topos. June Hall McCash, "Mutual Love as a Medieval Ideal," *Courtly Literature: Culture and Context*, Proceedings of the 5th Triennial Congress of the International Courtly Literature Society, Dalfsen, the Netherlands, 1986, eds. Keith Busby and Erik Kooper (Amsterdam/Philadelphia: Benjamins, 1990), pp. 429–38.

23. Sister Mariella quotes a sermon by the Spanish canon regular St. Martin of Léon (d. 1203), whom she still thought to be the first to use the rib-topos (Sister Mariella, OSB., "The Parson's Tale and the Marriage Group," *Modern Language Notes* 53 [1938]: 251–56). His wording is different from Hugh's but the general meaning is the same: "Mulier non de qualibet parte corporis viri, sed de latere ejus formata est, ut ostenderetur quia in consortium creabatur dilectionis; ne forte si de capite fuisset, viro ad dominationem videretur praeferenda, aut si de pedibus, ad servitutem subjicienda. Quia igitur jure nec domina, nec ancilla probatur, sed socia; nec de capite, nec de pedibus, sed de latere fuerat producenda, ut juxta se ponendam cognosceret, quam de suo latere sumptam didicisset" (*PL* 208.583). It was only after this article went to the press that I became aware that D. W. Robertson, Jr., discusses the rib-topos briefly in his paper "Certain Theological Conventions in Mannyng's Treatment of the Com-

mandments," *Modern Language Notes* 61 (1946), 505–14; rpt. in his *Essays in Medieval Culture* (Princeton: Princeton University Press, 1980), pp. 105–13, esp. pp. 110–11. Robertson here traces the topos from Mannyng through Robert de Sorbon to Peter Lombard's *Sententiae* (4.28.4). Since these were finished some twenty years after Hugh of St. Victor's *De sacramentis*, the latter remains the oldest source known to me.

24. Considering that both Hugh and Robert, as well as Martin of Léon, were canons regular, it would have been more appropriate to speak of the "regular" line. I decided against that because of the equivocalness of the word in this context.

25. Haréau, 1:189.

26. Translated from Thomas Aquinas, *Summa contra Gentiles* (Rome: Forzani, 1894).

27. Thomas Aquinas, *Summa Theologiae*, eds. Thomas Gilby, O.P., and T. C. O'Brien, O.P. (New York: Fathers of the Church, 1955).

28. Schillebeeckx, *Het huwelijk*, p. 234. He refers here to Thomas's commentary on Peter Lombard's *Sententiae in IV libris distinctae* (4.26.2).

29. References in the text are to Thomas Aquinas, *In decem libros Ethicorum Aristotelis ad Nicomachium expositio*, ed. Raymundo M. Spiazzi (Taurini: Marietti, 1949), with parallel references following to the translation by Litzinger.

30. Thomas comments on this: "He says that in all friendships involving inequality of one person to the other, love is given proportionately, so that the superior party is loved more than he loves. . . . For when each person is loved by reason of the worth he manifests, an equality of proportion that apparently pertains to friendship will ensue" (Litzinger, p. 737).

31. Thomas writes extensively on ideal friendship in more general terms in the section of the *Summa Theologiae* devoted to the emotion of love. He distinguishes there between *amor concupiscentiae* and *amor amicitiae*. The former is mostly for objects which are loved because they can contribute to one's well-being; with the latter a person is loved as if he were another self. In either case love can lead to a union with the object or person loved, but one that is appropriate to the nature of love (*secundum convenientiam amoris*), by which in respect to people he means that they cannot literally become one but merely want to be together, talk together and the like. Nowhere in this discussion does Thomas link *amor amicitiae* with marriage (*STh* 1a2ae.26,4).

32. See above n. 5.

33. I have excluded the collection of Humbertus de Romanis (d. 1277); in the strictest sense, d'Avray and Tausche say, they "are not *ad status* sermons, but sermons for particular occasions" (d'Avray, 82), and

probably because of that Humbertus does not probe very deeply into basic questions (d'Avray, 84). The collection of Guibert was the most widely circulated of the three (d'Avray, 85); P. Glorieux, *Répertoire des Maîtres en Théologie de Paris au xiiie siècle*, 2 vols. (Paris: J. Vrin, 1933, 1934), lists 18 manuscripts (2:57).

34. d'Avray, 77.

35. Martin of Léon (late twelfth century) still says that woman was created "in consortium dilectionis" (see n. 23 above).

36. d'Avray, 85. My impression is that Robert de Sorbon made use of one or more of Jacques's *ad status* sermons and that Guibert in his turn may have used the marriage sermons of both Jacques and Robert.

37. d'Avray, 177.

38. *Ibid.*, 106.

39. *Ibid.*, 114.

40. *Ibid.*, 115.

41. Aelred, *De spirituali amicitia*, 3.91.

42. d'Avray, 115.

43. *Ibid.*, 116; cf. Aelred, *De spirituali amicitia*, 3.102–109, and Aristotle's *Ethics*, 8.8.1650.

44. A. Hoste, ed., *De spirituali amicitia*, 281–85.

45. D. L. Douie, *The Conflict Between the Seculars and the Mendicants at the University of Paris in the Thirteenth Century*, The Aquinas Society of London, Aquinas Paper 23 (London: Aquin Press, 1954), p. 8; cf. Rolf Köhn, "Monastisches Bildungsideal und weltgeistliches Wissenschaftsdenken: Zur Vorgeschichte des Mendikantenstreites an der Universität Paris," in *Die Auseinandersetzungen an der Pariser Universität im XII. Jahrhundert*, ed. Albert Zimmerman, Miscellanea Mediaevalia, Band 10 (Berlin: De Gruyter, 1976), pp. 1–37.

46. Thus P. Glorieux, *Répertoire des Maîtres*, p. 340. In his later work on Robert he is less certain about these dates (see the work quoted in the next note, p. 21), but professor or not, from 1256 Robert was actively engaged in the founding of his college and as such known to all.

47. Glorieux, *Aux origines de la Sorbonne: 1. Robert de Sorbon: L'homme—Le Collège—Les documents*, Études de Philosophie Médiévale 53 (Paris: J. Vrin, 1966), p. 28.

48. *Ibid.*, pp. 35–39, 52–53.

49. d'Avray, 75.

50. *Ibid.*, 117.

51. Vernon J. Bourke, "The *Nicomachean Ethics* and Thomas Aquinas," in *St. Thomas Aquinas 1274–1974: Commemorative Studies*, 2 vols. (Toronto: Pontifical Institute of Mediaeval Studies, 1974), 1:240.

52. Lecoy, ed., *Le roman de La Rose*, 1:viii.

53. For a beginning of such criticism, see John V. Fleming, *The Roman de La Rose: A Study in Allegory and Iconography* (Princeton: Princeton University Press, 1969).

54. Cf. e.g. Fleming, pp. 121–23; E. S. Kooper, "Love, Marriage and Salvation in Chaucer's *Book of the Duchess* and *Parlement of Foules*" (Diss., Utrecht University, 1985), pp. 81–97.

55. Apart from Grosseteste's complete translation of the *Ethics*, which was available in Paris before 1250, "[a]t least six courses on the *Ethica vetus* and *nova*, given by Masters in the Arts faculty at Paris, have now been identified in manuscript," Bourke has said (p. 244). Moreover, between 1248 and 1252, when he was still a student, Thomas attended the lectures of Albert the Great on the *Ethics* (*ibid.*, p. 247), and Jean could easily have done the same.

CHAPTER 4

1. I quote Chaucer, and also *The Romaunt of the Rose*, from *The Riverside Chaucer*, ed. Larry D. Benson, 3rd ed. (Boston: Houghton Mifflin, 1987). The present paper, a first sketch for what I hope may be a more extended study, was originally written for delivery as a lecture at the Pennsylvania State University and at Harvard University in March 1986. It has been revised and expanded for publication, but I have not attempted to remove all traces of oral delivery. I am grateful to my audiences for several helpful suggestions of which I have made use, but I owe a special debt to Professor Vickie Ziegler of the German Department of the Pennsylvania State University, for arranging my visit there for Medieval Studies Week, for her generous hospitality, and for calling my attention to the poem by Walther von der Vogelweide and translating and annotating it for me.

2. *Andreas Capellanus on Love*, ed. and trans. P. G. Walsh (London: Duckworth, 1982), p. 32 ("an inborn suffering which results *from the sight of*, and uncontrolled thinking about, the beauty of the other sex"); my italics.

3. *Die Gedichte Walthers von der Vogelweide*, ed. Hugo Kuhn (Berlin: De Gruyter, 1965), pp. 52–53.

4. Trans. Michael Benedikt, in *The Medieval Age*, ed. Angel Flores (New York: Dell, 1963), pp. 142–43.

5. Sigmund Freud, *On Sexuality*, ed. Angela Richards (Harmondsworth: Penguin, 1977), pp. 69–70. In the *Standard Edition*, the *Three Essays* are found in volume VII.

6. David Stafford-Clark, *What Freud Really Said* (Harmondsworth: Penguin, 1967), p. 99.

7. *Rates of Exchange* (London: Secker & Warburg, 1983), ch. 8.II.

8. The word "auditeur" would be a useful term to refer to the person who applies an ear rather than an eye to the bedroom keyhole.

9. See R. Howard Bloch, *Medieval French Literature and Law* (Berkeley: University of California Press, 1977).

10. See for example the misericord carvings at Lincoln and Chester, reproduced by M. D. Anderson in *The Choir Stalls of Lincoln Minster* (Lincoln: Friends of Lincoln Cathedral, 1951), plate 14, and *Misericords: Medieval Life in English Woodcarving* (Harmondsworth: Penguin, 1954), plate 31, or the fine French ivory casket in the Metropolitan Museum of Art.

11. Beroul is quoted from *The Romance of Tristran*, vol. I, ed. A. Ewert (Oxford: Blackwell, 1939).

12. Trans. Alan S. Fedrick, *The Romance of Tristan* (Harmondsworth: Penguin, 1970).

13. Gottfried von Strassburg's treatment of this moment in his *Tristan* (based on the French version of Thomas, now lost for this scene) expands its voyeuristic element still further. Gottfried's lovers, lying on the bed of Venus in an elaborate *Minnegrotte*, are spied on through a little window first by a huntsman and then by Mark. To Mark, Isolde, with her glowing cheeks and lips, has never before seemed so alluring, and Gottfried ensures that we shall participate in the king's voyeuristic excitement by encouraging us to imagine versions of the story in which Isolde's flush would be caused by recent love-making, only to tell us that in fact it was the result of a stroll through the dew! Thus we are forced to face the fact that it is our fantasies that are responsible for any pornographic element in the scene. (See Gottfried von Strassburg, *Tristan*, trans. A. T. Hatto [Harmondsworth: Penguin, 1960], pp. 270–73.)

14. Cf. Evan Carton, "Complicity and Responsibility in Pandarus' Bed and Chaucer's Art," *PMLA* 94 (1979):47–61.

15. Cf. Sheila Delany, *Writing Woman* (New York: Schocken Books, 1983), p. 67.

16. Note 20 below indicates a small exception. For an excellent recent account of the relationship between the French and English versions, see Caroline D. Eckhardt, "The Art of Translation in *The Romaunt of the Rose*," *Studies in the Age of Chaucer* 6 (1984):41–63.

17. C. S. Lewis, *The Allegory of Love* (Oxford: Clarendon, 1936), p. 126; L. T. Topsfield, "*The Roman de la Rose*," in *Medieval Literature: the European Inheritance*, ed. Boris Ford (Harmondsworth: Penguin, 1983), pp. 223–35, p. 228.

18. D. W. Robertson, Jr., *A Preface to Chaucer* (Princeton, N.J.: Princeton University Press, 1962), p. 104.

19. Topsfield, p. 224.

20. Line 1284 has no equivalent in the French.

21. MS. Douce 213, f.l^r. It is reproduced by, for example, Elizabeth Salter and Derek Pearsall, "Pictorial Illustration of Late Medieval Poetic Texts," in *Medieval Iconography and Narrative*, ed. Flemming G. Andersen et al. (Odense: Odense University Press, 1980), pp. 100–23, p. 115, and A. J. Minnis, *Medieval Theory of Authorship* (London: Scolar Press, 1984), p. 194.

22. Dunbar is quoted from *The Poems of William Dunbar*, ed. James Kinsley (Oxford: Clarendon, 1979).

23. Cf. Pamela M. King, "Dunbar's Goldyn Targe: A Chaucerian Masque," *Studies in Scottish Literature* 19 (1984):115–31.

24. See my *Medieval to Renaissance in English Poetry* (Cambridge: Cambridge University Press, 1985), pp. 215–23.

CHAPTER 5

1. Peter Abelard, *The Story of Abelard's Adversities: A Translation with Notes of the "Historia calamitatum,"* trans. J. T. Muckle (Toronto: Pontifical Institute of Mediaeval Studies, 1954), pp. 11–12.

2. Mary Martin McLaughlin, "Abelard as Autobiographer: The Motives and Meaning of His 'Story of Calamities,'" *Speculum* 42 (1967): 481–82.

3. The text is quoted from Chrétien de Troyes, *The Knight with the Lion, or, Yvain*, ed. and trans. William Kibler (New York: Garland, 1985).

4. The translation is from Marie de France, *The Lais of Marie de France*, trans. Robert W. Hanning and Joan M. Ferrante (New York: Dutton, 1978, reprint Durham, N.C.: Labyrinth, 1984).

5. "Pwyll, Prince of Dyfed," in *The Mabinogion*, trans. Gwyn Jones and Thomas Jones (London: Dent; New York: Dutton, 1949), p. 9.

6. Henry James, *The Europeans* (New York: Penguin, 1984), p. 17.

CHAPTER 6

A much longer version of this paper was published in Italian "La cagna la mula la menade, e Nastagio degli Onesti" in *Comunità* 189–190 (July 1988), pp. 380–429. It contains an analysis of other classical and medieval traditions of the motif and a more detailed discussion of its form and content structures.

1. On this important subject, see the extensive study by Aldo Scaglione, *Nature and Love in the Late Middle Ages* (Berkeley: University of California Press, 1963).

2. L. Russo, *Letture critiche del Decamerone* (Bari: Laterza, 1956), p. 199.

3. On this subject, see Scaglione, ch. 4.

4. The final reconciliation of love and chastity achieved by Nastagio's decision forestalls the possibility of parody that some scholars have seen. See V. Sklovskij, *Lettura del Decamerone* (Bologna: Il Mulino, 1969), p. 226 and C. Segre, "La novella di Nastagio degli Onesti: i due tempi della visione," *Semiotica filologica* (Turin: Einaudi, 1979), pp. 95–96.

5. *Kathâ-sarît-sâgara or Ocean of the Streams of Story*, trans. C. H. Tawney, 2d ed., 2 vols. (Delhi: Munshiram Manoharlal, 1968), 1:87–91; see also *The Ocean of Story*, rev. ed. by N. M. Penzer, 10 vols. (London: C. J. Sawyer, 1924–28), 1:153–64, 169–71 n.

6. On the subject, J. G. Frazer, *Adonis, Attis, Osiris* (= *The Golden Bough*, Part IV), 3d ed. (New York: University Books, 1935), chs. 3 and 4; for married women as sacred prostitutes in India, see especially p. 63. See also N. M. Penzer, *Poison-Damsels, and Other Essays in Folklore and Anthropology* (London: C. J. Sawyer, 1952), pp. 129–84.

7. *The Ocean of Story*, 1:169.

8. *Poison-Damsels*, pp. 131–23, 137–40.

9. *Die Çukasaptati: Textus simplicior*, trans. R. Schmidt, (Leipzig: F. A. Brockhaus, 1893), p. 23; in the Persian abridged version of the book, *Tûtî-nameh*, the trick of the bitch is missing from the story, and in the Turkish version of the story is omitted altogether; see Domenico Comparetti, *Researches respecting the Book of Sindibad*, trans. H. C. Coote (London: E. Stock, 1882), pp. 47–49.

10. For the place occupied in the story in the various collections, see Comparetti, p. 25; J. Bédier, *Les Fabliaux*, 5th ed. (Paris: Champion 1925), p. 136; M. Landau, *Die Quellen des Dekameron* (Stuttgart: J. Scheible, 1884), p. 340; H. A. Keller, *Li Romans des Sept Sages* (Tübingen: L. F. Fues, 1836), p. cxxxi f.; W. A. Clouston, *The Book of Sindibad* (Glasgow: J. Cameron, 1884), pp. 217–18.

11. Respect., ed. Burton, 6:152–56, and *Le mille e una notte*, ed. F. Gabrielli (Turin: Einaudi, 1948), II: 107–10. For other oriental versions derived from the same sources, see V. Chauvin, *Bibliographie des ouvrages arabes ou relatifs aux arabes publiés dans l'Europe chrétienne de 1810 à 1885*, 12 vols. (Liège: Vaillant-Carmanne, 1892–1922), 8:45–46, n. 13.

12. *PL* 212:754.

13. Vincent de Beauvais, *Speculum historiale*, Bk.39, ch. 120, in vol. 4 of *Speculum quadruplex sive majus* (rpt. Graz: Akademische Druck und Verlaganstalt, 1965), p. 397. See also P. Toldo, *Archiv für das Studium der Neueren Sprachen und Literaturen* 19 (1907–08): 367–68, and A. Monteverdi, *Studi e saggi sulla letteratura italiana dei primi secoli* (Milan-Naples: R. Ricciardi, 1954), pp. 190–94. Similar stories are noted by Toldo, pp. 261–71; Aleksei Veselovskij, *La fanciulla perseguitata*, ed. D'Arco Silvio Avalle (Milan: Bompiani, 1977), pp. 62–73; F. L. W. Schwartz, *Die poetischen Naturanschauungen der Griechen, Römer und Deutschen in ihrer beaiehung zur mythologie* (Bern: 1864), 1:256–57.

14. Reprinted in Toldo, pp. 365–66.

15. See *Scrittori di religione del Trecento: testi originali*, ed. G. De Luca, 2d ed. (Turin: Einaudi, 1977), 1:84–85.

16. L. Di Francia, *Giornale storico della letteratura italiana* 49 (1907): 257–80.

17. Reprinted in Toldo, p. 366 n. 1.

18. K. J. Simrock, *Handbuch der deutschen Mythologie mit Einschluss der nordischen* (Bonn: A. Marcus, 1855), pp. 223–24.

19. H. Jeanmarie, *Dionysos, histoire du culte de Bacchus* (Paris: Payot, 1978), p. 256.

20. Hesiod, *Catalogue of Women*; see also *Apollodorus, the Library*, trans. J. G. Frazer (New York: G. P. Putnam's Sons, 1956); 1:147–49, and Jeanmarie, pp. 203–5.

21. Ovid, *Metamorphoses*, 6.1–40, 390–415; Antonius Liberalis, *Metamorphosen synagoge* 10; Aelianus, *Varia historia* 3.42. See also Jeanmarie, pp. 202–3 and *The Greek Questions of Plutarch*, trans. W. H. Halliday (Oxford: Clarendon Press, 1928), pp. 165–68.

22. A mention of the story remains, in fact, in a fragment of Nicander's *Heteroeumena* 4; see *The Poems and Poetical Fragments*, ed. A. S. F. Gow and A. F. Scholfield (Cambridge: Cambridge University Press, 1953), p. 207.

23. Fragment 665, in *Poetae Melici Graeci*, ed. D. L. Page (Oxford: Clarendon Press, 1962).

24. Jeanmaire, pp. 280–85, 310–11.

25. L. R. Farnell, *The Cults of the Greek States*, 5 vols. (Oxford: Clarendon Press, 1896–1909), 5:111.

26. Jeanmaire, p. 139.

27. *The Greek Questions of Plutarch*, p. 164.

28. Jeanmaire, pp. 254–56.

29. John B. Titchener, *The Manuscript-Tradition of Plutarch's "Aetia Graeca" and "Aetia Romana"* (Urbana: University of Illinois Press, 1924).

30. See Segre, pp. 89–91.

31. Taken from the same source, Dante's *Purgatorio* 14.98, 107–8; see V. Branca, ed., *Decamerone* (Milan: Mondadori, 1976), 5:8, 4 n. 3, and 5, n. 5.

32. See Branca, 31, n. 15.

33. Segre observes, "The pine woods do not represent an intermediate area, but an area of mediation" (p. 94).

34. Segre says, "Guido's story has the temporal status of a *factum*, whereas the story in which it is immersed has the status of a *fieri*" (p. 92).

35. On this subject, see Scaglione, pp. 96–97.

CHAPTER 7

1. There is a great deal written on this episode. Two interesting recent studies are Mark Musa's "Behold Francesca Who Speaks So Well" in *Advent at the Gates* (Bloomington: Indiana University Press, 1974), pp. 19–55, and Stephen Popolizio's "Literary Reminiscences and the Act of Reading in *Inferno V*," *Dante Studies* 98 (1980): 19–33. Except for *The Vita Nuova*, all citations for Dante are to *Le Opere di Dante Alighieri*, ed. by E. Moore and rev. by Paget Toynbee, 5th ed. (Oxford: The University Press, 1963). For *The Vita Nuova*, I have gone to the more conventional division into 42 chapters. I have used William Armistead Falconer's edition of Ci-

cero's *De Senectute, De Amicitia, De Divinatione* (Cambridge, Mass.: Harvard University Press, 1959) for my citations to *De Amicitia.*

2. See, in especial, A. G. H. Spiers, "*Dolce Stil Novo*—The Case of the Opposition," *PMLA* 25 (1910):657–75; Maurice Valency, *In Praise of Love* (New York: Macmillan Co., 1961); A. G. Ferrers Howell, "Dante and the Troubadours," *Dante: Essays in Commemoration 1321–1921* (1921; rpt. Freeport, NY: Books for Libraries Press, 1968); pp. 189–223; J. E. Shaw, *Essays on the Vita Nuova* (Princeton: Princeton University Press, 1929), pp. 77–108; and Jerome Mazzaro, *The Figure of Dante: An Essay on The Vita Nuova* (Princeton: Princeton University Press, 1981), pp. 71–74.

3. A. J. Denomy, *The Heresy of Courtly Love* (1947; rpt. Gloucester: Peter Smith, 1965), pp. 30, 31, 46, 85. For Dante's knowledge of Andreas, see Maria Simonelli, "Il tema della nobiltà in Andrea Cappellano e in Dante," *Dante Studies* 84 (1966): 51–64 and Domenico De Robertis, *Il libro della "Vita Nuova"* (Florence: G. C. Sansoni, 1961).

4. Kenelm Foster, *The Two Dantes* (Berkeley: University of California Press, 1977), pp. 16, 18, 23, 25, 32, 33, 34.

5. Foster, p. 25. Étienne Gilson, *The Mystical Theology of Saint Bernard*, trans. A. H. C. Downes (New York: Sheed and Ward, 1940), pp. 171, 172, 181, 184, 193.

6. John C. Moore, *Love in Twelfth-Century France* (Philadelphia: University of Pennsylvania Press, 1972), pp. 31, 38.

7. Leo M. Bond, "A Comparison between Human and Divine Friendship," *The Thomist* 3 (1941):54–94. See, also, St. Thomas Aquinas, *Commentary on the Nicomachean Ethics*, trans. C. I. Litzinger, O. P. (Chicago: Henry Regnery, 1964), 2:700–855.

8. Moore, pp. 39, 42, 72. In stating that Dante would have known the views on friendship expressed by Ambrose, Jerome, Cassian, and Aelred, I do not mean to convey that he necessarily knew the texts of these writers or recognized the views' credited authors. The views on friendship expressed by Ambrose, Jerome, and Cassian had by Dante's day become part of the fabric of Christian and monastic thought, and Marie Magdeleine Davy has argued that Aelred's ideas on friendship which Peter of Blois plagiarizes for his "De Amicitia" (c. 1200) are "indispensable" in tracing the origins of Thomas Aquinas's thought. See M. M. Davy, *Un Traité de l'Amour du XIIe Siècle* (Paris: E. De Boccard, 1932), p. 81. See, also, E. Vansteenberghe, "Deux théoriciens de l'amitié au XIIe siècle, Pierre de Blois et Aelred de Riéval," *Revue des sciences religieuses* 12 (1932):577–88.

9. For an excellent summary of the qualities of and argument about Beatrice and the "donna gentile," see Étienne Gilson, *Dante and Philosophy*, trans. David Moore (New York: Harper Torchbooks, 1963), pp. 50–82, 86–98.

10. Charles S. Singleton, *Commentary to the Inferno of The Divine Comedy* (Princeton: Princeton University Press, 1970), 2:32. Howard R. Patch, *The Goddess Fortuna in Mediaeval Literature* (Cambridge, Mass.: Harvard University Press, 1927), pp. 13, 19, 39–40.

CHAPTER 8

1. *The Legend of Good Women*, F 280, in *The Riverside Chaucer*, ed. Larry D. Benson et al., 3d ed. (Boston: Houghton Mifflin Co., 1987), p. 595; all quotations will use this text and be cited internally. The Prologue exists in two versions, designated F and G, which are thought to have been composed in 1387 and 1394, respectively. Unless indicated otherwise, references will be to the F version. For recent discussion of the textual problems, see George Kane, "The Text of *The Legend of Good Women* in CUL MS Gg.4.27," in *Middle English Studies Presented to Norman Davis in Honour of His Seventieth Birthday*, ed. Douglas Gray and E. G. Stanley (Oxford: Clarendon Press, 1983), pp. 39–58. John H. Fisher, "The Revision of The Prologue to the *Legend of Good Women*: An Occasional Explanation," *South Atlantic Bulletin* 43 (1978): 75–84, reasserts the traditional claim that the Prologue was revised because of the death of Queen Anne.

2. James I. Wimsatt, "Chaucer and French Poetry," in *Geoffrey Chaucer*, ed. Derek Brewer (Athens: Ohio University Press, 1975), p. 113 proposes that Cupid is derived from Guillaume de Lorris's God of Love in the *Roman de la Rose*. Lisa J. Kiser, *Telling Classical Tales* (Ithaca, N.Y.: Cornell University Press, 1983) interprets Cupid as "a parody of the kind of poetic artifice that Chaucer wished to reject" (p. 65), while Alceste is a figure for a kind of writing that stands between "making" and "poetrie" (pp. 74–75) and the daisy is a figure for the poet's art (p. 44).

3. *OED*, s.v. "translation" cites, among other sources relating to Scripture, passages from the Wycliffite Bible.

4. Text in T. Atkinson Jenkins, "Deschamps's Ballade to Chaucer," *Modern Language Notes* 33 (1918): 268–78. Like Wimsatt ("Chaucer and French Poetry," p. 110), André Crépin, "Chaucer and the French," in *Medieval and Pseudo-Medieval Literature*, ed. Piero Boitani and Anna Torti (Cambridge: D. S. Brewer, 1984) relates Chaucer's translation to a larger cultural project: "It amounts to a whole policy, or to accept a word in fashion today, a deliberate strategy, of importing and implanting" (p. 62). He goes on to remark that the metaphor of the garden in Deschamps's balade is a figure for French poetry (p. 63) and that Deschamps's mention of Chaucer's " 'rethorique' is meant both to echo and surpass" the praise he had given Machaut on his death in 1377—"Machault le noble rethorique" (p. 66).

5. I am grateful to the late Donald Sutherland for explaining the details of Chaucer's legalism in the passage and for pointing out the rather strict emphasis here on legal procedure.

6. Robert Worth Frank, Jr., *Chaucer and* The Legend of Good Women (Cambridge, Mass.: Harvard University Press, 1972) and Robert O. Payne, *The Key of Remembrance: A Study of Chaucer's Poetics* (New Haven, Conn.: Yale University Press, 1963). Payne extends his views in "Making His own Myth: The Prologue to Chaucer's *Legend of Good Women,*" *Chaucer Review* 9 (1974–75): 197–211. Russell A. Peck, "Chaucerian Poetics and the Prologue to the *Legend of Good Women,* " in *Chaucer in the Eighties,* ed. Julian N. Wasserman and Robert J. Blanch (Syracuse, N.Y.: Syracuse University Press, 1986), pp. 45–46, contends: "Desire, intuition, and a primary and secondary imagination are essential elements in Chaucerian poetics." Peck identifies three opposing epistemologies in the Prologue—empirical, bookish, and inspirational.

7. My reading of Alceste's defense differs in its emphasis from Kiser's: "Clearly, Alceste's excuses for Chaucer are all fabricated to disguise the fact that Chaucer's heresy against the law of love is probably real, and, more than that, is surely a matter of choice" (p. 86).

8. The usual distinction is between "making" (composition in the vernacular) and "poetry" (writing by the Latin *auctores* and, by extension, vernacular poetry, such as Dante's, which employs classical lore); see Glending Olson, "Making and Poetry in the Age of Chaucer," *Comparative Literature* 31 (1979): 272–90. Chaucer's distinction here and elsewhere in his writing registers a felt difference between two kinds of aesthetic creation, but the difference is expressed in local distinctions rather than a programmatic theory or consistent terminology.

9. A literary precedent for Chaucer's divergence from Cupid's law is given by Ovid at the beginning of the *Remedia Amoris* where the poet rehearses his dedicated service to love before taking on his new task of providing remedies for lovers. I am grateful to Robert Hollander for pointing out the parallel. Chaucer's problematic treatment of Cupid and the fallibility of both the god and the narrator are discussed in Sarah Stanbury Smith, "Cupid's Sight in the Prologue to the *Legend of Good Women,*" *Centerpoint* 4 (1981): 95–102.

10. John Lawlor, "The Pattern of Consolation in *The Book of the Duchess,*" *Speculum* 31 (1956): 633.

11. In his *Boece,* V, m. 4, Chaucer recounts and rejects the position of the Stoic philosophers. In "Against Women Unconstant," a poem of disputed attribution, he gives the counter-example to the image of the white wall: "Right as a mirour nothing may impresse, / But, lightly as it cometh, so mot it pace, / So fareth your love, your werkes beren witnesse" (8–10).

12. *The Riverside Chaucer,* p. 776. The extensive verbal and thematic parallels with Machaut are listed by Wimsatt, *Chaucer and the French Love Poets: The Literary Background of the* Book of the Duchess (Chapel Hill: University of North Carolina Press, 1968) and R. Barton Palmer, ed. and trans., *The Judgment of the King of Bohemia (Le Jugement dou Roy de Behaingne)* (New York: Garland, 1984).

13. Guillaume de Machaut, *Remede de Fortune,* lines 26–34, in *Oeuvres de Guillaume de Machaut,* ed. Ernest Hœpffner, 3 vols. (Paris: Champion, 1921), II:2.

14. The clearest poetic enunciation of this notion is in Guido Guinizelli's canzone "Al cor gentil rempaira sempre amore" ("Love always resides in the noble heart"), a line which Dante echoes in *Vita Nuova* 20 and Chaucer in *Troilus and Criseyde* 3.5, probably drawing on *Convivio* 4.20.7.

15. The assertion is repeated in comparison with Penelope and Lucrece, the classical models of virtue: "She was as good, and nothyng lyk" (1085).

16. D. W. Robertson, Jr., "The Historical Setting of Chaucer's *Book of the Duchess,*" in *Mediaeval Studies in Honor of Urban Tigner Holmes, Jr.,* ed. John Mahoney and John Esten Keller (Chapel Hill: University of North Carolina Press, 1965), p. 186.

17. "The Complaint of Mars" also takes up the themes of governance, binding, and mutability.

18. *Le Jugement dou Roy de Behaingne,* 148–53, ed. Palmer, p. 8. For discussion of the patterns and meaning in Chaucer's borrowings from the *Remede* and *Behaingne,* see my *The Dream of Chaucer: Representation and Reflection in the Early Narratives* (Durham, N.C.: Duke University Press, 1989), pp. 82–88.

19. *Teseida delle nozze di Emilia,* ed. Alberto Limentani, in *Tutte le opere di Giovanni Boccaccio,* ed. Vittore Branca, 12 vols. (Florence: Mondadori, 1964), II: 255. The translation is from N. R. Havely, ed. and trans., *Chaucer's Boccaccio: Sources of Troilus and the Knight's and Franklin's Tales* (Cambridge: D. S. Brewer, 1980), p. 106.

20. Robert A. Pratt, "Chaucer's Use of the *Teseida,*" *PMLA* 62 (1947): 603, holds that the "two suitors are virtually indistinguishable." W. H. French, "The Lovers in the *Knight's Tale,*" *Journal of English and Germanic Philology* 48 (1949): 326, contends that in their preference for arms and love, "the two knights were distinguishable; in others, Chaucer permitted no important differences." H. S. Wilson, "*The Knight's Tale* and the *Teseida* Again," *University of Toronto Quarterly* 18 (1949): 131–46,

argues that in Boccaccio the figures are distinguished only by their fate. Wilson believes that Boccaccio's theme of earthly and divine love governs his characterization and Chaucer's reading of the story: "It is not a competition of rival merits that is being presented to us but an *exemplum* of the power of love which overrules all fellowship, even that of the truest of knights and devoted friends. The force of the *exemplum* depends upon our seeing the antagonists as *equally* illustrating this theme" (p. 143). Among recent critics, Piero Boitani, "Style, Iconography and Narrative: the Lesson of the *Teseida*," in *Chaucer and the Italian Trecento* (Cambridge: Cambridge University Press, 1983), p. 187, has argued that "Arcite is a pensive, lyrical, melancholy, courteous figure; Palamon is more violent." Boitani offers an extended analysis of characterization in *Chaucer and Boccaccio* (Oxford: Society for the Study of Mediaeval Languages and Literature, 1977), pp. 135–47. In *The Two Noble Kinsmen*, Shakespeare intensifies the close relation of Arcite and Palamon after their capture (I, ii) and John Fletcher reduces the appearance of specious reasoning in Arcite when he proclaims his love for Emily in opposition to Palamon. Arcite says, "You play the child extremely. I will love her, / I must, I ought to do so, and I dare— / And all this justly" (II.ii.204–6).

21. Limentani suggests that Farinata is the source for Boccaccio's characterization of Arcita and Palemone (II: 891 n.50) as well as Creon (II: 238, 890 n.41). Boitani, *Chaucer and Boccaccio*, p. 38, contends, however, "Boccaccio uses Dante's words only in order to add dramatic quality to his scene."

22. René Girard, *Deceit, Desire, and the Novel*, trans. Yvonne Freccero (Baltimore: Johns Hopkins University Press, 1965) describes the basic model of mediated desire. Eve Kosofsky Sedgwick, *Between Men: English Literature and Male Homosocial Desire* (New York: Columbia University Press, 1985), pp. 21–27, objects that Girard's account of erotic triangulation accepts patriarchal values without attending to their historical contexts and ignores the importance of differences in gender. David Anderson, *Before the Knight's Tale: Imitation of Classical Epic in Boccaccio's* Teseida (Philadelphia: University of Pennsylvania Press, 1988), pp. 207–12, observes that one of the mythological subtleties Chaucer weaves into the tale is that Arcite and Palamon extend the genealogy of Oedipus's line and repeat its internecine conflict. Boitani, *Chaucer and Boccacio*, p. 21, sees the Theban story as chiefly "decorative," hence an element of Boccaccio's style rather than his theme. Alan T. Gaylord, "The Role of Saturn in the *Knight's Tale*," *Chaucer Review* 8 (1973–74): 178–79, observes that Chaucer passes over places in Boccaccio's text that might suggest that Arcite and Palamon were determined to reenact Theban history.

23. V. A. Kolve, *Chaucer and the Imagery of Narrative: The First Five* Canterbury Tales (Stanford, Ca.: Stanford University Press, 1984), pp. 85–157, draws on iconographic evidence to show the proximity and juxtaposition of the tower and garden, and argues that the adjacent locations

intensify the theme of freedom by showing how physical confinement gives way to the entrapment of desire.

24. OED cites *merci* as a noun ("thanks") and *merciede* as a verb ("to give thanks") from *Piers Plowman*, A 3.21. *MED* records the meaning "expressing gratitude, thanks" from late fourteenth century sources, including *Piers Plowman* A 1.41.

25. For an insightful contrast between the *Knight's Tale* and the *Franklin's Tale* on the matter of contradiction, see Alan T. Gaylord's essay "From Dorigen to the Vavasour: Reading Backwards" in this volume.

26. David Aers, *Chaucer, Langland and the Creative Imagination* (London: Routledge & Kegan Paul, 1980). Aers repeats the point in *Chaucer* (Brighton, Sussex: The Harvester Press, 1986), p. 24: " . . . the *Knight's Tale* is not an unequivocal celebration of Theseus as the principle of law and order we are to worship. It is a critical, often highly ironic, exploration of secular rule, its forms of power and its uses of language." This reading differs from the generally-accepted view argued by Charles Muscatine, *Chaucer and the French Tradition* (Berkeley: University of California Press, 1957), p. 181: "The story is immediately concerned with those two noble activities, love and chivalry, but even more important is the general tenor of the noble life, the pomp and ceremony, the dignity and power, and particularly the response and assurance with which the exponent of nobility invokes order." Paul Olson, *The* Canterbury Tales *and the Good Society* (Princeton, N.J.: Princeton University Press, 1986), pp. 66–69, holds that Theseus is a judge and leader who reconciles Athenian and Theban history and so offers a model for ending warfare between England and France.

CHAPTER 9

I presented a version of this essay at the conference that Thomas Hahn organized on "History/Text/Theory: Reconceiving Chaucer," at the University of Rochester (April 21, 1988).

1. The classic statement of this perception is in Simone de Beauvoir, *The Second Sex*, trans. H. M. Parshley (New York: Knopf, 1953), p. xv: "In actuality the relation of the two sexes is not quite like that of two electrical poles, for man represents both the positive and the neutral, as is indicated by the common use of *man* to designate human beings in general; whereas woman represents only the negative, defined by limiting criteria, without reciprocity." Also see p. 713: "It is in man and not in woman that it has hitherto been possible for Man to be incarnated."

Caroline Walker Bynum makes the interesting observation that "From Hildegard of Bingen and Elizabeth of Schönau to Catherine of Siena and Julian of Norwich, women theologians in the later Middle Ages used *woman* to symbolize *humanity." Holy Feast and Holy Fast: The Religious Significance of Food to Medieval Women* (Berkeley: University of California Press, 1987), p. 264.

2. For an interesting and often amusing account of such issues—including false etymologies of "woman," generic and sex-specific uses of "man," and the pronouns "he" and "she"—in more recent grammatical theory, see Dennis Baron, *Grammar and Gender* (New Haven: Yale University Press, 1986).

3. Gavin Douglas, trans., *The Aeneid of Virgil* (1839; rpt. New York: AMS Press, 1971), 1:18.

4. See Mary Nyquist's exceptionally interesting essay "Gynesis, Genesis, Exegesis, and Milton's Eve," in *Cannibals, Witches, and Divorce: Estranging the Renaissance,* ed. Marjorie Garber, English Institute Essays, n.s. 11 (Baltimore: Johns Hopkins University Press, 1987), pp. 147–208, esp. pp. 153–55.
I have used the Douay-Rheims translation of the Vulgate.

5. These examples are cited by Bosworth and Toller's *Anglo-Saxon Dictionary* and the *OED,* which also remarks, in the headnote to the word "man," that English differs from other Germanic languages in not having developed a derivative word for "human being," as differentiated from "adult male human being."

6. See especially Phyllis Trible, *God and the Rhetoric of Sexuality* (Philadelphia: Fortress Press, 1978), and her earlier essay, "Depatriarchializing in Biblical Interpretation," *Journal of the American Academy of Religion* 16 (1973): 30–48. See Nyquist, pp. 155–57, and the article she cites by Phyllis A. Bird for an effective demolition of such arguments.
Elaine H. Pagels, in *Adam, Eve, and the Serpent* (New York: Knopf, 1987), makes the analogous argument that a revolutionary claim for human equality, including sexual equality, was an important feature of many early Christian and Gnostic documents, but gave way to the patriarchal interpretation proposed by St. Augustine, and confirmed in later Church doctrine.

7. In his translation of the four Gospels, Jerome always uses *vir* to translate *aner,* with four exceptions: Matt. 15.38; Luke 5.8, 6.8, and 19.7. The first of these, distinguishing the "men" from the "children and women" at the miracle of the loaves and fishes, most noticeably uses "homo" with a limited male reference.
See Augustine's interpretation of Matthew 19.4–6 (*De Civitate Dei* 14.22), arguing from it that "male" and "female" cannot simply be interpreted allegorically in Genesis, and that God instituted marriage before the Fall.

8. Augustine, *The City of God,* trans. Henry Bettenson (Harmondsworth: Penguin Books, 1972), p. 626. Cf. Jerome, *PL* 23:946.

9. Augustine, trans. Bettenson, p. 943. Also see his argument on why God created only one man, when He had created many in each species of beast: *De Civ. Dei* 12.22, trans. pp. 502–03; also 13.14, p. 523.

Gregory of Tours has an interesting discussion of why the generic term "homo" must be considered to include both men and women, at Book 8.20 of his *Libri Historiarum X*, ed. Bruno Krusch and Wilhelm Levison, MGH: Scriptores Rerum Merovingicarum (Hannover: Hahn, 1942), 1:1:386–87. Also see the first volume of *A History of Private Life*, ed. Philippe Ariès and Georges Duby, *From Pagan Rome to Byzantium*, ed. Paul Veyne (Cambridge, Mass.: Harvard University Press, 1987), pp. 534–35, for an account of the synod of Mâcon in 585, at which a bishop protested that "a woman cannot be called man (*homo*)," and was answered by the citation of Gen. 1.27. (Cf. Augustine, *De Genesi ad Litteram* 3.22 [PL 34:294]: "in ipsa prima conditione hominis, secundum id quod et femina homo erat.") This example is used to illustrate the loss of the word "vir" in the shift from Latin to proto-French, and the effects of that loss. That such effects were felt later is illustrated by Nicole Oresme's concern that a translator from Latin into French does not always have equivalent words at his disposal. See Serge Lusignan, *Parler Vulgairement: Les Intellectuels et la Langue Française aux XIII⁰ et XIV⁰ Siècles* (Montréal: Les Presses de l'Université de Montréal, 1986), p. 164: "Les exemples que fournit Oresme ont trait aux mots latins *homo* et *animal*, que les mots français 'homme' et 'beste' ne rendent pas de façon exacte. Le mot 'homme' ne recouvre pour Oresme que les seuls humains de sexe masculin, alors que 'beste' désigne uniquement les êtres animés non raisonnables. Par conséquent, les propositions latines *homo est animal* ou *mulier est homo* deviennent fausses si on les traduit par 'homme est beste' et 'femme est homme.' "

10. *The City of God* 22.18, trans. Bettenson, p. 1059. This passage is cited by Kari Elisabeth Børresen, *Subordination and Equivalence: The Nature and Rôle of Women in Augustine and Thomas Aquinas*, trans. Charles H. Talbot (Washington, D.C.: University Press of America, 1981), p. 86. Børresen also discusses Aquinas's distinction of *homo* from *mas* (*S.T.* I, 92, 1, c.): see p. 158.

11. There is a summary of Pope John Paul II's letter *Mulieris Dignitatem* in the issue of *The Tablet* for 1 October 1988.

The usual exegetical maneuver to make these two texts congruent is to distinguish, as Augustine does, between the seminal creation (*informatio*) of the human being (*homo*) and the formation in time (*conformatio*) of the two sexes (*vir* and *femina*): see Børresen, pp. 20–21, and Nyquist, p. 168, for discussion.

12. John Skinner, *A Critical and Exegetical Commentary on Genesis*, rev. ed. (New York: Scribner's, 1925), p. 67.

13. See Augustine, *De Gen. contra Manichaeos* 2.11 (PL 34:205). According to Augustine (copied by Bede in PL 91:51), Adam shows his supe-

riority to the animals by the very act of naming them, because that act displays his reason. J. M. Evans quotes a similar passage in St. John Chrysostom: Paradise Lost *and the Genesis Tradition* (Oxford: Clarendon Press, 1968), p. 95. Also see Alcuin, *Interrogationes et Responsiones in Genesin* (*PL* 100:522); Bede, *PL* 91:51; and Peter Comestor, *Historia Scholastica*, ch. 16 (*PL* 198:1070).

14. St. Ambrose, *De Paradiso, PL* 14:299. Also see *The Pentateuch and Rashi's Commentary: A Linear Translation into English*, trans. Rabbi Abraham Ben Isaiah and Rabbi Benjamin Sharfman (Brooklyn, N.Y.: S.S. and R. Publishing Co., 1949).

15. Jacobus de Voragine, *The Golden Legend*, trans. William Caxton (London: Dent, 1900), 1:170.

16. All citations from Chaucer are to *The Riverside Chaucer*, ed. Larry D. Benson, 3rd ed. (Boston: Houghton Mifflin, 1987).

17. For the analogues of this interpretation in the Jewish commentarial tradition, see Gilbert Dahan, "Interprétations juives chez Pierre le Chantre," in *The Bible in the Medieval World: Essays in Memory of Beryl Smalley*, ed. Katherine Walsh and Diana Wood (Oxford: Blackwell, 1985), pp. 136 and 144. Philo gives a specifically sexual interpretation of the division from an original unity, applying it to the Creation of Adam and Eve: see Richard A. Baer, Jr., *Philo's Use of the Categories Male and Female* (Leiden: E. J. Brill, 1970), pp. 36–37.

18. See, e.g., Remigius of Auxerre, *Commentarius in Genesin* (*PL* 131:63).
Bede notes the grammatical aspect of the standard comparison between the creations of Eve and the Church (*PL* 91:51–52; copied by Rabanus, *PL* 107:485): just as Adam "wished the woman created from his flesh to become the sharer of his own name [*nominis sui participem*]," so Christ offered the partaking of his own name [*participium sui nominis*] so that the Christian might be named after Him. (There is probably a hint here of the grammatical meaning of "participium," i.e., "participle.") The best edition of the text is Bede, *Libri quatuor in principium Genesis . . .* , ed. Charles W. Jones, *Corpus Christianorum, Series Latina*, 118A (Turnholt: Brepols, 1967), p. 57.

19. *De Gen. contra Man.* 2.13 (*PL* 34:206); also see pseudo-Eucherius, *PL* 50:909. Isidore comments on the differences in meaning between *virgo* and *virago*, in his *Differentiae* (*PL* 83:68); also see *Etymologiae* 11.2.22. His remarks are copied in the later medieval dictionaries of Papias (see, e.g., B. L. MS Harl. 2735, fol. 196) and Johannes Balbi de Janua (B. L. MS Stowe 981, fol. 313).

20. See Jerome's comments in *Liber Hebraicarum Quaestionum in Genesim, PL* 23:942; Bede (*PL* 91:52) notes the parallel with the Hebrew

wordplay (copied by Rabanus Maurus, *PL* 107:485); also see Peter Comestor (*PL* 198:1070–71), and Abelard, in Jean Barthélémy Hauréau, *Notices et Extraits de quelques manuscrits latins de la Bibliothèque Nationale* (Paris: C. Klincksieck, 1892), 5:243.

21. For the *Vocabularium Biblicum* of Guilelmus Brito, see, e.g., B. L. MS Additional 10350, fol. 191; for the *Catholicon* of Johannes Balbi de Janua, see B. L. MS Stowe 981, fol. 313. Also see Nicholas Trivet, *Chronicles*, B. L. MS Arundel 56, fol. 2ᵛ.

22. Nicholas of Lyra, *Expositiones librorum Veteris et Novi Testamenti* (Rome: C. Sweynheim and A. Parmartz, 1471). Nicholas seems to be quoting at this point from the twelfth-century commentary of Andrew of St. Victor (Corpus Christi College, Cambridge, MS 30, fol. 7).

23. There are pictorial representations of the serpent with a woman's face in the works of the Boucicaut Master, in the *Tres Riches Heures* of the Duc de Berry, in the Chapter House of Salisbury Cathedral, and in one of the roof bosses in Norwich Cathedral.

24. Milton exploits most effectively the potential puns have as mirrors of dissimilitude. Milton's modern critics have pointed out the importance of punning and etymological wordplay as a demarcation of the Fall in *Paradise Lost:* see Arnold Stein, *Milton's Answerable Style* (Minneapolis: University of Minnesota Press, 1953), pp. 66–67, on "error"; Christopher Ricks, *Milton's Grand Style* (Oxford: Clarendon Press, 1963), p. 66, quoting Landor: " 'It appears then on record that the first overt crime of the refractory angels was *punning:* they fell rapidly after that' "; and Stanley Eugene Fish, *Surprised by Sin* (New York: St. Martin's Press, 1967).

25. Bede says that Adam names her Eve "by divine instinct" [divino instinctu] (*PL* 91:60) (copied by Rabanus, *PL* 107:499), and that the name is appropriate to Holy Church as the gate to life. (Cf. Augustine, *PL* 34:215 and 450–51). Bede presumably has in mind Ephesians 5.31–32, which reads Gen. 2.24 as a mystery of Christ and the Church.

26. *The Middle English Genesis and Exodus*, ed. Olof Arngart, Lund Studies in English 36 (Lund: C. W. K. Gleerup, 1968), p. 60. (I have normalized the spelling of th.) The poet seems, in line 235, to be suggesting an etymological link between "mayden" and "mad of man," to complement the Hebrew and Latin ones.

27. Martin Luther, *Uber das Erst Buch Mose* (Wittemberg, 1527), fol. 52ᵛ.

28. Isidore of Seville, *Etymologiae*, 7.6.5–6; copied by Huguccio of Pisa, *Liber Derivationum* (B. L. MS Additional 18380, fol. 38ᵛ) and Johannes Balbi de Janua (B. L. MS Stowe 981, fol. 136ᵛ); also see pseudo-Eucherius, *PL* 50:909 and Bodl. MS 186, fol. 87ᵛ. The wordplay here is

complicated. Isidore elsewhere uses the same sentence "A cadendo enim nomen sumpsit calamitas" to explain the orthographical substitution of "calamitas" for the earlier "cadamitas" (1.27.14). And he so explains the word for grammatical "case": "Casus a cadendo dicti; per eos enim inflexa nomina variantur et cadunt" [Cases are named from "falling" or "ending"; for by them inflected nouns are changed and terminate] (1.7.31).

29. Paul Lehmann, *Die Parodie im Mittelalter* (1922; rpt. Stuttgart: A. Hiersemann, 1963), pp. 53, 108. These examples and many others are catalogued by John A. Alford, "The Grammatical Metaphor: A Survey of Its Use in the Middle Ages," *Speculum* 57 (1982): 728–60. Also see Jan Ziolkowski, *Alan of Lille's Grammar of Sex: The Meaning of Grammar to a Twelfth-Century Intellectual,* Speculum Anniversary Monographs 10 (Cambridge, Mass.: Mediaeval Academy of America, 1985), pp. 66 and 74.

30. A number of examples of this wordplay on "Eva" and "Ave" have been assembled by Yrjö Hirn, *The Sacred Shrine* (1912: rpt. Boston: Beacon Press, 1957), pp. 520–21. Also see Ernst Guldan, *Eva und Maria* (Graz-Köln: Böhlau, 1966); and Rosemary Woolf, *The English Religious Lyric in the Middle Ages* (Oxford: Clarendon Press, 1968), pp. 115–16.

31. Lotario dei Segni (Pope Innocent III), *De Miseria Condicionis Humanae,* ed. Robert E. Lewis (Athens: The University of Georgia Press, 1978), pp. 102–03. The editor notes (p. 288) that most manuscripts of the work read the fourth sentence "Quid est igitur 'Eva' nisi heu a?" This explanation of babies' cries appears in Peter Comestor (*PL* 198:1071), who is quoted by Guilelmus Brito, *Vocabularium Biblicum,* B. L. MS Additional 10350, fol. 1ᵛ. Also see Stephen Langton, *Expositio moralis,* Paris B. N. lat. 14414, fol. 116ᵛ; and the late thirteenth-century translation of Peter Comestor in the *Bible Historiale* of Guyart Desmoulins: e.g., B. L. MS Harley 4381, fol. 8; and B. L. MS Royal 17.E.VII, fols. 7ᵛ–8.

32. Peter Riga, *Aurora,* ed. Paul E. Beichner, C.S.C., University of Notre Dame Publications in Medieval Studies 19 (Notre Dame, Ind.: University of Notre Dame Press, 1965), 1:39 (vv. 321–28).

33. *De Vulgari Eloquentia* 1.4, in *Opere Minori,* ed. Alberto del Monte (Milan: A. Vallardi, 1946), pp. 531–32; trans. Robert S. Haller, *Literary Criticism of Dante Alighieri* (Lincoln: University of Nebraska Press, 1973), p. 7.

34. Richard Verstegan, *A Restitution of Decayed Intelligence* (Antwerp: Robert Bruney, 1605), p. 194. This etymology survives in Noah Webster's *American Dictionary of the English Language* (1828): see Dennis Baron, *Grammar and Gender,* p. 33.

35. *The Chester Mystery Cycle,* ed. R. M. Lumiansky and David Mills, EETS S.S. 3 (London: Oxford University Press, 1974), p. 24.

36. Robert Southey, *The Doctor* 7:77, quoted by Dennis Baron, *Grammar and Gender*, p. 39.

37. Chaucer's procedure in quoting Jerome was unraveled by Germaine Dempster, "Chaucer at Work on the Complaint in *The Franklin's Tale*," *Modern Language Notes*, 52 (1937): 16–23.

38. The phrase "sone of Eve" has usually been understood as a vestige of Chaucer's own voice, since as he implies in the *Prologue* to the *Legend of Good Women* (F 426), he had translated the life of Saint Cecilia before he began work on the *Canterbury Tales*. But the Second Nun could also thus refer to herself: see Florence H. Ridley's note to v. 62 in the *Riverside Chaucer*. It is at least true, in the context of St. Cecilia's version of female heroism, that the masculinization of the female has a particular aptness: it is noticeably a feature of early narratives of Christian women's martyrdom, and indeed, of most defenses of women—such as Boccaccio's or Thomas Elyot's—through the Renaissance. St. Perpetua, strikingly, dreams of her approaching death in the arena: "My clothes were stripped off, and suddenly I was a man [facta sum masculus]": *The Acts of the Christian Martyrs*, ed. Herbert Musurillo (Oxford: Clarendon Press, 1972), pp. 118–19. There are also some notable efforts among early Christian writers to describe saintly women as essentially male. See Elizabeth Castelli, "Virginity and Its Meaning for Women's Sexuality in Early Christianity," *Journal of Feminist Studies in Religion* 2, 1 (1986): 61–88. Castelli notes that "Many of the ascetic women whose stories remain are considered laudable because they escaped the bonds of their feminine nature: thus, Olympias and Melania are both called *hē anthrōpos* (the [feminine article] hu/man [generic, masculine noun])" (p. 75). And, citing Cora Lutz's work on Musonius, she argues that the description of female courage as *andreia* probably has the connotation of "manliness" (p. 77). On this latter issue, also see Elizabeth A. Clark, "The Virginal *Politeia* and Plato's *Republic*," in *Jerome, Chrysostom, and Friends: Essays and Translations* (New York and Toronto: Edwin Mellen, 1979), pp. 15 and 19; and in the same volume, "Friendship Between the Sexes," pp. 56–57. There are some very interesting comments on this issue as it pertains to later medieval women's spirituality in Bynum, *Holy Feast and Holy Fast*, p. 263; p. 380, n. 171; and p. 417, n. 47.

Given the tone of the work, Boccaccio appropriately dedicates *De Mulieribus Claris* to Andrea Acciaiuoli: because of "the name you bear (since in Greek *andres* means 'men'), I felt that you should be set equal to the worthiest of men, even among the ancients." *Concerning Famous Women*, trans. Guido A. Guarino (New Brunswick, N.J.: Rutgers University Press, 1963), pp. xxxiii–iv.

39. Both "womanly" and "womanish," in the Middle English examples given by the *OED*, can have either favorable or unfavorable connotations: indeed, one of the *Troilus* manuscripts reads "womanliche" for "wommanysshe" at 4.694. "Womanish" is the more likely to be straight-

forwardly derogatory; and Chaucer seems to make a distinction between the two words by reserving "womanly" for favorable contexts.

40. *A Chaucer Glossary*, ed. Norman Davis et al. (Oxford: Clarendon Press, 1979), glosses the phrase "mannysh wood," I think incorrectly, as "man–mad." It seems more likely to mean "mad in a violently masculine manner." The more recent gloss also appears in the *Middle English Dictionary* and as a possible gloss in the *Riverside Chaucer*; it was proposed by Francis L. Utley, "Mannysch Wood—*Merchant's Tale* (IV) 1530–1536," *Modern Language Notes* 53 (1938): 359–62. For examples of the older gloss, see the *OED* and the editions of Skeat and Robinson.

41. Thomas Usk, *The Testament of Love*, in *Chaucerian and Other Pieces*, ed. Walter W. Skeat (London: Oxford University Press, 1897), p. 54, lines 34–36, and p. 56, lines 90–92.

42. Baldesar Castiglione, *The Book of the Courtier*, trans. Charles S. Singleton (Garden City, N.Y.: Anchor Books, 1959), p. 193. Castiglione has some interesting remarks on the relation between the species man [l'omo], male and female, and Genesis 1.26: see pp. 216–17.

43. See *Chaucer and Ovid* (New Haven: Yale University Press, 1979), pp. 96–123.

44. See *Le Livre des Faicts du Mareschal de Boucicaut*, ed. J. F. Michaut and J. J. P. Poujoulat, ser. 1, vol. 2, Nouvelle collection des mémoires . . . (Paris, 1836; reprinted Lyon: Guyot, 1851), p. 507: " . . . tout chevalier est tenu de droict de vouloir garder et deffendre l'honneur, l'estat, les biens, la renommée et la loüange de toutes dames et damoiselles de noble lignée."

45. Carla Bozzolo and Hélène Loyau, *La Cour Amoureuse Dite de Charles VI* (Paris: Léopard D'Or, 1982), p. 42.
There is a very interesting account of the issues involved here by Richard F. Green, "Chaucer's Victimized Women," *Studies in the Age of Chaucer* 10 (1988): pp. 3–21.

46. "Domesticating the Exotic in the *Squire's Tale*," *ELH* 55 (1988): 1–26.

47. For a fuller discussion of this passage, see "Domesticating the Exotic," pp. 15–17.

48. See Marie-Thérèse d'Alverny, "Comment les théologiens et les philosophes voient la femme," *Cahiers de Civilisation Médiévale* 20 (1977): 105–129, for a masterly account relevant to many of the issues I have discussed in this essay. Among other texts, she cites Rupert of Deutz's discussion of the spiritual equality of men and women, both included within the noun "homo," both created in God's image (p. 121). Wayne A. Meeks has a fascinating discussion of androgyny as a symbol of

the time before sexual division, and the image of its possible transcendence: "The Image of the Androgyne: Some Uses of a Symbol in Earliest Christianity," *History of Religions* 13 (1973–74): 165–208; and he mentions a rabbinical text of Genesis 1.27 that reads "male and female he created *him*" (p. 185). Augustine's discussion of Gen. 1.27, in *De Genesi ad Litteram* 3.22 (see d'Alverny, p. 109), rejects the idea of an original hermaphrodite, and proclaims that woman too is created in God's image, but paraphrases this passage, oddly, as "Fecit illum masculum et feminam" [He made him male and female].

49. Lee Patterson, " 'For the Wyves love of Bathe': Feminine Rhetoric and Poetic Resolution in the *Roman de la Rose* and the *Canterbury Tales*," *Speculum* 58 (1983): 689.

50. Cf. Monica McAlpine's comment on this passage: *The Genre of Troilus and Criseyde* (Ithaca, N.Y.: Cornell University Press), p. 234.

51. The classic statement of these ambivalences in the ending remains E. Talbot Donaldson, "The Ending of 'Troilus,' " in *Speaking of Chaucer* (London: Athlone Press, 1970), pp. 84–101.

CHAPTER 10

1. D. W. Robertson, Jr., *A Preface to Chaucer* (Princeton, N.J.: Princeton University Press, 1962), p. 278; Henrik Specht, *Chaucer's Franklin in the Canterbury Tales*, Publications of the Department of English, University of Copenhagen, 10 (Copenhagen: Akademisk Forlag, 1981), p. 146; Derek Pearsall, *The Canterbury Tales*, Unwin Critical Library (London: George Allen & Unwin, 1985), p. 150.

2. George Lyman Kittredge, *Chaucer and His Poetry* (Cambridge, Mass.: Harvard University Press, 1915), p. 155.

3. "The Promises in the Franklin's Tale," *English Literary History* 31 (1964): 334.

4. Nicolas Jacobs, review of Gerald Morgan, ed., *Geoffrey Chaucer: the Franklin's Tale, Medium Aevum* 52 (1983): 126.

5. All quotations from Chaucer's works are taken from Larry D. Benson, gen. ed., *The Riverside Chaucer*, 3rd ed. (Boston: Houghton Mifflin, 1987).

6. John M. Manly and Edith Rickert, eds., *The Text of the Canterbury Tales, Studied on the Basis of All Known Manuscripts* (Chicago: University of Chicago Press, 1940), 4:488.

7. David Lawton, *Chaucer's Narrators*, Chaucer Studies 12 (Cambridge: D. S. Brewer, 1985), p. 98. See his useful bibliographic review in n.5 to ch. 4, "Voices of Performance," pp. 153–54. His "A Modern Preface," along with ch. 1, "Apocryphal Voices," pp. ix–xiv and 1–16, provides one of the better medieval/modern/post-modern illuminations of the theoretical questions behind "the oral and the written" (p. 16).

8. The richest illustrations of the speaker-who-writes and the writer-who-speaks, of course, occur in the *Troilus*. See also Alan T. Gaylord, "The Moment of *Sir Thopas:* Towards a New Look at Chaucer's Language," *The Chaucer Review* 16 (1982): especially 322–23.

9. The strongest opposing view is that of N. F. Blake. As part of his attempt to dismantle the textual authority of the Ellesmere ms. and stand with the Hengwrt, he argues that "scribes were quite willing and able to turn out lines in the Chaucerian manner to fill in what they considered gaps in the poem" (*The Textual Tradition of the Canterbury Tales* [London: Edward Arnold, 1985], p. 56). The passage I have quoted in this section he believes "may almost certainly be ascribed to its scribe" (p. 141). He does not discuss the miracle of literary history he has discovered: the existence of one—or several!—ghost-writers, composing in small fragments with pungent wit, yet apparently never writing a full scale composition of their own. (His opinion of the passage, however, is—tendentiously?—much lower than mine: "rather fussy moral comment" [p. 197]).

10. Germaine Dempster, *Dramatic Irony in Chaucer*, Stanford University Publications, University Series, Language and Literature, 4, 3 (Stanford, Ca.: Stanford University Press, 1932), p. 65.

11. Here I put in a note what deserves treatment in a separate essay: the extent to which my terms, "reading forwards" and "reading backwards," might be related to postmodern theories of the text. Certainly, the later writings of Roland Barthes suggest certain affinities, as with *S/Z*'s development of the concept of "readerly" and "writerly" texts; and yet I would recommend caution. The deconstruction that is suggested in my essay would hardly merit notice in the pages of *Tel Quel*. Insofar as I treat the "reading forwards" process as reaching a goal of meaning that is discoverable, fixed, and authoritarian (in the several senses of the word), one could cite Barthes's concept of "the text of pleasure . . . linked to a *comfortable* practice of reading" (*The Pleasure of the Text*, trans. Richard Miller [New York: Hill and Wang, 1975], p. 14). The problem comes with the second term, "reading backwards." Barthes has described "The Death of the Author" (in *Image, Music, Text*, ed. and trans. Stephen Heath [New York: Hill and Wang, 1977], pp. 142–48); and the *signifiance* he looks for in the perusal of modern texts does not permit an authorial rhetoric to become a partner with the reader's perverse play (*Pleasure of the Text*, pp. 12, 39; "From Work to Text," *Textual Strategies: Perspectives in Post-Structuralist Criticism*, ed. and trans. Josue V. Harani [Ithaca, N.Y.: Cornell University Press, 1979], pp. 76, 78, 79; "Theory of the Text," trans.

Stephen Heath, in *Untying the Text: A Post-Structuralist Reader*, ed. Robert Young [Boston: Routledge & Kegan Paul, 1981], p. 37). As I understand Barthes, my "reading backwards," for whatever else it might come to, will not come to *jouissance*.

12. See also Robert. B. Burlin, *Chaucerian Fiction* (Princeton, N.J.: Princeton University Press, 1977), p. 67; Russell A. Peck, "Sovereignty and the Two Worlds of the *Franklin's Tale*," *The Chaucer Review* 1 (1967): 259–60; D. W. Robertson, Jr., "Chaucer's Franklin and his Tale," *Costerus* n.s. 1 (1974): 20–21; J. Terry Frazier, "The Digression on Marriage in the *Franklin's Tale*," *South Atlantic Bulletin* 43 (1978): 77–79; Robert P. Miller, "Augustinian Wisdom and Eloquence in the F-Fragment of the *Canterbury Tales*," *Mediaevalia* 4 (1978): 265; Jacobs, p. 130; Paul Olson, *The Canterbury Tales and the Good Society* (Princeton, N.J.: Princeton University Press, 1986), pp. 271, 274.

13. Here I believe I am sophisticating my earlier position, where I spoke of a tale's being "turned back against its teller" ("The Promises in the Franklin's Tale," p. 334); for reading backwards dissolves (deconstructs) the fictional composites of the forwards-narrative.

14. Donald R. Howard, *The Idea of the Canterbury Tales* (Berkeley: University of California Press, 1976), p. 268.

15. Jill Mann, "Chaucerian Themes and Style in the *Franklin's Tale*," *The New Pelican Guide to English Literature* 1. Medieval Literature, Part One: Chaucer and the Alliterative Tradition, ed. Boris Ford (Harmondsworth: Penguin Books, rev. ed. 1982), p. 135.

16. See, for example, Kittredge, pp. 209–10; Paul G. Ruggiers, *The Art of the Canterbury Tales* (Madison, Wis.: University of Wisconsin Press, 1965), pp. 227–28; Gertrude M. White, "The Franklin's Tale: Chaucer or the Critics," *Publications of the Modern Language Association* 89 (1974): 456, 461; Mary J. Carruthers, "The Gentilesse of Chaucer's Franklin," *Criticism* 23 (1981): 293–94; Mann, p. 152; Kathryn Jacobs, "The Marriage Contract of the *Franklin's Tale*: The Remaking of Society," *The Chaucer Review* 20 (1985): 134, 142; Pearsall, pp. 158–60.

17. Cf. Effie Jean Mathewson: "Arveragus cannot literally be accused of assuming mastery over Dorigen against her will. But in fact he is Dorigen's master. He commands and Dorigen obeys" ("The Illusion of Morality in the Franklin's Tale," *Medium Aevum* 52 [1983]: 31).

18. Alfred David, *The Strumpet Muse: Art and Morals in Chaucer's Poetry* (Bloomington: Indiana University Press, 1976), p. 183.

19. pp. 267–68, citing Chiapelli's *Opere* 235.

20. Benjamin S. Harrison, "The Rhetorical Inconsistency of Chaucer's Franklin," *Studies in Philology* 32 (1935): 61.

21. Constance R. Wright, "On the Franklin's Prologue, 716–721, Persius, and the Continuity of the Mannerist Style," *Philological Quarterly* 52 (1973): 741–42 and 743–45. The marginal glosses in some mss. that cite Persius must be discounted as knee-jerk pedantry or its parody. For a witty reading that nonetheless concentrates on Persius, see Miller, p. 249.

22. To provide a more sophisticated literary and historical context for Specht's apologetics see Roy J. Pearcy, "Chaucer's Franklin and the Literary Vavasour," *The Chaucer Review* 8 (1973): 36, 53; Robertson, "Chaucer's Franklin and his Tale," p. 20; P. R. Coss, "Literature and Social Terminology: The Vavasour·in England," *Social Relations and Ideas: Essays in Honour of R. H. Hilton*, ed. T. H. Aston *et al.* (Cambridge: Cambridge University Press, 1983): 148; Nigel Saul, "The Social Status of Chaucer's Franklin: A Reconsideration," *Medium Aevum* 52 (1983): 14, 21, 25 (n. 67); and Olson, pp. 264–66.

23. Cf. Kittredge: " . . . the Pilgrims do not exist for the sake of the stories, but *vice versa*. Structurally regarded, the stories are merely long speeches expressing, directly or indirectly, the characters of the several persons" (p. 155).

24. Or more: consider Robertson's sweeping statement, that "Chaucer had no way of knowing that the spiritual descendants of the Franklin would one day rule the world" (*Preface to Chaucer*, p. 472)!

CHAPTER 11

1. "Supertext" is a happy coinage of John V. Fleming, *Reason and the Lover* (Princeton, N.J.: Princeton University Press, 1984), pp. 69–70. As he says, the concept "has a particular vitality with regard to medieval literary culture, which in many ways fostered real or feigned subservience of original genius to literary authority and encouraged complex patterns of literary dependence, appropriation, imitation, and what in our day would be downright plagiarism." The discussion here will show that the *Roman de la Rose* and *Remede de Fortune* add their weight to the *Consolation* to form an especially powerful supertext for the Boethian situations in Chaucer's *Troilus*. For the Boethian affinities of Pandarus, see Alan T. Gaylord, "Uncle Pandarus as Lady Philosophy," *Papers of the Michigan Academy of Science, Arts and Letters*, 46 (1961), 571–95.

2. References to Chaucer follow *The Riverside Chaucer*, ed. Larry D. Benson, 3rd ed. (Boston: Houghton Mifflin, 1987). The *Consolation* is quoted from the translation by Richard H. Green, *Boethius: The Consolation of Philosophy*, The Library of Liberal Arts (New York: Bobbs-Merrill, 1962). The text of the *Roman* cited is Félix Lecoy, ed., *Le Roman de la Rose*, 3 vols. (Paris: Champion, 1970). The text of *Remede de Fortune* is

found in Ernest Hœpffner, ed., *Oeuvres de Guillaume de Machaut*, 3 vols., Société des Anciens Textes Français (Paris: Firmin-Didot, 1908–21), II; the translation quoted is that of James I. Wimsatt and William W. Kibler from their edition, *Le Jugement du roy de Behaigne* and *Remede de Fortune*, The Chaucer Library (Athens, Ga.: University of Georgia Press, 1988).

3. See Fleming, *Reason and the Lover*, pp. 56–63.

4. Though Machaut's description attributes numinous aspects to Esperance, the theological virtue of Hope is not primarily in question in the *Remede*; Esperance in action embodies the lover's aspiration for a worldly object.

5. For Chaucer's use of the *Remede* in *Troilus*, see James I. Wimsatt, "Guillaume de Machaut and Chaucer's *Troilus and Criseyde*," *Medium Aveum*, 45 (1976): 277–93.

6. In adapting elements of Boethius's treatise to an entirely new dialogue, Machaut perhaps was inspired by the appearance of Nature in Alan of Lille's *Complaint of Nature*. At the same time that Alan's opening situation is clearly based on the *Consolation*, his use of the Boethian elements is quite original.

7. See *Roman*, II. 4709–12; *De Spirituali Amicitia*, 2:28–40, 69; *De Amicitia*, 37, 40. Aelred is quoted herein from Aelred of Rievaulx, *Spiritual Friendship*, trans. Mary Eugenia Laker, SSND, Cistercian Fathers Series 5 (Kalamazoo: Cistercian Publications, 1974); Latin text, *Aelredi Rievallensis, Opera Omnia*, I, *Opera Ascetica*, ed. A. Hoste, *Corpus Christianorum, Continuatio Mediaevalis*, I (Turnholt: Brepols, 1971), pp. 279–350.

8. While all of the examples of friendship in Cicero's *De Amicitia* involve only males, several in Aelred's treatise in addition to Adam and Eve concern females. See *De Spirituali Amicitia*, 1:29 (Theodora of Alexandria); 3:47 (Jael); and 3:100 (Ruth). Aelred's discussions, furthermore, often seem to assume male-female relationships; see, e.g., 1:35–42, 55; 11:23–24, 40. Other Christian writers also recognized the possibility of female friendship; see, e.g., St. Ambrose, *De Officiis Ministrorum Libri III, PL*, 16: 189–90 (Esther).

9. Jean's Raison does recognize the possibility of a proper relationship between lovers, different from that which the Amant feels. See *Roman*, 11.4567–69.

10. "With regard to friendship, the most sacred kind belongs to the goods of virtue, not of Fortune." Book III, Prose 2.

11. Jean's postulation of the opposition between Mastery and Love, interestingly, itself probably originates in a quite different context in the

Metamorphoses. When Jove is about to descend to make love to Europa, says Ovid, he assumed the shape of a bull, since "non bene conveniunt nec in una sede morantur / maiestas et amor" (11.847–48).

12. George L. Kittredge, *Chaucer and His Poetry* (Cambridge, Mass.: Harvard University Press, 1915), p. 185.

13. The dependability of Reason's statements is strongly argued by Fleming in *Reason and the Lover*, as well as in his earlier *The Roman de la Rose* (Princeton, N.J.: Princeton University Press, 1969).

CHAPTER 12

1. *The Riverside Chaucer*, gen. ed. Larry Benson, 3rd ed. (Boston: Houghton Mifflin, 1987), VII, 467–72. All subsequent quotations from Chaucer's works are taken from this edition.

2. *The Myroure of oure Ladye*, EETS ES 19 (1873), ed. John Henry Blunt, p. 296.

3. The word *ravyshedest* in its primary senses suggests "took by force," and, most extremely, "raped." James Winny, for example, glosses the word as "seized, took possession of" (*The Prioress' Prologue and Tale* [Cambridge: Cambridge University Press, 1975]). Even rendered in its mildest sense as "drew, attracted," this word attributes a far more active role to Mary than she has in the Gospel story (compare Latin *raptus* and Paul's use of the word in 2 Cor. 12. 1–4). The verb *lighten* means not only "make light, render cheerful" or "illumine," the possible renderings in Robinson, or "cheer, gladden," the gloss in the *Chaucer Glossary*, but also "set on fire." These senses, following the image of the burning bush, sustain the paradox of sexualized asexuality that characterizes the passion of the prayer.

4. D. S. Brewer, *Chaucer* (London: Longmans, 1953; reprint. ed. 1961), p. 151.

5. E. T. Donaldson, *Chaucer's Poetry* (New York: Ronald Press, 1958; reprint ed. 1975), p. 1096.

6. Alan T. Gaylord, "The Unconquered Tale of the Prioress," *Papers of the Michigan Academy of Science, Arts, and Letters* 47 (1962): 632; Ian Robinson, *Chaucer and the English Tradition* (Cambridge: Cambridge University Press, 1972), p. 153.

7. D.W. Robertson, Jr., *A Preface to Chaucer* (Princeton, N.J.: Princeton University Press, 1962), p. 246.

8. Gordon H. Harper, "Chaucer's Big Prioress," *Philological Quarterly* 12 (1933): 310.

9. Muriel Bowden, *A Commentary on the General Prologue to the Canterbury Tales* (London: Macmillan & Co., 1948; 2nd ed. 1969), p. 95; Donaldson, *Chaucer's Poetry*, p. 1044; John Block Friedman, "The Prioress's Beads 'Of Smal Coral,'" *Medium Aevum*, 39 (1970): 301; cf. Thomas Blake Clark, "Forehead of Chaucer's Prioress," *Philological Quarterly*, 9 (1930): 312–14.

10. Sister M. Madeleva, "Chaucer's Nuns" in *Chaucer's Nuns and Other Essays* (New York: D. Appleton, 1925), pp. 21 ff.

11. G. K. Chesterton, *Chaucer* (London: Faber & Faber, 1932; reprint ed., 1965), pp. 202–3.

12. John Livingston Lowes, "Simple and Coy," *Anglia* 33 (1910): 440–51.

13. Madeleva, pp. 13–15.

14. Bowden, p. 99; Jill Mann adds that medieval satirists traditionally contrasted excessive tenderness for animals with indifference to human suffering (*Chaucer and Medieval Estates Satire* [Cambridge: Cambridge University Press, 1973], p. 132).

15. John M. Steadman, "The Prioress' Dogs and Benedictine Discipline," *Modern Philology* 54 (1956): 3.

16. Robertson, p. 246.

17. Chauncey Wood, "Chaucer's Use of Signs in His Portrait of the Prioress," in *Signs and Symbols in Chaucer's Poetry*, eds. John P. Hermann and John J. Burke, Jr. (University, Alabama: University of Alabama Press, 1981), pp. 89–91.

18. George Lyman Kittredge, *Chaucer and His Poetry* (Cambridge, Mass.: Harvard University Press, 1925), pp. 175–78.

19. Chesterton, p. 171; Nevill Coghill, *The Poet Chaucer* (London: Oxford University Press, 1949), pp. 22, 138.

20. Florence H. Ridley, *The Prioress and the Critics* (Berkeley and Los Angeles: University of California Press, 1965), p. 2.

21. John Livingston Lowes, "The Prioress's Oath," *Romanic Review* 5 (1914): 368; "Simple and Coy," 442.

22. Sister Madeleva says that the tale tells just the sort of story "that Sisters are telling to the smaller and even the grown children in Catholic boarding schools the world over to-day ... that the children clamor for again and again and never tire of hearing" (pp. 37–38). Robert Kilburn Root, in discussing the Prioress's tale in 1906, attributed the "senseless persecution" of the Jews in European history to the "fact" that

the Jews were rich while the Christians were poor. He added that the Christians' belief in the Jews' murderous practices "could hardly have sprung up without some sort of foundation" in fact (*The Poetry of Chaucer*, [Boston: Houghton Mifflin, 1906], p. 191)! Thomas R. Lounsbury, by contrast, as early as 1891 denounced the "folly and fanaticism" that underlie the tale (*Studies in Chaucer* [New York: Harper & Brothers, 1891; reprint ed., 1962], 2:490–91).

23. R. J. Schoeck, "Chaucer's Prioress: Mercy and Tender Heart," in *Chaucer Criticism*, eds. Richard Schoeck and Jerome Taylor (Notre Dame: Notre Dame Books, 1960; reprint ed. 1965), I, 245–58; George K. Anderson, "*Beowulf*, Chaucer, and Their Backgrounds," in *Contemporary Literary Scholarship*, ed. Lewis Leary (New York: Appleton-Century-Crofts, 1958), p. 41. The term "antisemitism" is appropriate to a modern rather than a medieval context; see n. 51 below.

24. Donaldson notes that unlike the narrowly limited Prioress, Chaucer, an intelligent man and a great poet, was in no way limited (*Chaucer's Poetry*, p. 1097). Ian Robinson (p. 152) says that it would be surprising if a responsible public servant like Chaucer were as simpleminded and savage as the Prioress. Alfred David, drawing the valid analogy between the tale and a fairy story, says that Chaucer, unlike the Prioress, is "very much aware that fairy-tale justice and Christian mercy are incompatible" (*The Strumpet Muse* [Bloomington: Indiana University Press, 1976], p. 209); Donald R. Howard in *The Idea of the Canterbury Tales* (Berkeley: University of California Press, 1976), p. 277, says that it is out of the question that the tolerant, open-minded, and empathetic Chaucer could have failed to note the Prioress's moral blindness.

25. Ridley, pp. 5ff.; Albert B. Friedman, "The *Prioress's Tale* and Chaucer's Anti-Semitism," *Chaucer Review* 9 (1974–75): 118–29.

26. Brewer, p. 151; David, p. 207; Robert Worth Frank, Jr., observes that anti-Semitism is a standard constituent element in the Miracle of the Virgin genre ("Miracles of the Virgin, Medieval Anti-Semitism, and the 'Prioress's Tale,'" in *The Wisdom of Poetry: Essays in Early English Literature in Honor of Morton W. Bloomfield*, eds. Larry D. Benson and Siegfried Wenzel [Kalamazoo: Medieval Institute Publications, 1982]), p. 179.

27. Frank also cites examples of tolerance and benevolence toward Jews, however. See his "Chaucer's Prioress and the Blessed Virgin," *Chaucer Review* 13 (1978–79): 355, 358. Compare Schoeck, pp. 255–56, and Howard, p. 279.

28. See Lee Patterson, *Negotiating the Past* (Madison: University of Wisconsin Press, 1987), ch. 1. Patterson asserts (p. 74) that the *Canterbury Tales* stood in ideological opposition to the dominant formations of its period. I take this to support the contention I develop below that Chaucer need not have shared in the prevailing intolerance of his time.

29. James Parkes observes that Christian texts had, since the early days of the Church, portrayed Jews not in terms of their contemporary relationships or circumstances, but rather in accordance with their Scriptural roles (*The Conflict of the Church and the Synagogue* [New York: Atheneum, 1969; reprint ed. 1977], pp. 220, 374f.) In Augustine's formulation, the Jew remained doctrinally "stationary in useless antiquity." This characterization of the Jew as frozen in time applied, of course, to the characterization itself. By the thirteenth century, however, Church scholars had to respond to the realization that Judaism had in fact evolved since the first century; see Jeremy Cohen's "Scholarship and Intolerance in the Medieval Academy: The Study and Evaluation of Judaism in European Christendom," *American Historical Review* 91 (1986): 592–613.

30. This argument differs in emphasis from Donaldson's in his famous essay "Chaucer the Pilgrim," which reaches somewhat different conclusions about the distinctions between Chaucer the pilgrim, the poet, and the man. Though these three figures bore a close resemblance to one another and "frequently got together in the same body," Donaldson says, Chaucer the poet subsumed the other two. Interestingly, much of this discussion treats the portrayal of the Prioress. Donaldson asserts that Chaucer the man, like his pilgrim persona, would have found the Prioress charming; Chaucer the poet, by contrast, noted her many imperfections, and incorporated her inharmonious parts into an inseparable whole (*Publications of the Modern Language Society* 69 [1954]: 928–36; reprinted in *Speaking of Chaucer* [New York: W. W. Norton, 1970], pp. 1–12). Responses to Donaldson have included the observation that writers project some element of themselves into any character, and the question as to whether anyone knows his "real" self well enough to present or conceal it (see Donald R. Howard, "Chaucer the Man," *PMLA* 80 [1965]: 337–43; reprinted in *Chaucer's Mind and Art*, ed. A. C. Cawley [New York: Barnes and Noble, 1970], pp. 31–45). But the disjunction between the suggestion of the poet's personality in the text and the historical indications about Chaucer the man has also been noted. See, for example, George Kane, *Chaucer* (Oxford: Oxford University Press, 1984), pp. 9–10.

31. Gaylord (p. 631) cites the brutality of attitude, action, and imagery in the tale, and observes that the brutality of the Prioress's language in the tale "tends to belie the total softness and sweetness of the lady who swears by Saint Loy." Albert B. Friedman denies this, and argues that the line "I seye that in a wardrobe they hym threwe" (572) reveals the Prioress's "fastidious hesitation in mentioning this unpleasant but necessary detail" (p. 126). I disagree: the line can equally well be read as charged with indignation.

32. John Lawlor, *Chaucer* (London: Hutchinson University Library, 1968), p. 131.

33. Edward H. Kelly, "By Mouth of Innocentz: The Prioress Vindicated," *Papers on Language and Literature*, 5 (1969): 363. In this essay I

attempt to occupy a middle ground between Kittredge's claim (p. 155) that the tales exist for the sake of developing the pilgrims as characters, and more recent arguments that the pilgrims are not recognizably motivated characters. I contend that in portraying the Prioress, Chaucer developed a stock literary figure in surprising ways, in part by matching her with a tale that both inspired and complicated his characterization of her.

34. Donaldson, *Chaucer's Poetry*, p. 1097. Cf. Howard, who says that the Prioress's simplicity and air of elegance lead her into a deplorable frame of mind (p. 276).

35. Bertrand H. Bronson, *In Search of Chaucer* (Toronto: University of Toronto Press, 1960), p. 78.

36. Gaylord, p. 632; Robinson, p. 150.

37. See Marie Padgett Hamilton, "Echoes of Childermas in the Tale of the Prioress," in *Chaucer: Modern Essays in Criticism*, ed. Edward Wagenknecht (New York: Oxford University Press, 1959), 88–97.

38. Audrey Davidson notes the unusual beauty of the *Alma redemptoris mater* and its emphasis on the motherliness of Mary, factors that make the anthem appropriate in a tale told by Madame Eglentyne ("*Alma Redemptoris Mater:* The Little Clergeon's Song," *Studies in Medieval Culture* 4 [1974]: 459–66).

39. See Beverly Boyd, "Young Hugh of Lincoln and Chaucer's 'The Prioress's Tale,' " *The Radford Review* 14 (1960): 1–5.

40. Donald W. Fritz interprets this assertion in terms of the topos of the "inexpressible" in "The Prioress's Avowal of Ineptitude," *Chaucer Review* 9 (1974–75): 166–81.

41. Other scholars have also noted the Prioress's affinity with the child, but have reached different conclusions from mine. Gaylord, in his perceptive and good-humored "The Unconquered Tale of the Prioress" (p. 634), says that the Prioress keeps the tale at the emotional and intellectual level of a child, evidencing her "arrested development." Maurice Cohen says that Eglentyne's sado-masochism toward the Jews is anal-erotic ("Chaucer's Prioress and Her Tale, A Study of Anal Character and Anti-Semitism," *Psychoanalytic Quarterly* 31 [1962]: 232–49). Sherman Hawkins takes her spiritual childishness as the starting point for the clergeon too, and develops a learned patristic argument about the child's spiritual growth: the pit and the murder represent, he says, the literal understanding of Scripture and death to the law ("Chaucer's Prioress and the Sacrifice of Praise," *Journal of English and Germanic Philology* 63 [1964]: 599–624). Albert B. Friedman (pp. 124–25) concludes that the Prioress's sentimental sympathy with the clergeon leads her to enter too completely into the child's world and to identify with him. He attributes this only to a

lack of mature judgment, however, and rejects Gaylord's interpretation of arrested development; he adds that Bronson's assertion that sentimentality is the obverse of cruelty is not relevant here. George J. Engelhardt conjectures that the Prioress, assuming the persona of the child, imagines herself singing unto death the plaint of litigation over the redemption of her convent's liberties ("The Ecclesiastical Pilgrims of the *Canterbury Tales:* A Study in Ethology," *Mediaeval Studies* 37 [1975]: 292–93). And Robert W. Hanning adopts a very interesting feminist perspective, in which the Jews and the child's teachers represent male domination and authority, and the tale expresses the Prioress's vulnerability to men ("From *Eva* and *Ave* to Eglentyne and Alisoun: Chaucer's Insight into the Roles Women Play," *Signs* 2 [1977]: 580–99). I attribute to the Jews their more traditional religious significance.

42. As Gavin I. Langmuir says, psychological (as opposed to cognitive) explanations of intolerance rely heavily on the Freudian concepts of displacement and projection ("Prolegomena to Any Present Analysis of Hostility against Jews," *Social Science Information* 15 [1976]: 701). For a review of Sartre's use of this theory and its application to medieval Biblical drama, see Stephen Spector, "Anti-Semitism and the English Mystery Plays," in *The Drama of the Middle Ages*, eds. Clifford Davidson, C. J. Gianakaris, John H. Stroupe (New York: AMS Press, 1982), pp. 329–30. Freud himself proposed that anti-Semitism is projected resentment against the Church by the "badly christened": those who had Christianity forced on them and deal with their own hostility by identifying similar sentiments in the Jews and vilifying them for it. See Sigmund Freud, *Moses and Monotheism*, trans. Katherine Jones (New York: Vintage Books, 1939; reprint ed., 1967), pp. 116–17.

43. Spector, "Anti-Semitism and the English Mystery Plays," pp. 328–41.

44. One could argue in Derridean terms that the invagination of the text creates a marginal graft, thereby dislocating the text and undermining the narrative intention.

45. Hardy Long Frank, in his fine discussion of the ambiguity in Madame Eglentyne's name, cites two figurative references to the Virgin as the eglantine in the poetry of Gautier de Coinci. In the present context, however, the contrast between the floral symbols is appropriate to the dichotomy between the Prioress and Mary.

46. The Wife's impulse to join in marriages that inevitably result in struggle recalls the joining of restless elements in Chaucer's art itself.

47. Salo Wittmayor Baron comments that when considered as "a single list of pogroms and expulsions, the attacks on Jews appear indeed as an uninterrupted succession of catastrophes. But one must realize that during the thirteenth century (until 1290 in England and 1298 in Ger-

many) there were but relatively few local anti-Jewish attacks with little bearing on Jewish conditions elsewhere. . . . Only the Black Death generated a mass hysteria . . . which had ominous implications for the very survival of European Jewry. . . . However, the then most populous Jewish settlements in Spain, Sicily, southern France, and the Papal States, as well as in Bohemia, Hungary, and Poland, suffered relatively little" (*A Social and Religious History of the Jews*, 2nd ed. [New York: Columbia University Press; Philadelphia: Jewish Publication Society of America, 1967], 11:281–82).

48. Guido Kisch argues, however, that nationalism in the modern sense of the word did not influence the treatment of the medieval Jew (*The Jews in Medieval Germany* [Chicago: University of Chicago Press, 1949], pp. 335–37).

49. The Jews and the devil were represented as having a common interest in maintaining the old law. For popular beliefs about the Jews' supposed association with the devil and the Antichrist, see especially Joshua Trachtenberg, *The Devil and the Jews* (New Haven: Yale University Press, 1943).

50. Not all angels wear halos: Gentiles who risked their lives to save Jews during the 1940s sometimes seemed to be unlikely choices for their roles. Many Jews survived the Holocaust because of the protection of the German industrialist Oskar Schindler, for example. They had good reason to be grateful that the brave and resourceful—but not conventionally moral or religious—Schindler was more faithful to his Jews than to his wife; see Thomas Keneally, *Schindler's List* (New York: Simon and Schuster, 1982). The influence of the Protestant pastor André Trocmé constitutes a partial explanation of why the people of Le Chambon courageously protected Jewish children while other French villagers took no such risk; see Philip P. Hallie, *Lest Innocent Blood Be Shed* (New York: Harper & Row, 1979).

51. The etiology of modern anti-Semitism is complex and disputed, but I use the term here as a means of distinction from medieval anti-Jewishness. Langmuir (p. 691) asserts that the hostility against Jews about 1900 was very similar to the hostility about 1400; and to the recipient, hostility no doubt does feel the same regardless of its rationalization. But medieval hostility to Jewishness was in large measure theologically inspired: the putative defects it attributed to the Jew could, at least in theory, be washed away by baptism. The most virulent modern "anti-Semitism," by contrast, postulates Jewish racial inferiority that cannot be effaced. Hitler, for example, denounced religiously-based political anti-Jewishness as sham anti-Semitism (Lucy S. Dawidowicz, *The War against the Jews 1933–1945* [New York: Bantam Books, 1975; reprint ed., 1978], ch. 1). The term "anti-Semitism," in the sense that Hitler used it, would be anachronistic in discussing medieval attitudes. Another term, "Ritual

Blood Libel," is also inappropriate to the Prioress's tale, which does not refer to the ritualized slaughter of a Christian child at Passover. The genre of the tale is Miracle of the Virgin.

52. One cannot discover the essence of Jewish-Christian relations in a brief survey of the present kind, and that is not my purpose here in any case. I intend only to refute the globally negative assertions about the possibility of amity and respect toward Jews during the period under consideration. I therefore present chiefly positive evidence.

53. Neither legislators nor jurists attempted to define Jewish serfdom clearly. Jews were also referred to as *servitus Judaeorum* and as chests (*cofres*) or treasures of the King (Baron, 11:4–5).

54. Jacob Katz, *Exclusiveness and Tolerance* (New York: Behrman House, 1961), p. 6. In this argument Katz depends on Kisch, *Germany*, pp. 119–28.

55. Israel Abrahams says that twelfth-century Jews read Christian love songs and ballads (*Jewish Life in the Middle Ages* [Philadelphia: Jewish Publication Society of America, 1896; reprint ed. New York: Atheneum, 1978], p. 361). H. H. Ben-Sasson adds that the influence of Christian romances led the author of the *Sefer Hasidim* to draw a comparison between service to God and a knight's loyalty to his lord (*A History of the Jewish People* [Cambridge, Mass.: Harvard University Press, 1969; English translation, 1976], p. 555). It is worth noting in a study of the *Prioress's Tale* that despite its negative stereotypes about Christian morality, the *Sefer Hasidim* holds the life of Gentiles sacred. It adds that if a Jew is conspiring against a Gentile, every other Jew must foil the plot (see Katz, p. 101, who follows F. Y. Baer in his discussion of this book). Katz (p. 93) and Ben-Sasson (p. 546) note shared, or at least parallel, religious movements between Jews and Christians.

56. Kisch observes that Jews in northern France dressed indistinguishably from Christians from the twelfth to the fourteenth century, and typically walked bare-headed. In Germany and the rest of central Europe, by contrast, Jews were distinguished by their horned hats, which they wore of their own free will according to old tradition, as well as by their beards. The famous thirteenth-century miniature of the Jewish minnesinger Süsskind von Trimberg, for example, shows him in fashionable dress except for his pointed hat and beard. In Spain and Italy, Jews had assimilated in dress, though Johannes Purgoldt's early sixteenth-century German lawbook asserts that Italian Jews were required to wear different clothes from those of Christians. See Kisch, *Germany*, pp. 296–98, and *Forschungen zur Rechts-, Wirtschafts- und Sozialgeschichte der Juden* (Sigmaringen: Thorbecke, 1979), pp. 119–20; also Baron, 11:101, 137. For their own safety, Jews wore the same clothes as Gentiles when travelling, and sometimes even dressed as priests and nuns! (See Ben-Sasson, p. 623;

also Kisch, *Forschungen*, p. 118.) Jews achieved a high degree of linguistic assimilation in their host countries, though dialectic differences eventually emerged under the influence of Hebrew and talmudic thinking (Baron, 11:188, 377n). Bernhard Blumenkranz observes that Rashi used some 2,000 French words in his Biblical and talmudic commentaries and demonstrated a perfect mastery of French (*Histoire des Juifs en France*, ed. Edouard Privat [Toulouse: Collection Franco-Judaïca, 1972], p. 26. Kisch says that Jews employed the German language of their native province to annotate and translate Scripture (*Germany*, p. 309). Abrahams (p. 425) notes that Jews in the late Middle Ages also bore the same names as Christians. But compare Blumenkranz, pp. 27–28.

57. The Jew Badge was required in 1215 because in many provinces Jews were indistinguishable from Christians, and so might "by error" have intercourse with them (see Baron, 9:28). The badge was not generally worn in France until 1269, and in Castile until the mid-fourteenth century. In Italy, distinguishing marks were common only in the fifteenth century (though earlier in Sicily). In Germany the distinctive Jewish hat was made obligatory in the thirteenth century; the hat obviated the need for a badge, and no mention is made of the red or yellow wheel as Jewish badge until the fifteenth century. See Kisch, *Forschungen*, pp. 126–27, and *Germany*, pp. 296–97; also Cecil Roth, *A History of the Jews* (New York: Schocken, 1954; revised ed. 1970), p. 277.

58. See Baron, 11:186. In Provence, c. 1300, R. Menahem Ha-Me'iri said that giftgiving to Christians was not only permissible but meritorious (Katz, p. 117). See R. Israel Isserlein's similar position, discussed below.

59. Quoted from Abrahams, p. 420. It is worth noting that Dante expressed an antagonistic position toward Jews as a people when he urged Pope Boniface VIII to make war on the Jews and Saracens rather than on the Colonnas (Baron, 11:131).

60. Baron, 11:81. In Spain the Church too tried to prevent such illicit relations (see Baron, 9:26).

61. In one noteworthy case, the provost of Paris, Hughes Aubriot, was denounced in 1381 for alleged sexual relations with Jewish women, as well as for allowing baptized Jewish children to be returned to the Jews (see Baron, 11:85, who concedes that such allegations could have been political; also 11:80). Noting that sexual contacts between Jews and Christians were often cited to demonstrate "la tendance habituelle des Juifs à la débauche," Blumenkranz cites the act of contrition presented in 1300 by Bonfils, "Juif de la Grasse, pour s'excuser des 'crimes quil avoit commis iusqua ce iour la en iouant ou en baisant, embrassant ou connoissant les femmes chrestiennes' " (p. 49).

62. Baron, 11:186. Abrahams (p. 425) cites the instance of a German knight who reportedly removed the crucifix from his mantel on the

frequent occasions that he received Jewish visitors. This, of course, may represent nothing more than an isolated case of politic behavior.

63. Isserlein's ruling on the cakes gave Jews general permission to eat bread prepared by Gentile bakers, except during the Ten Days of Repentance between the New Year and the Day of Atonement (Baron, 11:186–87).

64. See Abrahams, p. 409, and Baron, 9:26.

65. Baron, 11:85. Such illicit relationships continued in Germany: one German lawbook of c. 1500 provided that children born to a Jewish father and a Christian mother be removed from the father, baptized, and educated at the father's expense (Kisch, *Germany*, p. 207).

66. Baron, 11:81, 241; Abrahams, p. 428.

67. Chaucer's response, if he did meet Jews, would also be wholly conjectural. He might have had contact with Jews in 1366, when he was granted a three-month safe conduct in Navarre. This trip may have been connected with the Black Prince's alliance with King Pedro in the civil war in Castile, and perhaps concerned the recall of English mercenaries serving Pedro's opponent, Henry of Trastamara. If Chaucer had dealings with either party, he may well have had contact with Jews. Pedro's court physician and royal treasurer were Jewish, and Henry called Pedro the "Judaized king," who confided only in Jews. Henry for his part was later noted for having many Jewish officials and intimates, and during his reign Jews were accorded great liberty and power in the royal household. Chaucer could also have encountered Jews in France, where one Jewish family was received with esteem at the court of Charles V at the time of Chaucer's diplomatic missions to Paris, Montreuil, and "parts of France" (if, in fact, Chaucer did conduct these missions in 1377, as Froissart reports). Chaucer could have met Jews in Italy, where, Abrahams tells us, friendships between Christians and Jews extended into literary circles. And he may even have come into contact with Jews in England, where they occasionally came to the attention of the court. In 1390 a Sicilian Jew was baptized in the presence of Richard II. In 1392, according to Montagu Frank Modder, a Jewish physician was called to the court to attend Richard. And during most of Chaucer's lifetime, a *domus conversorum* was occupied by converted Jews on the street now known as Chancery Lane in London. Essentially a royal institution, the *domus*, at least earlier in the century, had attracted the warm interest of the king. See Baron, 11:122, 231; Heinrich Graetz, *History of the Jews* (Philadelphia: Jewish Publication Society of America, 1894; reprint ed., 1941), 4:129, 150; *Chaucer Life–Records*, eds. Martin M. Crow and Clair C. Olson (Oxford: Oxford University Press, 1966), pp. 44–53; Haldeen Braddy, "Froissart's Account of Chaucer's Embassy in 1377," *Review of English Studies* 14 (1938): 63–67; Martin M. Crow and Virginia E. Leland, "Chaucer's Life," in *Riverside*

Chaucer, pp. xvii–xviii; Leon Poliakov, *The History of Anti-Semitism* (New York: Vanguard Press, 1961; reprint ed., 1973), 2:150–51; John A. Crow, *Spain* (New York: Harper & Row, 1963), p. 110; Michael Adler, *Jews of Medieval England* (London: Jewish Historical Society of England, 1939), pp. 307–39; Albert M. Hyamson, *A History of the Jews in England* (London: Jewish Historical Society of England, 1908), pp. 127, 130–31; and Montagu Frank Modder, *The Jew in the Literature of England* (Philadelphia: Jewish Publication Society of America, 1944), p. 12 (cited by Ridley, p. 13).

68. For a more developed argument that the Jews "were not viewed as ministers of Satan by those Englishmen capable of moral reflection," see Richard Rex, "Chaucer and the Jews" *Modern Language Quarterly* 45 (1984): 107–22.

69. See Schoeck, p. 256; *Piers the Plowman,* ed. Walter W. Skeat (London: Oxford University Press, 1886; reprint ed., 1965), B. IX. 81–88. Ridley (p. 10) correctly points out that in this passage, Langland cites the Jews' virtue in order to shame Christians for failing to behave as well as "Iudas felawes" did (IX. 84).

70. See G. R. Owst, *Literature and Pulpit in Medieval England* (Oxford: Basil Blackwell, 1933; reprint ed., 1966), pp. 177, 418; and his letter to *The Jewish Guardian* (London), 6 August 1926, p. 5 (cited by Rex, pp. 115–16).

71. Cf. Rex, who says (p. 115) that Chaucer must have heard Brunton sermonize on numerous occasions. Rex observes that Gower praised Jews for observing the Sabbath. In response to claims that the *Confessio Amantis* is anti-Jewish, Rex cites Ruth M. Ames, "The Source and Significance of 'The Jew and the Pagan,' " *Mediaeval Studies* 19 (1957): 37–47, and notes Gower's praise for "the good Jew Mordecai" in *Mirour de l'Omme.*

72. Rex's admirable and well intentioned survey attributes this view of salvation to *Mandeville's Travels* and the *Parson's Tale,* but the passages he cites from these texts do not explicitly demonstrate this point. Compare Ridley's discussion (pp. 10–11) of Langland's position on the salvation of the Jews. R. W. Southern considers the growing concern to include unbelievers in the scheme of salvation to be "one of the most attractive features of the period" (*Western Views of Islam in the Middle Ages,* 2nd. ed. [Cambridge, Mass.: Harvard University Press, 1978], p. 76; cited by Rex, p. 118).

73. See Kisch, *Germany,* pp. 325, 539–40.

74. Although there is no proof that Chaucer ever read the *De-cameron,* it was, as Larry Benson observes, the most famous prose work

of his favorite Italian poet. He must have heard of it, and it may well have offered suggestions that inspired the frame of the *Canterbury Tales* (*Riverside Chaucer*, p. 3).

CHAPTER 13

1. *The Riverside Chaucer*, ed. Larry D. Benson *et al.*, 3rd ed., (Boston: Houghton Mifflin, 1987), p. 487. Further quotations, identified in the body of the text by line number, will be from this edition.

2. It should be observed that the phrasing of her allusion to St. Nicholas, early in her tale, implies that she is in the habit of meditating on this miracle of the Virgin and its associations:

> But ay, when I remembre on this mateere,
> Seint Nicholas stant evere in my presence. . . .
> [513–14]

3. Sumner Ferris, in "The Mariology of *The Prioress's Tale*" (*American Benedictine Review*, 32 [1981]: 232–54), shows that in both Prologue and tale, Chaucer consistently represents the Virgin's place in the supernatural order in accordance with Catholic doctrine. She is "supreme among God's creatures" yet, in that she herself is one of those creatures, she is "infinitely inferior to [God]. . . . [She] does not share in the kind of worship reserved for him" (235). He notes that in the Prologue God literally takes precedence over the Virgin (234), and that in describing the Virgin as "the roote / Of bountee," Chaucer, in the person of the Prioress, adds "next hir Sone" (465–66). As for the tale itself, "although this is by genre a Miracle of the Blessed Virgin, the words of the narrator and of the (Christian) characters in the tale acknowledge, without exception, that the power and glory belong to God" (242). Ferris further quotes lines 652–55, from the martyred boy's speech to the abbot, to show that "even [he] respects and observes the proper order of precedence" (243).

4. For the Latin text, see the notes to lines 36–56 in *The Works of Geoffrey Chaucer*, ed. F. N. Robinson, 2nd ed. (Boston: Houghton Mifflin, 1957), p. 757. *The Riverside Chaucer* substitutes a modern translation: "The womb (*claustrum*) of Mary bears Him, ruling the threefold fabric (*trinam machinam*), Whom earth, stars, sea, honor, worship, proclaim."

5. The word *labour*, which occurs earlier in the Prologue ("To telle a storie I wol do my labour" [463]), may anticipate the theme of pregnancy which, I am arguing, is implied in lines 481–83, though its relevant modern meaning was not yet established in Chaucer's time. The earliest citation for *labour* sb. in the meaning "the pains of childbirth" (sense 6) in *SOED* is dated 1545. No such definition for noun or verb appears in *MED*. (Cf., however, the phrase "labour of birthe" under sense 4(b), "pain, sick-

ness, disease," of *labour* n., and the phrase "labouren of child" under sense 3(a) "to endure pain, suffer" or *labouren* v.)

6. Donald Fritz, in "The Prioress's Avowal of Ineptitude" (*Chaucer Review*, 9 [1974]: 174–79), sees the Prioress's professed inability to "declare" the worthiness of the Virgin as having its source in the "inexpressibility topos." He does not associate her comparison of herself to an infant, capable of praising the Virgin only through the intercession of the Virgin herself, with the miraculous spreading of God's praise by infants suckling at the breast.

7. See Robert Worth Frank, Jr., "The *Canterbury Tales* III: Pathos," in *The Cambridge Chaucer Companion*, ed. Piero Boitani and Jill Mann (Cambridge: Cambridge University Press, 1986), pp. 143–47, 153–54. According to Frank, the Prioress's Tale, among others, exemplifies a mode of religious pathos which "in fourteenth- and fifteenth-century literature and art . . . was powerful and persuasive" (144). Frank emphasizes the absence of irony and complexity in Chaucer's "tales of pathos"; his "principal artistic concern [in these tales] is to produce a strong emotional effect" (143). Alfred David, in "An ABC to the Style of the Prioress," *Acts of Interpretation*, ed. Mary J. Carruthers and Elizabeth D. Kirk (Norman, Oklahoma: Pilgrim Books, 1982), remarks on the "pervasive emotionalism," associated with "the clash of opposites: good and evil, innocence and cruelty, the hope of salvation and the fear of damnation," characteristic of late fourteenth-century works of courtly and religious art (p. 152). John C. Hirsh, in "Reopening the *Prioress's Tale*," *Chaucer Review* 10 (1975): 30–45, finds a "non-biblical source for [the Prioress's Tale] . . . which is of utmost importance," namely, "the background of affective piety which informs the tale throughout" (37). He quotes from a modern description, applicable to medieval devotional practice, of "affective prayer" as characterized by the predominance of emotion over "argument," by the substitution of intuition for logical deduction, and, to a greater or lesser degree, by "simplification" of the soul (35–36). Hirsh also argues that "the Prioress's own allegations against the Jews are more restricted than is usually assumed." He notes that the Provost puts to death "only those Jews 'that of this mordre wiste' " (1820), and that "neither the Provost nor the Prioress institutes a pogrom," citing Thomas Aquinas's distinctions among the rulers of the Jews, the Jews of lesser rank, and the soldiers who carried out the execution as deserving of greater and lesser blame for the crucifixion of Jesus (39–40). But it is exactly such distinctions, I should argue, that are ruled out by the affective or pathetic simplicity pervading the narration of the tale. It is "the Jews" of the ghetto generally, not a small high-ranking group, who are incited by Satan to have the boy killed (565–66), and who therefore, we must assume, knew of the murder.

8. Sister Nicholas Maltman, O. P., in her essay "The Divine Granary, or the End of the Prioress's 'Greyn' " (*Chaucer Review*, 17, [1982]: 163–170), convincingly argues that the "greyn" laid upon the boy's tongue

by the Virgin has its source in a responsory and versicle and a prosa, or extension of the responsory, used in the second vespers of that Feast. The latter, which she quotes in full, includes the following lines: "the marble pavement of Christ's sanctuary is rubied with the stream of holy blood. The martyr, given the laurel wreath of life, is, like the grain purged from the chaff, transported into divine granaries" (Sister Nicholas's translation). Though she does not mention the image of the marble stones specifically, I take its appearance in the prosa in conjunction with the ruby (and the grain) as evidence that the marble in Chaucer's poem is a further echo of the liturgical passage.

9. This dungheap, it should be noted, is more than a gratuitously sensational detail; it acquires symbolic resonance in opposition to the marble sepulcher in which the "litel body sweete" of the martyr is appropriately entombed. The former suggests the medieval denigration of the bodies of sinful men that we hear in the *Pardoner's Tale:* "O wombe! O bely! O stynkyng cod, / Fulfilled of dong and of corrupcioun!" (VI 534–35); the latter represents the incorruption and splendor of the heavenly realm to which the soul of the martyred "innocent," whose virgin body was likewise pure, has been translated. See also the preceding note.

10. For Fritz, both "song" in the *Prioress's Prologue and Tale* and the Latin of the *Alma redemptoris* convey a "reality . . . different in *kind* from the reality of the world of the young boys [and, presumably, that of the Canterbury pilgrimage]" thus contrasting with "the vernacular language . . . [of] ordinary communications" (p. 173). The difficulty, for the Prioress, of finding language adequate for devotional praise, and the difficulty, for the little boy, of understanding Latin, point toward "a belief that God always transcends anything man can think or say of him" (173–74).

Contributors

MARIE BORROFF is the William Lampson Professor of English at Yale University. She is the author of *Sir Gawain and the Green Knight: A Stylistic and Metrical Study* and *Language and the Poet*, and of verse-translations of *Sir Gawain* and *Pearl*.

ELIZABETH A. CLARK is John Carlisle Kilgo Professor of Religion at Duke University. She has published several books, including *Women and Religion: A Feminist Sourcebook of Christian Thought* (with Herbert Richardson); *Jerome, Chrysostom, and Friends: Essays and Translations; Women in the Early Church;* and, most recently, *Ascetic Piety and Women's Faith: Essays on Late Ancient Christianity*. She has held fellowships from the NEH, the National Humanities Center, and the Guggenheim Foundation. Professor Clark is currently at work on a book on the Origenist controversy.

ROBERT R. EDWARDS is Professor of English and Comparative Literature at the Pennsylvania State University. He has taught at SUNY, Buffalo, where he chaired the Department of English, and at the Université de Bordeaux. Edwards has held research fellowships from the Mellon Foundation, NEH, and the SUNY Research Foundation, and in 1985–86 was a Fellow at the National Humanities Center. In 1987 he was awarded the Norman L. and Roselea J. Goldberg Prize by Vanderbilt University Press. Edwards is the author of *The Dream of Chaucer: Representation and Reflection in Chaucer's Early Narrative, Ratio and Invention: A Study of Medieval Lyric and Narrative, The Poetry of Guido Guinizelli,* and *The Montecassino Passion and the Poetics of Medieval Drama.*

JOHN M. FYLER is Professor of English and Chair of the English Department at Tufts University. He has published *Chaucer and Ovid* and edited the *House of Fame* in the *Riverside Chaucer,* and is currently interested in theories of language in the Middle Ages and medieval biblical commentaries. He has been awarded fellowships by the ACLS and the Guggenheim Foundation.

ALAN T. GAYLORD is Winkley Professor of English at Dartmouth College. His scholarly interests include medieval cultural and intellectual history as well as film criticism. He is editing the *Knight's Tale* for the Chaucer Variorum, and completing a book on Chaucer's prosody.

R. W. HANNING is Professor of English and Comparative Literature at Columbia University. His publications include *The Vision of History in Early Britain*, *The Individual in Twelfth-Century Romance*, and *The Lais of Marie de France* (co-translated with Joan M. Ferrante). He is currently completing a study of the *Canterbury Tales*.

ERIK KOOPER is senior lecturer in Medieval English at Utrecht University. His interests center on the relationships between individuals, and between individuals and the community; the cultural, social, and historical background to medieval literature; and the "internationality" of the literature of the Middle Ages. He has published widely, in English and Dutch, on a range of topics, mostly concerning Middle English literature.

JEROME MAZZARO is Professor of Modern Languages at SUNY, Buffalo. He is the author of *The Figure of Dante: An Essay on the Vita Nuova* and is currently writing on the question of sincerity in poetry.

MICHAEL M. SHEEHAN is Senior Fellow of the Pontifical Institute of Mediaeval Studies and Professor at the Centre for Medieval Studies at the University of Toronto. His research and publications have been principally in social and legal history, especially on subjects touching family and marriage in medieval Europe.

GIOVANNI SINICROPI is Professor of Italian Literature at the University of Connecticut. He is interested in aesthetics and literary criticism, Italian contemporary theater, and structural semiotics. His books and articles include studies of Boccaccio and Lope de Vega.

A. C. SPEARING, formerly Research Fellow of Gonville and Caius College, Cambridge, has, since 1960, been a Fellow of Queens' College. He was successively Assistant Lecturer and Lecturer in English, and Reader in Medieval English Literature, at Cambridge. In 1987 he left Cambridge for the University of Virginia, where he is William R. Kenan Professor of English. Among his books are *Criticism and Medieval Poetry*, *The Gawain-Poet: A Critical Study*, *Medieval Dream-Poetry*, *Medieval to Renaissance in English Po-*

etry, and *Readings in Medieval Poetry*. He is at work on a book-length study of watching and listening in medieval love-narratives.

STEPHEN SPECTOR, Professor of English at SUNY, Stony Brook, has edited the N-town Cycle of mystery plays for the EETS. His other publications include *The Genesis of the N-town Cycle, Essays in Paper Analysis*, and essays on the Jew in medieval literature as well as analytical and historical approaches to manuscript study. He has held fellowships and a grant from the NEH, an ACLS Fellowship, and positions as Research Fellow at the Center for Humanities, Wesleyan University, and the National Humanities Center. In 1980 the Medieval Academy of America awarded him the Elliott Prize.

JAMES I. WIMSATT, Temple Centennial Professor of English Literature at the University of Texas at Austin, is best known for his studies of the French background of Geoffrey Chaucer, including *Chaucer and the French Love Poets* and *Chaucer and the Poems of "Ch,"* and an edition (with William W. Kibler) for the Chaucer Library of *Guillaume de Machaut: Le Jugement du Roy de Behaigne and Remede de Fortune*. His comprehensive treatment of Chaucer's relationship to the Middle French lyric poets is to be published by the University of Toronto Press.

Index

A

Abelard, Peter, 88–90
Abrahams, Israel, 225, 226
Aelred of Rievaulx, 48–49, 52, 54, 55;
   and Chaucer, 208–9; and Dante,
   130; and Jean de Meun, 205–6
Aers, David, 150
Alan of Lille, 39, 52, 53
Albert the Great, Saint, 125
Alexander III, Pope, 4, 37
Alfonsi, Petrus, 108, 109, 113
Alighieri, Dante, 10, 121–37, 162;
   and Chaucer, 143, 174–75; in
   Decameron, 112, 113, 119, 147
Ambrose, 18, 130, 131
Anderson, George K., 217
Andreas Capellanus, 6, 9, 57, 96,
   125, 126, 137, 238n.11
Antoninus Liberalis, 114–115
Aquinas, Saint Thomas, 4, 49–51,
   53–56 passim, 263n.31; and
   Dante, 125, 129–30, 133, 136; on
   toleration of Jews, 224
Arabian Nights, 101, 102, 109
Ariès, Philippe, 2–3
Aristotle: and Chaucer, 142; and
   Dante, 125, 127, 128, 131, 136; on
   friendship in *Nichomachean
   Ethics*, 4, 10, 45, 49, 50–52, 55, 56
Arnaut Daniel, 123, 133, 134
Augustine, Saint, 3–4, 15–31; *City
   of God*, 131; *Confessions*, 48,
   128; and Dante, 10; on Genesis,
   155–60 passim; and medieval
   marriage theory, 45, 46, 52; and
   Roman de la Rose, 201
Averroes, 125

B

Balbi, Johannes, de Janua, 158
Baron, Salo, 224–26 passim
Bede, 157
Benson, Larry D., 8
Benton, John F., 5
Bernard of Clairvaux: in Dante,
   126, 134; on marriage, 4, 46–47,
   48, 52; on toleration of Jews, 224
Beroul, 9, 63–69, 71, 72, 76
Boccaccio, Giovanni, 10, 83, 166, 170;
   and Chaucer, 146–48, 150, 186;
   Decameron, 104–6, 117–20, 228
Boethius: and Chaucer, 12, 147,
   173, 186–88 passim, 194, 201–3
   passim; on friendship, 205; and
   Machaut 206
Bonaventura, 55
Book of Sindibâd, 108, 109
Boucicaut, 171
Bowden, Muriel, 213, 214, 219
Bradbury, Malcolm, 61–62, 67
Brewer, Derek S., 7, 212, 217
Brihat-Kathâ, 108, 116
Brito, Guilelmus, 158
Bromyard, John, 110–112 passim,
   227
Bronson, Bertrand, 219
Brunton, Thomas, 227
Burke, Kenneth, 17

C

Cassian, 130, 132
Cato, 131
Cavalcanti, Guido, 122, 123, 135